W9-AHN-881

Problems
in
Hospital Law

Fifth Edition

Robert D. Miller, J.D., M.S. Hyg.
Shutts & Bowen
West Palm Beach, Florida

AN ASPEN PUBLICATION®
Aspen Publishers, Inc.

1986

Rockville, Maryland
Royal Tunbridge Wells

This publication is designed to provide accurate and authorative information in regard to the Subject Matter covered. It is sold with the understanding that the publisher is not engaged in rendering legal, accounting, or other professional service. If legal advice or other expert assistance is required, the service of a competent professional person should be sought. *(From a Declaration of Principles jointly adopted by a Committee of the American Bar Association and a Committee of Publishers and Associations.)*

Library of Congress Cataloging-in-Publication Data

Miller, Robert D. (Robert Desle), 1947-
Problems in hospital law.
Includes bibliographical references and index.
1. Hospitals—law and legislation—United States.
KF3825.M53   1986   344.73′03211   86-1160
ISBN:0-87189-353-3   347.3043211

Editorial Services: Ruth Bloom

Aspen Publishers, Inc. grants permission for photocopying for personal or internal use, or for the personal or internal use of specific clients registered with the Copyright Clearance Center (CCC). This consent is given on the condition that the copier pay a $1.00 fee plus $.12 per page for each photocopy through the CCC for photocopying beyond that permitted by the U.S. Copyright Law. The fee should be paid directly to the CCC, 21 Congress St., Salem, Massachusetts 01970.
0-87189-353-3/86 $1.00 + .12.

This consent does not extend to other kinds of copying, such as copying for general distribution, for advertising or promotional purposes, for creating new collective works, or for resale. For information, address Aspen Publishers, Inc., 1600 Research Boulevard, Rockville, Maryland 20850.

Library of Congress Catalog Card Number: 86-1160
ISBN: 0-87189-353-3

Printed in the United States of America

1 2 3 4 5

Table of Contents

Acknowledgments

This updating of *Problems in Hospital Law* was made possible by the support and encouragement of many individuals and institutions.

The comments and questions of my health and law students at the University of Miami and the University of Iowa have helped to identify some of the weaknesses of the previous edition. I have tried to address them in this edition, but I am certain that future students and other readers will continue to find areas needing improvement.

The facilities of the law libraries of the University of Miami, the University of Iowa, the Fourth District Court of Appeals of Florida, and my law firm, Shutts & Bowen, have made the research for this book possible. Special thanks are due to Jeanne Waters, the librarian for Shutts & Bowen, who provided assistance with locating some of the information for this book.

My colleagues in the health law section of Shutts & Bowen have been very supportive.

Although I did most of the updating directly on my personal computer, the secretarial support of Lisa Picardy who inputted the fourth edition to serve as a first draft and of Patricia Cote who has helped with the required correspondence has been invaluable.

The strong support and cooperative attitudes of Barbara Tansill and the Aspen staff have made the production of the book an enjoyable process.

Finally, and most importantly, I acknowledge the strong support of my family—my wife, Jill, and my daughter, Katie. A project of this magnitude, while editing a new journal *(Topics in Hospital Law)*, teaching a course, and conducting a full professional practice, takes family sacrifices which my family has willingly made. I dedicate this book to my family whose sacrifices, encouragement and support make this book and my other endeavors possible and meaningful.

Robert D. Miller
March 1986

Chapter 1

Introduction to the American Legal System

Many of the decisions that health care administrators, professionals, and technical staff must make each day are affected by legal principles and have potential legal consequences. Since it is impossible to obtain legal advice before each decision, health care providers must develop an understanding of the law so that problems requiring legal counsel can be identified and other decisions can be made consistent with applicable legal principles.

The purpose of this introductory chapter is to provide the reader with some general information about law, including the workings of the legal system and the roles of the branches of government in creating, administering, and enforcing the law.

THE NATURE OF LAW

Law has been defined in a variety of ways. The essence of most definitions is that law is a system of principles and processes by which people who live in a society attempt to control human conduct in an effort to minimize use of force to resolve conflicting interests. Through law, society specifies standards of behavior and means to enforce those standards. The purpose of law is to avoid conflict between individuals and between government and individuals. Since conflicting interests are inevitable, the law also provides a way to resolve disputes.

Law is not an exact science. Lawyers are frequently unable to provide a precise answer to a legal question or to predict with certainty the outcome of a legal conflict because much of the law is uncertain. Some questions have never been precisely addressed by the legal system. Even when questions have been addressed and answered through the law, the legal system may change those answers in response to changing conditions. The ability of the law to adjust is one of its strengths. Legal uncertainty is similar to the uncertainty encountered in making medical and nursing diagnostic and treatment decisions. When dealing with systems as complicated as the human body or human society, uncertainty is inevitable. A lawyer's advice is still valuable, just as a physician's advice is valuable, because the lawyer can apply knowledge of how the law has addressed similar questions to predict the most probable answer. After a dispute has arisen, a lawyer can play a valuable role as an advocate to assure that the dispute resolution mechanisms of the law are used to the advantage of the client.

In daily life, the law serves as a guide to conduct. Most disputes or controversies between persons or organizations are resolved without lawyers or the courts. The existence of the legal system is a stimulus to orderly private resolution of disputes. Legal principles reinforce the compromises reached. The likelihood of success in court affects the willingness of parties to negotiate private settlements. Knowledge of the law is important for those who may become involved in resolving disputes.

Laws govern the relationships of private individuals with each other and with government. Law that deals with the relationships between individuals is called private law, while public law is the law dealing with the relationships between private individuals and government. Many laws have both private and public law aspects, so it is not always possible to assign a law to only one of these classifications. However, it is not important to be able to classify laws as public or private. The distinction has little significance other than to focus attention on these two roles of law.

Private law involves the definition and enforcement of rights and duties of private individuals and organizations. Private law can be divided into contract law and tort law. Contract law is concerned with the enforcement of certain agreements among private individuals and with the payment of compensation for failure to fulfill those agreements. Tort law defines and enforces duties and rights among private individuals that are not based on contractual agreement.

Public law defines, regulates, and enforces the relationships of individuals with government and governmental agencies. One example of public law is criminal law, which forbids conduct deemed injurious to the public order and provides for punishment of those who engage in the forbidden conduct. Public law also includes an enormous variety of regulations designed to advance societal objectives by requiring private individuals and organizations to act or not to act in specified ways. While there are criminal penalties for violating some regulations, the primary goal of public law is to obtain compliance and attain the goals of the law, not to punish offenders.

Public law at both the federal and state level addresses many societal problems. Public law addresses an increasing number of areas affecting hospitals, including health planning, containment of health care costs, quality of clinical laboratory operations, medical device safety, labor relations, employment policies, facility safety, and other important topics. Hospitals have entered the arena of legislative debate concerning the formulation of public policy in these areas to assure that lawmakers understand the implications of proposals for the health care system.

GOVERNMENTAL ORGANIZATION AND FUNCTION

This section addresses the structure of the three branches of government—the legislative, executive, and judicial branches—and how the functions of one branch relate to the functions of the other two. An overly simplified summary of the functions of the three branches is that the legislature makes the laws, the executive enforces the laws, and the judiciary interprets the laws. The actual functions of the three branches overlap in practice. The separation of powers is a vital concept in the constitutional framework of the United States government and of the various state governments. This separation means that no one of the three branches of government is clearly dominant over the other two; each branch may, in the exercise of its functions, affect and limit the functions of the others.

The concept of separation of powers—sometimes called a system of checks and balances—is illustrated by the process for enacting legislation. On the federal government level, statutes are enacted by Congress; however, until a bill enacted by Congress is signed by the president (or passed over his veto by a two-thirds vote of each house of Congress), the bill does not become law, except in the situation where the president allows it to become law by failing to veto or approve it within the time allowed. Thus, by his veto the president can prevent a bill from becoming law temporarily and possibly prevent it from becoming law at all. A bill that has become law may ultimately be declared invalid by the United States Supreme Court or other courts in the judicial branch of government, if the court decides that the law violates the Constitution.

The president's nominees to be federal judges, including the United States Supreme Court justices, must be approved by the Senate. Over time, both the executive and legislative branches can affect the composition of the judicial branch of government. In addition, while a Supreme Court decision is final concerning the specific controversy before the Court, Congress and the president may enact revised legislation to change the law. Another method for overriding a Supreme Court decision, while complex and often time-consuming, is an amendment to the Constitution.

Each of the three branches of government has a different primary function. The function of the legislative branch is to enact laws, which may be new laws or amendments to existing laws. It is the legislature's responsibility to determine the nature and extent of the need for new laws and for changes in existing laws. Legislatures generally assign legislative proposals to committees charged with oversight of the areas addressed by the proposals. The committees investigate, holding hearings at which interested persons may present their views. These hearings provide information to assist the committee members in their consideration of the bills. Some bills eventually are released from the committee and reach the full legislative body, where after consideration and debate the bills may be either approved or rejected. The Congress and every state legislature, except Nebraska, consist of two houses. (Nebraska has only one house.) Both houses must pass identical versions of a bill before it can be brought to the chief executive. Differences in the versions passed by the two houses are sometimes resolved by a joint conference committee.

The primary function of the executive is to enforce and administer the law. The chief executive, whether the governor of a state or the president of the United States, also has a role in the creation of law through the power to either approve or veto a legislative proposal, except in North Carolina, where the governor has no veto power. If the chief executive approves a bill, it becomes a statute, a part of the enacted law. If the chief executive vetoes the bill, it can become a law if the legislature overrides the veto.

The executive branch of government is organized into departments. The departments are assigned responsibility for specific areas of public affairs and enforce the law within their assigned areas. Much of the federal law affecting hospitals is administered by the Department of Health and Human Services. In most states there is a department assigned responsibility for health and welfare matters, including the administration and enforcement of most laws affecting hospitals. Other departments and governmental agencies may also affect hospital affairs. On the federal level, for example, laws concerning wages and hours of employment are enforced by the Department of Labor.

The function of the judicial branch of government is adjudication, the deciding of disputes in accordance with law. For example, courts decide suits against hospitals by patients seeking compensation for harm they feel was caused by the wrongful conduct of hospital personnel. While news of malpractice suits and suits by the government against hospitals frequently receives the greatest attention, hospitals also sue to enforce a right or to protect a legally protected interest. Hospitals initiate suits to challenge exercises of authority by governmental agencies and departments, to have legislation concerning hospitals declared invalid, to collect unpaid hospital bills, and to enforce contracts.

Many disputes are resolved by negotiation or arbitration without resort to the courts. However, in many situations, there is no way to end the controversy without submitting to the adjudicatory process of the courts. A dispute brought before a court is decided in accordance with applicable law; this application of the law to dispute resolution is the essence of the judicial process.

SOURCES OF LAW

The four primary sources of law are constitutions, statutes, decisions and rules of administrative agencies, and decisions of courts.

Constitutions

The Constitution of the United States is the supreme law of the land. It establishes the general organization of the federal government, grants certain powers to the federal government, and places certain limits on what the federal and state governments may do.

The Constitution establishes the three branches of the federal government—the legislative, executive, and judicial branches—and grants certain powers to them. The functions of the branches and their interrelationships are discussed in the preceding section of this chapter.

The Constitution is a grant of power from the states to the federal government. The federal government has only the powers that the Constitution grants expressly or by implication. The express powers include, for example, the power to collect taxes, declare war, and regulate interstate commerce. The federal government is also granted broad implied powers to enact laws "necessary and proper" for exercising its other powers. When the federal government establishes law, within the scope of its powers, that law is supreme. All conflicting state and local laws are invalid.

The Constitution also limits what the federal and state governments may do. Many of these limits on federal power appear in the first ten amendments to the Constitution, the Bill of Rights. The rights protected by the Bill of Rights include the right to free speech, free exercise of religion, freedom from unreasonable searches and seizures, trial by jury, and the right not to be deprived of life, liberty or property without due process of law. Some of most frequently applied limits on state power are stated in the Fourteenth Amendment, as follows: " . . . nor shall any state deprive any person of life, liberty or property, without due process of law; nor deny to any person within its jurisdiction the equal protection of the laws." These clauses of the Fourteenth Amendment are frequently referred to as the due process clause and the equal protection clause. Another constitutional limit on state and federal governmental power that affects hospitals and health care professionals is the right of privacy.

Due Process of Law

The due process clause restricts state action, not private action. Actions by state and local governmental agencies, including public hospitals, are considered to be state actions and must comply with due process requirements. Actions by private individuals at the behest of the state can also be subject to the requirements. In the past, private hospitals were sometimes considered to be engaged in state action when they were regulated or partially funded by governmental agencies. As discussed in Chapter 7, it is now rare for private hospitals to be found to be engaged in state action. The due process clause applies to state actions that deprive a person of "life, liberty or property." This is interpreted to include such liberty and property interests as a physicians' appointment to the medical staff of a public hospital and a hospital's institutional license from the state. Thus, in some situations public hospitals must provide due process, and in other situations hospitals are protected by the requirement that governmental agencies provide due process. The process that is due varies depending on the situation. The two primary elements of due process are: (1) the rules being applied must be reasonable and not vague; and (2) fair procedures must be followed in enforcing the rules. Rules that are too arbitrary or vague violate the due process clause and are not enforceable. The primary procedural protections that must be offered are notice of the proposed action and an opportunity to present information why the action should not be taken. The phrase "due process" in the Fourteenth Amendment also has been interpreted by the Supreme Court to include nearly all of the rights in the Bill of Rights. Thus, state governments may not infringe on those rights.

Equal Protection of the Laws

The equal protection clause also restricts state action, not private action. Equal protection means that like persons must be dealt with in a like fashion. The equal protection clause addresses the justifiability of the classifications used to distinguish persons for various legal purposes. The determination whether a difference between persons can justify a particular difference in rules or procedures can be difficult. In general courts require that the governmental agency justify the difference with a "rational reason." The major exceptions to this standard are the strict scrutiny courts apply to distinctions based on "suspect classifications," such as race, and the intermediate level of scrutiny applied to sex-based classifications.

Right of Privacy

In 1965, in the case of *Griswold v. Connecticut,* the Supreme Court recognized a constitutional right of privacy.[1] The Court has ruled that the right of privacy limits governmental authority to regulate contraception, abortion, and other decisions affecting reproduction. These reproductive issues are discussed in Chapter 15. Several state courts have ruled that the right of privacy permits terminally ill patients and those acting on their behalf to choose to withhold or withdraw medical treatment. These issues are discussed in Chapter 16.

State Constitutions

Each state has its own constitution. The state constitution establishes the organization of the state government, grants certain powers to the state government, and places certain limits on what the state government may do.

Statutes

Another major source of law is statutory law, which is the law enacted by a legislature. Legislative bodies include the United States Congress, state legislatures, and local legislative bodies, such as city councils and county boards of supervisors. Congress has only the powers delegated by the Constitution, but those powers have been broadly interpreted. State legislatures have all powers not denied by the United States Constitution, by federal laws enacted within the authority of the federal government, or by the state constitution. Local legislative bodies have only those powers granted by the state. Some states have granted local governments broad powers either through statutes or constitutional amendments authorizing "home rule."

When there is a conflict between federal and state or local law, valid federal law supersedes. Federal law preempts some areas of law and in those areas state law is superseded even when it is not in direct conflict. Some laws, such as the bankruptcy law, explicitly forbid dual state regulation. In other laws, the courts find that preemption is implied from the aim and pervasiveness of the federal scheme, the need for uniformity, and the likelihood that state regulation would be obstructive to the full goals of the federal action. Courts tend not to find implied preemption when the state is exercising its police power to protect the public health. For example, in 1960 the Supreme Court ruled that the extensive federal regulation and licensing of shipping did not preempt a city ordinance concerning smoke emissions. Therefore, a federally licensed vessel could be prosecuted for violating the pollution ordinance.[2] In 1985, the Supreme Court ruled that county ordinances regulating blood plasma collection were not preempted by the federal regulation of drugs through the FDA.[3]

When there is a conflict between state and local laws, valid state laws supersede. State law can preempt an entire area of law so that local law is superseded even when it is not in direct conflict. For example, the highest court of New York ruled that the state had preempted the regulation of abortions, prohibiting additional regulation by local authorities.[4]

Decisions and Rules of Administrative Agencies

The decisions and rules of administrative agencies are another source of law. Legislatures have delegated to administrative agencies the responsibility and power to implement various laws. The delegated powers include the quasi-legislative power to adopt regulations and the quasi-judicial power to decide how the statutes and regulations apply to individual situations. The legislature has delegated these powers because it does not have the time or expertise to address the complex issues concerning many areas it decides to regulate. Examples of federal administrative agencies include the Food and Drug Administration (FDA), the National Labor Relations Board (NLRB), and the Internal Revenue Service (IRS). The FDA is empowered to promulgate regulations and apply them to individual determinations concerning the manufacturing, marketing, and advertising of foods, drugs, cosmetics, and medical devices. The NLRB has the power to decide how the national labor law applies to individual disputes, and the IRS has the power to promulgate regulations and apply them to individual disputes concerning federal taxation. Many administrative agencies, such as the NLRB, seek to achieve some consistency in their decisions by following the position they adopted in previous cases involving similar matters. This is similar to the way the courts develop the common law discussed later in this chapter. When dealing with these agencies, it is important to review previous decisions, as well as rules.

Administrative regulations are valid only to the extent that they are within the scope of the authority validly granted by legislation to the agency. Delegations are invalid when they violate the constitutional requirement of separation of powers by not sufficiently specifying what regulations the administrative body may make. In the past, courts often declared delegations to be unconstitutional unless there was considerable specificity. Today the courts interpret the Constitution to permit much broader delegation, but the general area of law must still be specified.

The Congress and many state legislatures have passed administrative procedure acts. These laws specify the procedures administrative agencies must follow in adopting rules and in reaching decisions in individual cases, unless another law specifies different procedures for the agency to follow. Generally, these laws provide that most proposed rules must be published to allow individuals an opportunity to comment before they are finalized. Many federal agencies must publish both proposed and final rules in the *Federal Register.* Many states have similar publications that include proposed and final rules of state agencies. Those involved with hospitals should monitor proposed and final rules through these publications, their professional or hospital associations, or other publications. Despite their expertise, administrative agencies do not know all the implications of their proposals. They rely on the public and those regulated to alert them to potential problems through the comment process.

Court Decisions

Judicial decisions are the fourth source of law. The role of the courts is to resolve disputes. In the process of deciding individual cases, the courts interpret statutes and regulations, determine whether specific statutes and regulations are permitted by state or federal constitutions, and create the common law when deciding cases not controlled by statutes, regulations, or a constitution.

There is frequently disagreement over the application of statutes or regulations to specific situations. In many situations, there is an administrative agency that has the initial authority to decide how they shall be applied, but its decision can usually be appealed to the courts. Courts generally defer to the decisions of administrative agencies in discretionary matters. Courts review whether the delegation to the agency was constitutional and whether the agency acted within its authority, followed proper procedures, had a substantial basis for its decision, and acted without arbitrariness or discrimination. Even when an administrative agency is involved, the court may still have to interpret a statute or regulation or decide which of several conflicting statutes or regulations apply. Courts have developed rules for interpreting statutes. Some states also have a statute specifying interpretation rules. These rules or statutes are designed to help determine the intent of the legislature.

The courts also determine whether statutes or regulations violate the Constitution. All legislation and regulations must be consistent with the Constitution. The case of *Marbury v. Madison* established the power of the courts to declare legislation invalid when it is unconstitutional.[5]

Many of the legal principles and rules applied by the courts in the United States are the product of the common law developed in England and the United States. The term *common law* refers to the principles that evolve from court decisions. Common law is continually being adapted and expanded. During the colonial period, English common law applied. After the Revolution, each state adopted part or all of the existing common law.

Subsequent common law in the United States has been developed by each state, so the common law on specific subjects may differ from state to state. Statutory law has been enacted to restate many legal rules and principles that initially were established by the courts as part of common law. Many cases, especially disputes in private law areas, are decided according to common law rules. Common law rules may be changed by statutes that modify the rules or by court decisions that establish different common law rules.

Courts generally adhere to the doctrine of *stare decisis*, which is frequently described as "following precedent." By applying the rules and principles developed in previous similar cases, the court arrives at the same ruling in the current case as in the preceding one. Slight differences in the circumstances can provide a reason for the court not to apply the previous rule to the current case. Even when such differences are absent, a court may conclude that a particular common law rule is no longer in accord with the needs of society and may depart from precedent. An example of this overruling of precedent is the reconsideration and elimination of the common law principle of charitable immunity, which had provided nonprofit hospitals with virtual freedom from liability for harm to patients.[6] Courts in nearly every state overruled precedents that had provided immunity, so now nonprofit hospitals can generally be sued.[7]

Another doctrine that courts follow to avoid duplicative litigation and conflicting decisions is *res judicata*, which means "a thing or matter settled by judgment." When a legal controversy has been decided by a court and no more appeals are available, those involved in the suit may not take the same matters to court again. This is different from *stare decisis* in that *res judicata* only applies to those involved in the prior suit and to the issues decided in that suit. The application of the doctrine of *res judicata* can be complicated by disagreements over whether specific matters were actually decided in the prior case.

ORGANIZATION OF THE COURT SYSTEM

The structure of the court system determines which court decisions serve as precedents in a geographic area. There are over 50 court systems in the United States, including the federal system, each state's system, the District of Columbia's system, and the systems of Puerto Rico and the territories. These courts do not all reach the same decisions concerning specific issues. Frequently, a majority approach and several minority approaches exist on each issue. Careful review is necessary to find the court decisions applicable to an individual hospital and, if there are no such court decisions, to predict which approach the courts are likely to adopt.

The federal court system and many state court systems have three levels of courts—trial courts, intermediate courts of appeal, and a supreme court. Some states do not have intermediate courts of appeal.

State Court System

The trial courts in some states are divided into special courts that deal with specific issues, such as family courts, juvenile courts, probate courts, and limited courts that deal only with lesser crimes, such as misdemeanors, or with civil cases involving limited amounts of money. Each state has trial courts of general jurisdiction that may decide all disputes not assigned to other courts or barred from the courts by valid federal or state law.

At the trial court level, the applicable law is determined, and the evidence is assessed to determine what the "facts" are. The applicable law is then applied to those facts. It is the judge's role to determine what the law is. If there is a jury, the judge instructs the jury as to what the law is, and the jury determines what the facts are and applies the law. If there is no jury, the judge also determines what the facts are. In either case, the determination of the facts must be based on the evidence properly admitted during the trial, so the "facts" are not necessarily what actually happened.

In some cases, everyone agrees on the facts, and the court is asked only to determine what the law is. In other cases, everyone agrees what the law is, but there is disagreement over the facts. To determine the facts for purposes of deciding the case, the credibility of the witnesses and the weight to be given to other evidence must be determined. Many cases involve both questions of law and questions of fact. The judge has significant control over the trial even when a jury is involved. If the judge finds that insufficient evidence has been presented to establish a factual issue for the jury to resolve, the judge can dismiss the case or, in civil cases, direct the jury to decide the case in a specific way. In civil cases, even after the jury has decided, the judge can decide in favor of the other side.

Most state court systems have an intermediate appellate court. Usually, this court decides only appeals from trial court decisions. In some states, a few issues can be taken directly to the intermediate appellate court. When an appellate court is deciding appeals, it does not accept additional evidence. It uses the evidence presented in the record from the trial court. Appellate courts almost always accept the determination of the facts by the jury or judge in the trial court because the jury and judge see the witnesses and can better judge their credibility. Usually the appellate court bases its decision on whether proper procedures were followed in the trial court and whether the trial court properly interpreted the law. However, an appellate court will occasionally find that a jury verdict is so clearly contrary to the evidence that it will either reverse the decision or order a new trial.

Each state has a single court at the highest level, usually called the supreme court. In some states the name is different. For example, in New York the highest court is called the Court of Appeals, while trial courts are called supreme courts. The highest level court in each state decides appeals from the intermediate appellate courts or, in states without intermediate appellate courts, from trial courts. The highest level court frequently has other duties, including adopting rules of procedure for the state court system, determining who may practice law in the state, and disciplining lawyers for improper conduct.

Federal Court System

The federal court system has a structure similar to the state court system. The trial courts are the United States District Courts and special purpose courts, such as the Court of Claims, which determines certain claims against the United States. Federal trial courts are fundamentally different from state trial courts because they all have limited jurisdiction. A suit must either present a federal question or be between citizens of different states. In many types of cases, the controversy must involve at least $10,000. Federal questions include cases involving the application of federal statutes and regulations and cases involving possible violations of rights under the United States Constitution. When a federal trial court decides a controversy between citizens of different states, it is acting under what is called its "diversity jurisdiction." In diversity cases, federal court procedures are used, but the law of the applicable state is used, rather than federal law.

Sometimes federal trial courts will decline to decide state law questions until they have been decided by a state court. This is called *abstention*. It is designed to leave state issues for state courts and minimize the workload of the federal courts. Federal courts will generally not abstain when there are also important federal questions not affected by the state law question. Some states have procedures by which the federal courts can directly ask the highest state court to decide a question of state law.

Appeals from the federal trial courts go to a United States Court of Appeals. The United States is divided into twelve areas, called circuits, numbered one through eleven, plus the District of Columbia Circuit.

The highest level court in the United States is the United States Supreme Court. It decides appeals from the United States Courts of Appeals. Decisions of the highest state courts may also be appealed to the Supreme Court if they involve federal laws or the United States Constitution. Sometimes when the courts of appeals or the highest state courts decline to review a lower court decision, the decision can be directly appealed to the Supreme Court.

The Supreme Court has the authority to decline to review most cases. With only a few exceptions, a request for review is made by filing a petition for a *writ of certiorari*. If the Court grants the writ, the record of the lower court decision is transmitted to the Supreme Court for review. In most cases, the Court denies the writ, which is indicated by *"cert. denied,* [vol.] U.S. [page] ([year])" at the end of the case citation. Denial of a *writ of certiorari* does not indicate approval of the lower court decision; it merely means the Court declined to review the decision.

Stare Decisis

When a court is confronted with an issue, it is bound by the doctrine of *stare decisis* to follow the precedents of higher courts in the same court system that have jurisdiction over the geographic area where the court is located. Each appellate court, including the highest court, is generally also bound to follow the precedents of its own decisions, unless it decides to overrule the precedent due to changing conditions. Thus, decisions from equal or lower courts or from courts in other court systems do not have to be followed. One exception is when a federal court is deciding a controversy between citizens of different states and must follow the state law as determined by the highest court of the state. Another exception is when a state court is deciding a controversy involving a federal law or constitutional question and must follow the decisions of the United States Supreme Court. Another reason that a court may change its prior position is that controlling statutes or regulations are changed.

When a court is confronted with a question that is not answered by statutes or regulations and the question has not been addressed by its court system, the court will usually examine the judicial solutions reached in other systems to help decide the new issue. When a court decides to reexamine its position on an issue it has addressed, the court will often examine the judicial decisions of the other systems to decide whether to overrule its position. There is a general tendency toward consistency among court systems. A clear trend in decisions across the country can form a basis for a reasonable legal assessment of how to act even when the courts in a hospital's area have not decided the issue. However, a court is not bound by the decisions from other systems, and it may reach a different conclusion.

There can be a majority approach to an issue that many state court systems follow and several minority approaches that other states follow. State courts show more consistency on some issues than others. For example, nearly all state courts have completely eliminated charitable immunity. However, while nearly all states require informed consent to medical procedures, some states determine the information that must be provided to patients by reference to what a patient needs to know, while other states make the determination by reference to what other physicians would disclose. A few states have not yet decided which reference to use.

Courts in different states may reach different conclusions because state statutes and regulations differ. For example, the Georgia legislature enacted a statute that states that a physician need only disclose "in general terms the treatment or course of treatment" to obtain an informed consent.[8] In 1975 a Georgia court interpreted the statute to eliminate the requirement that risks be disclosed to obtain an informed consent.[9] Therefore, Georgia courts no longer will base liability on failure to disclose risks.[10] Courts in other states are very unlikely to consider Georgia court decisions concerning this issue because the decisions are based on Georgia statutes, not on a change in the common law of Georgia.

In summary, while it is important to be aware of trends in court decisions across the country, legal advice should be sought before taking actions based on decisions from court systems that do not have jurisdiction over the geographic area in which the hospital is located.

NOTES

1. 381 U.S. 479 (1965). (The case citations following case names are explained at the beginning of the Index of Cases at the end of this book.)

2. Huron Portland Cement Co. v. Detroit, 362 U.S. 440 (1960).

3. Hillsborough County v. Automated Medical Laboratories, 105 S. Ct. 2371 (U.S. 1985).

4. Robin v. Incorporated Village of Hempstead, 30 N.Y.2d 347, 285 N.E.2d 285, 334 N.Y.S.2d 129 (N.Y. 1972).

5. 5 U.S. (1 Cranch) 137 (1803).

6. *E.g.*, Mikota v. Sisters of Mercy, 183 Iowa 1378, 168 N.W. 219 (1918) [establishing charitable immunity].

7. *E.g.*, Haynes v. Presbyterian Hosp. Ass'n, 241 Iowa 1269, 45 N.W.2d 151 (Iowa 1950) [overruling charitable immunity].

8. Ga. Code Ann. §31-9-6(d) (1982).

9. Young v. Yarn, 136 Ga. App. 737, 222 S.E.2d 113 (1975).

10. *E.g.*, Padgett v. Ferrier, 172 Ga. App. 335, 323 S.E.2d 166 (Ga. Ct. App. 1984). The Georgia Supreme Court has interpreted a similar statute concerning consent to sterilization as limiting the applicability of the informed consent doctrine: Robinson v. Parrish, 251 Ga. 496, 306 S.E.2d 922 (1983).

Chapter 2

The Legal Basis and Governance of Hospitals

A hospital is a legal entity that derives its powers and many of the limitations on its powers from its legal basis. Familiarity with a hospital's legal basis is essential to an understanding of its organization and powers. A hospital can be one of five types of organizations—a governmental agency, a nonprofit corporation, a for-profit corporation, a partnership, or a sole proprietorship. These legal organizations are discussed in more detail in this chapter.

The organization of most hospitals, regardless of their type, includes a governing body, an administrator, and an organized medical staff. The governing body has the ultimate responsibility and authority to establish goals and policies, select the administrator, and appoint the members of the medical staff. The administrator is delegated the responsibility and authority to manage the day-to-day business of the hospital within the policies established by the governing body. The organized medical staff is delegated the responsibility and authority to maintain the quality of medical services in the hospital, subject to the ultimate responsibility of the board. The duties, authority, liability, selection, and rights of the governing body, administrator, and medical staff are discussed in more detail in this chapter and Chapter 7.

The hospital is a unique organization in that most decisions concerning the use of its staff, equipment, and supplies are made by physicians who are not employees or agents of the hospital. Physicians are usually legally independent of the hospital and accountable primarily through the organized medical staff.

LEGAL BASIS

The powers of the hospital and its governance structure are derived from its legal basis, which also imposes limitations on those powers. The hospital

15

can be a governmental entity, a corporation (nonprofit or for-profit), a partnership, or sole proprietorship. Each form of organization has its own implications for the governance of the hospital. While the powers of the hospital usually cannot be expanded without changing its underlying legal basis, many additional limitations may be imposed by contract, by government, or by restrictions in gifts and bequests that the hospital accepts. This section discusses the powers and limitations imposed by the legal basis of the hospital.

Governmental Hospitals

The legal basis of governmental hospitals is found in state and federal statutes. Governmental hospitals are not corporations in most states. They are created by a special statute for the specific hospital or by a governmental unit pursuant to a statute explicitly or implicitly authorizing units of that type to create hospitals. Examples of the second type are (a) a hospital created by a county pursuant to a law authorizing counties to establish hospitals and (b) a state university hospital created by a board of regents under its implied authority to take steps necessary to provide a medical education.

The statute that provides the legal basis for a governmental hospital often includes specific duties or limitations on actions. For example, in some states, county hospitals are required to care for indigent residents. Some county hospital statutes prohibit purchases from trustees and restrict how and to whom property of the hospital may be sold or leased. Another example is the Illinois law giving the board of commissioners of each county the power to establish an absolute limit on the expenditures of county hospitals regardless of the source of funds.[1]

Challenges to asset transfers or facility leases from public hospitals to corporations have been frequent. For example, a North Carolina court ruled in 1985 that a county hospital could not be leased to a for-profit management company because (1) there was no statutory authority for the lease and (2) the lease violated a restriction in the deed to the property that would have caused the loss of the property.[2] In 1985, the Georgia Supreme Court upheld the restructuring of a county hospital in which the hospital was leased to a nonprofit corporation governed by a board controlled by members of the county hospital authority.[3] The court found that public hospitals needed to be more competitive and that the lease would enable the hospital to better serve the public health needs of the community. In another case, the Kansas Supreme Court upheld transfer of assets of a county hospital to a nonprofit corporation because the transfer was authorized by a constitutional statute.[4]

When a governmental entity acts outside its authority, its actions are usually void. For example, the Missouri Supreme Court ruled in 1971 that a bank could not collect on certain debts that a public hospital had endorsed because the hospital did not have the authority to endorse them.[5]

Corporations

A corporation is a separate legal entity distinct from the individuals who own and control it. In the past, each corporation was created by an individual act of the legislature granting articles of incorporation. Today states have general corporation laws that authorize a state official to create a corporation by issuing articles of incorporation. One of the legal benefits of incorporation is that the owners' liability exposure is limited to their investment in the corporation. They cannot be individually liable beyond their investment except when they cause the injury by their personal acts or omissions. The corporation itself is liable from its resources, which include the owners' investments. Another benefit is corporate perpetual life. Death of an owner does not terminate the corporation; only the ownership is changed. Unless the corporation is tax exempt or elects another special tax status, the corporation must pay taxes on its earnings, but in most situations the owners of the corporation do not have to pay personal income tax on the corporation's earnings until the earnings are distributed to them.

Corporations may be for profit or nonprofit. A for-profit corporation is operated with the intention of earning a profit that may be distributed to its owners. The earnings of a nonprofit corporation may not be distributed for the benefit of individuals. A nonprofit hospital is sometimes called a charitable hospital, while a for-profit hospital is sometimes called an investor-owned or a proprietary hospital.

The powers of the corporation include only those powers expressed or implied in the articles of incorporation. Some corporations have articles that limit the type of business the corporation may conduct. When a hospital corporation plans to start a new line of business or abandon a present activity, the articles must be examined. Many modern corporations have articles that do not limit the scope of their activities; they authorize any business that a corporation may lawfully conduct. Other corporations may find it necessary to amend their articles before substantially changing their scope of business.

Express Corporate Authority

Any business corporation derives its authority to act from the state that creates it. The articles of incorporation state the purposes of its existence and the express powers the corporation is authorized to exercise in order to carry out its purposes. The state corporation laws also grant some express authority. Acts performed within the scope of this express authority are clearly proper. Similarly, performance of expressly prohibited acts is clearly improper.

Implied Corporate Authority

In addition to the express authority, implied powers can be inferred from corporate existence. Examples of implied authority include the power to have a corporate name, a corporate seal, and perpetual existence; the power to enact corporate bylaws; and the power to purchase and hold property. These powers are often enumerated in the incorporation statutes and become express authority.

Corporations have implied authority to do any acts necessary to exercise the express authority and to accomplish the purposes of the corporation. The act must tend directly to accomplish the corporation's purpose in a manner not otherwise prohibited by law. Benefit or profit to the corporation is not sufficient. The act need not be usual or indispensably necessary, but it must be reasonably adapted and appropriate to accomplish the corporation's purpose.

Some hospital corporations have articles of incorporation that limit them to hospital-related activities. It is often important to determine whether an activity will be viewed as sufficiently related to and, thus, necessary for hospital purposes.

Some activities that are usually considered closely related to patient care include the operation of a cafeteria, gift shop, or parking lot. While these activities provide income for the hospital, they have the primary function of providing a service for patients, their families, and other hospital visitors. Authority for these activities is usually implied.

While the general purpose of the hospital corporation has remained the same over the years, the methods by which this purpose is fulfilled may vary, depending upon changing conditions. Thus, activities that might have seemed totally unrelated to the purpose of a hospital in the past now have a definite, if not essential, relationship.

Once the activity questioned is found to have a definite relation to the accomplishment of the hospital's purpose, the fact that it is conducted at a profit is immaterial. Conducting these related activities is within the implied authority of the corporation in the same manner as operating a hospital laboratory that bills for its services.

When nonprofit hospitals maintain a nurses' residence or offices for physicians, their authority is sometimes challenged because these facilities also provide a direct benefit to the nurses and physicians who use them. The challengers assert that the nonprofit hospital's implied authority is limited to actions for the benefit of patients. Courts weigh the utility of the facilities to the hospital against the utility to the benefited groups and determine if the facilities are primarily intended to accomplish the hospital's purpose and only incidentally to benefit the users. Nurses' residences are now generally recognized as primarily accomplishing the hospital's purposes because they place nurses within easy call of the hospital and help attract competent nurses to staff the hospital. Implied authority is generally found. The same reasoning is generally applicable to the maintenance of physicians' offices on the premises, although this development is more recent.

In 1966 a Connecticut court allowed a hospital to construct a medical office building on land that had been donated to it for maintaining and carrying on a general hospital.[6] The court recognized the trend toward providing private offices for rental to staff members and the fact that offices aid in the work of general hospitals. The court found it to be within the discretion of the governing board to use this method to improve patient care.

As a hospital moves into other activities, such as ownership of an oil well, a manufacturing company, or a fast food outlet, it is much less likely that a court will find implied authority if the articles of incorporation narrowly define the corporation's purpose. Hospitals considering these activities must consider changes in the articles of incorporation or creation of subsidiary corporations. Without these changes, they risk acting outside their powers.

Even when a corporation has authority for an activity, many other factors must be considered. For example, if the hospital has exemption from property or income taxes, it must be determined whether the new activity will risk loss of this exemption. There are also regulatory constraints, such as zoning laws that limit the uses of land or licensing and certificate-of-need laws that require permission before certain activities can be started. Hospitals also need to apply business judgment to decide whether it is prudent to engage in the activity.

Consequences of Ultra Vires *Acts*

When a corporation acts outside its authority, the act is said to be *ultra vires*. In some states, an *ultra vires* contract cannot be enforced. The courts will not require the parties to complete what they have agreed to do, nor will they order one party to pay the other for its injuries when the contract is not fulfilled. In some states, the defense of *ultra vires* has been abolished, so these contracts are enforced. The state or the members of the corporation generally have the right to obtain an injunction to prevent the performance of an *ultra vires* act. This is illustrated by the case of *Queen of Angels Hospital v. Younger,* in which the court ruled that the articles of incorporation required the corporation to continue operating a hospital, so the governing board could not lease the hospital and use the rent to operate clinics.[7] *Ultra vires* acts can also justify revocation of the articles of incorporation by the state, thus dissolving the corporation.

If an *ultra vires* act is already completed, courts will normally permit it to stand, unless the state intervenes. The state may obtain an order for the corporation to erase the *ultra vires* act by disposing of property, discontinuing services, or taking other steps.

Some courts have imposed a stricter standard on nonprofit corporations because of the public interest in their charitable activities.

Changing Corporate Documents

Articles of incorporation and bylaws of corporations are changed for many reasons, including (1) to permit expansion into new activities; (2) to reorganize the corporation, frequently in an effort to shelter activities from various regulations; and (3) to adapt to other changes in the environment. Corporate document changes are usually possible as long as proper legal procedures are followed and other members of the corporation are not treated too unfairly.

A 1967 Vermont case illustrates changing the articles for reasons other than altering the business of the corporation. The court upheld an amendment to the articles that required a one-dollar contribution from members. Previously, any adult resident of a certain area of Vermont had been a member without making any contribution. The hospital made the change so it could more easily determine its membership.[8]

When basic corporate documents are changed, the hospital has a duty to deal fairly with other members of the corporation. If this duty is violated, the changes may be declared void. For example, an Arizona court ruled that an amendment to the articles of incorporation was void because of the unfair way it was adopted.[9] A few hours before the vote on the amendment, the board of directors designated 159 new members of the corporation from among their friends, relatives, and associates so that together they would have more votes than the 60 physicians who were the other members of the corporation. Even though the board had the authority to appoint the new members, the court found the appointment of the new members, plus the way their proxy votes were used, to be too unfair.

The legislature that creates the corporation reserves the power to amend the corporation laws and the articles even if the corporation or its members do not want the change. This power is illustrated by a ruling of the highest court of New York upholding a legislative amendment to the articles of a hospital requiring the outgoing members of the governing board to be replaced by persons selected by the remaining members of the board rather than by a vote of the corporation's membership.[10]

Some legislatures have considered controlling the composition of the governing board. West Virginia enacted a law that requires 40 percent of the boards of each nonprofit and local governmental hospital to be composed of consumer representatives, selected in equal proportions from small businesses, organized labor, elderly persons, and lower income persons. Special consideration must also be given to women, racial minorities, and the handicapped. Failure to comply can result in loss of the hospital's license, fine, or imprisonment.[11] A federal district court found the statute constitutional.[12] The decision is being appealed.

Corporations have broad powers to change their bylaws as long as they comply with procedures and restrictions set forth in their articles and the state's corporation law. For example, the Illinois Supreme Court ruled that a board could amend the bylaws to end elections of board members and to provide for replacement board members to be selected by present board members, since the articles of incorporation did not forbid the change.[13]

Bylaws and bylaw amendments can be adopted orally or in writing, or by acts as well as words, except where a statute or the articles of incorporation require a certain mode of adoption. Courts have found implied adoption of bylaws from a uniform course of conduct.[14]

Partnership

A business can be organized as a partnership of several individuals or organizations. One benefit of a partnership is that income tax is paid only by the partners; no separate income tax is paid by the partnership. However, there is no limitation on the potential liability of the partners, and it is more difficult to arrange the affairs of the partnership to survive the death or withdrawal of a partner. The potential liability of some of the partners can be limited through what is called a limited partnership, but there must be at least one partner whose liability is not limited. It is unusual for hospitals to be operated as partnerships.

Sole Proprietorship

A business can also be organized as a sole proprietorship, which means it is owned by one individual who has not incorporated the business. All the income of the business is taxed as the personal income of the owner, and there is no limitation on the potential liability of the owner. It is unusual for hospitals to be operated as sole proprietorships.

GOVERNANCE

The organization of most hospitals includes a governing body, an administrator, and an organized medical staff. Their duties, authority, liability, selection, and rights are discussed in the rest of this chapter and in Chapter 7.

Governing Body

The governing body has the ultimate legal responsibility for the operation of a hospital. In the past, members of governing bodies of many community hospitals did not take an active role in hospital governance. They viewed their positions as honorary and delegated the operation of the hospital to the hospital administration and medical staff. They reluctantly became involved to resolve internal disagreements. Today, active involvement of the members is essential as communities, governmental agencies, and the courts hold the governing body accountable for the activities of the hospital.

The same general duties of supervision and management are applicable to members of governing bodies of for-profit and nonprofit hospitals. The governing bodies of most governmental hospitals have similar duties. Each member has a duty to act as a reasonably prudent person would act under similar circumstances when faced with a similar problem.

Duty To Act with Due Care

Members of the governing board have a duty to exercise reasonable care and skill in the management of corporate affairs and to act at all times in good faith and with complete loyalty to the corporation. This general duty applies to the governing boards of governmental, nonprofit, and for-profit hospitals.

The general duty of due care requires any member of a hospital governing board to fulfill the functions of a member personally. The member must attend meetings and participate in the consideration of matters before the board. All board members assume responsibility for decisions made by the board that they do not oppose.

These principles were applied in a 1947 Minnesota case involving an agreement by two individuals that if they were elected to the hospital board, they would take no part in the management of hospital affairs. The court ruled that they had a duty to the corporation that they could not legally bargain away, so the agreement was void.[15] A more recent case involving failure of board members to use due diligence is *Stern v. Lucy Webb Hayes National Training School for Deaconesses and Missionaries.*[16] The hospital board had delegated investment decisions to a committee of board members. The delegation would have been proper if the board had supervised the committee and periodically scrutinized its work. Since they failed to do this, they had not fulfilled their duty to use due diligence. The actual investment decisions involved conflicts of interest that will be discussed later in this chapter.

Preservation of Assets

The general duty to act with due care and loyalty requires reasonable steps to preserve the hospital's assets from injury, destruction, and loss. Appropriate protection varies with the circumstances. Many forces are beyond the control of the hospital, so it is not always possible to preserve specific property. Sometimes the cost of preservation may exceed the value of the property to the hospital. The law does not expect the impossible, but instead requires prudent judgment in deciding how to provide for the preservation of the hospital's property. The duty to preserve property applies not only to the land, buildings, equipment, and investments of the hospital, but also to its rights under contracts, wills, and other legal claims. It also includes protection against liability losses.

Buildings and equipment should be maintained in good repair, and necessary expenditures of hospital funds should be authorized for this purpose. Adequate insurance against fire and other risks should also be maintained.

Most governing boards have a duty to protect the hospital from liability losses. This duty can be satisfied by purchasing insurance against this risk. Most hospitals face a greater risk of loss from liability judgments than from fires or other disasters. Many hospitals have elected to self-insure a large part of their risk exposure by setting aside funds for this purpose, but they still generally purchase insurance against larger losses.

Hospitals in some states still enjoy complete or partial immunity from liability based on their governmental or charitable nature. In some of these states, it may not be necessary to secure liability insurance. However, except where specifically forbidden by statute, it is unlikely that a decision by the board to carry liability insurance would be considered beyond its authority. Purchase of insurance protects the hospital if immunity is ended, provides legal counsel to defend claims, and may promote good public relations and social responsibility, especially if the policy requires the insurance company to waive the immunity defense.

The governing board has a duty to pay all taxes due on the hospital property so that no penalties are incurred. If the corporation qualifies for a tax exemption, the governing board must treat this exemption as an asset of the corporation to be preserved and protected like any other asset.

The governing board must enforce rights to which the hospital is entitled. This includes supervising collection of bills or hospital services and authorizing appropriate legal suits when justified. If the hospital is entitled to property under a will, the interest of the hospital should be protected. The board has a corollary duty to defend the hospital from the claims of others. However, in all situations the board must act reasonably under the circumstances. Some claims are not worth pursuing or should be settled out of court. The board's duty will generally be satisfied if the board conforms to sound business practices.

Basic Management Functions

The governing board has general authority to manage hospital business. This authority is absolute as long as the board acts within the law. Questions of policy and internal management are usually left by the courts wholly to board discretion. When departure from board duties is clear, the courts will intervene.

The basic management functions of the governing board include (1) selection of corporate officers and agents; (2) general control of the compensation of such agents; (3) delegation of authority to the administrator and subordinates; (4) establishment of policies; (5) exercise of businesslike control of expenditures; and (6) supervision and vigilance over the welfare of the whole corporation.

Specific management duties peculiar to hospitals include (1) determining the policies of the hospital in connection with community health needs; (2) maintaining proper professional standards in the hospital; (3) assuming a general responsibility for adequate patient care throughout the institution; and (4) providing adequate financing of patient care.

The authority to manage hospital business may be delegated to the administrator or to committees. In practice, much of this authority is expressly or implicitly delegated. If authority is not delegated or is not conferred on officers by statute or by the articles or bylaws, the governing board is the only body authorized to exercise the authority and to represent the corporation. The governing body is under no obligation to delegate any of its management functions. Any delegation of the policy-making function is subject to revocation by the governing board at any time. Since there is no obligation to delegate any part of the function, there is no obligation to continue a delegation once made. If revocation breaches a contract, the hospital may have to pay for injuries the revocation causes.

The directors cannot delegate their responsibility. The power to delegate authority is implied from the business necessities of managing the corporation. To avoid abdicating its responsibility, the governing body must have some mechanism to retain accountability through oversight of the exercise of the delegated authority.

Inherent in the management function is the authority of the board to establish policies for the hospital. The board may directly exercise its policy-making authority by adopting rules or it may delegate the authority. Hospital administrators, their subordinates, or hospital committees may be permitted to make policies or formulate rules and regulations, subject to review by the board. One example of the policy-making power is a Georgia Supreme Court decision upholding a hospital rule requiring that all computerized tomography (CT) scans of hospital patients be performed with the hospital machine, not with a machine outside the hospital.[17] Chapter 7 includes a discussion of the court decisions addressing the broad powers of the governing body to establish policies concerning the medical staff.

Courts do not always approve board policies. For example, some hospital policies concerning pregnancy termination and sterilization have been declared unconstitutional. This is discussed in Chapter 15.

Courts have reviewed several board actions concerning affiliation, relocation, sale, or dissolution of hospitals. In 1950, the Attorney General of Missouri challenged a proposed affiliation of Barnard Free Skin and Cancer Hospital with Washington University Medical Center that involved relocation of Barnard Hospital.[18] The Attorney General asserted that the proposal violated several provisions of the gifts and will of Mr. Barnard that established and supported Barnard Hospital. The Missouri Supreme Court found that the affiliation contract was a reasonable exercise of the board's discretionary powers and did not violate any conditions imposed by the gifts and bequests of Mr. Barnard. In the 1960s a New Jersey city sought to enjoin a hospital from relocating outside the city limits.[19] The court denied the injunction because the hospital had legally amended its articles of incorporation to give the board the authority to relocate, and the board had found the relocation to be in the best interests of the hospital. When a nonprofit hospital corporation sought approval in Illinois to sell all of its assets to another nonprofit corporation and to dissolve, the court ruled that the sale was permitted in Illinois because (1) the purchaser was a nonprofit corporation with similar purposes and (2) the purchaser contracted to continue to devote the property to hospital purposes.[20] Note that in the *Queen of Angels Hospital* case discussed earlier in this chapter, the California court decided that the hospital corporation could not abandon the hospital by leasing it and using the rents to operate another business unless the articles of incorporation were changed. In another Missouri case, a nonprofit hospital association chartered to provide hospital services to the employees of a railroad company had sold its hospital and was distributing the assets to the members.[21] Several members challenged the dissolution of the association. The court found the dissolution to be beyond the authority of the board under Missouri law because it was not expressly authorized by the articles of incorporation, not approved by a sufficient percentage of the membership, and not of imperative necessity due to the lack of a reasonable prospect of successfully continuing the business. These cases illustrate that questions concerning the board's authority frequently arise when it is contemplating a major change in the corporation's business. When state law is not clear, it is prudent to seek ratification from a court before attempting relocation, sale, or dissolution.

Duty To Provide Satisfactory Patient Care

The duty to provide satisfactory patient care is an essential element of the board duty to operate the hospital with due care and diligence, applying equally to for-profit and nonprofit hospitals. Through fulfillment of this duty, the basic purpose of the hospital is accomplished. Actions required by this duty extend from the purchase of suitable equipment for patient treatment (subject to the hospital's financial ability) to the hiring of competent employees. Two important required actions are (1) selection and review of the performance of the medical staff and (2) selection and supervision of a competent hospital administrator, which is discussed later in this chapter.

The duty to select members of the medical staff is legally vested in the governing board as part of its duty to manage the hospital and maintain a satisfactory standard of patient care. To fulfill its duty, the governing board, while cognizant of the importance of hospital staff membership to physicians, must meet its obligation to maintain standards of good medical practice in dealing with matters of staff appointment and discipline.

In *Darling v. Charleston Community Memorial Hospital,*[22] the court held that the hospital governing board has a duty to establish mechanisms for the medical staff to evaluate, advise, and, where necessary, take action when an unreasonable risk of harm to a patient arises from the treatment being provided by a physician.

In *Johnson v. Misericordia Community Hospital,*[23] the hospital was found liable for failing to exercise due care in evaluating and checking the claimed credentials of an applicant for medical staff membership. Hospitals should have appropriate mechanisms for evaluating the competency of candidates for staff appointments and for determining the privileges to be given to physicians.

Hospital responsibilities and physician rights concerning medical staff matters are discussed in detail in Chapter 7.

Duty of Loyalty

The governing body's duty of loyalty to the hospital can be violated by seizing corporate opportunities, self-dealing, and not disclosing conflicts of interest.

A governing body member who becomes aware of an opportunity for the corporation has a duty not to seize that opportunity for private gain unless the corporation elects not to pursue the opportunity. One clear case of seizure of a corporate opportunity concerns a professional service corporation that contracted to provide services to a hospital in Illinois.[24] While the corporation was negotiating with the hospital to continue the contract, one of the two members of the corporation created a competing corporation that contracted with the hospital to provide the services. The court found that the new contract was a seizure of a corporate opportunity, violating the duty of loyalty to the first corporation.

Self-dealing is a contract between the corporation and an entity in which a director has a financial interest. Statutes in some states specifically forbid some types of self-dealing transactions. For example, it is a crime in North Carolina for trustees or officers of a public hospital to own stock in any company that does business with the hospital.[25] However, forbidding all self-dealing may be disadvantageous to the hospital because sometimes the most advantageous contract is with a director or with a company in which a director has an interest. Unless there is a statutory prohibition, most hospitals permit contracts between the corporation and a director if (a) the contract is fair, (b) the interested director does not speak or vote in favor of the contract, and (c) the director makes full disclosure of all important facts concerning the interest. The courts generally believe that the disinterested remainder of the board is able to protect the corporate interest.

Courts have the power to declare any self-dealing contract void. If the fairness of the contract is questioned, the burden of proving fairness falls upon the director with the financial interest. The North Carolina Supreme Court addressed this in a case in which a board had leased an entire hospital to one of the directors.[26] The court said that this could legally be done under certain circumstances, but that those involved would have to overcome a presumption against the validity of the lease. The court ordered further proceedings to give those involved an opportunity to prove the fairness of the lease. Another example is a South Carolina case in which two directors challenged the sale of some land owned by the hospital to another director.[27]

Although the purchaser did not participate in the final vote on the sale, his business associate, who was also a director, did actively participate. The court declared the sale void because the directors did not meet the expected high standard of loyalty.

An extremely strict view of the responsibility of board members of governmental hospitals is often taken by the courts. In a 1960 Arkansas case the court held that a contract between a board member and a governmental hospital for laundry service was improper although the board member's bid was the lowest bid among the several submitted.[28] The court allowed the hospital to pay the fair value of the services that had already been performed. Membership on the board of a governmental hospital is a public office. The danger of conflicts of interest of public officers is considered sufficient, by many courts, to justify holding all contracts between board members and governmental hospitals improper and invalid, even when otherwise advantageous to the hospital.

Conflict of interest is closely akin to self-dealing. While no actual self-dealing may be involved, nondisclosure of conflicting interests may be subject to penalty under statute or result in a breach of common law fiduciary duties. All hospital boards should require periodic disclosure of all potentially conflicting interests.

One of the most extensive judicial discussions of the duties of hospital board members concerning self-dealing and conflicts of interest was *Stern v. Lucy Webb Hayes National Training School for Deaconesses and Missionaries,*[29] involving Sibley Hospital. The court considered allegations that directors of Sibley Hospital, a nonprofit hospital, breached their duties of care and loyalty. The board of trustees routinely approved financial arrangements made by two of its members, the treasurer and hospital administrator. When the administrator died, the other trustees became more active and discovered that much of the hospital's assets were in savings and checking accounts drawing inadequate or no interest at all. The monies were deposited in institutions with which several of the hospital board members were associated.

The court held that board members who had general financial responsibility breached their duty to the hospital if (1) they failed to supervise the actions of persons to whom responsibility for making those decisions had been delegated; (2) they allowed the hospital to conduct a transaction with a business in which they had a substantial interest or held a significant position without disclosing their interest and any facts they were aware of that would indicate such a transaction would not be in the hospital's best interest; (3) they voted in favor of or actively participated in making a decision concerning a transaction with a business in which they held a substantial interest or held a significant position; or (4) they failed to perform their duties honestly, in good faith, and with a reasonable amount of care and diligence.

Although the court found that the trustees had breached their duty to the hospital, it did not remove them from their positions. It required that written financial procedures and policies be established and that trustees be required to disclosure their interests in financial institutions with which the hospital had dealings. Written financial statements were to be issued to the trustees before each board meeting. In addition, the court required newly elected board members to read the order and memorandum issued with its decision.

Liability of Directors

Although members of hospital governing boards are sometimes called trustees, they are usually not held to the strict standard of a trustee of a trust but instead are judged by the standard applicable to directors of other business corporations. Trustees of trusts are generally liable for simple negligence. Directors of business corporations are generally not liable for mere negligence in exercising their judgment concerning the business of the corporation; they are liable only for gross or willful negligence. This "business judgment" rule offers directors wide latitude for their actions taken in good faith. The *Stern* case involving Sibley Hospital is an example of courts applying the business corporation standard to hospital directors. The directors were not personally liable for the money the hospital lost while the hospital's funds were earning inadequate interest. A 1948 decision by a federal court of appeals also clearly stated that hospital directors were not personally liable for mere mistakes of judgment.[30]

Directors of hospitals are sometimes named as personal defendants in malpractice suits involving the hospital. The general rule is that a director is not personally liable for medical malpractice unless the director individually participated in or directed the wrongful act that caused the injury. This rule is illustrated by a 1980 South Carolina decision, in which the court ruled that the directors could not be sued for the death of a patient during an operation due to the erroneous installation of a new medical gas system in which the oxygen and nitrous oxide lines were crossed.[31] The court said that the directors would not be personally liable even if the plaintiff's allegations—that the directors had failed to hold meetings, failed to oversee the hospital management, and failed to confirm inspection of the medical gas unit—were correct. While the hospital could be liable for the consequences of the crossed lines, the directors could not. However, when a corporate officer knows that the corporation is violating the standard of care and fails to take any action, the officer may be personally liable. For example, a District of Columbia court ruled in 1984 that a corporate officer of a clinic could be personally liable to a patient harmed by overnight treatment in violation of local law where the officer knew of the practice and did nothing to stop it.[32]

Even though these general rules limit the liability exposure of directors, defense of these suits can be costly. It is not reasonable to expect directors to serve without pay unless the corporation protects them from the costs of defense and from liability for good faith actions. The general rule is that a corporation may indemnify a director for the costs of defense, judgments, fines, and other expenses resulting from a civil or criminal action if the director acted in good faith and reasonably believed the actions to be lawful and in the best interests of the corporation. Many hospitals purchase insurance to protect directors from these costs. However, some insurance policies may not provide the protection they appear to provide. A federal district court ruled in 1984 that one officer's misrepresentations in the application for the insurance invalidated the coverage for all directors and officers.[33]

Directors can also be criminally liable for certain acts. For example, a federal court affirmed the criminal convictions of several members of a county council, which served as the governing body of a county hospital, for soliciting and receiving kickbacks from architects in return for awarding contracts for a hospital project financed with federal funds. They were each sentenced to one year in prison.[34]

Selection and Dismissal of Directors

Board members are selected in several ways. In many hospitals, the board is self-perpetuating. When there is a vacancy on the board, the remaining members of the board select a new replacement member. Another selection mechanism is for the stockholders or members of the corporation to elect the members of the board. Board members for governmental hospitals are frequently elected by a vote of the people in the governmental subdivision that owns the hospital. In some states, the boards of certain governmental hospitals are appointed by elected officials.

Usually the terms of office of board members are staggered so that all members are not replaced at the same time. This assures that there will be experienced members who can provide continuity of governance.

If board members are not selected in accord with applicable laws, articles of incorporation, and bylaws, courts may declare actions of the board void. For example, in a Tennessee case board members were not selected as specified in the articles, and several members did not satisfy the membership qualifications.[35] The court declared the vote of the board to transfer the hospital to the county to be void.

When board members are selected by the proper procedure, they must still satisfy the qualifications for membership before they can become board members. This is illustrated by a 1980 California case, in which one person's membership on a public hospital board was challenged.[36] He had been elected to the board by the proper procedure. However, he was also president of a nonprofit private hospital serving the same area. Under California law, anyone who is an officer of a private hospital serving the same area is not qualified to be a member of a public hospital district board. The court set aside the election.

As discussed earlier in this chapter in the section on changing corporate documents, it is possible to change the method of selecting board members.

Sometimes boards try to remove a member. The procedure specified in the articles and bylaws must be followed. In at least one state, a director of a private hospital must be provided with notice of the reason for the action and an opportunity to be heard, whether or not the articles and bylaws require these steps. New Jersey established this rule in a 1897 case in which the court ordered the person restored to the board because this procedure had not been followed.[37] However, in a 1979 Oregon case involving a public hospital, the court affirmed the removal of a hospital board member by the board of county commissioners after he was provided with notice and opportunity to be heard pursuant to a lower court order.[38] The court found that there was substantial evidence supporting the commissioners' decision that the member's lack of candor caused a lack of trust that diminished his effectiveness as a hospital board member and that this was sufficient reason to remove him from the board.

ADMINISTRATOR

As chief executive officer of the hospital, the administrator is concerned with all of the topics covered in this book. The administrator's personal intervention will probably be required when many legal problems discussed in this book arise. In this section the duties, authority, qualifications, and personal liability of the administrator will be covered.

Duties of the Administrator

The administrator of a hospital is the executive officer directly in charge of the hospital, responsible only to the governing board. The administrator is the general supervisor of all hospital operations and is delegated powers by the board to fulfill this responsibility. Although specific areas of responsibility may be delegated to subordinates, the administrator is primarily responsible for the successful, efficient, and orderly management of the hospital. The administrator is the agent and often employee of the governing board and is subject to its superior authority. Even when the administrator is also a board member or a part owner of the hospital, the administrator is an agent of the board and has a duty to carry out the policies adopted by the board.

The multiple hospital system has become a more prevalent form of hospital management and ownership. Both for-profit and nonprofit organizations have established a systems approach for managing multiple hospitals owned or managed by the organization. The organization applies a systematic policy of management designed to be appropriate for various sizes, types, and locations of institutions. To promote efficiency, the organization uses shared services, uniform accounting procedures, centralized support services, and other management methods made possible by the umbrella structure. An administrator in a multiple hospital system may or may not be an employee of the larger organization, but will be subject to its policies.

In governmental hospitals, administrators are usually appointed public officials. Whether public officials or hired supervisors, they are directly responsible to the federal, state, or local body that controls the health facility. In some instances, their conditions of employment may fall within the civil service laws.

The administrator has only the duties either delegated expressly or by implication by the hospital governing board or imposed by law. To fulfill its responsibility, the board appoints an administrator who is charged with certain general hospital management duties. In addition, by resolution, bylaw, or order, the board may assign the administrator other specific duties. Following are examples of duties often delegated by the board.

As board representative, the administrator has the general duty to oversee every activity taking place in the hospital. The administrator is responsible for implementing the board's policies, including obtaining required regulatory agency approvals. The administrator transmits and interprets the board's policy to the medical staff and other personnel and is responsible for informing patients, visitors, hospital personnel, medical staff members, and others of hospital rules. The administrator is also responsible for taking appropriate corrective action concerning noncompliance with hospital rules, except in cases where disciplinary authority has been retained by the board or delegated by the board to others. The administrator also has the general duty to make periodic reports to the board concerning hospital operations.

Normally, administrators will be authorized to select or recommend selection of administrative department heads. Some administrators delegate to department heads the authority to select their assistants, while reserving the authority to coordinate the overall operation of the departments. Administrators are normally made responsible for employment in the hospital and, within budgetary limits, are generally given the authority to fix individual salaries and wages.

When duties are delegated to subordinates, the administrator remains responsible for the duties. The administrator's responsibility is to the board, which ultimately is legally responsible for the hospital.

Administrators are generally responsible for the care of patients. While they should not usurp the functions of the medical and other professional staff, they must make sure that proper admission and discharge procedures are formulated and carried out. They must also cooperate with the medical and professional staff in maintaining satisfactory standards of medical care. In addition, they must see to it that hospital departments work in coordination with each other and with the medical staff to provide satisfactory patient care. The administrator also assists the medical staff with its organizational and administrative problems and responsibilities.

The administrator is usually responsible for the operating funds of the corporation. The administrator's duties include planning and analysis for the governing board. The administrator has the responsibility to advise the board on matters of policy formation, to propose plans of organization of the hospital, to prepare plans for achieving the hospital's objectives, to submit for approval an annual budget, to recommend rates to be charged for hospital services, and to submit various periodic and special reports to the board showing the service and financial experience of the hospital and dealing with other matters as requested by the board.

Unless otherwise directed by the board, the administrator or a delegate is expected to attend all meetings of the board and its committees and to advise the board of significant trends that it needs to know to fulfill its policy-making function. These can include societal, economic, legal, medical, and technical trends, as well as changing conditions in the hospital and in the hospital field.

In some hospitals, administrators fill a dual role by also serving as governing board members. Administrators frequently serve as secretaries of boards. As long as the administrators are nonvoting members, their positions on the boards do not present legal difficulties. When the administrator serves as a voting member of a nonprofit hospital board, caution is required; administrators cannot vote on any question concerning their status or compensation.

In addition to delegated duties, duties are imposed on administrators by state statute or regulation, or by municipal ordinance. Such duties should be obeyed. These duties may include reporting vital statistics information to health authorities and furnishing communicable disease and gunshot wound treatment reports, unless state law imposes the duty on an entity other than

the hospital. Sometimes it is not possible to obey all of the legal requirements because they conflict with each other or because of other reasons.
Legal advice should be sought in these situations to determine the proper
procedure for resolving the conflict or to seek appropriate temporary or
permanent waivers to the requirements.

The most important skill needed to accomplish these varied responsibilities is the art of negotiation. Hospital administration is a series of negotiations. Arrangements must be made that are in the interest of the institution
and the community it serves and that appropriately accommodate the many
groups having an interest in hospital activities. The following partial list of
these groups suggests the complexity of the negotiations required: patients,
their families, physicians, nurses, other hospital staff, hospital directors,
community groups, insurers, other third party payers, bankers, other
lenders, politicians, government officials, and reporters. It is always possible for an adversary or any other interested party to find fault with the
administrator's assessment of the situation, the strategy chosen to solve
problems, or the decision made and the subsequent actions taken. The
performance of an administrator should be judged as a whole, since in the
circle of diverse negotiations, somebody is always on the other side. The
administrator has many persons to deal with and many interests to attempt
to satisfy. Not every negotiation will be successful. The governing board to
whom the administrator is responsible should take into account the complexity of tasks and the inherent difficulties in successful negotiation when
evaluating the actions of their administrator.

Authority of the Administrator

The primary source of the administrator's authority is the governing
board, which normally delegates to the administrator the duty and responsibility of managing the hospital, together with the authority to accomplish
this duty. As a practical matter, the administrator may be able to do many
things that are not challenged, either because people are unaware of the
actions or because people with the right to challenge or forbid them do not
care to do so. Acts that could be successfully challenged are said to be
beyond the scope of the administrator's authority. An administrator acting
beyond authority is subject to several possible legal consequences, including
being dismissed by the board in accordance with its established rules; sued
by the hospital for breach of the employment contract and for any resultant
financial damage to the hospital; held liable by employees or other persons
for damages resulting from negligence or intentional wrongdoing; and subjected to prosecution for any specific criminal laws violated. Insurance is
available to provide protection from some of the exposure to civil liability.

Resolutions of the board may from time to time enlarge the administrator's authority or grant special authority to deal with certain problems. Some of the administrator's authority may be provided in the legal documents organizing the hospital, such as the hospital articles or bylaws. Some aspects of the administrator's authority may be covered in an employment contract. State statutes or regulations may provide for certain administrative powers.

Authority may be either express or implied. Express authority is a written or oral grant giving the administrator responsibility and power to accomplish certain ends. Implied authority consists of those powers that are deemed to be conveyed along with express authority so desired ends may be accomplished. If, for example, the administrator is given responsibility for maintenance of hospital safety, authority to promulgate specific rules is implied, such as one requiring the wearing of specific clothing in certain hospital areas.

The scope of the administrator's express authority may be as broad or as limited as the governing body desires. Authority is implied to the extent necessary to accomplish express responsibilities and duties. The administrator will be deemed to possess only those powers and duties that can be properly delegated. The governing board cannot delegate authority that it does not possess, nor can it delegate certain responsibilities that are nondelegable.

Selecting, Evaluating, and Discharging the Administrator

Governing boards are responsible for selecting administrators to act as their agents in hospital management. Governing boards that try to run hospitals without administrators are subject to extensive criticism and risk legal liability.[39] The governing board must select a competent administrator who will set and maintain satisfactory patient care standards. Minimum standards for administrators are contained in some hospital licensing statutes and regulations and in some statutes creating governmental hospitals. Where legal requirements exist, the administrator appointed by the governing board must at least satisfy the requirements. Governing boards, especially those of hospitals with more complex operations, often find it necessary to appoint administrators with qualifications that exceed the minimum.

Even when no statutory or regulatory standards exist, the board still has a duty to select a competent administrator. This governing board responsibility was the subject of lengthy discussion in a federal court case. A county hospital board had selected an administrator who had had no prior hospital management experience. The administrator padded the bills of patients covered by hospitalization insurance policies, and the insurance company sued to recover the amount of the overcharges. The court criticized the hospital board for selection of the administrator.

> To select a governing board for an institution as complex as a hospital in the manner used here, chosen as political patronage by County Supervisors from their respective districts without any requirement of training, experience or knowledge of what was expected of them was calculated to bring about the very result which developed here. Failing to appreciate their duties and responsibilities led these Trustees to feel, according to their testimony, that they had discharged their duties by picking as Administrator, Salter, a former school teacher, apparently as ignorant of operating a hospital as they themselves were. Their attachment to him was such that, despite the refusal of other agencies to deal with Salter in certain respects, and his dismissal, these Trustees again rehired and restored him to the position of Administrator of the hospital. They seemed to think because Salter had changed the hospital's financial position from a deficit of several thousand dollars to one of approximately the same amount on the black side of the ledger, this justified his restoration.[40]

After appointing an administrator, the governing board must periodically evaluate the administrator's performance. The governing board will be liable if the level of patient care becomes inadequate because of the board's failure to properly supervise the administrator's management. When not satisfied with the performance, the board should take appropriate corrective action, including replacement, if necessary. Failure to remove an incompetent administrator or agent is as much a breach of the duty of due care and diligence as the failure to appoint a competent one.

To assure continuing accountability, the board should set performance standards and mechanisms for measuring administrative performance. Some of the possible indices for judging the performance of a hospital's administrative staff include

- Budgets compare favorably with actual expenditures.
- Costs per patient day compare favorably to those of similar hospitals with a similar case mix.
- Costs per case by department compare favorably to those of similar hospitals with a similar case mix.
- Cash on hand, payables, and receivables are in appropriate relationship with revenue.

- Ratios of payroll to total expense, staff to patients, and work performed per employee work-hour are appropriate.
- In addition to fiscal indices, quality of care, patient relations, and relationships with medical staff, hospital staff, and the community should be considered.

When the board is considering whether to replace the administrator, it should follow the procedures in applicable law, the articles of incorporation, and the bylaws. Some courts have declined to intervene even when the bylaws are not followed. For example, in 1979 the Louisiana Supreme Court declined to order that the administrator of a public hospital be reinstated even though the bylaws had not been followed.[41] The bylaws required a warning and an opportunity to correct any deficiencies before dismissal. The court ruled that it would order reinstatement only if the administrator could prove that he had relied on the bylaws to his detriment. Similarly, the Minnesota Supreme Court refused to intervene when an administrator was discharged.[42] The applicable law provided that the administrator served "at the pleasure of the county board," so he was not entitled to a hearing.

Under the laws of some states, it may be possible for someone other than the board or a court to order the removal of an administrator. For example, in 1982 a state court ruled that the New York Department of Health has the authority to order the removal of a new hospital administrator for not being sufficiently qualified by education or experience.[43]

Liability of the Administrator

Administrators, like other members of society, may be personally liable for their own wrongful actions that injure others.

Administrators can be liable for injuries inflicted by a subordinate only where it is shown that the administrator is at fault due to negligent supervision or careless hiring of the subordinate. An administrator who is not personally at fault is not liable for injuries caused by subordinates. Employers are liable for the injuries wrongfully caused by their employees, but hospital administrators are not the employers of their subordinates. Since administrators are employees of the hospital, the hospital may be liable for the wrongful acts of the administrators. If the hospital is liable, it usually has the right to require the employee who caused the injury to repay the amount of money it has paid to the injured person. In actual practice hospitals rarely exercise this right of indemnification. Liability issues are discussed in more detail in Chapters 10 and 11.

Administrators are not personally liable for contracts made on behalf of the hospital when acting within their authority to contract. However, when administrators exceed their authority and make a contract that the hospital has not empowered them to make, the hospital is not bound by the contract. The administrators are personally liable to the other party to the contract for the loss resulting from the failure to bind the hospital. The administrators are not liable if the hospital ratifies the contract and adopts it as its own. Administrators are not liable for unauthorized acts if they innocently believe they have the power to make the contract and the hospital clothed their position with such apparent, although not real, authority that the other contracting parties reasonably believed the administrators had power to bind the hospital to the contract. If the hospital creates this apparent authority so that innocent third parties are misled, then the law imposes liability on the hospital. However, if the other contracting parties should have suspected the administrator did not have authority, they are legally required to make appropriate inquiries. If the inquiries would have disclosed the administrator's lack of authority, no recovery is allowed against the hospital. The administrator is liable to the other contracting party, even when the administrator has apparent authority, if the administrator made the contract with the intent to defraud.

In a 1957 federal district court case, an insurance company sought to recover the excessive amounts it had paid to a Mississippi hospital because the administrator had padded the bills.[44] The court found both the administrator and the hospital liable to repay the overcharges.

Administrators may be liable civilly or criminally for the breach of duties imposed on them by statute. For example, where the law requires a license or permit before certain acts may be performed and the administrator is required to obtain the license or permit, failure to obtain it may lead to fine or imprisonment. The administrator may also be required to make certain reports to the state. It is doubtful that a hospital administrator would, in actual practice, be fined personally for failure to discharge a statutory duty of this nature, but the possibility exists.

In a 1958 Mississippi Supreme Court case, involving the same administrator and hospital as the 1957 federal case discussed above, a state auditor sought to force the administrator and the hospital board to repay county hospital funds that had been spent without authority.[45] The court analyzed each type of expenditure that the state auditor claimed to be unauthorized and found that several were unauthorized, requiring personal repayment by the administrator and board members.

When the administrator breaches a duty imposed by statute, the administrator may be liable civilly to a person harmed by the statutory violation. Thus, if a statute imposed a positive duty upon officials in charge of mental institutions to keep the contents of medical records confidential, an official who made such records public could be held liable to one who was injured by the violation of the statute.

The federal government and some states, however, have provided a degree of official immunity from personal civil liability for some public officials when following a legal mandate (i.e., performing a "ministerial duty") or when exercising administrative judgment (i.e., performing a "discretionary duty"). The rules vary considerably, and the courts tend to restrict the application of immunity doctrines.

Administrators who become involved in fraudulent schemes can be held criminally liable, as those in other industries can. For example, a Florida administrator who caused a hospital to issue 21 checks, fraudulently endorsed them, and appropriated the proceeds in excess of $850,000 was sentenced to 25 years in prison.[46]

Some prosecutors have pursued criminal charges against administrators when patients have died. In 1984 the Wisconsin Supreme Court upheld the conviction of a nursing home administrator for abuse of residents, but reversed a decision for reckless conduct causing death.[47] One resident had died of exposure after walking away from the facility. Other residents lost weight and had bed sores. The state claimed this was due to understaffing by the administrator.

NOTES

1. County of Cook v. Ayala, 76 Ill.2d 219, 390 N.E.2d 877 (1979).

2. National Medical Enterprises, Inc. v. Sandrock, 72 N.C.App. 245, 324 S.E.2d 268 (1985).

3. Richmond County Hosp. Auth. v. Richmond County, 336 S.E.2d 562 (Ga. 1985).

4. Ullrich v. Board of County Comm'rs of Thomas County, 234 Kan. 782, 676 P.2d 127 (1984).

5. Fulton Nat'l Bank v. Callaway Memorial Hosp., 465 S.W.2d 549 (Mo. 1971).

6. Charlotte Hungerford Hosp. v. Mulvey, 26 Conn. Super. 394, 225 A.2d 495 (1966).

7. 66 Cal. App.3d 359, 136 Cal. Rptr. 36 (1977).

8. Langrock v. Porter Hosp., Inc., 126 Vt. 233, 227 A.2d 291 (1967).

9. Hatch v. Emery, 1 Ariz. App.142, 400 P.2d 349 (1965).

10. In re Mt. Sinai Hosp., 250 N.Y. 103, 164 N.E. 871 (1928).

11. W.Va.Code §16-5B-6a (1984 Supp.).

12. American Hosp. Ass'n v. Hansbarger, 594 F. Supp. 483 (N.D. W. Va. 1984).

13. Westlake Hosp. Ass'n v. Blix, 13 Ill.2d 183, 148 N.E.2d 471 ((1958), *appeal dismissed* 358 U.S. 43 (1958).

14. *E.g.,* In re Rye Psychiatric Hosp. Center, Inc., 101 A.D.2d 309, 476 N.Y.S.2d 339 (1984).

15. Ray v. Homewood Hosp., 223 Minn. 440, 27 N.W.2d 409 (1947).

16. 381 F. Supp. 1003 (D. D.C. 1974).

17. Cobb County v. Prince, 242 Ga. 139, 249 S.E.2d 581 (1978).

18. Taylor v. Baldwin, 247 S.W.2d 741 (Mo. 1952).

19. City of Paterson v. Paterson Gen. Hosp., 97 N.J. Super. 514, 235 A.2d 487 (Ch. Div. 1967).

20. Holden Hosp. Corp. v. Southern Ill. Hosp. Corp., 22 Ill.2d 150, 174 N.E.2d 793 (1961).

21. McDaniel v. Frisco Employes' Hosp. Ass'n, 510 S.W.2d 752 (Mo. Ct. App. 1974).

22. 33 Ill.2d 326, 211 N.E.2d 253 (1965), *cert.denied* 383 U.S. 946 (1966).

23. 99 Wis.2d 708, 301 N.W.2d 156 (1981).

24. Patient Care Servs., S.C. v. Segal, 32 Ill. App.3d 1021, 337 N.E.2d 471 (1975).

25. N.C. Gen. Stat. §14-234 (1983 Supp.); N.C. Atty. Gen. Op. Dec. 6, 1982.

26. Fowle Memorial Hosp. v. Nicholson, 189 N.C. 44, 126 S.E. 94 (1925).

27. Gilbert v. McLeod Infirmary, 219 S.C. 174, 64 S.E.2d 524 (1951).

28. Warren v. Reed, 231 Ark. 714, 331 S.W.2d 847 (1960).

29. 381 F. Supp. 1003 (D. D.C.1974).

30. Beard v. Ackenbach Memorial Hosp. Ass'n, 170 F.2d 859 (10th Cir. 1948).

31. Hunt v. Rabon, 275 S.C. 475, 272 S.E.2d 643 (1980).

32. Vuitch v. Furr, 482 A.2d 811 (D.C. 1984).

33. Shapiro v. American Home Assurance, 584 F. Supp. 1245 (D. Mass. 1984).

34. United States v. Thompson, 366 F.2d 167 (6th Cir. 1966).

35. Bedford County Hosp. v. County of Bedford, 42 Tenn.App. 569, 304 S.W.2d 697 (1957).

36. Franzblau v. Monardo, 108 Cal. App.3d 522, 166 Cal. Rptr. 610 (1980).

37. State ex rel. Welch v. Passaic Hosp. Ass'n, 59 N.J.L. 142, 36 A. 702 (1897).

38. Coldiron v. Board of Comm'rs of Curry County, 39 Or. App. 495, 592 P.2d 1053 (1979).

39. *Community Hospital's Questionable Ethics,* and Barkholz, *Maryland System's Board Refutes Allegations, Promises Improvements,* 15 MOD. HEALTHCARE, June 7, 1985, 5, 44 [hospital operated 18 months without administrator].

40. Reserve Life Ins. Co. v. Salter, 152 F. Supp. 868, 870 (S.D. Miss. 1957).

41. Lamm v. Board of Comm'rs for Vermilion Hosp. Serv. Dist. No. 1, 378 So.2d 919 (La. 1979).

42. State v. Board of County Comm'rs of Hennepin County, 273 Minn. 361, 141 N.W.2d 499 (1966).

43. Harlem Hosp. Center Medical Bd. v. Hoffman, 84 A.D.2d 272, 445 N.Y.S.2d 981 (1982).

44. Reserve Life Ins. Co. v. Salter, *supra* note 40.

45. Golding v. Salter, 234 Miss. 567, 107 So.2d 348 (1958).

46. Bronstein v. State, 355 So.2d 817 (Fla. Dist. Ct. App. 1978); see Touche Ross & Co. v. Sun Bank of Riverside, 366 So.2d 465 (Fla. Dist. Ct. App. 1979) [effort by the hospital to recover the losses due to administrator's crimes].

47. State v. Serebin, 119 Wis.2d 837, 350 N.W.2d 65 (1984).

Chapter 3

Regulation and Accreditation

Hospitals are among the most extensively regulated institutions in the United States. They are regulated by all levels of government and by numerous agencies within each level. As a result of this multiple regulation, hospitals occasionally are confronted with conflicting mandates. Since this problem has received more attention, relief has been provided in some areas. However, conflicts still remain because of the underlying conflicts in societal goals. One example of such conflict is the tension between the cooperation sought by the health planning laws and competition sought by the antitrust laws.

The terms *licensure* and *accreditation* are often confused. Licensure is governmental regulation. The state legislature grants an administrative agency authority to adopt standards hospitals must meet, to grant licenses to institutions that meet the standards, and to enforce continuing compliance. Hospitals that do not have licenses are barred from operating. Those who operate hospitals that violate the standards can lose their licenses or be fined or penalized in other ways. The important features of licensure that distinguish it from accreditation are that (1) it is a function of government; and (2) it is mandatory for hospitals.

In contrast, accreditation is granted by a private authority and is not legally mandated. Many hospitals are accredited by the Joint Commission on Accreditation of Hospitals (JCAH), an organization that includes representatives from the American College of Physicians, the American College of Surgeons, the American Dental Association, the American Hospital Association, and the American Medical Association. Hospitals wishing to be accredited apply to JCAH, pay a fee, and submit to a survey to determine whether they satisfy the standards established by the JCAH and published in its *Accreditation Manual for Hospitals*.[1] The American Osteopathic Association (AOA) accredits osteopathic hospitals and functions similarly to the JCAH. Several states accept JCAH or AOA accreditation as a basis for either full or partial licensure without further state inspection. This acceptance is part of an effort to reduce duplicative hospital inspections.

The Medicare program also has standards for hospital operations, called "conditions of participation."[2] They are not licensing standards, but hospitals must comply with them to qualify for payment from the Medicare program for most services to Medicare beneficiaries. The Medicare law and regulations provide that hospitals accredited by JCAH or AOA are deemed to meet most of the conditions of participation unless a special Medicare inspection finds noncompliance.[3]

Some regulatory or accrediting agencies focus on the entire institution. Other agencies focus on individual services or activities of the hospital, such as the pharmacy or the elevators. Some agencies can focus on the entire institution or individual areas of the institution depending on the circumstances. For example, the certificate-of-need granting agency must give its permission before a new hospital or many new services can be started. Numerous other regulations apply to other aspects of the hospital, such as financing, taxation, planning, waste disposal, communications, transportation, and labor relations.

Other regulatory agencies focus on licensing individuals, and these agencies are discussed in Chapter 8.

LICENSURE OF INSTITUTIONS

The state regulates each hospital as an institution through licensure. The major legal issues concerning licensure are the authority for licensure, the scope of regulations, and the penalties for violations.

Authority

The police power provides state governments with the authority to regulate hospitals. All states have enacted hospital licensing statutes. These statutes usually grant an agency the authority to adopt standards, to grant licenses, and to revoke licenses or impose other penalties when the standards are violated. Licensing statutes and regulations must be a reasonable exercise of the police power and must not deny due process or equal protection of the laws. For the agency's rules to be enforceable, the rules must be within the authority properly delegated to the agency in the statute. The rules must be adopted using the procedure the state specifies for administrative rule making. The procedure usually includes public notice of the proposed rule and an opportunity for the public to comment before it becomes final. However, some states require additional steps before a rule becomes enforceable, such as an economic impact statement.[4]

If the agency has the statutory authority, if the rules do not violate due process by being vague or arbitrary, and if the proper procedures were followed to adopt the rule, challenging the rules will be difficult regardless of the actual impact of the rule. For example, extremely detailed hospital licensing rules were contested in Pennsylvania on the ground that they were an attempt by the Department of Health to take away the "management prerogatives" of hospital governing bodies and administrators. In 1980 the Pennsylvania Supreme Court decided that the department had the statutory authority and upheld the rules, even though they might supplant part of the traditional authority of hospital management.[5]

Scope of Regulations

Hospital licensing regulations usually address the organization of the hospital, requiring an organized governing body or some equivalent, an organized medical staff, and an administrator. The relationship among these elements usually is also addressed. The regulations may require that general hospitals provide certain basic services, including laboratory, radiology, pharmacy, and some emergency services. The regulations generally require that adequate nursing personnel be available. They also may establish standards for facilities, equipment, and personnel for specific services, such as obstetrics, pediatrics, and surgery. The standards may also address safety, sanitation, infection control, record preparation and retention, and other matters.

All standards do not have to be in objective numerical terms to satisfy due process requirements, but courts are reluctant to uphold overly subjective rules. In 1978 a New York court found that several nursing home rules violated due process requirements because they were so subjective that they did not provide adequate notice of the conduct required.[6] The invalidated rules required sewage facilities, nursing staff, and linen laundering to meet the "approval" and "satisfaction" of the Commissioner of the Department of Health. No objective standard was included in those rules. In the same decision, the court upheld another rule concerning the nursing staff that was based on the "needs of the patients." The court considered this to be an objective standard because it believed the needs would be "reasonably well identifiable by all competent observers." Courts recognize that in some areas objective standards are either impossible or would themselves be too arbitrary. Thus, courts have upheld enforcement of subjective standards if fairly applied. This is illustrated by another New York nursing home case,

in which somewhat vague standards were upheld because the actual violations clearly deviated from the objective of the rules and the agency had
provided written explanations of the violations to the owners.[7]

One focus of hospital licensure is the integrity of hospital buildings.
Numerous special building code and fire safety code regulations apply to
hospitals and are frequently enforced through the licensing mechanism.
These codes can provide for inspections of the hospital by building inspectors and fire marshals who may either have authority to initiate action
through their own agencies or refer the matter to the licensing agency to
initiate action.

Often administrative agencies have the authority to permit exceptions to
their rules by granting a waiver or variance. Undue hardship may result
from unbending application of the rules, and the public's best interest may
not be served by inflexibility. For example, one state required all hospital
rooms to have showers for patients. When the rules were written, apparently no one thought of intensive care units where patients could not use
showers, so it was necessary for hospitals in the state to obtain waivers until
the rule could be changed. The need for waivers sometimes arises because
some systems of rules, especially building and fire codes, are so complex
that individual rules contradict each other when applied to unusual situations. It may be necessary to obtain an authoritative determination of which
rule to follow and a waiver of the rule that is not to be followed. Waivers
may also be necessary to implement innovative practices. In general, waivers are granted only when (1) there is a substantial need for relief from the
rule; (2) the public purpose will be better served by the exception; and (3)
the exception will not create a hazard to the health and well-being of
patients or others that is excessive in light of the public purpose being
served.

Violations and Sanctions

Two of the fundamental elements of due process are notice and an
opportunity to be heard. Unless the deficiencies of a hospital immediately
threaten life or health, the state can close a hospital or impose other
penalties for licensing law violations only after giving the hospital adequate
notice of the violations and an opportunity to be heard. For example, in
1961 a New York court ordered the hospital licensing agency to provide a
hearing before deciding not to renew a hospital's license even though the
hospital lacked many basic services.[8]

Some state statutes and regulations require licensing agencies to give a
hospital an opportunity to correct deficiencies before imposing sanctions.

Although this opportunity is not constitutionally required, it must be provided when guaranteed by state law, or any sanctions will be invalid unless immediate action is justified by life- or health-threatening deficiencies.

Some hospital licensing statutes recognize that it may not be in the public interest to revoke a hospital's license for minor violations. These statutes provide a range of lesser penalties and reserve license suspension or revocation for "substantial" violations. States vary in how they define a substantial violation. In every state sufficiently serious violations lead to license revocation.[9]

When a licensing agency makes an adverse decision, the hospital can generally seek judicial review. In most states, the courts will only review the administrative hearing record and will not accept additional evidence. Courts will overrule the agency only if the decision was beyond the agency's authority, the agency did not follow proper procedures, or evidence was insufficient to justify the decision.

In addition to the possibility of fines or license suspension or revocation, some hospital licensing statutes provide criminal penalties for violations. For example, the operation of a hospital without a license may lead to criminal prosecution.

CERTIFICATE-OF-NEED AND ZONING LAWS

A license is no longer sufficient authority to start a new hospital in most states. Certificate-of-need laws require that the hospital also obtain a permit entitled a *certificate of need* before it can begin construction or operations. Existing hospitals must also obtain a certificate of need before they can begin some new services or make large capital expenditures. Certificate-of-need laws are discussed in more detail in Chapter 5.

Zoning is another potential barrier to starting a new hospital or substantially changing an existing hospital's services. Zoning ordinances are laws adopted by local governmental subdivisions to provide for the safe and orderly development of the locality by specifying where certain types of land use are permitted. Usually, local ordinances are not permitted to exclude hospitals from the governmental subdivision entirely. However, an ordinance that reasonably specified available areas where hospitals could locate would be difficult to attack when a hospital wanted to locate in a forbidden area. Zoning ordinances also limit the height, size, and design of buildings. These limitations often either restrict expansion or require time-consuming efforts to obtain waivers, variances, or amendments to zoning ordinances.

LICENSURE AND PERMITS FOR SERVICES

Hospitals that have institutional licenses may also be required to obtain licenses or permits for individual departments or services. For example, many state and local governments require that separate licenses or permits be obtained for hospital pharmacies, clinical laboratories, radiological equipment, renal dialysis facilities, substance abuse centers, food services, vending machines, elevators, hospital vehicles, waste disposal, and other services. Some states exempt hospitals from having to obtain licenses or permits for some of these services. If the hospital offers the service to other hospitals or to persons other than hospital patients and staff, the exemption may be lost in some states, so it is important to examine applicable laws carefully before offering services to others.

Other Regulations

Many types of laws and regulations do not require licenses and permits. They mandate certain conduct and specify the sanctions for failure to comply. Many regulations are associated with the governmental financing and taxation laws discussed in Chapter 4 and the labor laws discussed in Chapter 9.

REGULATION OF DRUGS AND MEDICAL DEVICES

One of the most heavily regulated activities of the hospital is the use of drugs and medical devices. State laws regulate the operation of pharmacies. Federal laws regulate most aspects of the production, distribution, and use of drugs and medical devices, especially drugs and medical devices involved in interstate commerce. Many states have laws that regulate intrastate commerce involving drugs that is not regulated by the federal laws. Operation of hospital pharmacies is also addressed in the standards of the JCAH and the Medicare conditions of participation.[10]

Modern medicine cannot be practiced without the availability of necessary drugs, so hospitals must provide pharmaceutical services. The Medicare conditions of participation, the JCAH, and hospital licensing laws require pharmaceutical services. They also require that the pharmaceutical services be under the direction of a professionally competent and legally qualified pharmacist.

State Regulation

Some states require hospitals to obtain a separate license or permit for hospital pharmacies. In those states, hospitals must comply with the pharmacy licensing regulations. Other states regulate hospital pharmacies through the hospital licensing system, exempting hospital pharmacies from the pharmacy licensing system. In some states, the exemption applies only to certain activities such as dispensing and administering drugs to patients in the hospital and dispensing take-home drugs in conjunction with an inpatient or outpatient hospital visit, but not to other refills. Hospitals that operate pharmacies under an exemption should limit the pharmacy's operations to stay within any restrictions. In states that use the hospital licensing system, the regulations concerning hospital pharmacies usually are included in the hospital licensing regulations.

Most states require licensed pharmacies to maintain chronological records. Some states require a patient profile system, in which prescriptions are filed by patient name along with some patient information, rather than in chronological order. This system helps to identify possible drug interactions or contraindications. Hospitals might benefit from developing their own programs to incorporate this system, whether or not government regulations mandate it.

Technical Staff

Regulatory and accrediting agencies require that a sufficient number of staff members be assigned to the hospital pharmacy according to the hospital's size and scope of services. There is still some controversy over the use of unlicensed technical staff. Medicare and JCAH have permitted the practice, when there is supervision by a pharmacist, to the extent it is not forbidden by state law. Since pharmacists must be licensed, the central legal issue is whether the manipulative and mechanical tasks performed by technical staff fall within the definition of practicing pharmacy. This question may continue to be a point of dispute in some jurisdictions. Hospitals should comply with accepted practices under applicable law until there is an authoritative resolution in their jurisdictions. However, as cost-conscious lawmakers and regulators recognize the cost-effectiveness of properly supervised technical staff, substantial barriers to use of technical staff will probably be eliminated in many jurisdictions.

Hospital Formularies

One area of controversy in the past has been the promotion of rational drug use through a hospital formulary system that selects the drugs to be available for use. When a medical staff committee determines that two or more drugs are equivalent, only one is primarily stocked. It is selected by negotiation with or bidding from competing suppliers to arrange the lowest cost. When a physician prescribes a drug for which an equivalent is stocked, the equivalent drug is dispensed, unless the physician specifies on the prescription form or order that no substitutions are permitted.

The basic formulary system was established many years ago by the American Society of Hospital Pharmacists, the American Hospital Association, the American Medical Association, and the American Pharmaceutical Association.[11] The system has also been incorporated in the standards of the JCAH[12] and the Medicare conditions of participation.[13] Formulary systems have been adopted in a majority of hospitals. They have controlled the increase in drug costs, especially when competition is promoted among multiple suppliers.

Periodically, drug manufacturers and others have challenged formulary systems. The primary legal attacks have been based on state antisubstitution or generic substitution laws, federal or state drug laws, or trademark laws. These attacks have not been successful when there is an understanding or agreement between the prescriber and dispenser that an equivalent drug may be dispensed.

Some states have laws that preclude retail pharmacies from substituting drugs for those prescribed by physicians. Many states have enacted drug product selection or generic substitution laws that permit retail pharmacies to substitute lower-priced, equivalent drugs under some circumstances. One type of attack on hospital formularies has been based on the assertion that hospital pharmacies may dispense equivalent drugs only under the circumstances specified in these new laws. This attack has generally not been successful because the hospital formulary system is authorized by agreement of the physician and hospital pharmacy, not by these new laws. Hospital formulary systems were legally operated prior to the new laws, while the antisubstitution laws were still in effect. Of course, antisubstitution and generic substitution laws apply when a pharmacy fills a prescription that was written by a physician who is not a member of the hospital medical staff.

Some attacks on the formulary system have asserted that the dispensed drugs are adulterated or misbranded because they are different from the ones prescribed, or that trademark rights are violated if the prescribed brand is not dispensed. These attacks have failed because substitution must take place to establish a violation. When the prescriber has an agreement with the dispenser that the order may be filled with an equivalent drug specified in a formulary, there is no substitution. The equivalent drug is what is actually being prescribed by the symbols on the form or order. Usually the agreement is embodied in the hospital's or medical staff's bylaws or rules which each medical staff member has agreed to accept as part of the process for obtaining and retaining medical staff membership.

Price Advertising

Many states used to have laws limiting prescription price advertising. In 1976 the Supreme Court declared any law unconstitutional that prohibited or unnecessarily restricted the advertising of prescription price information. The Court left room for states to control some aspects of advertising, including restrictions on time, place, manner, and false or deceptive practices.[14] Some states now require the posting of prices in pharmacies.

Controlled Substances Act

The Comprehensive Drug Abuse Prevention and Control Act of 1970,[15] commonly known as the Controlled Substances Act, replaced virtually all preexisting federal law dealing with narcotics, depressants, stimulants, and hallucinogens. The Act directly affects hospital distribution systems and also deals with rehabilitation programs, research in and treatment of drug abuse, and importation and exportation of controlled substances. The Act should be carefully reviewed when hospitals create or revise procedures for handling and administering controlled substances.

Hospitals are defined as "institutional practitioners" in the implementing regulations and must register with the government as specified in the Act. Each registrant must take a physical inventory every two years. In maintaining inventory records, a perpetual inventory is not required, but a separate inventory is required for each registered location and for each independent activity registered. In addition to inventory records, each registrant must maintain complete, accurate records of all controlled substances received and disposed of.

Controlled substances are classified into lists, called *schedules*, by the degree to which they are controlled. Schedule I has the tightest controls. Controlled substances in Schedules I through IV may, for all practical purposes, be dispensed only upon the lawful order of a practitioner. For outpatients, the order must be a prescription that complies with the requirements of the law. For inpatients, a chart order satisfies the requirement for a lawful order, so a separate prescription is not required. The practitioner who signs the order must be registered with the Drug Enforcement Administration (DEA) of the Department of Justice. State law determines which professionals may be practitioners.

All institutions and individual registrants must provide effective controls and procedures to guard against theft and diversion of controlled substances. The central storage area in a hospital should be under the direct control and supervision of the pharmacist. Only authorized personnel should have access to the area. When controlled substances are stored at nursing units, they should be kept securely locked, and only authorized personnel should have access.

Substantial federal criminal penalties, including fines and imprisonment, are imposed for violating the Controlled Substances Act. In addition, violators can lose the authority to possess, prescribe, or dispense controlled substances.

Most states have controlled substances acts that closely parallel the federal law.

Food and Drug Administration

The Food and Drug Administration (FDA) enforces a complex system of federal controls over the testing, manufacturing, labeling, and distributing of drugs, cosmetics, and devices. These controls appear in the Federal Food, Drug and Cosmetic Act, which includes the Medical Device Amendments of 1976, and in FDA regulations.[16]

The definitions of *drug* and *device* are broad, so the applicable statutes, regulations, and court decisions should be consulted to determine whether a particular item is included. For example, human blood is considered a drug. Virtually all equipment and supplies used in patient care are regulated as devices. In addition to such obvious devices as hip prostheses, pacemakers, and artificial hearts, the term includes common equipment and supplies such as catheters, endoscopes, hospital beds, specimen containers, support stockings, scissors, adhesive tape, elastic bandages, tongue depressors, and sutures.

The FDA has broad discretion to decide whether to use its powers to investigate or penalize specific activities. When the FDA declined to investigate the drugs used to execute condemned criminals, the Supreme Court was asked to order an FDA investigation. In 1985 the Court ruled that the FDA and other federal agencies had prosecutorial discretion to decide whether to exercise their discretionary powers in individual cases, so the courts could not review such decisions in most situations.[17]

Investigational Drugs and Devices

Before new drugs and devices may enter general use, an elaborate procedure must be followed to establish their safety and effectiveness. The investigational new drug (IND) and investigational device exemption (IDE) requirements must be met to use investigational drugs and devices lawfully. With few exceptions, these drugs and devices can be used only in research projects approved by an institutional review board, conducted by a qualified investigator, and sponsored by an appropriate company or institution.[18]

Approved Drugs or Devices

When the FDA is convinced that a new drug or device is safe and effective for certain uses, it approves the drug for general sale. The approval may permit either over-the-counter sales or sales by order of a practitioner. Approval of devices may include additional restrictions on the use of the device.

The approval specifies the uses of the drug or device that are to be included in the labeling. Frequently medical practice changes more rapidly than FDA approvals, so the use of a drug or device is often different from the approved uses listed on its label. For example, drugs are given for other conditions or in different dosages. It is not a violation of federal law for physicians to order such unapproved uses or for pharmacists to dispense drugs pursuant to such orders. However, unapproved uses that result in injuries to patients may result in liability. Many courts consider the FDA approved labeling to be sufficient evidence of proper use, so that no further expert testimony is required.[19] However, when defendants introduce evidence that the FDA approved uses lag behind current medical practice, the deviation from FDA approved uses alone does not conclusively prove negligence. Juries are permitted to consider the FDA position along with other testimony concerning accepted practice in deciding whether the use was negligent.[20] The most prudent practice is for the physician to explain the unapproved use of the drug and the reasons for its use to the patient and to obtain the patient's informed consent to the use.

Prescriptions

Prescriptions must be properly documented. When prescription drugs are ordered in writing, the documentation requirement is clearly satisfied. The physician either writes a prescription or writes an order on the patient's chart, which serves as the written prescription. The Act requires oral orders for drugs to be ". . . reduced promptly to writing and filed by the pharmacist . . . ." Hospitals should review these requirements and other state requirements, such as hospital licensing regulations, to assure that telephone orders are accepted only by proper personnel. It is prudent to require that a registered nurse or a pharmacist personally accept telephone orders.

Manufacturing

Every person who owns or operates any establishment engaged in the interstate or intrastate "manufacture, preparation, propagation, compounding or processing" of drugs must register name, place of business, and all such establishments with the Secretary of Health and Human Services.[21] The terms *manufacture, preparation, propagation, compounding,* and *processing* include prepackaging or otherwise changing the container, wrapper, or labeling of drugs for distribution to others who will make the final sale or distribution to the ultimate consumer. In addition to registration, the Act requires manufacturers to maintain certain records, file specified reports, be periodically inspected, and satisfy other requirements. Manufacturers must file a list of all drugs they manufacture. The FDA exempts hospitals from these requirements if the hospitals are "in conformance with any applicable local laws regulating the practices of pharmacy or medicine" and "regularly engage in dispensing prescription drugs, other than human blood or blood products, upon prescription of practitioners licensed by law to administer these drugs to patients under their professional care."[22] If the hospital pharmacy supplies compounded or repackaged drugs to other institutions or pharmacies under circumstances other than emergencies, it will probably be considered a manufacturer.

Hospital blood banks must register and comply with the regulations concerning good manufacturing practices for blood and blood components.[23]

Poison Prevention Packaging Act

The Poison Prevention Packaging Act[24] is an example of the other federal laws that regulate the pharmacy area. This Act requires most drugs to be dispensed in containers designed to be difficult for children to open. Exceptions are permitted when authorized by the prescribing physician.

ANTITRUST LAWS

Federal and state antitrust laws are designed to preserve the private competitive market system by prohibiting various anticompetitive activities. The primary federal laws are the Sherman Anti-Trust Act,[25] the Clayton Act,[26] the Federal Trade Commission Act,[27] and the Robinson-Patman Act.[28] These laws forbid many anticompetitive activities, including conspiracies to restrain trade; monopolization or attempts to monopolize; some exclusive dealing arrangements; acquisitions and mergers that have an anticompetitive effect; unfair or deceptive practices affecting competition; and discriminatory pricing that lessens competition.

In the early 1970s, many aspects of the federal antitrust laws were not thought to apply to hospitals because it was believed that (1) hospitals were not engaged in interstate commerce; (2) activities of the learned professions were exempt; and (3) the federal health planning laws created an implied exemption for health planning activities. In a series of decisions, the Supreme Court has made it clear that health care providers are treated in the same way as other industries for antitrust purposes. In 1976 the Court ruled that Mary Elizabeth Hospital, a 49-bed proprietary hospital operated by Hospital Building Company, was involved in interstate commerce because it purchased $100,000 worth of medicines and supplies from out-of-state vendors and received considerable revenues from out-of-state insurance companies and federal payers.[29] Thus, the trustees of Rex Hospital could be sued under the antitrust laws for an alleged conspiracy to restrain trade by blocking the expansion of Mary Elizabeth Hospital. In 1975 the Court ruled that the learned professions were not excepted from the antitrust laws.[30] In 1981 the Court ruled that implied exemptions to the antitrust laws are not favored and will be applied only to the limited extent necessary to fulfill the purposes of other laws.[31] Blue Cross had refused to enter a participating hospital agreement with a hospital that had not obtained approval for its new building from the local health planning agency. State law did not require approval. The hospital claimed that the refusal by Blue Cross was a restraint of trade, and Blue Cross claimed the refusal was protected by the national health planning law. The Court ruled that the refusal by Blue Cross was not protected. Other laws provide implied protection from antitrust sanctions only when there is a clear repugnancy between the antitrust laws and the regulatory system under the other law. The protection will be recognized only to the minimum extent necessary to make the other law work. This principle was applied by a federal court in 1984, when it ruled that a certificate-of-need is just one step in the process of starting a facility or service.[32] The provider must still comply with all other laws, including antitrust laws. The certificate-of-need does not protect the provider from being charged with monopolization.

The law has recognized some exemptions from antitrust liability for state actions, activities intended to induce governmental action, and the business of insurance. In 1943 the Court ruled that state-compelled activities were immune from antitrust liability to preserve the state's authority to supervise economic activity within the state.[33] The state action doctrine was clarified in 1980, when the Court ruled that state authorization is not enough. The actions must be pursuant to a clearly articulated and affirmatively expressed state policy actively supervised by the state.[34] The doctrine was further defined in 1985, when the Court ruled that the clearly defined state policy did not have to compel the actions to bring them under the state action immunity.[35] Collective ratemaking by motor carriers was found to be protected as state action because the states expressly permitted the ratemaking and actively supervised it. On the same day the Court ruled that active state supervision is not a requirement for exemption when the actor is a municipality rather than a private individual.[36]

In two cases in 1961 and 1965 the Court ruled that the antitrust laws do not apply to most activities intended to induce governmental action, such as lobbying.[37] This concept is called the Noerr-Pennington doctrine and is based on the right under the First Amendment to petition the government and on a judicial interpretation that lobbying activities are not restraint of trade. The petitioning must be for a legitimate purpose of influencing governmental policy. Sham efforts to bar the access of competitors to the government are not protected.

The McCarran-Ferguson Act created a statutory exemption for the "business of insurance" when it is regulated by state law and does not constitute coercion, boycott, or intimidation.[38] The Court has taken a restrictive view of what constitutes the business of insurance entitled to this exemption. For example, in 1979 the Court limited the exemption to the business of insurance, not the business of insurers.[39] It defined the "business of insurance" as limited to the procedures and activities related to the spreading of risk among policy holders. It held that special reimbursement arrangements between Blue Shield and participating pharmacies were not within the business of insurance, but instead were merely the business of insurers.

The courts have established that some practices are unlawful regardless of the rationale supporting the practices. These are called *per se* violations of the antitrust laws. Examples include price fixing, division of markets, group boycotts, and tying arrangements. In 1982 the Court ruled that a maximum fee schedule for physicians was price fixing and, thus, a *per se* violation.[40] The courts have concluded that the practices considered *per se* violations are unreasonable and will not usually examine the actual impact of the practice being challenged. When a practice is not considered a *per se* violation, the practice is analyzed by the court under the "rule of reason," which means that the court determines under the circumstances of the case whether the restrictive practice actually imposes an unreasonable restraint on competition. The scope of *per se* violations is still being defined. In 1982 a Federal Circuit Court found an exclusive contract with an anesthesiology group to be a *per se* violation as a tying arrangement, but the Supreme Court reversed the decision, finding the exclusive contract not to be a *per se* violation.[41] This decision is discussed in Chapter 7.

An activity does not automatically violate the antitrust laws just because it is not exempt. In 1980 a Federal Circuit Court held that the different compensation formulas used by Blue Cross for participating and nonparticipating hospitals were not exempt under the McCarran-Ferguson Act "business of insurance" exemption, but that the arrangement did not violate the antitrust laws because it was reasonable.[42] Similarly, Rex Hospital won the suit by Mary Elizabeth Hospital discussed earlier in this section. Initially a jury awarded Mary Elizabeth Hospital $7.3 million, but the appeals court ordered a new trial for the jury to consider whether Rex Hospital's participation in planning activities was in good faith and reasonable. In the second trial the jury ruled in favor of Rex Hospital.[43]

The Robinson-Patman Act prohibits discriminatory pricing that lessens competition, but there is a statutory exemption for purchases by nonprofit institutions "for their own use." Due to this exemption, hospital pharmacies in nonprofit hospitals usually buy drugs from manufacturers at a discount not available to commercial pharmacies. These drugs can be used only "for their own use." In 1976 the Supreme Court defined "for their own use" to be limited to the following uses: (1) treatment of inpatients at the hospital; (2) treatment of admitted emergency patients in the hospital; (3) personal use by outpatients on the hospital premises; (4) personal use away from the premises by inpatients or emergency patients upon their discharge; (5) personal use away from the premises by outpatients; (6) personal use by hospital employees, students, and their immediate dependents; and (7) personal use by medical staff members and their immediate dependents.[44] Thus, hospitals must limit sales of discount drugs to these groups to avoid possible civil liability, including treble damages and loss of the valuable discount.

Purchasers who do not qualify include (1) former patients who wish to renew prescriptions given when they were inpatients, emergency facility patients, or outpatients; (2) physicians who are medical staff members and intend to dispense the drugs in the course of their private practices away from the hospital; and (3) walk-in customers who are not hospital patients. To avoid liability, hospitals should refuse to sell to these groups or set up a separate order system to fill the requests of these purchasers.

In 1983 the Supreme Court ruled that governmental hospitals are not exempt from these restrictions on resale of discount drugs.[45] In 1984 a federal appellate court ruled that resales of drugs by health maintenance organizations to their own members are "for their own use."[46]

In addition to suits by private individuals, the government can challenge some actions of hospitals as violations of the antitrust laws. For example, in 1984 the Federal Trade Commission (FTC) found that a chain of hospitals had acquired so many of the hospitals in an area that there was a tendency toward a monopoly, so the FTC ordered the chain to sell one of the hospitals.[47]

Hospitals must consider the antitrust implications when entering group purchase or shared services agreements, entering mergers or agreements not to duplicate services, entering exclusive contracts with a physician or group of physicians, or exchanging information with other hospitals. Many of these actions can be permissible under the antitrust laws. Hospitals must understand what they are permitted to do and must be prepared to defend their actions before engaging in these or other activities that might appear to have some anticompetitive effect. It is difficult to obtain dismissal of antitrust suits involving health care providers, so defense of these actions in a full trial is increasingly possible.

NOTES

1. Joint Commission on Accreditation of Hospitals, ACCREDITATION MANUAL FOR HOSPITALS (1986 ed.) [hereinafter cited as JCAH 1986].

2. 42 U.S.C. §1395x(e) (1982); 42 C.F.R. §§405.1011-405.1041 (1984).

3. 42 U.S.C. §§1395aa(c) and 1395bb (1982), as amended by Pub. L. No. 98-369, 98 Stat. 1096, 1101 (1984).

4. Department of Health and Rehabilitative Servs. v. Delray Hosp. Corp., 373 So.2d 75 (Fla. Dist. Ct. App. 1979).

5. Hospital Ass'n of Pa. v. MacLeod, 487 Pa. 516, 410 A.2d 731 (1980).

6. Koelbl v. Whalen, 63 A.D.2d 408, 406 N.Y.S.2d 621 (1978).

7. Eden Park Health Servs., Inc. v. Whalen, 73 A.D.2d 993, 424 N.Y.S.2d 33 (1980).

8. Woodiwiss v. Jacobs, 125 Misc. 584, 211 N.Y.S.2d 217 (N.Y. Sup. Ct. 1961).

9. Harrison Clinic Hosp. v. Texas State Bd. of Health, 400 S.W.2d 840 (Tex. Civ. App. 1966) aff'd, 410 S.W.2d 181 (Tex. 1966) [multiple violations of fire and safety rules and multiple citations for poor sanitation justified license revocation].

10. 42 C.F.R. §405.1027 (1984).

11. Statement of Guiding Principles on the Operation of the Hospital Formulary System, 21 AM. J. HOSP. PHARM. 40 (1964).

12. JCAH 1986, supra note 1 at 170.

13. 42 C.F.R. §405.1027(f)(3) (1984).

14. Virginia State Bd. of Pharmacy v. Virginia Citizens Consumer Council, 425 U.S. 748 (1976).

15. Pub. L. No. 90-513, 84 Stat. 1236 (codified as amended in scattered sections of 18, 21, 26, 31, 42, 46, and 49 U.S.C.).

16. Title 21 of the United States Code and Title 21 of the Code of Federal Regulations.

17. Heckler v. Chaney, 105 S.Ct. 1649 (U.S. 1985).

18. 21 C.F.R. pts. 50, 56, 312, 812, and 813 (1985); for a summary of FDA actions for scientific misconduct from 1975 through 1983, see Shapiro & Charrow, Scientific Misconduct in Investigational Drug Trials, 312 NEW ENG. J. MED. 731 (1985).

19. E.g., DePaolo v. State, 99 A.D.2d 762, 472 N.Y.S.2d 10 (1984).

20. E.g., Young v. Cerniak, 126 Ill. App.3d 952, 467 N.E.2d 1045 (1984).

21. 21 U.S.C. §360 (1982).

22. 21 C.F.R. §207.10 (1985).

23. 21 C.F.R. pt. 607 [registration]; 21 C.F.R. pt. 606 [manufacturing practices] (1984).

24. Pub. L. No. 91-601, 84 Stat. 1670 (codified as amended in scattered sections of 7, 15, and 21 U.S.C.).

25. 15 U.S.C. §§1–7 (1982).

26. 15 U.S.C. §§12–27 and 44 (1982), as amended by Pub. L. No. 98-443, 98 Stat. 1708 (1984) and Pub. L. No. 98-620, 98 Stat. 3358 (1984).

27. 15 U.S.C. §§41–58 (1982), as amended by Pub. L. No. 98-620, 98 Stat. 3358 (1984).

28. 15 U.S.C. §13c (1982).

29. Hospital Bldg. Co. v. Trustees of Rex Hosp., 425 U.S. 738 (1976).

30. Goldfarb v. Virginia State Bar Ass'n, 421 U.S. 773 (1975).

31. National Gerimedical Hosp. and Gerontology Center v. Blue Cross of Kansas City, 452 U.S. 378 (1981).

32. North Carolina v. P.I.A. Asheville, Inc., 740 F.2d 274 (4th Cir. 1984).

33. Parker v. Brown, 317 U.S. 341 (1943).

34. California Retail Liquor Dealers Ass'n v. Midcal Aluminum, Inc., 445 U.S. 97 (1980).

35. Southern Motor Carriers Rate Conference, Inc. v. United States, 105 S.Ct. 1721 (U.S. 1985).

36. Town of Hallie v. City of Eau Claire, 105 S.Ct. 1713 (U.S. 1985).

37. Eastern R.R. President's Conference v. Noerr Motor Freight, Inc., 365 U.S. 127 (1961), and United Mine Workers of Am. v. Pennington, 381 U.S. 657 (1965).

38. 15 U.S.C. §1012(b) (1982).

39. Group Life and Health Ins. Co. v. Royal Drug, 440 U.S. 205 (1979).

40. Arizona v. Maricopa County Medical Soc'y, 457 U.S. 332 (1982).

41. Hyde v. Jefferson Parish Hosp. Dist. No. 2, 686 F.2d 286 (5th Cir. 1982), *rev'd*, 104 S.Ct. 1551 (U.S. 1984).

42. St. Bernard Hosp. v. Hospital Servs. Ass'n of New Orleans, Inc., 618 F.2d 1140 (5th Cir. 1980).

43. Hospital Bldg. Co. v. Trustees of Rex Hosp., No. 4048 (E.D.N.C. Dec. 5, 1984).

44. Abbott Laboratories v. Portland Retail Druggists Ass'n, Inc., 425 U.S. 1 (1976).

45. Jefferson County Pharmaceutical Ass'n, Inc. v. Abbott Laboratories, 460 U.S. 150 (1983).

46. DeModena v. Kaiser Found. Health Plan, Inc., 743 F.2d 1388 (9th Cir. 1984).

47. In re Am. Medical Int'l, Inc., No. 9158 (F.T.C. July 2, 1984).

Chapter 4

Financing and Taxation

One of the duties of the governing body of a hospital is to maintain the financial integrity of the institution. Most actions necessary to accomplish this goal are the responsibility of the administrator, who must conceptualize and recommend actions to the governing body and then implement the governing body's decisions.

The financial requirements of the hospital must be met, or the hospital cannot continue to operate. This is accomplished through realistically establishing the scope of the hospital's activities within available resources; developing a realistic budget to allocate resources to carry out those activities; setting appropriate charges; obtaining payment from third parties and individuals; initiating appropriate cost-containment measures; arranging for appropriate capital financing; protecting the hospital's assets; and preserving tax exemptions.

FINANCIAL REQUIREMENTS

The full financial requirements of a hospital include its current operating needs plus an operating margin. In addition to caring for paying patients, many hospitals also provide charity care, education, and research, and these activities also contribute to current operating needs. An operating margin is necessary to provide working capital and meet other capital requirements. For-profit hospitals also seek profit so they can pay dividends to their investors. Working capital is needed to assure immediate stability and the ability to make timely payment of current obligations without costly excessive short-term borrowing. Other capital requirements include renovations and major repairs, replacement of buildings and equipment, expansion, and acquisition of new technology.

SETTING CHARGES

The goal in setting charges is to meet the financial requirements of the hospital. This is difficult to accomplish because many payers pay less than charges and because some patients are unable to pay the full charges for their care. This section focuses on some of the legal considerations in setting charges.

Rate Regulation

Many states have an agency that monitors, reviews, or establishes charges or revenue limits for hospitals. The role of this agency varies greatly among the states. Some programs are mandatory, while others are voluntary, so a hospital can elect not to participate. Some programs are regulatory and require the hospital to comply with the decision of the agency, while others are only advisory. In advisory programs, the hospital may still set the rates it chooses, but it must be willing to accept the resulting publicity. The programs vary in their scope of coverage. Some programs are limited to the rates paid by certain payers, and others apply only to rates for inpatient services. The programs also vary in the type of data they use as a basis for their evaluations. Some programs establish peer groups of hospitals and then make comparisons among the hospitals in each group. Courts have generally recognized the appropriateness of peer comparisons and the need for administrative agencies to have latitude in grouping hospitals for this purpose.[1] Other programs focus on historical data from the individual hospital, evaluating the current year by comparison to a base year.

The three basic approaches to evaluation of the data collected are (1) formulas; (2) budget analysis; and (3) negotiation. Some states use a combination of these approaches. Formula review involves comparing the submitted data to a standard that is calculated from a formula. Budget review involves analysis of the hospital's proposed budget to determine the appropriateness of particular expenditures. The hospital is permitted to set its own rates as long as the revenue generated does not exceed the approved budget. The negotiation approach uses a process for reaching agreement between the hospital and regulatory agency concerning appropriate rates.

Mandatory rate regulation has led to controversies over several issues, including the following:

1. Cross-subsidization, the use of revenue from one service to subsidize another service, has been controversial in some states. Some states have prohibited cross-subsidization, while others have not given their regulatory agencies authority to prevent it.

2. Some states require that rates be calculated at the level that would adequately reimburse the hospital if it were sufficiently utilized by having a certain occupancy rate. This requirement threatens the continuing existence of hospitals with low occupancy.

3. Depreciation and other capital needs have been a controversial area. In 1977 a Maryland court upheld the substitution of a capital facility allowance for depreciation when analysis established that it was appropriate for the individual hospital.[2]

4. A related issue has been whether the rate regulation agency must authorize rates that will permit the hospital to carry out projects approved through the health planning process. In some states, the rate regulation agency separately reviews the need for the service and asserts the power not to permit funding. Other states have sought to avoid this duplication and potential conflict by mandating cooperation or placing both functions in the same agency.

5. Use of foundation and other nonpatient revenue has been an issue when regulatory agencies have required that rates be set so low that unrestricted nonpatient income must be applied to expenses under the approved budget. This requirement has led some hospitals to reorganize their corporate structures, seeking to place control of unrestricted nonpatient income in an entity that is not subject to the control of the regulatory agency.

6. Bad debt and charity costs have been controversial in some systems, but many systems specifically recognize the appropriateness of providing for both of these in the setting of rates. Although some have questioned the appropriateness of subsidizing indigent care through higher charges to paying patients, government has been unwilling to accept the alternatives of either no care for those unable to pay or sufficiently increased governmental subsidies.

The Massachusetts Nurses Association challenged the state rate regulation system, claiming the payment restrictions illegally interfered with collective bargaining efforts with hospitals. A federal appellate court ruled in 1984 that the law did not violate the nurses' collective bargaining rights because it affected labor-management relations only indirectly.[3] Another federal appellate court reached the same conclusion in 1985 in a similar case brought by the Washington State Nurses Association challenging its state's rate regulation system.[4]

Some third party payers have challenged rate regulation systems. For example, a pension plan challenged a New York system that prevented self-insured employee benefit plans from negotiating rates lower than those set by the system. A federal appellate court upheld the law in 1984,[5] finding it not to be preempted by the federal Employee Retirement Income Security Act of 1974 (ERISA)[6] because the impact on the pension plans was only tangential.

Bonding Covenants

When the hospital borrows money through bonds or other mechanisms, it usually pledges certain property or revenues to guarantee repayment of the loan. One of these pledges is usually a promise to set rates sufficiently high to repay the loan and maintain the operation of the hospital until the loan is repaid. These pledges must be considered and complied with, to the extent permitted by law, in setting rates.

REIMBURSEMENT

Medicare

The 1965 Amendments to the Social Security Act[7] added Title XVIII to the Act. Title XVIII established a two-part program of health insurance for the aged known as Medicare. Persons are eligible to participate in Part A, the hospital insurance program, if (1) they are 65 or older and are receiving retirement benefits under Title II of the Social Security Act or the Railroad Retirement Act; (2) they qualify under a special program for persons with endstage renal (kidney) disease; or (3) they qualify under the special transitional program. Persons not qualifying otherwise who are 65 or older may still participate in Part A by paying the premiums themselves. Anyone age 65 or older who is a United States citizen or has been a permanent resident alien for five years may elect to enroll in Part B, a program of supplementary medical insurance. Medicare applies to all qualified people without regard to financial need. It is administered federally, so its benefits are uniform across the country. Provider relations and payments are federally administered on a regional basis, so some regional variations exist.

Part A, which hospitals are most often concerned with, is a program of hospital insurance benefits for the aged and selected others that is financed by a special tax on employers, employees, and the self-employed. The coverage includes a specified number of days of care in hospitals and extended care facilities for each benefit period plus posthospital home care. Claims must be presented to trigger reimbursement. Until 1983, reimbursement under Part A was based on the allowable costs of the facility providing the care but was subject to several reimbursement limits. This was changed by the Social Security Amendments of 1983.[8] Beginning in 1983–84, payment to hospitals for inpatient care is based on a prospectively determined amount per discharge according to the patient's diagnosis and the facility's location. During a transitional period of three years, the amount is modified based on the hospital's historical costs. In addition to the payments by the Social Security system, beneficiaries have to pay certain deductible and coinsurance payments. A deductible is the amount of health care charges that the patient must incur and owe before Medicare pays for any of the remainder. Medicare will pay only a percentage of some of the remaining allowable payments for some services; the percentage not paid by Medicare is called a coinsurance payment and is owed by the patient.

Part B is a program of supplementary medical insurance covering a substantial part of physician and other practitioner services, medical supplies, and x-rays and laboratory tests incident to physician services, as well as other services not covered under Part A, such as ambulance services and prosthetic devices. Enrollment is voluntary. The program is funded from contributions by beneficiaries and the federal government. Beneficiaries must pay a deductible and a 20 percent coinsurance amount. Provider payment under Part B is based on "reasonable charges," which are subject to numerous arbitrary limits. The Deficit Reduction Act of 1984 placed a freeze on fees that nonparticipating physicians could charge Medicare patients. Federal courts upheld the freeze.[9]

The Secretary of the Department of Health and Human Services (HHS) has overall responsibility for the program. The operation of the program has been assigned to the Health Care Financing Administration (HCFA). Congress authorized the delegation of much of the day-to-day administration to state agencies and public and private organizations operating under agreements with the Secretary of HHS. Most claims for payment are processed by agencies such as Blue Cross plans and commercial insurance companies on behalf of the government. These agencies have entered agreements to serve as "intermediaries" for Part A or "carriers" for Part B to make initial determinations whether services provided to beneficiaries are payable by the program and how much payment is due.

Hospitals must be very cautious in acting upon information provided by intermediaries and carriers. The Supreme Court ruled in 1984 that HCFA could recover Medicare overpayments from a provider despite the fact that the overpayments were due to erroneous information from the intermediary.[10] The Court stated that providers are expected to know the law and cannot rely on the information provided by government agents.

Participating Providers

To be a participating provider of services and receive payments from the Medicare program, a hospital must sign an agreement with HHS and meet the "conditions of participation."[11] The only exception is that Medicare will pay for some emergency services in hospitals that are not participating providers. The participating provider agreement specifies that the hospital will not bill Medicare patients for services, except for (1) deductible and coinsurance payments required by law; and (2) charges for services that the Medicare program does not cover. Charges can be made for noncovered services only if the patient has been given adequate notice that they are not covered. A hospital is deemed to meet the conditions of participation if it is accredited by the JCAH or the American Osteopathic Association, unless a Medicare inspection indicates noncompliance.[12]

Prospective Payment

The Social Security Amendments of 1983[13] established a Medicare prospective payment system based on diagnosis-related groups (DRGs) to pay hospitals for inpatient care. The system was modified a year later by the Medicare and Medicaid Budget Reconciliation Amendments of 1984.[14] The following is a summary of the system based on the statute and implementing regulations[15] as amended after the 1984 amendments. All Medicare inpatients are divided into 471 DRGs based on their principal diagnoses. The principal diagnosis is the one chiefly responsible for the admission. Medicare will pay for 469 of the groups. Groups 469 and 470 involve unacceptable diagnoses and invalid data. Group 471 was added in 1985 to encompass certain multiple joint procedures.

With a few exceptions, the hospital receives one payment for the entire admission based on the DRG and the facility's location. During a transition period the payment was composed of a component based on the hospital's historical costs and a component based on regional or national averages. There was considerable litigation over the historical cost component because HHS refused to make corrections of errors retroactive.[16]

There is no extra payment for longer stays or more procedures unless the patient becomes an outlier. An outlier is a patient with an extraordinarily long length of stay or high total cost of care. Medicare makes an extra payment for part of the additional costs of outliers. Another exception is that capital costs, direct educational costs, kidney acquisition costs, and costs of anesthesia services by certified registered nurse anesthetists are not included in the prospective payment; they are paid on a cost basis. The cost-based payment for capital costs is scheduled to end October 1, 1986.

An adjustment for indirect educational costs increases the payment to hospitals with medical residency programs. Children's hospitals, long-term hospitals, psychiatric hospitals, and rehabilitation hospitals are exempt from the prospective payment system, so they can continue to receive cost-based payment from Medicare. Psychiatric and rehabilitation units of general hospitals can be exempt if they apply for an exemption.

Congress directed HHS to provide exceptions and adjustments for hospitals that serve a disproportionate share of low-income or Medicaid patients, are sole community providers, or experience other extraordinary circumstances. After extensive litigation to force compliance, HHS published a definition of disproportionate share hospitals in 1985.[17]

The prospective payment system is prospective only in the sense that the amount paid is calculated based on circumstances at the time of admission. Payment is made only after the services are provided. This system completely changes the implicit incentives. Under the previous cost-based system, additional days in the hospital and additional services meant additional payment. Thus, there was an incentive to give patients all services that could possibly benefit them. In some situations, unnecessary services may have been provided, although if discovered, Medicare refused to pay for them.

Under the prospective payment system there is an incentive to minimize services and shorten the length of stay to the greatest extent possible. Hospitals lose money if services to patients exceed the prospective payment, and they can keep the savings if the services cost less than the payment. There is some indication that the incentives are working. The average length of stay for all Medicare patients in 1982–83, the year before the prospective payment system started, was 9.3 days. In the first year of the new system, the average length of stay for Medicare patients whose care was paid for under the prospective system was 7.6 days. However, this increased to 7.7 days in 1984–85.[18]

Interhospital transfers constitute another important practice that is likely to be affected by the change to prospective payment. Those fashioning the system wanted to make one payment to be shared by all hospitals that provided care to the patient, but the Act did not authorize shared payment. The hospital from which the patient is finally discharged receives a full prospective payment based on the patient's DRG. The hospital that cares for the patient before the transfer is paid a per diem rate equal to the prospective payment for the DRG divided by the average length of stay for that DRG. The transferring hospital can qualify for additional payment if the patient becomes an outlier due to high costs. It is likely that there will be efforts to change the law to permit one payment that all of the hospitals will share. Regardless of the approach used, the payment policy may affect decisions on whether and when to transfer a patient.

Prospective payment based on DRGs may be replaced with other payment mechanisms. Some HHS officials are considering proposals to shift to some form of capitation, in which an amount would be paid for each covered person regardless of the amount of services used.[19]

Appeals

Depending on the amount of money in controversy, hospitals may appeal payment decisions to the Provider Reimbursement Review Board (PRRB) in the case of larger amounts or to an intermediary hearing in the case of smaller amounts. When the issues being appealed apply to several hospitals, group appeals are frequently pursued to reduce the cost to individual hospitals. The Secretary of HHS has the authority to modify the decisions of the PRRB or the intermediary. The final decision of HHS concerning a payment issue can sometimes be appealed to the federal courts. However, the number of issues that can be appealed have been substantially limited.[20]

Medicaid

Medicaid is a joint federal-state program designed to provide medical assistance to individuals unable to afford health care. The Medicaid program is authorized by federal law (Title XIX of the Social Security Act)[21], but states are not required to have Medicaid programs. Each state must pass its own law to participate. Under Medicaid, the federal government makes grants to states to enable them to furnish (1) medical assistance to families with dependent children and to aged, blind, or disabled individuals whose income and resources are insufficient to pay for necessary health services; and (2) rehabilitation and other services to help such families and individuals obtain or retain the capability for independence or self-care. The Secretary of HHS is responsible for the administration of federal grants-in-aid to states under the Medicaid program.

Beneficiaries and Scope of Benefits

Any state adopting a Medicaid plan must provide certain minimum health benefits to the "categorically needy." The "categorically needy" include individuals receiving financial assistance under the state's approved plan for Supplemental Security Income (Title XVI of the Social Security Act[22]) or for Aid to Families with Dependent Children (Title IV-A of the Social Security Act[23]). Several other groups are included in the categorically needy if they qualify for financial assistance under the state plans except for certain characteristics that Medicaid requires to be ignored. States have the option of including other persons within their plan as "medically needy" if (1) they would qualify for assistance under one of the above programs if their incomes were lower; and (2) their incomes would be low enough to qualify for assistance under that program if they were permitted to subtract the health care expenses they have already incurred. This is sometimes called the "spend-down" option because the persons must in effect spend their income down to the threshold level for the other programs to be eligible for Medicaid.

Eligible recipients must apply to the designated state agency before Medicaid will pay for the services they receive. State Medicaid plans must meet many conditions before they can be approved, but states are permitted substantial flexibility in the administration of their own programs. States may decide, within federal guidelines, who in addition to the categorically needy will be eligible for medical assistance. In determining the scope of benefits, states are required to provide only five basic services to the categorically needy but are free to provide additional optional services. As a result of this flexibility, all states have developed Medicaid programs. Although the states are given wide latitude in the administration of their programs, they are sensitive to federal direction because 50 percent or more of the financial support for Medicaid comes from the federal government.

Institutional providers of services generally become participants in the Medicaid program by applying to the state agency responsible for the program and contracting with the state to provide services to Medicaid recipients in exchange for the payment permitted by the state. Payment cannot be collected from the patient except to the extent permitted by federal law. Noninstitutional providers generally are not required to enter into any contract with the state but participate merely by treating Medicaid recipients and then billing the state. States may directly reimburse physicians who provide covered services to the medically needy, or they may pay the individual beneficiaries, leaving them with the obligation to pay the physician. Payment for physician services can only be made if the physician agrees to accept charges determined by the state as the full charges.

The 1981 amendments to the Medicaid law increased the latitude of the states to determine the services to be covered and the amount of payments. States are free to establish their own methods of payment for inpatient hospital services as long as the costs do not exceed Medicare payment for the same services. Many states have reduced services. When Tennessee reduced the covered days of inpatient care from 20 to 14, the reduction was challenged as a violation of the federal laws prohibiting discrimination against the handicapped because they generally need longer lengths of stay. The Supreme Court rejected this challenge in 1985, ruling that the handicapped nondiscrimination law does not guarantee equal results from Medicaid services.[24] The Court did not rule on whether the limit was consistent with the Medicaid law. Lower courts have ruled that limits on the number of inpatient days, such as South Carolina's 12-day limit, are consistent with the Medicaid law.[25]

Other states placed new limits on payment to providers. Some states have adopted prospective payment systems for Medicaid similar to the Medicare system.[26] Minnesota went one step further in its nursing home payment system. Minnesota will pay nursing homes through its Medicaid system only when the nursing home agrees not to charge non-Medicaid patients more than Medicaid pays for comparable care. This system has been upheld by both the federal and state courts.[27] In 1985, a Minnesota court ruled that neither the state nor Medicaid patients could stop a nursing home from phasing out participation in Medicaid.[28]

Some states using cost-based systems calculate the average costs based on the assumption that the occupancy of the facility is at least a certain percentage, such as 85 percent or 90 percent. These formulas have generally been upheld by the courts.[29]

Medicaid is different from Medicare in that it provides medical assistance for categories of persons in financial need, while Medicare provides medical assistance primarily to people 65 years of age or older without regard to financial need. Medicaid varies widely among the states, while Medicare is uniform. Medicaid is financed by general federal and state revenues, while Medicare is financed by a special tax on employers and employees for hospital insurance and contributions by beneficiaries and the federal government for supplementary medical services. Medicaid is basically a welfare program, while Medicare is a form of social insurance.

Medicare and Medicaid Fraud and Abuse

In 1977, Congress enacted the Medicare-Medicaid Anti-Fraud and Abuse Amendments,[30] which strengthened the remedies for wrongful provider conduct. Many existing offenses were reclassified from misdemeanors to felonies, and the possible fines and prison sentences for violators were increased. For example, misrepresentations on cost reports, claims, and other reports were made felonies, increasing the maximum penalty to $25,000 and/or five years in prison. The amendments also declared some previously permitted conduct to be offenses. For example, the scope of conduct considered to constitute forbidden kickbacks, bribes, and rebates was expanded. One consequence is that hospitals must be more careful when structuring business relationships with physicians and other providers to assure that any payments are not considered forbidden kickbacks.[31] The Justice Department refused to issue a national ruling on whether routine waiver of Medicare copayments and deductibles constitutes a forbidden kickback.[32] Each United States Attorney will continue to decide individually whether to prosecute.

Abuse is a broader term than fraud. While fraud requires deliberate deceit, the government considers it abuse to operate a hospital in a manner that is inconsistent with accepted principles of medical practice and business and that results in excessive and unreasonable expenditures by Medicare and Medicaid. In general, abuse is subject to civil sanctions, such as suspension of payments, suspension from the program, and repayment of overpayments, rather than criminal sanctions.

In 1981, the Social Security Act was amended to permit HHS to impose civil money penalties and assessments for filing false claims. Penalties of $2000 per item or service and assessments of twice the amount claimed may be imposed.[33] A penalty of $1.5 million has been assessed against one provider.[34]

Other Third Party Payers

A large part of health care is paid for by nongovernmental third party payers. Private third party payers include Blue Cross and Blue Shield plans, commercial insurance companies, employers' self-funded health insurance plans, and various health maintenance organizations (HMOs), preferred provider organizations (PPOs), and other alternate delivery systems (ADSs).

Blue Cross and Blue Shield Plans

Blue Cross and Blue Shield are together the largest private third party payers. Blue Cross covers hospital and related services, while Blue Shield covers physician and related services. Blue Cross and Blue Shield plans each cover a local region and have widely different practices concerning payment and other matters. Most plans are different from the traditional commercial insurance that requires the patient to locate the provider and then reimburses the patient for all or part of the cost of the care. Blue Cross and Blue Shield plans usually contract directly with providers and include an agreement to provide services to Blue Cross and Blue Shield subscribers for the payment specified in the contract. Many plans use a formula to determine the payment for hospitals. A few Blue Cross plans contract with hospitals for payment based on costs, while some plans contract to pay all or part of billed charges. Under the contract, the hospital agrees to accept the amount determined by the contract as payment in full for all covered services. The subscriber can be responsible for paying a portion of the bill when the contract between the subscriber and Blue Cross requires certain out-of-pocket payments by the subscriber. The remainder of the amount is paid by Blue Cross.

Generally Blue Cross and Blue Shield will reimburse subscribers for covered care given by providers that have no direct contract, but the payment is at a lower rate. Blue Cross and Blue Shield contracts generally forbid assignment to these nonparticipating providers, so the payment is usually made to the patient rather than directly to the provider. This procedure has been used as an incentive for providers to sign participating contracts. Some providers have challenged the prohibition of assignment, but the courts have disagreed on whether these nonassignment provisions are enforceable.[35]

Plans that permit assignment generally allow it only when the provider agrees to accept the direct payment (plus permitted copayments) as payment in full. For example, in Michigan the form a physician signs to request direct payment states that the physician will accept the amount as payment in full. One Michigan physician crossed out this statement before signing the form, but a Michigan court ruled in 1984 that the physician was still bound by the statement.[36] Physicians in Massachusetts challenged the ban on billing the patient more than permitted by Blue Shield. They claimed that it was a violation of federal antitrust laws. A federal appellate court upheld the policy, ruling that it was not an unreasonable restraint of trade.[37]

Commercial Insurance and Self-Funded Health Insurance

Most commercial insurance and self-funded health insurance plans are different from Blue Cross in that they usually do not contract directly with hospitals. Instead, commercial insurers generally reimburse their insureds for some or all of the expenses they have incurred. However, most commercial insurers will make their payments directly to the hospital if the patient requests direct payment. If the insurer does not pay the entire bill, the subscriber is still responsible for the remainder of the charges. This traditional pattern is rapidly changing as commercial insurance companies and self-funded plans develop new approaches to control utilization and cost. Some of these new approaches are discussed in the next section.

Hospitals and physicians should determine the nature of a patient's insurance before providing nonemergency services. Many employers have adopted health care plans that pay for hospitalization and certain procedures only if prior approval is obtained from the plan. Some plans make a second opinion from another physician prior to the procedure a requirement for eligibility for payment.

Health Maintenance Organizations and Other Alternate Delivery Systems

A Health Maintenance Organization generally provides services directly to the patient through HMO employees and other providers with which the HMO contracts. In exchange the HMO receives a fixed premium payment from the patient. Except for some emergency services and some services provided while the patient is out of the HMO's service area, the HMO pays for services only if they are provided by HMO employees or contractors. While some HMOs own their own hospitals, most HMOs make arrangements with other hospitals. These arrangements vary widely, with some providing for payment of full charges and others providing for payment at a lower negotiated rate.

A preferred provider organization generally does not provide services directly. It contracts with other providers to provide care at an agreed rate. Patients are given a financial incentive to use these preferred providers. The PPO pays for services provided by other providers, but usually at a lower rate, so the patient pays higher out-of-pocket expenses. PPOs are usually marketed to self-insured employers on a cost-plus-processing-fee basis. Thus, the PPO does not assume the risk of higher health care costs; the PPO is usually an administrative service, not an insurer. PPOs must have effective utilization control systems to be competitive. Some providers have attempted to convince courts and regulators that PPOs are violations of federal antitrust laws, but these attacks have generally been unsuccessful.[38]

Various hybrid Alternative Delivery Systems have also developed. Review of antitrust law and state law is necessary before a hospital enters arrangements with HMOs, PPOs, or ADSs because some types of arrangements are forbidden.

The Medicare regulations concerning payment of HMOs and other competitive medical plans were revised in 1985.[39]

Collections

A difficult area for hospital administrators is control of the amount of money owed to the hospital, called *accounts receivable*. Even though third party payers may generally owe the majority of accounts receivable, collection from individual patients is a vital source of operating revenue. To ensure that collection of a bill can be pursued to the full extent permitted by law, the bill must be accurately prepared and maintained. The correct name and address of the patient and the person responsible for payment must be obtained; the services rendered and the dates must be clearly described; and any payments or other credits must be promptly reflected on the account.

Responsibility for Payment

An adult patient is responsible for paying his or her hospital bill. This responsibility is based on either an express or implied contract to pay for accepted services. The adult patient is responsible for the reasonable value of services furnished in good faith, even if the patient is unconscious, mentally incompetent, or incapacitated at the time the services are provided. The major exceptions are when the competent, oriented adult has explicitly refused to accept the services or when the law entitles the patient to free care.

In most states a husband is responsible for paying for necessary care for his wife. In most states, the wife has a reciprocal duty to pay for necessary care for her husband.[40] Most states make the father responsible for payment for necessary care for minor children. In many states, the mother is also responsible. In some states, minors are not legally responsible for paying for care they receive, unless they are emancipated. However, in other states, minors are also responsible for paying for their necessary care. When there is doubt under state law concerning parental responsibility, the parents' express promise to pay is frequently obtained. When parents are divorced or separated, special rules concerning parental responsibility apply in some states, so that an express promise is frequently required to make the noncustodial parent responsible.[41]

Absent a statute or an express promise, other relatives or friends are not responsible for paying for care. Some state statutes make adult children responsible for the cost of their parents' care when their parents are unable to pay. By expressly promising to pay, a relative or friend may become responsible for paying for care, especially if the promise is written. The promise must be carefully written because some forms have been successfully challenged.[42] In most states, merely arranging for care or bringing a person to the hospital does not make a relative or friend responsible for payment.

Under the statutes of some states, counties or other units of local government are responsible for paying for some health care on behalf of their residents who are unable to pay. Some of these statutes provide that prior authorization must be obtained from appropriate government officials. Other statutes do not require prior approval to create an obligation, especially in emergencies.[43] In many states police departments have a statutory obligation to pay for care of persons in their custody who are charged with crimes.[44] However, police generally do not assume financial responsibility by bringing someone who is not in custody to a hospital.[45]

Collection Mechanisms

Two special legal collection mechanisms are hospital liens and estate claims. Many states have hospital lien laws to assist hospitals in collecting for services rendered to victims of compensable accidents. A *lien* is a legal claim attached to property. If the property is sold, the claim can ultimately be paid from the proceeds. If a patient is treated for injuries caused by a person who is insured or otherwise capable of paying damages, the hospital may place a lien on the proceeds of any court judgment or settlement of the patient's personal injury action against the responsible individual. Appropriate documents must be filed with the court, the negligent party, the insurer, and the patient's attorney. The second special legal mechanism applies when the patient dies. The estate of the patient is responsible for the debts of the deceased if the estate is given timely notice of the debt. Many states assign a high priority to the payment of the expenses for care of the deceased during the last illness. Thus, many of the other debts of the deceased cannot be paid until the hospital's bill has been paid.

When a hospital's internal collection procedures fail to produce payment, hospitals frequently use collection agencies. Usually the hospital enters a written agreement with one or more collection agencies specifying the terms and conditions for collection activities to assure compliance with applicable laws and hospital policies. In some states, questions have been raised concerning the authority of public hospitals to use collection agencies. Absent a specific statutory prohibition, courts have ruled that they can use collection agencies. One example is a 1976 California decision in which the court ruled that a county could assign its delinquent accounts to a private collection agency, provided it first evaluated the patient's ability to pay and reserved the right to adjust or cancel any bill that would work undue hardship on the debtor.[46]

In the past, Medicare did not permit hospitals or their collection agencies to threaten or use court action to collect Medicare deductible or coinsurance amounts. This restriction has been removed.

A bill is evidence of a contract to pay for services rendered and as such is enforceable by legal action. Although small bills are usually not worth the cost of judicial proceedings, legal action taken by the hospital may sometimes help educate patients about their obligation to pay medical bills just as they pay other bills. In some states small claims courts, either with or without an attorney, can enforce legal obligations. If a court judgment is obtained, then there are several ways to enforce the judgment, including having a sheriff seize the debtor's property or imposing garnishment of the debtor's wages. Garnishment of a debtor's wages is a court order to an employer to pay a portion of the debtor's paycheck to the creditor until the debt is paid. The federal Consumer Credit Protection Act[47] and various state laws limit the portion of a paycheck that may be garnisheed.

Other Regulation of Collection Efforts

The Federal Debt Collection Practices Act[48] and various state laws regulate techniques that may be used to seek payment of delinquent accounts. Some of these laws apply only to collection activities of collection agencies, while others also apply to the hospital's internal collection activities. All persons involved in the hospital's collection activities should be familiar with these laws to assure compliance. In some situations, failure to comply can make the debt unenforceable and even subject the hospital and individuals involved to civil liability and criminal penalties. In 1984 a collection agency attempting to collect a $552.40 bill for the Mayo Clinic was required to pay the debtor $14,400 for his emotional distress, out of pocket expenses, and attorney's fees because the agency violated the Fair Debt Collection Practices Act.[49]

When a hospital receives a notice that a patient has obtained discharge of debts in bankruptcy, collection efforts must cease. Federal law forbids efforts to collect debts that have been discharged in bankruptcy. A hospital can be fined for violating this law.

Truth-in-Lending

Hospitals also need to be aware of the Truth-in-Lending Act and its implementing regulations,[50] called "Regulation Z," which specify the disclosures that must be made by entities that lend consumers money. These rules are applicable to the credit practices of some hospitals. A federal appellate court ruled in 1980 that the law and regulations do not apply to most informal "workout" arrangements between hospitals and patients, even if a late fee is charged for delinquent payments.[51] Thus, the credit practices of some hospitals are not affected by the rules.

UNCOMPENSATED CARE

Many hospitals are required by law to provide uncompensated care to certain patients. State law requires many governmental hospitals to provide uncompensated care, especially to patients who are residents of the area providing tax support to the hospital and who are unable to pay. Federal law imposes this obligation on all hospitals that have received Hill-Burton grants or loans.

The federal Hill-Burton Act[52] provided public and nonprofit community hospitals with funding for construction and modernization. Hospitals that accepted this funding are required to provide a reasonable volume of services to persons unable to pay. For many years, this obligation was met by either (a) certifying that an amount of free care was provided equal to 10 percent of all Hill-Burton assistance; (b) certifying that the amount was 3 percent of hospital operating costs, excluding costs for Medicare and Medicaid patients; or (c) maintaining an open door policy so that no person was turned away for lack of money. The obligation continued for 20 years after the construction was completed. The open door option was eliminated in 1979. Compliance became much more difficult in 1979, when HHS promulgated regulations,[53] specifying notice and record-keeping requirements, qualifications patients must meet for their care to count toward satisfying the obligation, an inflationary index so that the required amount under the 10 percent option increases each year, a requirement that any portion of the obligation not met in one year be added to the obligation for the next year, and numerous other changes. In 1983, a federal appellate court found the regulations to be authorized and constitutional.[54] In 1985, HHS proposed regulations to simplify the requirements for public health care facilities.[55]

Some patients have attempted to use a hospital's failure to comply with the Hill-Burton uncompensated care regulations as a defense to collection suits. Courts have tended to reject this defense.[56]

COST CONTAINMENT AND REVENUE PRODUCTION

Hospitals have responded to the increasing societal concern with rising costs through efforts to contain costs and seek revenue from sources other than patients and third party payers.

Cost Containment

Most of the internal programs of hospitals to reduce costs do not present legal problems as long as they are consistent with adequate care of patients the hospital continues to serve and implemented in a manner that does not violate licensing and permit laws or collective bargaining agreements. Legal consultations may be required for some programs, such as a shift from commercial insurance to a self-insurance mechanism or adoption of stricter security measures to reduce misappropriation of hospital property.

Group Purchasing

Many hospitals have joined together to purchase certain goods and services, such as food, drugs, equipment, and supplies. The size of the aggregate purchases can result in lower prices. Group purchasing arrangements must be designed to avoid antitrust violations. In 1983 a federal appellate court ruled that one of the largest group purchasing arrangements did not violate antitrust laws.[57]

Shared Services

Many hospitals share services, such as data processing, warehousing, billing and collections, and laboratory and clinical services. The sharing of some services has been facilitated by section 501(e) of the Internal Revenue Code,[58] which permits the formation of tax-exempt organizations to provide some of these services to several hospitals. Only the services listed in section 501(e) are entitled to exemption under the section, so it is not helpful for other services, such as shared laundry services, that are not listed.

Revenue Production

Hospitals are seeking increased revenues from sources other than direct hospital care to patients. For example, hospitals arrange fund-raising activities to obtain more philanthropic gifts. Some hospitals are selling their services to other providers and nonproviders through shared service arrangements and direct sales. Some are entering new businesses totally unrelated to the hospital's business solely for purposes of revenue production. Before entering these businesses, hospitals must determine that they have the legal authority to be involved in them. It may be necessary to establish a separate corporation to engage in the activity. Even when the hospital has the existing authority, it may be helpful to establish a separate corporation because of some tax and other considerations discussed later in this chapter.

Other Legal Considerations

Antitrust Laws

Hospitals are generally subject to federal and state antitrust laws. Since many cooperative arrangements for either group purchasing or shared services may violate these laws if the arrangements are not structured properly, antitrust implications must be reviewed before entering such arrangements.

Securities Laws

The creation of shares of an organization in which more than one entity participates may involve the creation or sale of a security. If securities are involved, federal and state laws regulating securities must be complied with.

Income Tax Exemption and Unrelated Business Income

When a tax-exempt hospital provides services directly to other hospitals or earns money from involvement in nonhospital endeavors, the hospital has to pay income taxes on its earnings from the services if the earnings are considered "unrelated business income." Tax-exempt hospitals lose their tax-exempt status for all of their activities if too large a portion of their revenues is unrelated business income. This has caused some tax-exempt hospitals that anticipate substantial unrelated business income to establish a separate corporation to conduct those activities.

Third Party Payment

Because the structure and operation of a hospital are greatly dependent upon the funds received through third party payment, hospitals need to consider the effects of acquisitions or organizational changes on payments from third parties. Three concerns under cost-based payment systems and some rate regulation systems are (1) subtraction of certain revenues from allowable costs; (2) requirements that a portion of otherwise allowable overhead costs be allocated to activities whose costs are not allowable; and (3) limitations on the payment for goods and services purchased from related organizations.

Loan, Gift, and Real Estate Documents

Documents concerning loans, gifts, bequests, leases, and real estate transactions may restrict the uses of certain land, buildings, or funds of the hospital. Before any hospital assets are transferred to other entities and before assets are devoted to new uses, applicable documents should be carefully reviewed.

CAPITAL FINANCING

Hospitals have substantial and growing needs for capital to modernize and expand. Internal financing from current net operating revenues or funded depreciation is one source of capital, but it has become increasingly difficult to accumulate. Historically, private philanthropy has been another primary source of capital for voluntary hospitals. Although the aggregate amount of funds provided by philanthropic sources has been increasing each year, the percentage of total hospital funds for capital expenditures from these sources has been continually decreasing. A third major source of capital was governmental grants, until the federal government discontinued its programs. Some states still have grant and loan programs to assist in the construction and improvement of medical facilities.

The sale of tax-exempt bonds is the predominant method for many nonprofit providers of health care to obtain funds for major capital expenditures. The principal advantage of tax-exempt bonds is the interest savings. The interest rate is usually less than the interest on taxable loans. Tax-exempt bonds are issued by state or local governmental entities. The bonds are usually revenue bonds repayable only from the revenues of the hospital, but bonds for governmental hospitals are sometimes payable from the general tax revenues of the governmental entity issuing the bonds. The exemption of bond interest from federal income taxation is based on section 103 of the Internal Revenue Code.[59] This law and its implementing regulations must be complied with to assure tax exemption. For example, federal directives place limits on the contracts that may be signed with management companies or with nonemployee physicians.[60] The Tax Equity and Fiscal Responsibility Act of 1982[61] added requirements for some types of tax-exempt bonds, including reports to the Secretary of Treasury and approval by a governmental unit.

Some states place additional limits on hospital use of tax-exempt bonds. One controversial area has been whether these bonds can be used to finance the capital needs of church-owned hospitals, but most courts have upheld such uses.[62]

Tax-exempt bonds are generally exempt from registration under federal securities laws,[63] but are subject to the penalties under those laws if fraudulent or deceptive practices are used. Tax-exempt bonds are not exempt from some state securities laws.

For-profit hospitals borrow money using taxable bonds and other taxable arrangements. In addition, they acquire equity capital by selling stock to investors.

The Federal Housing Administration (FHA) insures some conventional mortgages for constructing, modernizing, and equipping hospitals.[64] Rather than lending funds directly to the hospital, the FHA provides loan insurance. This minimizes the lender's risk, making it easier to borrow money. The FHA also guarantees and insures loans for some capital expenditures of hospitals in rural communities.[65]

While purchasing has been the more traditional method within the health care industry for obtaining capital assets, some hospitals lease assets. Although any type of capital asset may be leased, leases are most frequently used to obtain equipment.

ASSET PROTECTION

Hospital administrators must be concerned with protection against losses arising from injuries to patients or visitors and from damage to or destruction of physical facilities, equipment, and vehicles. Patients may sue the hospital if they are injured by the malpractice of professionals or the acts of the hospital's nonprofessional employees. Fire, theft, and other hazards may damage the hospital's physical property. A program to manage all risks includes attempts to minimize or eliminate the risks and proper insurance coverage against the risks that cannot be eliminated.

When negotiating insurance coverage, it is important for hospital administrators to be familiar with the range of options available, the constraints on insurance companies, and the actual scope of coverage being offered. Insurance companies are extensively regulated, but they have considerable latitude when the insured has sufficient bargaining power.

Hospital Professional and General Liability Insurance

Hospitals need professional and general liability insurance. Professional liability contracts generally are a combination of malpractice and product liability coverage. A typical insuring clause may state that the policy covers liability arising out of providing or failing to provide professional services, including medical, surgical, dental, or nursing treatment; provision of food or beverages to patients; furnishing and dispensing of medical, dental, or surgical supplies or appliances; or performance of postmortem examinations. General liability insurance usually covers losses from injury to patients or visitors arising out of negligence of personnel other than professionals. Disputes concerning which company is obligated to provide coverage for particular incidents sometimes arise between the insurance companies that provide professional and general liability protection. Hospitals should design their coverage to avoid gaps between the policies.

Other Types of Insurance

Hospitals are involved in many activities that are not covered by professional and general liability insurance, so separate coverage should be sought for these activities.

Since hospitals own and operate motor vehicles, they should purchase vehicle liability insurance and should consider collision, comprehensive, medical payments, and uninsured motorist coverages.

State worker's compensation laws establish the medical and compensation payments that must be paid by an employer to an employee who is injured on the job. Insurance is available to the employer to cover worker's compensation losses. Premium costs are usually based upon the hospital's own experience. The hospital's employee safety program can reduce both direct employee time loss and insurance premium costs. Worker's compensation insurance usually includes liability coverage to protect the hospital from suits by employees who are permitted to sue the employer in addition to, or in lieu of, receiving worker's compensation benefits.

A major element of property insurance is fire insurance. In addition, extended coverages, including flood, windstorm, and earthquake coverage, are frequently included in property insurance policies, depending on local risks.

Losses due to theft are frequently self-insured by the hospital because of the high premium cost for such insurance. The major type of "crime" coverage generally purchased is employee fidelity insurance to cover losses arising out of embezzlement, fraud, and other acts of employee dishonesty. Bonds are frequently purchased for hospital employees with financial responsibilities.

Hospitals frequently purchase protection for directors and officers, both in their group and individual capacities, to protect them against personal loss from lawsuits for acts in their official capacities. These policies also provide funds for the defense of these corporate officials in a class-action or other shareholder action. However, some insurance policies may not provide the protection they appear to provide. A federal district court ruled in 1984 that one officer's misrepresentations in the application for the insurance invalidated the coverage for all directors and officers.[66]

To reduce insurance premium costs, many hospitals have explored alternatives to commercial insurance policies. Some hospitals have found it advantageous to buy insurance on a group basis, while others have used "captive" insurance companies created by state hospital associations, state medical societies, groups of hospitals, or individual hospitals. Insurance companies are called "captive" when they are chartered to do business only for a particular group of patrons. Regardless of the manner in which insurance coverage is purchased, the premium is usually determined in part by the hospital's liability history. To control the premium cost, hospitals have implemented loss control programs, including a thorough incident reporting system and a system of addressing identified incident patterns and handling claims.

Some hospitals may be able to reduce their insurance costs through self-insurance of some risks. One approach to limited self-insurance is policies with larger than standard deductibles. Deductibles are the amounts the insured hospital must pay before the insurance company becomes responsible for paying the remainder up to the policy limits. The hospital self-insures all losses smaller than the deductible.

TAX EXEMPTION

Governmental and charitable institutions are granted exemption from many taxes at both the state and local levels for property, sales, and income taxes, and at the federal level for income taxes. Classification of a hospital as exempt depends upon several factors that vary depending on the type of tax.

Property Tax Exemption

Each state has the power to tax the properties within its boundaries. A hospital must prove that it is eligible for a specific tax exemption, or the property is taxable. In some states ownership by a nonprofit or governmental hospital is not sufficient to establish eligibility. In those states hospitals must also show that the property is used exclusively for hospital or other exempt purposes to qualify.

Governmental Hospitals

Hospitals belonging to the federal government are exempt from state and local taxation because the United States has the sovereign right to hold property free of taxation. The bases of this right are found in the Supremacy Clause of the Constitution and in the necessity for the federal government to be free from any interference by the states when dealing with its property. The federal government need not show that the property is exclusively devoted to government purposes since mere ownership is enough.

State, county, district, and municipal hospitals are usually also exempt from property taxation because they fall within state constitutional or statutory exemptions. These exemptions are usually based on ownership of the property by an exempt governmental entity. Hospitals owned by either the state or its local subdivisions are exempted in most states regardless of the use of the property. In some states, exemption from taxation is granted only when the governmental property is devoted to a "public use." Use for hospital purposes is generally considered to be a "public use." Questions may arise, however, about whether other uses of hospital land are valid public uses.

For-Profit Hospitals

Hospitals that are organized and operated for profit do not qualify for tax exemption because they are considered to be ordinary businesses for profit, regardless of whether a profit is actually earned. When for-profit hospitals are reorganized as nonprofit hospitals, some states consider the property to be tax exempt, even when the net revenue of the hospital is used to pay off bondholders who are the former stockholders in the predecessor for-profit hospital. However, some courts disagree.[67]

Nonprofit Hospitals

Nonprofit hospitals are frequently exempt from state and local property taxation by state constitutions and statutes. Most of these exemptions require that the institution serve a charitable purpose, but the specific wording determines the qualifications and extent of the exemption.

In many states a charitable organization's property must satisfy four tests to qualify for a tax exemption: (1) the organization must qualify as a charitable organization; (2) the property must be the type of property eligible for exemption; (3) the organization must demonstrate that it owns or has another qualifying interest in the property; and (4) the property must be used for a charitable purpose.

Qualifying As a Charitable Organization

The articles of incorporation or other organizational documents must state the charitable purpose and contain a provision forbidding any financial gain to private individuals from the operation of the hospital or from the distribution of its assets. It is not sufficient for these purposes merely to be reflected in the bylaws. The actual operation of the hospital may be scrutinized to see that it operates as a charitable enterprise.

Direct compensation to trustees for each meeting or each year is generally consistent with a charitable purpose, if the compensation is a reasonable amount and is not statutorily prohibited. Compensation can be provided to trustees when they provide services to the hospital, such as legal advice or financial management services. Compensation can also be provided to doctors for administrative or other actual services for the hospital. The prohibition of private gain does not prevent salaries to hospital staff, contracts with vendors and specialty physicians, and other payments for services rendered. When the payments do not bear a reasonable relationship to the services provided, courts may find that the charitable organization is being operated for private gain and refuse the exemption.

The beneficiaries of a charitable hospital may be restricted to some extent without loss of the tax exemption. For example, children's hospitals limit their care to children, specialty hospitals limit their care to certain types of disease, and some hospitals limit their services to members of an order, society, or association. An exception to this general rule was the Missouri decision that a hospital owned by a railroad and open only to railroad employees and their families was not exempt from taxation because the hospital was not open to the public.[68]

Some states accept health care services as sufficient evidence of a charitable purpose. Other states require that the hospital actually provide free care to those unable to pay.[69] Generally, exempt hospitals may charge for services and collect bills in an ordinary business manner. However, the Georgia courts have denied exemption to hospitals that collect payments from patients, because the statutory exemption requires the institution to be a "purely public charity."[70]

Type of Property

Some states tax both real property (e.g., land and buildings) and personal property (e.g., movable equipment and automobiles). The charitable exemption may only apply to certain types of property. Real estate owned by a charitable hospital and used for hospital purposes is usually exempt; however, personal property belonging to the hospital may not be exempt.

Ownership Requirements for Exemption

To be exempt, the hospital must demonstrate that it owns or has another qualifying interest in the specific property. In some states, the hospital must actually have title to the property. In other states, it is sufficient for the hospital to be leasing the property, although some states require the lease to be of a certain type or length to qualify.[71] The form of ownership may be closely examined because of the demand to widen the property tax base.

Use Requirements for Exemption

The charitable hospital must also demonstrate that the property is being used for an exempt purpose as defined in the statute granting the exemption. Most statutes require the property to be exclusively used for charitable purposes, but the interpretation of what is an exclusive use varies. Generally the use must be reasonably necessary for the charitable or educational work of the institution. Some states have questioned whether property used for purposes not directly related to patient care is entitled to exemption. Many such uses, though not specifically described in the exemption statute, have been held to be so closely related to the primary purpose of the hospital that they enhance or enlarge the primary use, entitling the property to exemption. Not all uses have been considered so closely related, so some property owned by charitable hospitals has been taxed. For example, property rented for commercial use is generally taxable, even when the income is used for charitable purposes. Some other specific issues concerning uses of hospital property are considered separately below.

A few states do not require the exclusive use of property for charitable purposes. For example, Kentucky's constitutional exemption of institutions of public charity has been interpreted to extend to property rented or leased by the charity for the purpose of obtaining income to be used for charitable purposes.[72] In these states, the use of the property is immaterial, as long as the income is used for charitable purposes.

Some states permit split listing of property, so that the portion used for tax-exempt purposes can retain its tax exemption, while other portions are taxed.[73] In other states, the tax exemption of the entire property is lost if a portion is being used for other than tax-exempt purposes. In the states that do not permit split listing, much greater care should be exercised to avoid nonexempt uses.

Noncommercial and Occasional Rental

Many exemption statutes forbid any rental of exempt property, only commercial rental, or use of the property for profit. Noncommercial rental calculated to cover no more than expenses on the property rented does not destroy the property's exemption in most states. Property usually also remains exempt when it is rented to another charitable organization.

Rentals that are infrequent and irregular and have no view to profit, generally called occasional rentals, will normally not affect the tax exemption if the property is rented for such purposes as meetings of civic groups.

Specific Uses

In most states hospital property that is used for private physician offices is not exempt.[74] Most taxing authorities view this private use of office space as primarily for the convenience and profit of the physicians. When office space is furnished to a physician in return for administrative services, it is usually still tax exempt for the hospital.[75]

Hospital property used to house hospital employees, trainees, and key administrative personnel is exempt in some states. Some states have specific statutory exemptions, while others have court decisions recognizing housing as an exempt purpose because it encourages more efficient operation of the hospital. However, when the rental is set too high, the property will probably be viewed as commercially rented and will be taxable in some states.

States vary in considering a cafeteria, pharmacy, or other patient and visitor amenity an exempt use because of a sensitivity to the commercial and competitive aspects of these activities. Exemptions frequently depend on whether (1) these enterprises are run on a nonprofit basis by the hospital itself; (2) net revenues are used only for the direct benefit of the hospital; and (3) sales or services are restricted primarily to the hospital's medical staff, employees, patients, and visitors.

States also vary in considering vacant land or unoccupied buildings exempt. In some states, a building must be in use to be exempt.[76] In other states, a building may be exempt when it is in the process of construction. In other states the property is exempt when plans are complete or a specific use is imminent.[77] Vacant land is considered to be used for a charitable purpose in some states either because the land is necessary to the hospital's quiet and successful enjoyment of other exempt property or because the land is necessary to fulfill the hospital's expansion plans.

In some states, hospital property used for tennis courts, playgrounds, and parks or walking areas for employees or patients has been held exempt because it is sufficiently related to the overall primary charitable use. Since recreation for patients is generally recognized as therapy, property used for this purpose is generally exempt. States vary in regarding property used for employee recreation as exempt. Such uses promote the health and well-being of employees and promote recruitment of hospital personnel. A Pennsylvania court found a tennis court, an apartment house for foreign nurses, and a lighted open area between them all exempt because they were "necessary for the occupancy and enjoyment of the charitable use."[78] However, at least one state has withdrawn the exemption for recreation facilities by statute.[79]

Most states view a hospital parking building as necessary to the efficient operation of the hospital as long as it is used primarily by hospital personnel, patients, and visitors and as long as an occasional parking fee from hospital visitors does not destroy the exemption.[80] However, in Massachusetts taxes must be paid on the portion of a parking building used by physicians and their staff in connection with their private practices in an adjacent medical building.[81]

As nonprofit hospitals have formed chains, the tax status of corporate headquarters has been questioned. In 1984, a court found the headquarters to be tax exempt in Illinois.[82]

Most states have not yet addressed whether property is exempt when owned by cooperatives or shared services corporations. In a 1976 Minnesota decision, the court found cooperative property to be exempt because the exempt member hospitals completely owned, managed, and financed the cooperative and received all the benefits from it.[83]

Payments in Lieu of Taxes

In some states, municipal taxing authorities have placed substantial pressure on hospitals and other tax-exempt organizations to make payments in lieu of taxes. Although there is usually no legal basis for these requests, they have sometimes succeeded in obtaining "voluntary" payments. Some have actually been made voluntarily. Others have been made as a result of threats to challenge the tax-exempt status of the property or to withhold approval of requests for building permits, zoning changes, and other variances, licenses, and approvals. Thus, hospitals may be confronted with the choice of negotiating a payment, accepting delays or denials of important approvals, or resisting through the political or legal process.

Sales and Use Taxes

States that have sales and use taxes vary considerably in their coverage and exemptions, so state and local law must be consulted to determine tax responsibilities and available exemptions. Hospitals must be aware of when they must pay taxes on their purchases and when they must collect on their sales. Some states exempt qualified charitable organizations from collecting sales taxes, while others grant exemption for specific products or services, rather than for entire institutions. There is usually an exemption for medicines and some medical products.

Federal and State Income Tax

Many nonprofit hospitals are eligible for exemption from federal income tax under section 501(c)(3) of the Internal Revenue Code.[84] It exempts organizations created and operated exclusively for certain purposes, including "charitable purposes." The scope of charitable purposes entitled to exemption from federal income tax is different from the scope used by states to determine exemption from state and local taxes. Thus, property may be exempt from one and not from the other.

All organizations seeking section 501(c)(3) tax exemption must meet the following six requirements:

(1) The organization must be organized and operated exclusively for one or more special purposes (religious, charitable, scientific, testing for public safety, literary, educational, prevention of cruelty to children or animals, or amateur sports).
(2) No part of the net earnings can inure to any private shareholder or individual.
(3) No substantial part of its activities can involve passing propaganda or otherwise attempting to influence legislation.
(4) The organization cannot participate in or intervene in any political campaign on behalf of any candidate for public office.
(5) The assets of the organization must be dedicated to charity, so that they go to another qualified charity if the organization is dissolved.
(6) The organization must apply for classification as a tax-exempt organization on forms furnished by the IRS.

Health care is accepted as a "charitable purpose" by the Internal Revenue Service (IRS). Before 1969, the IRS considered free care to the poor one of the essential characteristics a hospital must have to be "charitable." In 1969, the IRS issued a ruling that recognized promotion of health as one of the general purposes of the law of charity, so free or reduced rate services are not required.[85] A federal appellate court upheld this ruling.[86] The Supreme Court later reversed the decision on the grounds that the organization could not file the suit because it did not have sufficient interest in the outcome.[87] Thus, the 1969 ruling was left in effect. The characteristics that the 1969 ruling found to be important in determining whether the hospital was operated for a charitable purpose included

(1) The hospital provided care on a nonprofit basis to all persons in the community who were able to pay directly or through third party reimbursement.
(2) The hospital operated an emergency room that was open to all persons.
(3) Any surplus of receipts over disbursements was used to improve the quality of patient care, expand facilities, and advance training, education, and research.
(4) Control of the hospitals rested with a board of trustees composed of independent civic leaders.
(5) The hospital maintained an open medical staff, with privileges available to all qualified medical staff.
(6) The hospital permitted all members of the active medical staff to lease space in its medical office building.

This ruling was clarified by the IRS in a 1983 ruling that addressed a hospital that did not have all of the characteristics listed in the 1969 ruling.[88] The hospital did not have an emergency room because the state health planning agency had found it unnecessary. The IRS looked at other factors and concluded that the hospital was operated for the exclusive benefit of the community and, thus, was charitable and entitled to tax exemption. Additional flexibility is indicated in other areas, such as the approval of some profit sharing plans for nonprofit hospitals.[89] The minimum characteristics necessary to assure tax exemption are not yet clear, so hospitals that desire federal income tax exemption under section 501(c)(3) should seek advice from a competent tax lawyer before changing any of the characteristics listed in the rulings.

In 1983, the Supreme Court recognized a new requirement for exemption under section 501(c)(3). The Court ruled that organizations that violate an "established national public policy" are not entitled to an exemption.[90] Thus, the Court upheld the denial of tax exemptions to a school with a racially discriminatory admission policy and a school with a racially discriminatory code of conduct for students.

A tax-exempt hospital still must pay taxes on unrelated business income. For example, the profit from drug sales to outpatients who are private patients of the medical staff is usually unrelated business income.[91] If the unrelated business income is too large a portion of total revenues, the entire tax exemption can be lost.

A tax-exempt hospital may have a for-profit subsidiary if certain conditions assuring separation of the entities are met.[92] A 1985 IRS General Counsel Memorandum outlines the four factors that are examined to determine if the parent corporation's tax-exempt status is compromised

(1) The parent and the subsidiary should have separate boards of directors with minimal overlap,
(2) The parent should have no more than minimal involvement with the subsidiary's day-to-day management,
(3) The subsidiary should have a separate existence and a bona fide business purpose, and
(4) Any services provided between the parent and subsidiary should be on an arm's length basis.[93]

However, an IRS private letter ruling has indicated that the absence of one of the factors may not be fatal.[94] If the IRS finds that the factors have not been sufficiently met, the actions of the subsidiary will be attributed to the parent, so, for example, any dividends paid by the subsidiary could be fatal for the parent's tax-exempt status.

Some governmental hospitals are tax exempt under section 115 of the Internal Revenue Code[95] on the basis of being an instrumentality of the state, rather than under section 501(c)(3).

State income taxes (and city income taxes in larger municipalities) apply to all profits or net proceeds accruing to an organization unless it has been approved for exemption under the state tax laws. The state qualifications for exemptions may be different from the federal qualifications.

NOTES

1. *E.g.*, In re 1976 Hosp. Reimbursement Rate for William B. Kessler Memorial Hosp., 78 N.J. 564, 397 A.2d 656 (1979).

2. Health Servs. Cost Review Comm'n v. Franklin Square Hosp., 280 Md. 233, 372 A.2d 1051 (1977).

3. Massachusetts Nurses Ass'n v. Dukakis, 726 F.2d 41 (1st Cir. 1984).

4. Washington State Nurses Ass'n v. Washington State Hosp. Comm'n, 773 F.2d 1044 (9th Cir. 1985).

5. Rebaldo v. Cuomo, 749 F.2d 133 (2nd Cir. 1984).

6. Pub. L. No. 93-406, 88 Stat. 829 (1974) (codified in scattered sections of 5, 18, 26, 29, 31, and 42 U.S.C.).

7. Pub. L. No. 89-97, 79 Stat. 290 (1965).

8. Pub. L. No. 98-21, 97 Stat. 65 (1983), as amended Pub. L. No. 98-369, 98 Stat. 1073 (1984); the implementing regulations were published in 48 FED. REG. 39752 (Sept. 1, 1983), as amended 49 FED. REG. 234 (Jan. 3, 1984), and codified in 42 C.F.R. §§405.470–405.477 (1984) and scattered sections of 42 C.F.R. pts. 405, 409, and 489.

9. Whitney v. Heckler, 603 F. Supp. 821 (N.D. Ga. 1985); American Medical Ass'n v. Heckler, 606 F. Supp. 1422 (S.D. Ind. 1985).

10. Heckler v. Community Health Servs. of Crawford County, 104 S.Ct. 2218 (U.S. 1984).

11. 42 U.S.C. §1395x(e) (1982); 42 C.F.R. §§405.1011–405.1041 (1984). Proposed revised conditions of participation were published in 48 FED. REG. 299–315 (Jan. 4, 1983).

12. 42 U.S.C. §§1395aa and 1395bb (1982), as amended by Pub. L. No. 98-369, 98 Stat. 1096, 1101 (1984).

13. Pub. L. No. 98-21, 97 Stat. 65 (1983).

14. Pub. L. No. 98-369, 98 Stat. 1073 (1984).

15. Pub. L. No. 98-21, 97 Stat. 65 (1983), as amended Pub. L. No. 98-369, 98 Stat. 1073 (1984); the implementing regulations were published in 48 FED. REG. 39752 (Sept. 1, 1983), as amended 49 FED. REG. 234 (1984) and 50 FED. REG. 35691 (1985), and codified in 42 C.F.R. §§405.470–405.477 (1984) and scattered sections of 42 C.F.R. pts. 405, 409, and 489.

16. *E.g.*, St. Francis Hosp. v. Heckler, MEDICARE & MEDICAID GUIDE (CCH) ¶34, 918 (S.D. W. Va. Sept. 30, 1985) [prohibition of retroactive adjustments invalidated].

17. Samaritan Health Care v. Heckler, MEDICARE & MEDICAID GUIDE (CCH) ¶34862 (D.D.C. 1985); 50 FED. REG. S3398 (1985).

18. Health Care Financing Administration, BACKGROUND PAPER, Nov. 1985, MEDICARE & MEDICAID GUIDE (CCH) ¶35, 009 .

19. Baldwin, *Administration Expects to Begin Study to Find "Something Better" than PPS,* 15 MOD. HEALTHCARE, July 19, 1985, at 32; Wallace, *Capitation System Tops Agenda—HCFA Official,* 15 MOD. HEALTHCARE, July 5, 1985, at 52.

20. 42 U.S.C. 405(h) (1982); Heckler v. Ringer, 104 S.Ct. 2013 (U.S. 1984).

21. 42 U.S.C. §§1396a–1396q (1982 & Supp. I 1983), as amended by Pub. L. No. 98-369 (1984).

22. 42 U.S.C. §§1381–1383c (1982 & Supp. I 1983), as amended by Pub. L. No. 98-369 (1984).

23. 42 U.S.C. §§601–613 (1982 & Supp. I 1983), as amended by Pub. L. No. 98-369 (1984) and Pub. L. No. 98-378 (1984).

24. Alexander v. Choate, 105 S.Ct. 712 (U.S. 1985).

25. Charleston Memorial Hosp. v. Conrad, 693 F.2d 324 (4th Cir. 1982).

26. *E.g.,* Michigan, Ohio, Pennsylvania, South Dakota, Utah, and Washington, MEDICARE & MEDICAID GUIDE (CCH) ¶¶ 15600, 15626, 15632, 15640, 15646, and 15654.

27. Minnesota Ass'n of Health Care Facilities, Inc. v. Minnesota Dep't of Pub. Welfare, 742 F.2d 442 (8th Cir. 1984), *cert. denied,* 105 S.Ct. 1191 (U.S. 1985); Highland Chateau, Inc. v. Minnesota Dep't of Pub. Welfare, 356 N.W.2d 804 (Minn. Ct. App. 1984).

28. LaZalla v. Minnesota, 366 N.W.2d 395 (Minn. Ct. App. 1985).

29. *E.g.,* Haven Home, Inc. v. Department of Pub. Welfare, 216 Neb. 731, 346 N.W.2d 225 (1985). Note that these formulas do not require the state to take steps to furnish the specified occupancy: Humphrey v. State, Dep't of Mental Health, 14 Ohio App.3d 15, 469 N.E.2d 981 (1984).

30. Pub. L. No. 95-142, 91 Stat. 1185 (codified as amended in scattered sections of 42 U.S.C.).

31. *E.g.,* United States v. Greber, 760 F.2d 68 (3d Cir. 1985) *cert. denied,* 106 S.Ct. 396 (U.S. Nov. 12, 1985); United States v. Lipkis, 770 F.2d 1447 (9th Cir. 1985); *but see* United States v. Porter, 591 F.2d 1048 (5th Cir. 1979).

32. Letter from Stephen S. Trott, Ass't Att'y Gen., United States Dep't of Justice, to Richard P. Kusserow, Inspector Gen., HHS, Oct. 30, 1985, *reprinted in* 13 HEALTH LAW DIGEST, Dec. 1985, Supp. Pt. 2; *See also* Baldwin, *Justice Dept. Firm on Waiver Policy,* 15 MOD. HEALTHCARE, Nov. 11, 1985, at 33.

33. 42 U.S.C. §1320a-7a (1982); 45 C.F.R. pt.101 (1985).

34. In re Mayers, No.C-4 (Dep't Health and Human Servs. Aug. 11, 1985); 8 HEALTH LAW VIGIL, Sept. ??, 1985, at 10.

35. *E.g.,* Obstetricians-Gynecologists, P.C. v. Blue Cross, 219 Neb. 199, 361 N.W.2d 550 (1985) [prohibition of assignment enforceable]; Blue Cross Hosp. Serv., Inc. v. Frappier, 681 S.W.2d 925 (Mo. banc 1984) [state law requiring insurers to accept assignment upheld].

36. Oakland Neurosurgical Arts v. Blue Cross and Blue Shield of Mich., 135 Mich. App. 798, 356 N.W.2d 267 (1984).

37. Kartell v. Blue Shield of Mass., Inc., 749 F.2d 922 (1st Cir. 1984).

38. *E.g.,* Ball Memorial Hosp., Inc. v. Mutual Hosp. Ins. Co., 603 F. Supp. 1077 (S.D. Ind. 1985) [preliminary injunction of PPO denied]; Associated Foot Surgeons v. National Foot Care Program, Inc., No. 84-271367 CZ (Mich. Cir. Ct., Oakland County Feb. 1, 1984) [injunction of PPO denied]; Johns Hopkins Univ. v. Insurance Comm'r of Md., No. 84 209033/CL23414 (Md. Cir. Ct., Baltimore County Sept. 25, 1984) [PPO provider agreement approved by Insurance Commissioner upheld].

39. 50 FED. REG. 1314–1418 (Jan. 10, 1985), codified in 42 C.F.R. pts. 405 and 417.

40. *E.g.*, Iowa Code Ann. §597.14 (1981) [both spouses liable for necessary care provided to family members]; Richland Memorial Hosp. v. Burton, 282 S.C. 159, 318 S.E.2d 12 (1984) [both spouses liable for necessary care provided to spouses]; Schilling v. Bedford County Memorial Hosp., 225 Va. 539, 303 S.E.2d 905 (1983) [unconstitutional to require husband to pay for wife, but not wife for husband, thus, neither obligated. This ruling was partially reversed by legislation, S.B. 43 (New Laws 1984)]; Presbyterian Hosp. v. McCartha, 66 N.C. App. 177, 310 S.E.2d 409 (1984) [neither spouse obligated for care to the other].

41. Wagoner v. Joe Mater & Assocs., Inc., 461 N.E.2d 706 (Ind. Ct. App. 1984) [noncustodial parent not required to pay despite support order because he was willing to pay for care at another location, but opposed the particular provider].

42. *E.g.*, Memorial Hosp. v. Bauman, 100 A.D.2d 701, 474 N.Y.S.2d 636 (1984) [daughter not bound by signed commitment to pay because no evidence she intended to be personally bound]; Rohrscheib v. Helena Hosp. Ass'n, 670 S.W.2d 812 (Ark. Ct. App. 1984) [brother-in-law who signed admission form not personally responsible for bill because it did not contain express promise to pay]; McCarthy v. Weaver, 99 A.D.2d 652, 472 N.Y.S.2d 64 (1984) [form ambiguous because it contained both a promise to pay expenses not covered by insurance and promise to pay all expenses]; Texas County Memorial Found., Inc. v. Ramsey, 677 P.2d 665 (Okla. Ct. App. 1984) [promise by son to pay for nursing home care for indefinite term could be revoked with 30 days notice].

43. *E.g.*, University of Utah Hosp. and Medical Center v. Bethke, 101 Id. 245, 611 P.2d 1030 (1980) [Idaho county ordered to pay for emergency services to two indigent county residents].

44. *E.g.*, Health and Hosp. Corp. v. Marion County, 470 N.E.2d 1348 (Ind. Ct. App. 1984), *petition reh'g denied*, 476 N.E.2d 887 (Ind. Ct. App. 1985); *see also* Borgess Hosp. v. County of Berrien, 114 Mich. App. 385, 319 N.W.2d 354 (1982) [no obligation to pay for care of former prisoner after discharge from jail].

45. *E.g.*, Dade County v. Hospital Affiliates Int'l, Inc., 378 So.2d 43 (Fla. Dist. Ct. App. 1979); *but see* Albany General Hosp. v. Dalton, 69 Or. App. 204, 684 P.2d 34 (1984) [county responsible for cost of care of person injured in gunfight with police].

46. Lara v. Kern County Bd. of Supervisors, 59 Cal. App.3d 399, 130 Cal. Rptr. 668 (1976).

47. 15 U.S.C. §§1671–1677 (1982).

48. 15 U.S.C. §§1692–1692o (1982), as amended by Pub. L. No. 98-443, 98 Stat. 1708 (1984).

49. Venes v. Professional Serv. Bureau, Inc., 353 N.W.2d 671 (Minn. Ct. App. 1984).

50. 15 U.S.C. §§1601–1667e (1982), as amended by Pub. L. No. 98-443, 98 Stat. 1708 (1984) and Pub. L. No. 98-479, 98 Stat. 2234 (1984); 12 C.F.R. pt. 226 (1984).

51. Bright v. Ball Memorial Hosp. Ass'n, 616 F.2d 328 (7th Cir. 1980).

52. 42 U.S.C. §§291a–291o-1 (1982), as amended by Pub. L. No. 98-369, 98 Stat. 1112 (1984).

53. 42 C.F.R. pt. 124 (1984).

54. American Hosp. Ass'n v. Schweicker, 721 F.2d 170 (7th Cir. 1983), *cert. denied* 104 S.Ct. 2169 (U.S. 1984).

55. 50 FED. REG. 36454 (1985).

56. Falmouth Hosp. v. Lopes, 376 Mass. 580, 382 N.E.2d 1042 (1978); *contra* Hospital Center at Orange v. Cook, 177 N.J. Super. 289, 426 A.2d 526 (N.J. Super. Ct. App. Div. 1981).

57. White and White, Inc. v. American Hosp. Supply Corp., 723 F.2d 495 (6th Cir. 1983).

58. 26 U.S.C. §501(e) (1982).

59. 26 U.S.C. §103 (1982 & Supp. I 1983), as amended by Pub. L. No. 98-369, 98 Stat. 839 (1984).

60. Rev. Proc. 82-14 and 82-15 [limits on term of contract and compensation arrangements].

61. Pub. L. No. 97-248, 96 Stat. 466 (1982).

62. *E.g.*, Manning v. Sevier County, 30 Utah 2d 305, 517 P.2d 549 (1973); *contra* Board of County Comm'rs v. Idaho Health Care Facilities Auths., 96 Id. 498, 531 P.2d 588 (1975).

63. 15 U.S.C. §§77a–77aa (1982) as amended by Pub. L. No. 98-440, 98 Stat. 1691 (1984).

64. 12 U.S.C. §1715z-7 (1982 & Supp. I 1983), as amended by Pub. L. No. 98-479, 98 Stat. 2227, 2232 (1984).

65. 7 U.S.C. §§1926 and 1932 (1982).

66. Shapiro v. American Home Assurance, 584 F. Supp. 1245 (D. Mass. 1984).

67. *E.g.*, Benton County v. Allen, 170 Or. 481, 133 P.2d 991 (1943) [reorganized hospital not tax exempt].

68. Missouri Pac. Hosp. Ass'n v. Pulaski County, 211 Ark. 9, 199 S.W.2d 329 (1947).

69. Georgia Osteopathic Hosp. v. Alford, 217 Ga. 663, 12 S.E.2d 402 (1962); Utah County v. Intermountain Health Care, Inc., 709 P.2d 265 (Utah 1985).

70. St. Joseph Hosp. of August v. Bohler, 229 Ga. 577, 193 S.E.2d 603 (1972).

71. Cole Hosp., Inc. v. Champaign County Bd. of Review, 113 Ill. App. 3d 96, 446 N.E.2d 562 (1983) [sale-and-lease back as a financing device did not destroy exemption].

72. City of Louisville v. Presbyterian Orphans Soc'y, 299 Ky. 566, 186 S.W.2d 194 (1945).

73. *E.g.*, Fla. Stat. §196.192(2) (1985).

74. *E.g.*, Appeal of Lanchester Medical Center Ass'n, 23 Pa. Commw. 596, 353 A.2d 75 (1976); North Shore Medical Center, Inc. v. Bystrom, 461 So.2d 167 (Fla. Dist. Ct. App. 1984).

75. *E.g.*, Calais Hosp. v. City of Calais, 138 Me. 234, 24 A.2d 489 (1942).

76. Dade County Taxing Auth. v. Cedars of Lebanon Hosp. Corp., Inc., 355 So.2d 1202 (Fla. 1978).

77. Cleveland Memorial Medical Found. v. Perk, 10 Ohio St.2d 72, 225 N.E.2d 233 (1967).

78. Presbyterian-Univ. of Pa. Medical Center v. Board of Revision of Taxes, 24 Pa. Commw. 461, 357 A.2d 696 (1976).

79. Minn. Stat. §272.02(3) (1985 Supp.).

80. Allegheny General Hosp. v. Board of Property Assessment, 207 Pa. Super. 266, 217 A.2d 796 (1966).

81. Lynn Hosp. v. Board of Assessors, 383 Mass. 14, 417 N.E.2d 14 (1981).

82. Evangelical Hosp. Ass'n v. Novak, 125 Ill. App. 3d 439, 465 N.E.2d 986 (1984).

83. Community Hosp. Linen Servs., Inc. v. Commissioner, 309 Minn. 447, 245 N.W.2d 190 (1976).

84. 26 U.S.C. §501(c)(3) (1982).

85. Rev. Rul. 69-545, 1969-2 C.B. 117.

86. Eastern Kentucky Welfare Rights Org. v. Simon, 506 F.2d 1278 (D.C. Cir. 1974).

87. 426 U.S. 26 (1976).

88. Rev. Rul. 83-157, I.R.B. 1983-42,9.

89. *E.g.*, IRS Letter Ruling No. 8442064 (July 18, 1984).

90. Bob Jones Univ. v. Simon, 416 U.S. 725 (1983).

91. Carle Found. v. United States, 611 F.2d 1192 (7th Cir. 1979); *but see* IRS Letter Ruling 8349006 [not if physicians are in hospital-based group practice integrally part of hospital operations].

92. General Counsel Memorandum 39326 (Jan. 17, 1985); O'Brien & Marcino, *Quarterly Tax Report,* 8 HEALTH LAW VIGIL, Aug. 9, 1985, at 7, 10.

93. GCM 39326 (Jan. 17, 1985), IRS Positions Reports (CCH) ¶1608.

94. *E.g.,* Letter Ruling No. 8519037 (Feb. 12, 1985), *as discussed in* 8 HEALTH LAW VIGIL, Aug. 9, 1985, at 10.

95. 26 U.S.C. §115 (1982).

Chapter 5

Health Planning

Health care planning is a continuing process of assuring the community that resources are being properly used to meet the health care needs of the people. Effective planning focuses on the individual hospital, service area needs, and governmental health goals. This chapter focuses primarily on state and national governmental efforts to mandate and regulate health planning.

Planning involves an assessment of community desires and of community and institutional needs and capabilities. Since there is no precise way to assess either desires or needs, many aspects of planning remain administrative and require diplomatic skills. Economic and other considerations may force the hospital to choose between the satisfaction of apparent needs and the satisfaction of expressed desires. The hospital may be able to minimize this potential conflict through community participation in its planning process. When community leaders and representative community members are involved in analysis of needs and planning to address those needs, these individuals can assist in obtaining broader community support for changes in programs. Communities are involved in the planning process through broad-based representation on most hospital governing boards. An alternative or complementary approach is to include broad community representation on advisory committees, particularly those that advise on planning.

Health planning has been fostered through incentives, local planning funds, and mandates provided by a series of federal laws, including the Hill-Burton Act of 1946,[1] the Comprehensive Health Planning and Public Health Service Amendments of 1966,[2] the Social Security Amendments of 1972,[3] the National Health Planning and Resources Development Act of 1974,[4] and the Social Security Amendments of 1983.[5] The 1972 amendments promoted internal hospital planning by mandating that all hospitals participating in Medicare develop a capital expenditures budget.[6] They also promoted state planning by giving states the option, under section 1122,[7] of requiring state-level review of certain capital expenditures of hospitals. The 1974 Act stated several national health planning goals and criteria. It also created an elaborate structure to develop local health plans and to attempt to implement the plans through various steps, including the certificate-of-need laws discussed later in this chapter. Amendments to the 1974 Act, passed in 1979[8] and 1981,[9] reduced the number of projects subject to review, among other changes. Federal funding to reviewing agencies was drastically reduced over the same period, reducing the scope of their activities. The Social Security Amendments of 1983 modified section 1122 to require states to implement review by October 1986.[10] Further reductions in the federal role in health planning have been proposed. Other approaches to health planning are evolving, including community coalitions.

A HISTORICAL PERSPECTIVE

Hill-Burton Act

The Hill-Burton Act of 1946 created an incentive for state planning. As a prerequisite to receiving federal funds for hospital construction, each state was required to conduct a survey of existing facilities and to adopt a plan used to determine need. Before a hospital could receive federal assistance, a state agency had to determine that the proposed project was consistent with the needs identified by the state plan.

Comprehensive Health Planning and Public Health Services Amendments of 1966

The 1966 amendments provided financial assistance to states to promote coordinated health planning efforts. To receive funds, a state was required (1) to designate a state agency (the "A" agency) to supervise the state's health planning function and (2) to establish a state health planning council with certain governmental and consumer representatives. The "A" agency was required to review the program of each health care facility in the state periodically and recommend appropriate modification. The Act authorized federal assistance for hospital construction consistent with the state plan. The Act also authorized a wide range of federal grants, including project grants to local agencies (the "B" agencies) to develop local plans for coordination of health services.

Social Security Amendments of 1972

The 1972 amendments[11] require each Medicare provider, as a condition of participation in the program, to have a written plan, including an annual operating budget and a three-year capital expenditures budget.[12] The plan is to be prepared under governing body direction by a committee composed of representatives of the governing body, the hospital administration, and the medical staff. It must be internally reviewed and updated at least annually. Since the purpose of the requirement is to assure that providers conduct their own budgeting and planning, plans are not reviewed for substance by governmental authorities.

Section 1122 Review

The 1972 amendments also added section 1122,[13] which provides states the option of establishing a program to review capital expenditures by institutions participating in Medicare, to the Social Security Act. HHS enforces the required review in participating states by refusing to pay Medicare's share of the capital costs of an unapproved or disapproved hospital project. Nearly every state implemented this provision through an agreement between the Secretary of HHS and the governor. In return for funding and assistance, the governor designated a state agency to administer the section. The agency, called the designated planning agency (DPA), is required to have an advisory body with at least half its members representing consumer interests. These requirements are satisfied by the State Health Planning and Development Agency (SHPDA) with its advisory State Health Coordinating Council (SHCC) created under the National Health Planning and Resources Development Act discussed later in this chapter. Most states have either designated their SHPDA to be their DPA or have ended their section 1122 review programs to avoid duplicative review with their certificate-of-need programs. This trend away from section 1122 review will change because the 1983 amendments discussed below require such review.

Section 1122 originally provided for review of projects that change the bed capacity of the facility, substantially change the services of the facility, or cost more than $100,000. The Social Security Amendments of 1983 increased the $100,000 threshold to $600,000 and made section 1122 review mandatory by October 1986.[14]

The National Health Planning and Resources Development Act of 1974

The National Health Planning and Resources Development Act of 1974[15] added Titles XV and XVI to the Public Health Service Act. Title XV created a system of local planning agencies, called Health Systems Agencies (HSAs), that interfaced with state agencies called State Health Planning and Development Agencies (SHPDAs) and State Health Coordinating Councils (SHCCs). Their goal was to restructure and expand the health planning process, leading to the development of state health plans under a national health planning scheme and to efforts to implement those plans through certificate-of-need review and other mechanisms. Title XVI sought to integrate the federal hospital construction funding into the national health planning process of Title XV and at the same time redirect the flow of federal construction and modernization funds from inpatient to outpatient facilities. Although implementing regulations were promulgated,[16] Title XVI had relatively little impact because Congress declined to appropriate substantial funds.

The Act has been amended several times since its enactment. The most extensive amendments were in 1979[17] and 1981,[18] substantially modifying many elements of the law. Except where otherwise noted, the following discussion describes the Act as amended in 1981.

The health planning framework created by Title XV has federal, state, and local elements. In section 1502,[19] several national health priorities were listed. The original Act had ten priorities, and seven more have been added by amendment. The priorities include promotion of

   (1) primary care services;
   (2) multi-institutional systems;
   (3) health maintenance organizations and other alternative delivery systems;
   (4) physician's assistants;
   (5) shared services;
   (6) quality care;
   (7) geographic integration of care;
   (8) disease prevention;
   (9) accounting and reimbursement changes;
  (10) health promotion;
  (11) energy conservation;
  (12) discontinuance of unneeded services;
  (13) cost containment;
  (14) appropriate institutional mental health care;
  (15) appropriate outpatient mental health care;
  (16) attention to the emotional and psychological components of health care; and
  (17) strengthening of competitive forces.

Federal

At the federal level, the Secretary of HHS was directed to develop national guidelines for health planning in consultation with various groups. In 1977 the Secretary proposed guidelines on the number of hospital beds per 1,000 population and on utilization of several types of services.[20] The proposal stated that all state and local plans could differ from the numerical guidelines only by setting lower maximums or higher minimums.[21] A tremendous public reaction, particularly from rural states, resulted in over 50,000 comment letters and in a resolution unanimously passed by the House of Representatives expressing the sense of the Congress that there should be more flexibility allowed for local characteristics.[22] The final guidelines issued in 1978 were presented as benchmarks that could be adjusted to local conditions and needs.[23]

State

There are two entities at the state level. The first is a state governmental agency called the State Health Planning and Development Agency (SHPDA). It performs health planning and fund allocation functions. The SHPDA is responsible for implementing the state government's responsibilities under the state health plan, serving as the designated planning agency (DPA) for "section 1122 review," administering the state's certificate-of-need program, reviewing and publicizing the "appropriateness" of existing institutional health services periodically, and assisting the State Health Coordinating Council (SHCC) in performing its functions. The SHCC is the second entity at the state level. It is responsible for reviewing HSA budgets and applications for assistance, reviewing the HSA and SHPDA health plans, and approving the final state health plan. In addition, the SHCC reviews and approves all applications for funds under the Act. The SHCC is composed of persons named by the governor, partly from nominations made by the HSAs. The SHPDA and the SHCC must comply with the Act and regulations[24] applicable to their operations to qualify for federal funding.

Local

The Act required the Secretary to divide the nation into health service areas, so over 200 health service areas were designated. One HSA was established for each area. The HSA was responsible for collecting data concerning the health status of residents, taking inventory of health care resources and needs, and developing and implementing both a long-term Health Systems Plan (HSP) and a short-term Annual Implementation Plan (AIP).

The HSAs relied primarily on federal financing, although some were able to obtain some funding from other sources. They had to comply with the Act and the regulations[25] applicable to their operations to qualify for federal support. With the reduction in federal funding for HSAs, the 1981 amendments modified section 1536 of the Act to authorize HHS to approve an application of any governor to abolish the HSAs in a state and have the SHPDA perform its functions. Several states have obtained this approval and their HSAs have ceased to operate.[26] Some have reorganized to continue involvement in private health planning efforts, such as the community coalitions discussed later in this chapter.

Appropriateness Review

One responsibility of SHPDAs and HSAs under sections 1513(g) and 1523(a)(6)[27] is to review periodically the appropriateness of existing services for which goals have been established in the State Health Plan.[28] In 1982, the Secretary of HHS waived the requirement of HSA involvement. No official sanctions are attached to appropriateness review, but the publication of the findings alone may have significant implications for hospitals involved in providing services that are announced to be inappropriate.

Review of Proposed Uses of Federal Funds (PUFF)

One tool that each HSA is given to influence the evolution of the health care system is the authority to review and approve or disapprove the proposed use within its health service area of certain federal funds for health-related purposes.[29] Disapproval can be overridden by the Secretary of HHS if the funds come directly from the federal government and by the governor if the funds come through the state. Review by the HSA is optional. If the HSAs in a state are abolished under section 1536, the SHPDA may perform the HSA's review function.

CERTIFICATE-OF-NEED PROGRAMS

A certificate-of-need law is a state law that requires that a health care provider receive permission, called a *certificate of need* (CON), from a state agency before making certain capital expenditures or program changes. The state agency promulgates criteria to be used in evaluating the need for individual projects and evaluates individual proposals to determine whether they satisfy the criteria. The specific criteria, procedures, and scope of projects subject to review vary somewhat among the states, but federal incentives promoted substantial consistency in most features of these laws.

Some states began enacting certificate-of-need laws before federal incentives were enacted in 1975. New York pioneered the concept in 1964. In 1970 a federal court declared California's certificate-of-need law constitutional.[30] However, the North Carolina Supreme Court declared its own state law in violation of the state constitution as a deprivation of liberty without due process of law and as the establishment of a monopoly.[31]

Section 1523(a)(1)(4)[32] of the National Health Planning and Resources Development Act requires that each state have a certificate-of-need program or forgo federal funding for health planning and several other health-related functions. The state of North Carolina challenged the constitutionality of this requirement, pointing out that its state supreme court had ruled that it could not comply without changing its state constitution. The United States Supreme Court ruled that the certificate-of-need requirement did not violate the federal Constitution even as applied to a state that could not comply without amending its constitution. The state was free not to comply but would have to forgo the inducement of $50 million in federal health program funds.[33] With the reduction in federal financial incentives, a few states have eliminated their certificate-of-need programs.[34]

HHS reported that between 1979 and 1982 over 23,000 projects worth over $38 billion were approved, while nearly 3,000 projects totaling approximately $9 billion were not approved. This denial rate of about 19 percent increased to almost 28 percent in 1982.[35]

Scope of Projects Requiring Review

The regulations implementing the original federal law required review of (1) all capital expenditures by health care institutions in excess of $150,000; (2) establishment of new health care institutions; (3) certain changes in bed capacity; and (4) new health services of health care institutions regardless of cost. Review of physician office projects was not required, although some states chose to cover some office projects, such as purchase of major equipment. The 1979 amendments[36] specified in greater detail which projects needed to be reviewed and specified that a new service must be reviewed only if it involved annual operating expenses of at least $75,000. The amendments also created several exceptions to the review requirement and permitted states to increase the $75,000 and $150,000 thresholds each year by an inflation factor approved by the Secretary of HHS. The 1981 amendments[37] increased the threshold for review of (1) new services to $250,000 in annual operating expenses; (2) major medical equipment to $400,000; and (3) other capital expenditures to $600,000. These changes did not take effect in each state until they were implemented by changes in the state's law. In 1985 HHS announced that the inflation factor had increased the $250,000 to $306,750 and the $600,000 to $736,200.[38] Some states have established higher thresholds.[39] When services are discontinued for more than twelve months, a certificate-of-need must be obtained before the service is provided again.[40]

Review Criteria

Section 1532[41] of the federal Act requires each HSA and SHPDA to develop and publish criteria for evaluating CON applications. The criteria must include the following fourteen, listed in section 1532(c):

(1) relationship to applicable health plans;

(2) relationship to the institution's long-range plan;

(3) need of the service area's population;

(4) availability of alternative methods;

(5) relationship to the existing health care system;

(6) in the case of proposed services, availability of resources, impact on professional training programs, access of health professions schools, alternative uses of the resources, and accessibility to those to be served;

(7) special needs and circumstances of institutions serving multiple health service areas;

(8) special needs and circumstances of HMOs;

(9) in the case of construction projects, costs and methods of construction and impact on costs and charges;

(10) need for energy conservation;

(11) effect on competition;

(12) innovations in financing and delivery of services that promote competition, quality assurance, and cost effectiveness;

(13) efficiency and appropriateness of use of similar existing facilities; and

(14) quality of care provided in the past.

Additional criteria are required by the implementing regulations.[42]

The SHPDA must evaluate a proposed project based on properly defined standards. Courts have ordered the issuance of a CON when a SHPDA's denial was not based on defined standards. For example, a Michigan court ordered a CON for a new hospital because the SHPDA had used unpublished criteria that gave preference to existing facilities.[43] A New Jersey court ruled that the SHPDA must consider all applicable criteria and cannot base its evaluation solely on one criterion.[44]

Review Procedures

Section 1532(b)[45] of the federal Act requires the following procedures to be used in processing CON applications:

(1) written notice to affected persons;
(2) a limit on the time for the review of an application;
(3) a procedure for obtaining additional information from applicants;
(4) submission of applications to involved agencies;
(5) submission of periodic reports concerning proposals;
(6) written findings stating the basis for any final decision or recommendation;
(7) timely notice of the status of a review;
(8) public hearings;
(9) publication of reports or actions;
(10) public access to applications and certain related information;
(11) for construction projects, submission of a letter of intent prior to submission of an application;
(12) certain rights during hearings, including the right to present evidence and be represented by a lawyer;
(13) accordance of the final decision with published procedures and criteria and foundation of the decision solely on the information in the official report of the administrative proceedings concerning the application; and
(14) an opportunity to appeal adverse decisions to an administrative agency and to the courts.

Between the time a hearing starts and the time the decision is made, the rules restrict informal contacts between the applicant or an opponent and SHPDA staff or members responsible for the application.

The requirement that the decision be based on the record is designed to protect providers from unfounded speculation and from use of information the provider has no opportunity to challenge. The potential for such abuses is illustrated by a 1985 case in which the Massachusetts Department of Public Health (DPH) denied a certificate of need for a reconditioned CT scanner because DPH was skeptical that the cost was so low that the scanner must be too old to be accurate or functional.[46] An appeals board reversed the denial because the application met the standards and no evidence in the record supported DPH's skepticism.

Procedural requirements imposed by state law must also be followed. This principle is illustrated by the federal court decision addressing a section 1122 review in Nebraska in which the court ruled the state agency did not have authority to deny any applications because it had never published review rules as required by state law.[47] Compliance with federal procedures was not sufficient. Providers must also comply with state law requirements. For example, a Kentucky court ruled that a provider could not use the courts to challenge a CON issued to another provider when the challenger failed to participate in the administrative hearings concerning the application.[48]

Monitoring

The 1979 amendments[49] added a requirement that a CON specify the timetable for carrying out the approved project and the maximum amount of authorized capital expenditures. If a good faith effort is not made to meet the timetable, the certificate can be withdrawn. If the actual expenditures are expected to exceed the maximum, the project can be subject to further review. The withdrawal of a CON after a project is commenced could have a serious adverse effect on a hospital, so a realistic timetable and budget are essential elements of a prudent CON application.

Lenders

Since the adoption of section 1122 of the Social Security Act, financial institutions, bond underwriters, and other lenders have required providers seeking funds for construction, expansion, or modernization to obtain all necessary approvals from the state planning agency. Thus, lenders will expect a timely CON application, plus appropriate ongoing actions to preclude withdrawal of the CON. Prospective lenders want approval to assure that third party payments are not limited. In addition, planning agency approval helps assure the lender or the underwriter that the proposed capital expenditures will not result in duplication of facilities, making full utilization and repayment more likely. Planning agency approval does not guarantee financing. Lenders may require a feasibility study in addition to the planning process. In some instances, projects that have received planning approval have not been constructed because of unfavorable findings in feasibility reports.

CAPITAL EXPENDITURE LIMITS AND MORATORIA

Several states have enacted limits on the total capital expenditures in the state for health care. Other states have imposed moratoria prohibiting approval of all capital expenditures of certain types, such as expenditures for new hospital beds or new hospitals.[50] These moratoria and limits have been successfully challenged only when they were not authorized by state statute.[51]

THE FUTURE OF HEALTH PLANNING

Congress has drastically reduced the funding for health planning activities. Proposals to reduce the federal role in health planning further are receiving serious consideration. Internal planning by institutions will continue whether or not there are governmental mandates or incentives because planning is necessary to cope successfully with changing societal expectations, changing medical science and technology, and other aspects of the environment. Although a few states have discontinued health planning, most states will continue or restore their health planning activities even if the federal government removes its incentives. It is likely that more states will seek to fund their certificate-of-need programs by charging application fees. Local public and private programs, including health care coalitions, are also likely to continue to evolve.

Health Care Coalitions

In response to the declining federal support of health planning and the growing concern of some businesses over the costs of health care benefits for their employees, interest is growing in voluntary community coalitions that address local health care issues, especially costs. In January 1982, the American Hospital Association, the American Medical Association, the Blue Cross and Blue Shield Association, the Health Insurance Association of America, the AFL-CIO, and the Business Roundtable endorsed the concept of voluntary coalitions and encouraged participation by their members. Many coalitions have already been formed. These coalitions have focused on different issues, including data collection; utilization review; development and encouragement of HMOs and other alternative delivery systems; restructuring of insurance benefits; reduction of hospital capacity; health provider regulation; ambulatory care; increasing access for the poor and unemployed; mitigating the impact of cuts in government support of health care; and health promotion through wellness, exercise, and risk reduction programs. Hospitals and hospital associations are participating in many of these efforts because of their commitment to planning for broad community health care needs and because of the need to contribute their knowledge and expertise to help the coalitions develop realistic proposals.

Antitrust

Involvement by hospitals and hospital associations in coalitions and similar activities must be carefully structured to assure that antitrust laws are not violated.[52] Antitrust laws can be violated by some types of exchange of cost information, negotiations of fees and charges, health facilities and services planning enforcement, and utilization review. At one time it was thought that the National Health Planning and Resources Development Act might be interpreted to modify the antitrust laws and permit activities not permitted for other businesses when they were part of health planning. In 1981 the United States Supreme Court ruled that no broad exception to the antitrust laws had been created, leaving open the possibility that in the future smaller exceptions might be possible.[53] Subsequent antitrust decisions concerning health planning have tended to treat health care the same as other activities. For example, in 1984 a federal court ruled that a certificate of need does not protect a hospital from being charged with monopolization. The court ruled that the certificate was only one step in the approval process and that the hospital must still comply with other laws, including the antitrust laws.[54]

When hospitals or coalitions are considering engaging in these activities or other activities that might be perceived as anticompetitive, it is important to review the antitrust implications. Many of these activities will be found to be permissible as is illustrated by the 1985 Department of Justice ruling that hospitals could provide a broad range of cost and utilization data to a business health care coalition without violating antitrust laws.[55] Antitrust issues are discussed further in Chapter 3.

NOTES

1. Act of August 13, 1946, Ch. 958, 60 Stat. 1040.

2. Pub. L. No. 89-749, 80 Stat. 1180 (1966).

3. Pub. L. No. 92-603, 86 Stat. 1329 (1972).

4. Pub. L. No. 93-641, 88 Stat. 2225 (1975).

5. Pub. L. No. 98-21, 97 Stat. 171 (1983).

6. 42 U.S.C. §1395x(e)(8) and (z) (1982 & Supp. I 1983), as amended by Pub. L. No. 98-369, 98 Stat. 1063 (1984).

7. 42 U.S.C. §1320a-1 (1982 & Supp. I 1983), as amended by Pub. L. No. 98-369, §2354, 98 Stat. 1100 (1984).

8. Pub. L. No. 96-79, 93 Stat. 592 (1979).

9. Pub. L. No. 97-35, §§933–937, 95 Stat. 570-572 (1981).

10. Pub. L. No. 98-21, §607, 97 Stat. 171 (1983).

11. Pub. L. No. 92-603, 86 Stat. 1329 (1972).

12. 42 U.S.C. §1395x(e)(8) and (z) (1982 & Supp. I 1983), as amended by Pub. L. No. 98-369, 98 Stat. 1063 (1984).

13. 42 U.S.C. §1320a-1 (1982 & Supp. I 1983), as amended by Pub. L. No. 98-369, §2354, 98 Stat. 1100 (1984).

14. Pub. L. No. 98-21, §607, 97 Stat. 171 (1983).

15. Pub. L. No. 93-641, 88 Stat. 2225 (1975).

16. 42 C.F.R. pt. 124 (1985).

17. Health Planning and Resources Development Amendments of 1979, Pub. L. No. 96-79, 93 Stat. 592.

18. Omnibus Budget Reconciliation Act of 1981, Pub. L. No. 97-35, §§922–937, 95 Stat. 570.

19. 42 U.S.C. §300k-2 (1982).

20. 42 FED. REG. 48502-5 (Sept. 23, 1977).

21. 42 FED. REG. 48502 (Sept. 23, 1977).

22. Danaceau, *The Health Planning Guidelines Controversy: A Report from Iowa and Texas,* Health Resources Administration, U.S. Department of Health, Education, and Welfare, October 1978; 123 CONG. REC. 38383–89 (1977).

23. 42 C.F.R. §§121.201–121.211 (1984).

24. 42 C.F.R. pt. 123 (1985).

25. 42 C.F.R. pt. 122 (1985).

26. *E.g.,* see Hellman, *Status Report: Health Planning and Capital Expenditure Regulation,* 8 HEALTH LAW VIGIL, June 14, 1985 (Supp.), 1.

27. 42 U.S.C. §§3001-2(g) and 300m-2(a)(6) (1982).

28. 42 C.F.R. §§122.501–122.508 (1985) and 42 C.F.R. §§124.601–124.608 (1985).

29. 42 U.S.C. §3001-2 (1982); 42 C.F.R. §§122.401–122.415 (1985).

30. Simon v. Cameron, 337 F. Supp. 1380 (C.D. Cal. 1970).

31. In re the Certificate of Need of Aston Park Hosp., Inc., 282 N.C. 542, 193 S.E.2d 729 (1972).

32. 42 U.S.C. §300m-2(a)(1)(4) (1982).

33. North Carolina ex rel. Morrow v. Califano, 435 U.S. 926 (1978), *aff'g* 445 F. Supp. 532 (E.D. N. C. 1977).

34. Hellman, *supra* note 26, at 1.

35. *State CON Agencies Approve 23,000 Projects over 4 Years,* 15 MOD. HEALTHCARE, July 5, 1985, at 43.

36. Pub. L. No. 96-79, §§117 and 126, 93 Stat. 614–620, 628 (1979), codified in 42 U.S.C. §300m-6 (1982), as amended, and in 42 U.S.C. §300n (1982).

37. Pub. L. No. 97-35, §936(a), 95 Stat. 572 (1981), codified in 42 U.S.C. §§300n(5), (6), and (7) (1982).

38. 50 FED. REG. 14027 (1985).

39. *E.g.,* Colorado's capital expenditure threshold is $2 million. *See* Hellman, *supra* note 26, at 1.

40. *E.g.,* Kenley v. Newport News General and Nonsectarian Hosp. Ass'n, Inc., 227 Va. 39, 314 S.E.2d 52 (1984); Iowa State Dep't of Health v. Hertko, 282 N.W.2d 744 (Iowa 1979).

41. 42 U.S.C. §300n-1 (1982).

42. 42 C.F.R. §123.412 (1985).

43. Huron Valley Hosp., Inc. v. Michigan State Health Facilities Comm'n, 110 Mich. App. 236, 312 N.W.2d 422 (1981).

44. Irvington General Hosp. v. Department of Health, 149 N.J. Super. 461, 374 A.2d 49 (N.J. Super. Ct. App. Div. 1977).

45. 42 U.S.C. §300n-1(b) (1982).

46. Sommerville Hosp. v. Department of Public Health, DON Project No. 4-3251 (Health Facilities App. Bd. Sept. 9, 1985); 13 HEALTH LAW DIGEST, Nov. 1985, at 11.

47. First Fed. Sav. and Loan Ass'n v. Casari, 667 F.2d 734 (8th Cir. 1982).

48. Baptist Hosps., Inc. v. Humana of Kentucky, Inc., 672 S.W.2d 669 (Ky. Ct. App. 1984).

49. Pub. L. No. 96-69, §117(a), 93 Stat. 614 (1979), codified in 42 U.S.C. §300m-6 (1982), as amended.

50. Hellman, *supra* note 26, at 1.

51. *E.g.,* Balsam v. Department of Health and Rehabilitative Servs., 452 So.2d 976 (Fla. Dist. Ct. App. 1984).

52. *See* American Hospital Association, *Report of the Adjunct Task Force on Antitrust,* July 8, 1982, for a discussion of the antitrust implications of health care coalitions.

53. National Gerimedical Hosp. and Gerontology Center v. Blue Cross, 425 U.S. 378 (1981).

54. North Carolina v. P.I.A. Ashville, Inc., 740 F.2d 274 (4th Cir. 1984), *rev'g* 722 F.2d 59 (4th Cir. 1983).

55. Justice Department Business Review Letter, Aug. 30, 1985, *as discussed in* 18 HOSPITAL LAW, Nov. 1985, at 2.

Chapter 6

Reorganization and Closure

Many hospitals are in circumstances that will not permit them to continue to function as independent entities. Declining and shifting utilization, reimbursement constraints, and various governmental initiatives are already threatening the continued existence of some hospitals. In the early 1980s, an average of 40 hospitals closed each year.[1] The financial and planning issues discussed in the previous two chapters point to continued and increasing pressure on hospitals and other health care facilities to change. Each hospital will have to reevaluate its long-term mission in light of the increasing constraints on resources for health care and changing utilization patterns.

The shift to prospective per-admission payment based on diagnosis-related groups is accelerating the trend. Inpatient hospital utilization has dramatically declined, while utilization of outpatient services has grown. Some services have been regionalized to assure efficient use of expensive facilities and equipment and to facilitate better outcome rates by enabling hospital staff to gain and maintain specialized skills that come from treating a larger number of patients with related conditions. Regionalization has reduced the utilization of some local hospitals. Some payment formulas threaten hospitals with low utilization because they are designed to provide adequate payment only to hospitals with higher occupancy rates. The same effect is being achieved more directly by some states through modifications in their Medicaid reimbursement formulas. They have set a required minimum percentage occupancy level, and, when a hospital falls below the minimum, its average costs per patient for reimbursement purposes are calculated using the minimum percentage rather than the hospital's actual percentage. Most prospective payment systems go a step further by removing any link to the hospital's costs. Some states have taken other steps that may cause some hospitals to change. For example, the New Jersey Administrative Code forbids the building of a new hospital or the expansion of an existing hospital unless the project will result in a needed hospital of a least 100 beds with specific plans for reaching 200 beds.[2] The only exception is for satellite hospitals of larger hospitals.

These trends and others are leading hospitals to reevaluate their future missions. They must consider their capacities, the needs of their communities, and their other responsibilities in evaluating the available options. The options include (1) continuing their present missions, intensifying their relationships with their patients and community, their efforts to contain costs, and their efforts to seek new revenue sources; (2) retaining their independence but changing their focus in either minor or major ways; (3) seeking outside assistance through consultants, shared services, affiliations, or even management contracts; (4) combining with others in multihospital systems or in a single merged hospital, perhaps with satellite clinics; (5) relocating; (6) dissolving and closing; or (7) declaring bankruptcy. Frequently a combination of elements of several of these options will be employed.

The vast majority of hospitals will continue to operate in some form to provide their important services to society. However, some institutions will not be able to continue if the present trends persist. As pressure increases, the most responsible course for some hospitals will be to pursue orderly change while the hospital still has substantial bargaining power that can be used to preserve the interests of community and staff to the greatest extent possible, rather than waiting for involuntary reorganization, closure, or a decline in the quality of services provided to the community.

This chapter addresses some of the legal issues involved in merger, consolidation, and sale of assets; dissolution; relocation and closure; bankruptcy; and eminent domain.

MERGER, CONSOLIDATION, AND SALE OF ASSETS

Merger occurs when two or more hospitals combine, and one of the hospitals is the surviving organization. Consolidation occurs when two or more hospitals combine, and the result is an entirely new organization. In a merger or consolidation, the resulting organization assumes the assets and liabilities of the former hospitals. A merger or consolidation is different from a sale of assets, in which the liabilities are usually not assumed.

The proper procedures must be followed in a merger, consolidation, or sale of assets, including the procedures required by statutes applicable to the constituent hospitals, by their articles of incorporation, and by their bylaws. Some governmental hospitals have special requirements that may include a vote of the residents of the governmental unit. When one or more of the hospital organizations is dissolved in the process, the applicable procedures for dissolution must also be followed.

The selection of the proper approach requires a careful analysis that is beyond the scope of this book. Combining hospitals is often motivated by a desire for increased efficiency and improved access to capital funds. Combining hospitals is often difficult in practice due to (1) philosophical differences of the hospitals, especially religious orientations; (2) reduction in the number of leadership positions; (3) necessary changes in established relationships with physicians, employees, suppliers, the community, and others; and (4) the technical complexity of developing a mutually acceptable approach and obtaining necessary approvals. Some of the legal considerations in developing the proper approach are restrictions in state statutes, articles of incorporation, bylaws, deeds, grants, gifts, loans, collective bargaining agreements, and other legal documents. For example, if certain changes are made, Hill-Burton hospital construction grants must be repaid to the government, and some loans may require accelerated repayment. There are complex tax and reimbursement implications. One hospital had to take its case to the California Supreme Court to establish that it did not have to pay sales tax on the sale of its furnishings and equipment as part of the sale of all of the assets of the hospital.[3] Proper notification must be given to licensure, certificate-of-need, and other regulatory authorities, and in some cases licenses, certificates, or permits must be obtained. Some types of changes may even involve the federal securities law.

In any merger or consolidation, consideration must be given to antitrust implications. Some antitrust issues are discussed in Chapter 3.

DISSOLUTION

A hospital organization may dissolve as part of a reorganization, merger, or consolidation. The facility may continue to operate under another organization, or the services of the facility may be relocated. Alternatively, a dissolution may result in the discontinuance of the use of the facility without relocating the services. Proper procedures must be followed in any dissolution, including the procedures in applicable statutes, articles of incorporation, and bylaws. The procedures usually include (1) an approval mechanism, which may include a state administrative official, a court, the vote of a specified percentage of the stockholders or members of the corporation, or others; (2) notification of creditors and others; and (3) clearance by governmental tax departments. Some governmental hospitals have special requirements, including a vote of the residents of the district, city, or county that supports the hospital.

Dissolution may be voluntarily initiated by the hospital. In appropriate circumstances, dissolution of a hospital corporation may be involuntarily initiated by outside parties, such as the state attorney general, shareholders, directors, and creditors. A person called a "receiver" can be appointed to operate the hospital during the process of involuntary dissolution.

The hospital corporation continues for a period of time after it ceases to operate the hospital so that the affairs of the organization can be concluded. After satisfying any debts and liabilities that have not been assumed by other organizations, the assets of the corporation must be distributed. Some assets may have to be returned to those who gave them to the hospital or to others designated by the giver because of restrictions imposed on the grants or gifts. All other assets are distributed under a plan of distribution that may have to be approved by an administrative agency or court. Assets of for-profit corporations are distributed to their shareholders. Assets designated for charitable purposes must usually be distributed to a corporation or organization engaged in activities that are substantially similar to the dissolving corporation.

Some nonprofit hospital corporations choose not to dissolve after selling their assets. They continue as independent foundations and use the proceeds of the sale of the hospital for other charitable purposes, such as paying for indigent patient care.[4]

RELOCATION AND CLOSURE

A hospital building can close (1) as part of a relocation of functions; or (2) without transfer or replacement of the functions because they are viewed as excess capacity or are otherwise not viable. Some communities have challenged planned closures, causing costly delays. Although courts have seldom found the plans illegal, some of the challenges have resulted in voluntary modifications of the plans. It is important to determine community concerns when planning relocations and closures and to consider reasonable accommodations to avoid protracted challenges.

The wide variety of theoretically possible legal challenges to the closure of all or part of a hospital is illustrated by the Wilmington Medical Center (WMC) cases. Two private inner city hospitals in Wilmington, Delaware, planned to replace a large portion of their inner city facilities with one suburban hospital, and they obtained approval of the project under section 1122. Neighborhood groups, the National Association for the Advancement of Colored People (NAACP), the Center for Law and Social Policy, and others conducted an extensive legal challenge to the relocation. The plaintiffs claimed that section 1122[5] had been violated, that the relocation discriminated against minorities in violation of Title VI of the Civil Rights Act[6] and against the handicapped in violation of section 504 of the Rehabilitation Act of 1973,[7] and that an environmental impact statement was required under the National Environmental Policy Act of 1969.[8] The first reported court order required the Secretary of HEW to determine whether there had been any violation and report to the court.[9] In the second reported order, the courts ruled that an environmental impact statement was not required because there was no major federal action involved.[10] In the third reported order, the court ruled that it was constitutional to provide different administrative appeal procedures for recipients and complainants under Title VI and section 504.[11] In the next reported order, the courts ruled that the decision of the Secretary of HHS concerning section 1122 approval was not subject to judicial review and that it was constitutional not to provide an appeal mechanism for opponents.[12] In the next reported decision, the court ruled that there was a private right of action to challenge discrimination that violated Title VI or section 504. The court ordered a trial.[13] After the trial, the courts ruled that evidence was adequate to justify the reorganization and relocation plans, so they did not violate Title VI or section 504.[14]

Public hospitals frequently must obtain voter approval before closing. Some consumer groups have attempted to use these requirements to preclude the hospital from changing its services. For example, a group in Texas sought to bar the closure of an emergency room of a public hospital. They asserted that closure of the emergency room was equivalent to closing the hospital, so the requirement of a vote before the hospital could be closed should apply. In 1984 a Texas appellate court ruled that they were not equivalent, so no vote was required.[15]

Contractual barriers to closure can also arise. In 1984 an Arkansas court ordered a corporation to continue to operate a nursing home on certain property because it had promised to do so in the lease to the property.[16]

BANKRUPTCY

In the past, the question of insolvency and bankruptcy of hospitals did not seem to be a serious issue. Generally, if a hospital was in a rundown condition physically and financially, loan funds, Hill-Burton monies, or bond issues could bail out or rebuild the hospital. With increasing constraints on the expansion and modernization of hospital facilities and higher costs of doing business imposed by new technology, wages, safety codes, and other factors, the question of insolvency and bankruptcy is unfortunately relevant.

For bankruptcy purposes, the Federal Bankruptcy Reform Act of 1978 defines an entity to be "insolvent . . . when the sum of such entity's debts is greater than all of such entity's property, at fair evaluation, exclusive of (i) property transferred, concealed, or removed with intent to hinder, delay or defraud such entity's creditor's, and (ii) property that may be exempted. . . ."[17] When a hospital discovers that it is insolvent, it may be forced to consider going into bankruptcy to settle its accounts and obligations on an equitable and final basis.

Since bankruptcy proceedings are entirely a matter of federal law, they are conducted in the federal district courts under the provisions of the Federal Bankruptcy Act. A petition for bankruptcy may be voluntary (by the debtor) or involuntary (by the creditors).

Nonprofit corporations, including charitable hospitals, are not subject to involuntary bankruptcy; therefore, they cannot be forced into bankruptcy by creditors. The only remedy available to the creditors of a nonprofit organization is through applicable state law proceedings. Nonprofit corporations may voluntarily petition to be adjudicated bankrupt. Petitions may be filed with the federal court even after state insolvency proceedings have been instituted.

Bankruptcy does not necessarily require the hospital corporation to dissolve. While one form of bankruptcy does include dissolution, other forms permit the corporation to continue to operate through modification of its operations and debt structure.

Hospitals facing insolvency need to evaluate their options carefully to avoid personal liability for directors and to use the available bankruptcy proceedings properly to optimize the outcome. Directors can be personally liable for voting to authorize improper distribution of corporate assets when the corporation is insolvent.[18] Bankruptcy proceedings can sometimes be used to implement changes that permit the institution to survive.[19]

EMINENT DOMAIN

Federal and state governments have the power to take property for public uses. This is called the power of eminent domain. States may authorize local governmental entities to exercise eminent domain. The Fifth Amendment to the Constitution requires the payment of just compensation in exchange for the property. When there is no agreement on compensation, generally courts set the compensation.

In the past, hospitals usually confronted eminent domain only when highway authorities took a strip of land to widen a bordering road or when a public hospital authority took neighboring land for expansion. In 1985 the city and county of St. Louis, Missouri, decided that they needed to replace their inner city public hospitals. Instead of building a new hospital, they proposed to use eminent domain to take a hospital from a for-profit chain and convert it to a public hospital. Faced with the takeover, the chain sold the hospital to a new nonprofit corporation organized by the city and county to operate the hospital.[20]

NOTES

1. Gallivan, *Trends and Topics*, HOSPITALS, June 1, 1985, at 29.

2. N.J. Admin. Code, tit. 8, §8:43B-1.11 (1980).

3. Ontario Community Found., Inc. v. State Bd. of Equalization, 35 Cal.3d 811, 201 Cal. Rptr. 165, 678 P.2d 378 (1984).

4. *E.g.,* Coady, *Not-For-Profits, Beware—Foundation Formed by Sale Could Be Short Lived,* 15 MOD. HEALTHCARE, Mar. 29, 1985, at 138; Carland, *Computer Model Used to Evaluate Foundation Had Flawed Assumptions,* 15 MOD. HEALTHCARE, June 7, 1985, at 177.

5. 42 U.S.C. §1320a-1 (1982 & Supp. I 1983), as amended by Pub. L. No. 98-369, §2354, 98 Stat. 110 (1984).

6. 42 U.S.C. §§2000d–2000d-6 (1982).

7. 29 U.S.C. §794 (1982).

8. 42 U.S.C. §4332 (1982).

9. NAACP v. Wilmington Medical Center, Inc., 426 F. Supp. 919 (D. Del. 1977).

10. NAACP v. Medical Center, Inc., 436 F. Supp. 1194 (D. Del. 1977), *aff'd,* 584 F.2d 619 (3rd Cir. 1978).

11. NAACP v. Wilmington Medical Center, Inc., 453 F. Supp. 330 (D. Del. 1978).

12. Wilmington United Neighborhoods v. United States, 458 F. Supp. 628 (D. Del. 1978), *aff'd,* 615 F.2d 112 (3rd Cir. 1980), *cert. denied,* 449 U.S. 827 (1980).

13. NAACP v. Medical Center, Inc., 599 F.2d 1247 (3rd Cir. 1979), *rev'g* 453 F. Supp. 289 (D. Del. 1978).

14. NAACP v. Medical Center, Inc., 491 F. Supp. 290 (D. Del. 1980), *aff'd,* 657 F.2d 1322 (3rd Cir. 1981).

15. Jackson County Hosp. Dist. v. Jackson County Citizens for Continued Hosp. Care, 669 S.W.2d 147 (Tex. Civ. App. 1984).

16. Lonoke Nursing Home, Inc. v. Wayne and Neil Bennett Family Partnership, 676 S.W.2d 461 (Ark. Ct. App. 1984).

17. 11 U.S.C. §101(29) (1982), as amended by Pub. L. No. 98-353, §421, 98 Stat. 364 (1984).

18. Renger Memorial Hosp. v. State, 674 S.W.2d 828 (Tex. Ct. App. 1984).

19. *E.g.,* Quait & Cohen, *Effect of Chapter 11 Bankruptcy on a Hospital's Medical Staff and Bondholders,* 7 HEALTH LAW VIGIL, Dec. 21, 1984 (Supp.), at 1.

20. Punch, *Faced with Takeover, Charter Officials Will Sell St. Louis Hospital for $15 Million,* 15 MOD. HEALTHCARE, July 19, 1985, at 24; *New Corporation Purchases Charter Hospital in St. Louis,* 15 MOD. HEALTHCARE, Nov. 8, 1985, at 11.

Chapter 7

Medical Staff

Before a physician may practice in a hospital, the physician must obtain an appointment to the medical staff and be granted clinical privileges by the hospital governing board. Physicians may provide only the services for which they have clinical privileges. The governing board has the responsibility to exercise discretion in deciding whether to grant an appointment and what scope of clinical privileges to grant. The governing body should also assure that periodic review of the physician and adjustments in clinical privileges take place when needed. The governing body nearly always relies on the organized medical staff to conduct reviews and recommend board action.

Each hospital is required to have an organized medical staff to comply with licensing regulations, accreditation standards, and third party payer requirements, such as the Medicare conditions of participation.

This chapter discusses the responsibility of the organized medical staff, appointment to the medical staff, delineation of clinical privileges, periodic review, modification and termination of clinical privileges, the procedural due process rights of physicians, and the potential liability of those involved in the process of making medical staff appointment and clinical privilege decisions. This chapter also discusses contracts with physicians.

THE ORGANIZED MEDICAL STAFF AND ITS RELATIONSHIP WITH THE HOSPITAL GOVERNING BODY

An important element of the governance of any hospital is the organized medical staff. In most hospitals, physicians are not employees or agents of the hospital, but are accountable individually and collectively to the governing body for the quality of care they provide. Their collective accountability is fulfilled through a medical staff organization. JCAH accreditation standards,[1] Medicare conditions of participation,[2] and most hospital licensure rules require that the medical staff be organized.

The governing body of the hospital as discussed in Chapter 2 has the ultimate authority over the hospital, and the authority must be exercised consistent with satisfactory patient care. Through the bylaws, the governing body delegates to the medical staff the authority and duty to carry out the medical aspects of patient care. The governing board retains the authority and responsibility to approve appointments to the medical staff, to grant and decrease clinical privileges, and to assure that there is a mechanism for monitoring quality of care. The governing body normally looks to the medical staff to monitor the quality of care and to provide expert advice on appointment and clinical privilege decisions.

The medical staff organization usually includes officers, such as a president; an executive committee to act in matters that do not require approval of the entire staff; and committees to address specific issues, such as quality assurance, infection control, pharmaceutical utilization, credentials review, and other matters. In smaller hospitals, these functions are frequently performed by the entire medical staff as a committee of the whole. In larger hospitals, several specialty departments with their own organizations, are often coordinated by the medical staff organization at the hospital level.

Functions of the organized medical staff include (1) facilitating communication among the medical staff members and with the hospital; (2) implementing policies and procedures designed to provide patients with satisfactory patient care; (3) recommending appointments to the medical staff and scope of clinical privileges; (4) developing and implementing a quality assurance mechanism; (5) providing continuing medical education; and (6) taking other actions necessary to govern the medical staff and relate to the hospital governing board.

The governing body cannot abdicate its responsibility by relying completely on the medical staff. The JCAH accreditation standards, the Medicare conditions of participation, and most hospital licensing rules clearly require involvement of the governing body in these functions. Hospitals have been found liable for the actions of physicians when they failed to evaluate the physicians properly prior to medical staff appointment or failed to monitor physician performance properly after appointment. In *Johnson v. Misericordia Community Hospital* [3] the Wisconsin Supreme Court found the hospital liable for injuries to a patient by a physician because the hospital should never have appointed him to the medical staff. The hospital had not checked his professional credentials and references. A check would have alerted the hospital to discrepancies and misrepresentations that would have led the hospital to deny him appointment to the medical staff. In *Purcell v.*

Zimbelman[4] an Arizona court found a hospital liable for failing to curtail the clinical privileges of a physician who had several bad results with a procedure, resulting in suits. The failure of the medical staff to recommend curtailment of privileges to the hospital was not a sufficient justification. The court considered the organized medical staff to be an agent of the hospital, so the hospital was legally considered to know everything the organized medical staff knew. Whether or not all states adopt this position, it is likely that most states will find liability if a hospital fails to act when it has actual knowledge of serious problems or it has reason to suspect serious problems.

It is sometimes necessary for the governing body to employ outside experts to assist in the review of medical care. Usually this is done with the advice and concurrence of the medical staff. Most frequently, outside experts review specialists when other staff members do not feel able to review them or when those who are able to conduct the review appear to be biased. Some specialty societies have established programs to provide this kind of consultation.

Growing competition, changing payment mechanisms, changing legal accountability, evolving public expectations, and other changes in the legal and social environment have focused attention on the relationship of the organized medical staff and the hospital. In the early 1980s the American Medical Association (AMA) created a new Hospital Medical Staff Section. To help medical staffs to address the issues knowledgeably, in 1984 the AMA published a guide for medical staffs.[5] The JCAH completely revised its medical staff standards, effective January 1, 1985.[6] Many of the detailed requirements of the previous standards were deleted, leaving hospitals and medical staffs considerable flexibility to fashion their own structures and procedures. The most significant change was removal of the restrictions preventing other health professionals from being members of the medical staff, leaving the issue to be decided within each individual hospital. In 1985 the JCAH further amended its standards to require that medical staff bylaws be adopted and changed only with the mutual consent of the medical staff and the hospital.[7] Previously, some courts had recognized the legal right of the hospital governing board to change the medical staff bylaws unilaterally when necessary.[8] In many states hospitals will probably continue to have this legal authority and, in some circumstances, the legal duty to make required changes. However, exercising the authority may jeopardize JCAH accreditation. Even when the governing body has the authority to make unilateral changes, it is always best to seek mutually acceptable changes, even though this may require prolonged negotiations. The resulting changes will be more likely to be implemented fully when commitment to them is mutual. Unilateral changes are an extraordinary last resort, usually adopted at great cost to deal with impasses.

It is increasingly recognized that hospital and organized medical staff efforts must not be focused on defining ultimate legal rights; they must be focused on minimizing misunderstandings and conflicts, seeking mutually acceptable solutions, and resolving impasses without resort to the judicial process. A Joint Task Force on Hospital-Medical Staff Relationships of the AMA and the American Hospital Association published a report in 1985 outlining ways to achieve this focus.[9] Note, however, that while it is important to be fair to individual medical staff applicants and members, the same effort to reach mutually acceptable solutions to problems with individuals is not necessary. The hospital and the medical staff must take appropriate steps to maintain standards within the hospital.

Since virtually all hospitals have a medical staff organization, the two basic groups of medical staff issues include (1) facilitating modifications as requirements evolve; and (2) applying the rules and procedures in actual situations. The remainder of this chapter discusses some of the limitations on requirements that can be placed in the bylaws and the application of rules and procedures.

THE DISTINCTION BETWEEN PUBLIC HOSPITALS AND PRIVATE HOSPITALS

Lawsuits arising out of governing body decisions concerning appointments and clinical privileges of physicians usually focus either on the right of the governing body to impose the rules applied or on the procedures followed in reaching the decision. Governing boards of public hospitals have less discretion than boards of private hospitals in most states. However, there is a trend toward reducing the discretion of private hospitals.

Public Hospitals

Due Process

Public hospitals must satisfy the requirements of the Fourteenth Amendment to the United States Constitution, which says that no state shall "deprive any person of life, liberty, or property, without due process of law." Actions of public hospitals are considered actions of the state. Courts have determined that the interest of physicians in practicing in a hospital is a liberty or property interest, so physicians are entitled to "due process of law" when a public hospital makes a decision concerning appointment to the medical staff or clinical privileges. However, physicians do not have a right to practice in any public hospital. Physicians must demonstrate that they satisfy valid hospital rules before they may practice in the hospital.

To provide physicians with due process, hospital rules must be reasonable and must adequately express the intent of the hospital. Rules that are too arbitrary or vague may be unenforceable. Physicians must also be offered procedural protections, or an adverse action may violate due process requirements. (Procedural due process protections are discussed later in this chapter.)

Equal Protection

The Fourteenth Amendment also says that no state shall "deny to any person within its jurisdiction the equal protection of the laws." Equal protection means that like persons must be dealt with in like fashion. The equal protection clause is concerned with the justifiability of the classifications used to distinguish persons for various legal purposes. Determining whether a particular difference between persons can justify a particular difference in rules or procedures can be difficult. In general, the courts require that the government agency justify the difference with a "rational reason." The major exception to this standard is the strict scrutiny courts apply to distinctions based on "suspect classifications," such as race, and the intermediate level of scrutiny applied to sex-based classifications. Because of the comprehensive federal and state legislation prohibiting discrimination based on many characteristics, most challenges to alleged discriminatory actions are based on legislation rather than directly on this constitutional principle. Nondiscrimination legislation is discussed in Chapter 9.

Private Hospitals

Medical staff actions of most private hospitals are subject to fewer legal constraints than staff actions by public hospitals. The Fourteenth Amendment does not apply to private hospitals, except in the unusual circumstance when their activities are found to be state actions. In most states, private hospitals are required only to follow their own rules in medical staff actions. In a growing number of states, state legislatures and courts are requiring that medical staff members be provided some protections, although the protections are not always as formal as those required for public hospitals.

State Action

It is rare for private hospitals to be found engaged in state action and, thus, subject to the Fourteenth Amendment. Prior to 1974, some courts ruled that private hospitals were engaging in state action when they received federal construction funds, received Medicare and Medicaid payments, and were heavily regulated by the state.

In 1974, the Supreme Court ruled that regulation or funding was not enough to establish state action. The Court said that there must be a "sufficiently close nexus between the state and the challenged action of the regulated entity so that the action of the latter may be fairly treated as that of the state itself." The Court gave the following examples of such connection: (1) when the private entity exercises powers traditionally reserved for the state; (2) when the state directly benefits by sharing in the rewards and responsibilities of the private venture; and (3) when the state directs or encourages the particular act.[10] All federal courts now agree that funding or regulation alone is not enough to convert the actions of private hospitals to state action.[11]

In rare circumstances, private hospitals can engage in state action. If a majority of the governing body is appointed by a governmental agency, the courts will be likely to find the hospital to be engaged in state action.[12] Appointment of a minority of the governing body is not likely to be enough to establish state action.[13] If the hospital leases land from a governmental entity, it may be found to be engaged in state action. However, some courts have found that leasing government property is not enough to establish state action.[14]

Hospital Rules

Most private hospitals have rules concerning the criteria and procedures to be followed in making decisions concerning medical staff membership and clinical privilege delineation. These rules usually appear in the medical staff bylaws and are required for JCAH accreditation. After a private hospital has adopted rules concerning these actions, most courts will require the hospital at least to follow its own rules in making a decision.[15] However, courts are likely to overlook minor deviations when they do not significantly affect the fundamental interests of the physician.[16] A few courts have indicated that hospital rules do not have to be followed if due process is actually provided through other mechanisms.[17] It is prudent not to rely on courts to accept substantial deviations from hospital rules and instead to strive to comply with hospital rules.

Some courts have ruled that a physician must be a member of the medical staff before having a right to seek court enforcement of medical staff and hospital bylaws.[18] In those states, applicants cannot use violation of the bylaws as a basis to challenge denial of appointment. If the hospital is nonprofit, the state official who has the general supervisory power over nonprofit corporations may have the power to challenge violations of bylaws.

State Law Protections

There is a great range of state law protection for physicians in their relationships with private hospitals. Some states have not recognized any physician rights, but most states will enforce the rules of private hospitals. By statute or court decision, some states have limited the latitude of private hospitals. For example, New York requires hospitals to process all applications for membership or clinical privileges from physicians, podiatrists, and dentists.[19] Membership or clinical privileges may be denied, curtailed, or terminated only after the reasons have been stated. The only permissible reasons are "standards of patient care, patient welfare, the objectives of the institution or the character or competency of the applicant." The Public Health Council is authorized to investigate complaints alleging violations of the section and to order the hospital governing body to review the action if it finds "cause exists for the crediting of the allegations." The New York courts require physicians to pursue review by the Public Health Council before they will permit suit against the hospital.[20]

Some state courts require private hospitals to provide some procedural protections for medical staff members, including notice of alleged shortcomings and an opportunity to be heard.[21] New Jersey has extended detailed additional procedural protections, including the right to be represented by a lawyer.[22] Thus, it is important to be familiar with the law of the state in which action is being considered.

APPOINTMENT TO THE MEDICAL STAFF

Since the definition of a hospital and of a medically necessary admission to a hospital generally include the necessity of ongoing medical attention, an identified, competent practitioner must be responsible for the care of the patient. The practitioners will almost always be physicians, but they may be dentists and other practitioners in some situations. The discussion in the rest of this chapter concerning physicians also applies to other practitioners who may admit patients.

Hospitals must screen physicians before appointment to the medical staff and allow only physicians who are medical staff members to admit patients to the hospital. The physician then assumes the continuing responsibility for the medical care of that patient until the responsibility is transferred to another physician who is a member of the medical staff or until the patient is discharged.

A medical license does not give a physician the right to practice in a particular hospital. Each physician must apply for appointment to the medical staff. Each physician must prove that he or she satisfies the criteria of the hospital for appointment or that the criteria are not permitted. The burden of proof is on the applying physician, especially if the medical staff bylaws so provide.

Since hospitals must fulfill their responsibility to screen applicants and most physicians need access to a hospital to practice, many court cases have involved medical staff issues. Procedural issues will be discussed later in the chapter in the section on due process and fair procedure. This section reviews judicial decisions concerning selected criteria for decisions on initial appointment, reappointment, and termination.

Permitted Criteria

Complete Application Form

Hospitals require that the application form be completed with a full, frank disclosure of requested information and an agreement to abide by hospital rules. Courts have upheld denial of appointment based on false and incomplete statements on the application and on failure to complete the application.[23]

As part of the application process, physicians should be required, along with providing other information, to (1) present evidence of medical education, training, experience, current competence, current licensure, and health status; and (2) disclose professional liability actions and pending and completed governmental, institutional, and professional disciplinary actions against them.[24]

References

References may be required if the number of eligible writers is not limited inappropriately. Courts have not accepted a requirement of letters of recommendation from the present medical staff. In *Johnson v. Misericordia Community Hospital,* the Wisconsin Supreme Court found the hospital liable for the malpractice of a physician because the hospital failed to check his references. Checking the references would have led to discovery of adverse information about the physician, causing the hospital either to limit his clinical privileges or not to appoint him to the medical staff. The court ruled that Wisconsin hospitals must require references and check them.[25] It is prudent to require references and to check them. Generally hospitals are liable for failing to check applications only when a reasonable check would have led to rejection of the applicant.[26]

Ability To Work with Others

With the growing sophistication and multidisciplinary nature of patient care in hospitals, the ability of the medical staff applicant to work harmoniously with other physicians and hospital staff is an increasingly important criterion. The courts in many states have accepted this criterion. While most states have not delimited the degree of inability to work with others that justifies denial, a few states have placed limits. In 1967 a New Jersey court pointed out that "prospective disharmony" was a reasonable factor to consider as long as "valid and constructive criticism of hospital practice" is not equated with potential disharmony.[27] The court noted that "a person has a right to disagree with the policy or practice, but he does not have a right to be disagreeable in doing so." The California Supreme Court ruled in 1980 that inability to work with others could be the basis for denial of appointment, but only when it presents "a real and substantial danger that patients treated by him might receive other than a 'high quality of medical care' at the facility."[28] A few states have forbidden use of this criterion.[29]

Geographic Limit

Some bylaws require an applicant to live or practice within a certain distance of the hospital, stated in terms of miles, travel time, or location close enough for the applicant to be reasonably able to provide necessary care to patients. These rules are intended to assure that physicians can respond to the needs of patients, especially during emergencies. Courts have generally upheld such rules even when they result in denial of reappointment to a physician who relocates farther from the hospital.[30] The JCAH recognizes geographic location of the applicant as an appropriate criterion.[31] When political boundaries are used to describe geographic limits, it is less likely they will be enforceable.[32]

Malpractice Insurance

The hospital and its medical staff have a legitimate business interest in assuring that each physician practicing in the hospital has adequate malpractice protection. In a malpractice suit, it is likely that both the hospital and the physicians involved will be sued. If one defendant is not adequately insured, it is likely that the burden of any payment will fall disproportionately on the others. The JCAH recognizes adequate professional liability insurance as an appropriate criterion.[33] Since 1975 appellate courts have consistently upheld reasonable requirements of malpractice insurance as a condition of medical staff membership.[34] Some decisions have stated that there must be some flexibility in enforcing such rules because they might be unreasonable when applied in some situations, such as where no malpractice insurance is available to be purchased.[35]

Limits on the Size of the Medical Staff

A hospital policy, reasonably related to the operation of the hospital, that limits the number of medical staff can be a legitimate reason for denying medical staff privileges in certain circumstances. The policy should be set by the hospital governing board, and the reasons for it should be documented at the time the policy is adopted. Courts are concerned that these policies not be used simply to protect the economic interests of present medical staff members. Limitations on the number of staff members in certain specialties have been upheld in several court decisions.[36] However, in 1976 a New Jersey court invalidated a moratorium on new staff appointments because inadequate evidence had been presented that the moratorium was needed to assure appropriate patient care.[37] In 1985, a North Carolina appellate court ruled that a hospital could close a part of its medical staff if the moratorium was reasonable for the hospital and community and was fairly administered, but that the challenging podiatrist was entitled to a trial in which he could attempt to show the moratorium was unreasonable.[38] The JCAH recognizes the appropriateness of criteria related to the ability of the hospital to provide facilities and support services and to the need for additional members with the applicant's skill and training.[39]

Dues and Assessments

Some hospitals require physicians to pay various dues, fees, and assessments to apply for and retain medical staff membership.[40] In a 1984 decision, a Michigan appellate court upheld the suspension of a physician who refused to pay a $100 assessment levied by the executive committee of the medical staff to furnish a medical library.[41]

Unacceptable Criteria

Discrimination

Hospitals cannot base their refusal to appoint a physician on the applicant's race, creed, color, sex, national origin, or handicap. Alleged violations are usually addressed under the various federal antidiscrimination laws discussed in Chapter 9.[42] These laws generally apply to all institutions receiving federal funds, whether the institutions are public or private. Citizenship is another unacceptable criterion. Hospitals cannot exclude aliens solely because of their immigration status as long as they are appropriately licensed and possess a visa permitting the practice of medicine.

Medical Society Membership

Hospitals cannot require membership in a medical society.[43] Courts view such requirements as an abdication of the hospital's responsibility to screen applications and are concerned that membership in a medical society could be denied for discriminatory reasons. A few older court decisions accepted this criterion for private hospitals,[44] but it is doubtful that courts will permit this criterion today, except in the states that decline to review any of the criteria used by private hospitals.

Recommendations of Medical Staff Members

Courts will not permit hospitals to require applicants to present written recommendations from existing medical staff members.[45] This requirement is viewed as a way for the medical staff to discriminate arbitrarily against an unpopular applicant and assure that the application will not even be processed.

Preappointment Tests

A California public hospital adopted a requirement that applicants be given "such tests, oral and written, as the credentials committee shall in its discretion determine." A physician refused to take the examination and challenged it in court. A California appellate court invalidated the requirement because it was vague and ambiguous and provided no standards for what the examinations would be.[46] It is probable that courts will uphold a reasonable, relevant examination uniformly given to all applicants for certain clinical privileges. Another circumstance in which preappointment examinations would be acceptable is when they are mutually acceptable to the applicant and the hospital.

DELINEATION OF CLINICAL PRIVILEGES

When a physician is appointed to a hospital medical staff, the hospital must also determine the scope of practice the physician will be permitted. A licensed physician can act within the entire scope of medical practice without violating the medical licensing laws of most states. However, no physician is actually competent to perform all medical procedures. The hospital protects the patient and the physician by examining the physician's credentials and granting clinical privileges to engage in a certain scope of clinical practice. A physician who acts outside the granted scope, except in an emergency, is subject to discipline, including termination of medical staff membership. The hospital governing body usually looks to the organized medical staff for expert advice in delineating clinical privileges.

There are many ways to delineate clinical privileges.[47] The key element is a written definition that the medical staff understands. Some hospitals grant clinical privileges for individual procedures. Some hospitals use categories or levels of care. Broad categories of patient conditions and procedures are grouped into levels, and physicians are granted clinical privileges to perform everything in the appropriate group. Other hospitals grant clinical privileges by specialty, defining what each specialty is permitted to do. A hybrid of these approaches is also used.

Some hospitals require that a physician be certified by a specialty board before granting clinical privileges in the specialty. The JCAH recognizes board certification or board eligibility as "an excellent benchmark" for privilege delineation.[48] The Medicare conditions of participation prohibit an absolute requirement of board certification.[49] However, most courts have upheld private hospital requirements of board certification or completion of an approved residency before specialty clinical privileges are granted.[50] A few courts have invalidated board certification requirements of public hospitals.[51] One way to avoid controversy is to require board certification or equivalent experience. This requirement permits the hospital to avail itself of the strengths of the private certification system while complying with Medicare requirements and leaving open a channel to deal with individual applicants on a case-by-case basis.

Hospitals may place conditions on clinical privileges, such as a requirement that (1) a consultation be obtained before certain procedures are done; (2) assistants be used for certain procedures; or (3) certain procedures be supervised. Disciplinary measures may be taken for violating these conditions, as discussed later in this chapter. Hospitals may change their requirements so that physicians who already have clinical privileges must begin to meet these types of conditions. Some courts view such changes as a clinical privilege reduction and require that each affected staff member be given the same opportunity for a hearing as is offered for other reductions.[52] When establishing a consultation requirement, hospitals should consider that at least one court has ruled that a hospital with a consultation requirement must assist physicians in obtaining consultations.[53]

REVIEW AND REAPPOINTMENT

After physicians are appointed to the medical staff and granted clinical privileges, their performance is reviewed periodically as part of the process to determine whether to grant reappointment. Both the JCAH *Accreditation Manual for Hospitals* and the Medicare conditions of participation require review and reappointment.[54] Failure to review performance and take appropriate action can result in hospital liability. For example, in *Elam v. College Park Hospital*,[55] a California appellate court ruled that a hospital has the duty to select carefully and review periodically the performance of physicians and podiatrists granted clinical privileges.

The JCAH standards require that all appointments to the medical staff be provisional for a time specified in the bylaws.[56] During this period, the actual practice of the new medical staff member is observed. If the new member lacks the ability to exercise granted clinical privileges properly, action should be taken to modify the clinical privileges before the end of the provisional status.

After the provisional period, the hospital and its medical staff can use several different methods to review the performance of individual medical staff members. Traditionally, this has been accomplished through review by medical staff committees, such as the surgical case review committee, which reviews surgical procedures; the pharmacy and therapeutics committee, which reviews drug use; the medical records committee, which reviews compliance with requirements for timely, complete documentation; the blood usage review committee; the antibiotic usage review committee; and similar committees for other functions.

Although these committees continue to perform important functions, since the early 1970s there has been increasing focus on quality assurance programs that conduct patient care evaluations, problem-focused studies, and utilization review.[57] Patient care evaluations and problem-focused studies are directed toward evaluation of care provided for specific diseases or conditions or evaluation of clinical or administrative procedures. Criteria are established for the evaluative process, and many data sources are used to measure performance against the criteria. Variations are either justified or analyzed for appropriate corrective action, which is often an educational effort. A follow-up study can then be conducted to determine if the action was successful.

Utilization review focuses on the appropriateness of the admission of individual patients to the hospital and the appropriateness of their length of stay. Utilization review can be conducted retrospectively by reviewing medical records or concurrently with the time the patient is in the hospital.

Pressure to reduce expenditures for hospital care by reducing the number of admissions and the time patients are in the hospital has focused efforts on concurrent review.

If problems are discovered through this formalized review or the review provided by day-to-day interaction with other physicians and hospital staff, the hospital has a responsibility to determine what action is appropriate and to initiate that action. Usually educational efforts will be adequate, but sometimes steps such as suspension or termination of all or some clinical privileges may be necessary.

In addition to ongoing review, systematic review is necessary to determine whether each medical staff member is still fulfilling the responsibilities of medical staff membership and the clinical privileges granted. Thus, medical staff appointments are for a limited period, usually one or two years.[58] Before the expiration of the appointment, each member is reviewed. The review includes clinical performance, judgment, and skills; licensure; health statutes; compliance with hospital and medical staff policies; and fulfillment of other medical staff responsibilities, such as active involvement in assigned committees. Based on this review, a decision is made whether to reappoint the person to the medical staff and whether to maintain present clinical privileges or to modify them.

Difficult situations sometimes arise when a physician does not recognize declining capabilities. Fortunately, in most circumstances physicians will recognize the change when they are approached tactfully and will agree to adjust their scope of practice to fit their capabilities. However, if the physician will not agree to needed adjustments, the hospital and medical staff have the difficult duty of protecting patients by reducing the physician's clinical privileges to the appropriate scope.

Another difficult situation occurs when a physician is impaired by substance abuse. This situation is becoming easier to address because of the growing awareness that the first approach should be to promote rehabilitation. Physicians tend to attempt to cooperate with these efforts, including temporary reductions in clinical privileges, as necessary to protect patients. Unfortunately, it is sometimes extremely difficult to remain rehabilitated, and the hospital may be confronted with the question of how many rehabilitation opportunities should be given. If rehabilitation fails, permanent action must eventually be taken to preserve acceptable standards of patient care.

Peer Review Organizations

The 1972 amendments to the Social Security Act required patient care evaluations and utilization review for all federally funded patients.[59] The Secretary of Health, Education, and Welfare (now HHS) was directed to divide the nation into areas and then designate a Professional Standards Review Organization (PSRO) for each area. The PSRO conducted utilization review to determine the medical necessity of the care and the appropriate level of care required. The PSRO could delegate the patient care evaluation and utilization review functions to the hospital. The PSRO monitored the review activities of hospitals that had delegated status and could withdraw the status if the hospital did not perform the reviews properly. When the system of federally mandated review was challenged, the Supreme Court found that the law did not violate the Constitution because it provided standards only for the dispensation of federal funds.[60]

In 1982, the Tax Equity and Fiscal Responsibility Act[61] repealed the PSRO law, replacing it with a requirement of similar peer review by Utilization and Quality Control Peer Review Organizations (PROs). Transition provisions provided for each PSRO to continue to function until a PRO was established in its area.

The Social Security Amendments of 1983 modified the role of PROs to focus their efforts on the potential problems created by prospective per-case reimbursement based on diagnosis-related groups.[62] Many other third party payers mandate utilization review of the services for which they pay.

The federal review system and the other third party payer systems are focused primarily on expenditure reduction, so they do not fulfill the hospital's responsibility to review the quality of physician performance. Some elements of the review programs can assist, but hospitals must have their own systems of review.

MODIFICATION OR TERMINATION OF CLINICAL PRIVILEGES

The clinical privileges granted to a physician must sometimes be modified or terminated because of changes in the physician's capabilities, violation of hospital or medical staff policies, changes in hospital standards, or other reasons. When physicians challenge modification or termination of their privileges, they challenge the adequacy of the procedures followed and the reasons given for the action. The procedural issues are discussed in the next section of this chapter.

The most frequent reason for temporary suspension of clinical privileges is failure to complete medical records within the time limits established by hospital policy. Most hospitals temporarily restrict admitting privileges of delinquent physicians until they complete all overdue records. The rationale is that physicians do not have enough time to accept responsibility for additional patients if they do not have enough time to complete records for past admissions. Courts have generally upheld disciplinary actions for failure to complete records.[63]

Some bylaws require physicians to provide indigent care to fulfill institutional principles or to enable the hospital to fulfill its Hill-Burton obligations. In 1983 a Pennsylvania court upheld the suspension of a medical staff member who refused to treat the percentage of indigents required by the bylaws.[64]

Some physicians have challenged adverse actions on the basis that their due process rights were violated because the standards by which they were judged were too vague to inform them of what was expected. Courts have generally upheld actions taken on the basis of subjective standards when the standards are applied in a reasonable way. For example, in 1972 the Nevada Supreme Court upheld termination of clinical privileges based on the general standard of "unprofessional conduct."[65] The court recognized that it was not feasible to specify the variety of unprofessional conduct. The physician had touched a spinal needle without gloves before using it and had appeared for surgery in no condition to perform it, requiring cancellation of the surgery. The court found that the standard was properly applied in this case. In 1979 a New Jersey appellate court affirmed a physician's suspension based on a bylaws provision that permitted suspension "for cause."[66] The physician had negligently treated a patient. The court found that evidence in the case was sufficient, so that "for cause" was not too vague. The situation leading to the suspension demonstrated that all the grounds for suspension could not be specified in advance.

Public hospitals cannot terminate clinical privileges because of a physician's public criticism of the quality of care. In 1985 a federal court in Arkansas found such criticism to be protected by the First Amendment right of free speech.[67]

A hospital should carefully review the evidence it has of poor performance or violation of policies before deciding to take adverse action. The hospital should be prepared to substantiate the action.

As hospitals upgrade their standards, the clinical privileges of some physicians may be reduced. These changes will be upheld if they are reasonable. For example, the Ohio Supreme Court upheld a hospital's new requirement that physicians either be board certified, be board eligible, be a fellow in the American College of Surgery, or have ten years' experience to qualify for major surgical privileges.[68] Hospitals may have to demonstrate the reasonableness of new rules. In 1975 an Illinois appellate court refused to enjoin a hospital's new requirement that surgeons with general surgery clinical privileges consult with a gynecologist before doing major gynecological surgery. However, the court ruled that the physician was entitled to a hearing concerning the reasonableness of the rules.[69]

Many states require hospitals to report denials of medical staff appointments and modifications or terminations of clinical privileges to a state agency, frequently the medical licensing board.[70] In 1985 a federal court of appeals ruled that a hospital could not be sued for defamation for filing a required report of suspension of a medical staff member.[71] The hospital was found immune because the report was mandated.

DUE PROCESS

The due process procedures required of public hospitals are discussed in this section. In most states, private hospitals are not required to provide the due process that public hospitals must provide. The states that require private hospitals to provide a fair procedure may not include all of the elements discussed in this section.

Public hospitals are required by the Fourteenth Amendment to provide due process to both applicants and members. However, some courts recognize a distinction between the circumstances and, thus, the rights of applicants and medical staff members. The JCAH requires a fair hearing for applicants, but permits it to be different from the procedure for members.[72] As for private hospitals, some courts take the position that the physician's right to procedures specified in the bylaws is derived from membership on the medical staff. Since an applicant is not yet a member, an applicant does not have a legal right to make claims on the private organization. Some medical staff bylaws specify that applicants do not have procedural rights. Unless a hospital is in a state that recognizes this difference and the difference is specified in the bylaws, the most prudent practice is to follow the same procedures for both applicants and members.

Most courts recognize that due process procedures do not have to be provided at the earliest stages of investigation of potential medical staff problems. Informal investigations usually precede a decision to take action. Although it is often helpful to seek information from the affected physician early in the investigation, it is not until formal action is initiated that the physician has a legal right to notice and an opportunity to present information.

The full scope of due process procedures is usually required only for actions that directly affect the physician's practice, such as decisions concerning the scope of clinical privileges. A censure usually does not entitle the physician to a hearing.[73]

In 1971 the JCAH published an elaborate due process system in a pamphlet entitled *Guidelines for the Formulation of Medical Staff Bylaws, Rules and Regulations*. At that time, many hospitals established systems based on this model. In 1978 the JCAH rescinded the guidelines and published a new pamphlet, *JCAH Monograph: Medical Staff Bylaws,* that did not include model bylaws. The pamphlet emphasized that bylaws should be designed to meet the unique requirements of individual hospitals. The JCAH's *Accreditation Manual for Hospitals* contains many specific suggestions that provide guidance in developing medical staff bylaws.[74]

Summary Action

Situations involving potential immediate risk to patient well-being call for restrictions on a physician's practice before any due process procedures can be followed. Although usually due process procedures must be followed before adverse action is taken, courts recognize that summary action can be necessary and appropriate. For example, in 1980 the Alaska Supreme Court ruled that the fair hearing could be conducted within a reasonable time after the summary suspension of clinical privileges when there was immediate risk to patients.[75]

Courts have issued injunctions prohibiting summary suspension when the risk is not sufficiently immediate.[76] Courts will reconsider an injunction if the physician's conduct during the injunction indicates that summary suspension is needed.[77]

Reasonable Notice

The first step in providing due process is to give reasonable written notice of the reasons for the proposed action and of the time and place where the physician may present information. Reasonable notice must include sufficient information to permit preparation of a response, but a detailed and exhaustive listing of each perceived deficiency is not required.[78]

The hospital does not have to cater to the idiosyncrasies of the physician in giving notice. Standard methods such as personal delivery or registered mail are appropriate. In 1976 an Arizona appellate court ruled that registered mail provided adequate notice, even to a physician who had a known habit of refusing to open registered mail.[79]

Hearing

The second step of due process is to provide the physician with an opportunity to present information on his or her behalf. Often the physician will have had one or more opportunities to present information during the informal investigative steps that precede formal action. However, a formal opportunity to present information is usually required after the formal recommendation of adverse action. Courts vary on the degree of the formality that they require.

Physician Presence

The hospital may specify that the hearing be held only if the physician is present. Unexcused failure to appear can waive the right to the hearing and the right to object to other defects in the proceedings.[80]

Legal Counsel

There is disagreement on whether the physician should be represented by legal counsel at the hearing. Some believe an attorney can assist in assuring that information is provided in an orderly fashion. The attorney can help the physician understand the strength of the hospital's position and the outcomes that can reasonably be expected. Others believe many attorneys cannot adapt to the relative informality of the medical staff hearing and, thus, are disruptive to the process as they inappropriately attempt to apply the rules that apply in courts. Thus, some hospitals do not permit attorneys to be involved, while others encourage their involvement.

The few courts that have ruled on whether there is a legal right to legal representation have not agreed. New Jersey requires hospitals to permit representation by an attorney.[81] California hospitals do not have to permit representation by an attorney, especially when the hospital is not represented by an attorney.[82] Hospitals will have a difficult time convincing any court of the fairness of their procedures if only one side is permitted legal representation.

Hearing Body

The committee or individual conducting the hearing should not be biased against the physician. For example, in 1980 a California appellate court ruled that a physician had been denied due process because the committee that recommended his suspension was not impartial.[83] The court believed that there was too great a potential for bias because two members of the committee depended on the obstetrical expertise of the physician who brought the charges and his associate. The court did not believe that the risk of bias was overcome by the subsequent affirmation of the suspension by an appeal committee. Many courts have recognized the virtual impossibility of complete impartiality because all physicians in a hospital have a collaborative relationship. One federal appellate court required a demonstration of actual bias before a hearing body was considered to violate due process.[84] In 1979 an Illinois appellate court ruled that due process rights were not violated when a physician both assisted in the preparation of the charges and served on the credentials committee during the hearing because (1) there was no evidence of actual bias; (2) there was no evidence that the physician's vote was "based on something other than that which was learned from participation in the case"; and (3) the final decision was made by a board of directors composed of members who had not participated in the recommendation under review.[85] In 1985 the South Carolina Supreme Court found that a physician's due process rights were violated when three of the original accusing physicians were members of the joint conference committee that made the final recommendation to the governing board.[86] When selecting the hearing body, persons who have known biases should be excluded. To the extent feasible, it is helpful to also exclude those who were involved in earlier stages of the investigation and review process, but this is not essential in all jurisdictions. These steps will assure fairness and minimize the risk of successful challenge. In rare cases, hospitals with smaller medical staffs may have to arrange for someone from outside the hospital to conduct the hearing.

Opportunity To Present Information

The primary purpose of the hearing is to give physicians an opportunity to present information on their own behalf. Courts have disagreed on which hospital records of patient care and peer review the physician may obtain to prepare the presentation. Access to medical records is discussed in Chapter 14. Another issue is whether the physician is entitled to an opportunity to present witnesses. Some courts have ruled that the bylaws can require all submissions to the hearing body to be in writing.[87]

Opportunity To Cross-Examine Witnesses

Courts have recognized that hospitals do not have the power to compel witnesses to attend hearings because hospitals do not have subpoena power. Due process usually does not require an opportunity to cross-examine all those who have complained about the physician's conduct.[88] However, a few courts have found a right to cross-examine some witnesses.[89] The better practice is to permit cross-examination of witnesses who actually provide information at the hearing.

Record

It is prudent to make a record of the hearing proceedings. If the hospital's final decision is appealed to the courts, a record will be necessary to prove the fairness of the proceedings and evidence of the basis for the decision. A court reporter's transcript of the proceedings is expensive and usually not necessary. However, if the physician requests a court reporter and is willing to share the cost appropriately, a court reporter should be considered. Usually a tape recording or, in some situations, detailed notes will be sufficient.

Appeal

Courts have permitted only the affected physician to seek judicial review of adverse decisions. Courts have not permitted other medical staff members, patients, or the families of patients to challenge decisions to grant or deny medical staff membership.[90]

Courts generally require the physician to pursue all of the procedures available within the hospital before an appeal to the courts is allowed. If a physician refuses to participate in the hospital hearing, courts will usually not allow an appeal based on denial of procedural due process.[91] Hospital procedures usually do not have to be exhausted before court review when the procedures offered by the hospital clearly do not satisfy due process guarantees.[92]

When courts review hospitals' medical staff actions, they usually show great deference to the judgment of the hospital and its medical staff. They limit their review to a determination whether appropriate procedures were followed and whether the action appears arbitrary or capricious. If credible evidence supports the action and proper procedures have been followed, the judiciary will almost always approve hospital actions. A few states do not follow this principle. For example, in 1983 a Missouri appellate court ruled that Missouri courts do not have to show any deference to public hospitals' medical staff decisions.[93]

LIABILITY

When some physicians challenge adverse hospital actions, they seek payment of money in addition to reversal of the hospital action. They base their claims on several grounds, including lost earnings or emotional distress during the proceedings, defamation, malicious interference with their business, antitrust violations, and discrimination. Some legal doctrines provide those involved in these determinations with limited immunity from some of these claims. Many hospitals require all applicants to sign a waiver protecting those involved from liability, but some courts have declined to enforce these waivers.[94] Thus, those involved must be aware of the potential grounds for liability so they can tailor their actions to minimize the risk.

Refusing to take necessary actions also exposes the medical staff and the hospital to liability, so inaction does not avoid liability.

Lost Earnings or Emotional Distress

Courts will sometimes award physicians money for their lost earnings or emotional distress during the hospital review process if it is later found that due process rights were violated. In 1982 a federal court affirmed an award of $20,000 for emotional distress, but reversed an award for lost earnings because the physician would have been discharged even if proper procedures had been followed.[95] A California jury awarded another physician $200,000 when the governing body delayed resolution of his appeal for 14 months.[96]

Defamation

Wrongful injury to another person's reputation is defamation. Defamation is discussed in Chapter 10. One of the defenses to a defamation claim is called a "qualified privilege," which means that there is no liability for certain communications even if they injure another's reputation, as long as the communications were not made with malice. Most courts apply a qualified privilege to communications during medical staff peer review activities and during due process procedures for medical staff actions.[97] In 1982 a Pennsylvania court dismissed the portion of a defamation suit against the hospital because no malice had been shown, but refused to dismiss the portion against the physicians.[98] It was asserted that the physicians had made their statements because they wanted the financial benefit of keeping a competitor from obtaining clinical privileges. If proven at trial, the financial motive could establish malice.

Antitrust

Physicians frequently challenge medical staff actions by claiming they are a restraint of trade or an attempt to monopolize medical practice, violating the federal antitrust laws. The physician must first prove that there is an impact on interstate commerce for the federal antitrust laws to apply. In the past the courts took the position that activities in individual hospitals did not affect interstate commerce, so the courts dismissed the suits. Now courts often find an effect on interstate commerce based on factors such as referrals from out of state.[99] Thus, hospitals have had to defend their actions in a full trial. However, hospitals have generally been able to justify their actions at the trial. For example, *Robinson v. Magovern*[100] upheld the denial of clinical privileges to a qualified thoracic surgeon because the denial was consistent with the hospital's competitive strategy that included limiting appointments to physicians who would contribute to the institution's goals and objectives. Thoracic surgery services were provided in other hospitals in the market area.

Discrimination

As discussed in Chapter 9 and earlier in this chapter, medical staff decisions should not be based on discriminatory criteria, such as race, creed, color, sex, national origin, or handicap. Sometimes medical staff actions are challenged on the basis that they violate federal and state statutes barring discrimination. For example, a black female physician in the District of Columbia claimed she had been terminated from her position in a health maintenance organization because of her race, violating the federal Civil Rights Act. In 1981 a federal court found sufficient evidence that her termination was based on complaints of black and white coworkers and on failure to improve her performance after being warned, and not on her race, so no violation was found.[101]

Immunity

In some states persons involved in the medical staff review process may be entitled to some immunity from liability for their statements or actions in the process. The common law qualified privilege from liability for defamation previously discussed is an example. Some states have statutes that provide limited immunity from damages for actions in the peer review process.[102] In 1978 an Arizona appellate court ruled that the chief of staff and the hospital administrator could not be sued for the summary suspension of a surgeon's clinical privileges unless there was a showing that the primary purpose of the action was other than the safeguarding of patients.[103] Since a patient had died following "serious errors in judgment" by the surgeon and the surgeon had scheduled another patient for the same type of surgery, the court found the primary purpose was the safeguarding of patients.

As part of the application form for medical staff membership, some hospitals require physicians to sign an agreement waiving the right to sue for improper peer review decisions. It is prudent to have these agreements signed. However, some courts will not enforce these agreements.[104]

Because the degree of protection provided by these agreements is difficult to predict, those involved in the review process should be careful to respect the rights of the physician being reviewed.

PHYSICIAN-HOSPITAL CONTRACTS

There is a trend to formalize the relationship between hospitals and physicians who perform specialized services in those hospitals. The use of formal, written contracts helps to define the relationship to the mutual benefit of hospital and physician. Many questions must be considered in reaching agreement concerning the relationship. Will the contract be with an individual physician or a group of physicians? Will the physicians be hospital employees or independent contractors? This question will affect fringe benefits, applicability of personnel policies, potential liability, and responsibility for withholding taxes and paying worker's compensation. The qualifications that the physician must meet should be specified. What services will the physician perform? In addition to providing direct patient care, the physician will usually need to participate in professional review and other committees and may also have some administrative responsibilities, such as budgeting or reports. Space, equipment, and supply issues must be addressed. Who will be responsible for selecting, training, supervising, scheduling, and disciplining professional and technical personnel who work with the physician? What insurance or indemnification agreements should the parties require? How will the physician be compensated? Salary, percentage, and fee-for-service arrangements or combinations of these arrangements are possible. Often the physician is not compensated by the hospital and charges fees to the patient directly. How will the charges be established, and who will be responsible for billing them? How will changes in third party payer requirements, such as the adoption of mandatory global billing (one bill for both the physician and hospital services), be addressed? How can the agreement be amended or terminated? How are disagreements to be resolved? These and other questions must be considered in contracting with physicians.

The answers to the above questions will be influenced by reimbursement policies of Medicare and other third party payers and by tax implications, such as threats to tax exemption. For example, hospitals that desire to be eligible to raise funds from tax-exempt bonds must limit all contracts with physicians to a period of no more than five years and reserve the right to terminate the contract without penalty every two years.[105]

A special clause concerning access to records should be included in all contracts for services that have a value of $10,000 or more over a year.

Section 952 of the Omnibus Reconciliation Act of 1980[106] forbids Medicare payment of hospital costs under a service contract if the clause is not in the contract. The clause must allow the Secretary of HHS and the Comptroller General to have access to the subcontractor's books, documents, and records that are necessary to verify the costs of services furnished under the contract. The records must be retained for at least four years after the services are provided. This requirement will apply to many contracts with physicians.

Exclusive Contracts

Hospitals frequently enter contracts with specialists that specify their exclusive right to provide certain types of care, such as radiology, pathology, emergency room, and cardiac catheterization services. These contracts can help the hospital to optimize patient care. However, physicians who want to provide the same type of care have attacked these contracts as violations of equal protection, due process, and antitrust laws. Most courts have upheld these exclusive privilege contracts when it is clear that they are intended to foster good quality patient care.

In 1973 in *Adler v. Montefiore Hospital Association of Western Pennsylvania*,[107] the Pennsylvania Supreme Court upheld a contract that granted exclusive cardiac catheterization privileges to the full-time director of the cardiology laboratory. A physician who had been performing the procedure in the hospital challenged the contract. The court found the arrangement reasonable and related to the hospital's operation because (1) it assured the best training and supervision of the catheterization team; (2) it enabled the physician to maintain competence by performing more procedures; (3) it centralized responsibility for use and maintenance of the equipment; (4) it reduced scheduling problems for patients; (5) it improved the ability to monitor quality of care; and (6) it assured the presence of a physician in the event of complications.

Antitrust attacks on exclusive contracts have generally been unsuccessful. However, in 1982 the Fifth Circuit Court of Appeals, in the *Hyde* decision,[108] declared an exclusive contract for anesthesia services to be a violation of the antitrust laws and ordered the hospital to permit Dr. Hyde, who had been recommended for appointment by the medical staff, to provide anesthesia services. The court found the use of the operating room and anesthesia services to be two separate products that were illegally "tied" by the exclusive contract. An agreement to sell one product only on the condition that the buyer also purchase a different product is called a tying arrangement and is a *per se* violation of the antitrust law if the seller has sufficient market power to coerce purchase of the tied product. The court defined the market area as so small that the hospital had sufficient market power. The court focused on the fact that anesthesia services were predominantly being provided by nurse anesthetists employed by the hospital and supervised by the anesthesiologists, so the court believed the "actual basis for the hospital's actions in this case" was "increasing the hospital's profit." The court rejected the other "business justifications" for the contract because it believed there were less restrictive ways to accomplish the same ends.

The *Hyde* decision led many to question the viability of exclusive contracts, until in 1984 the Supreme Court reversed the decision with an opinion that refined the definition of tying arrangements considered to be *per se* antitrust violations.[109] The court concluded that the arrangement did not force purchases that would not otherwise have been made, so it was not a tying arrangement. Applying the rule of reason, the Court found the contract did not unreasonably restrain competition. The Court's decision should not be interpreted as an endorsement of all exclusive contracts. Exclusive contracts can probably still be successfully attacked in some circumstances. However, the decision does again make it possible in many settings to structure exclusive arrangements that are likely to survive antitrust attack.

The exemption from antitrust liability for state actions discussed in the antitrust section of Chapter 3 may protect exclusive contracts in states with appropriate statutes. For example, in 1984 a federal appellate court ruled that clinical privilege decisions of Indiana hospitals are protected by the state action doctrine because state statutes make hospitals responsible for physician privileges and the state provides active supervision through its regulation of the peer review process.[110] In 1985 a federal court in North Carolina ruled that a county hospital did not violate antitrust laws by entering an exclusive contract because state law allowed the hospital to base privilege decisions on reasonable objectives, including appropriate utilization.[111] Since the hospital was public, active state supervision was not required for the exemption to apply.

In some states, state law may be more restrictive than federal law. For example, when a Texas hospital sought a court determination that it could legally have an exclusive radiology contract, the state of Texas counterclaimed on the basis of violation of state law.[112] The hospital entered a consent judgment agreeing to abandon its exclusive arrangement.

Extensive litigation may be necessary to defend exclusive contracts,[113] so it is prudent to enter such contracts only when they are clearly necessary to accomplish the hospital's mission. Antitrust issues are discussed in more detail in Chapter 3.

NOTES

1. Joint Commission on Accreditation of Hospitals, HOSPITAL ACCREDITATION MANUAL (1986 ed.) [hereinafter cited as JCAH 1986], at 101.

2. 42 C.F.R. §405.1023 (1984).

3. 99 Wis. 2d 708, 301 N.W.2d 156 (1981); *see also* Sheffield v. Zilis, 170 Ga. App. 62, 316 S.E.2d 493 (1984) [hospital demonstrated adequate review of physician's credentials, so hospital was not liable].

4. 18 Ariz. App. 75, 500 P.2d 335 (1972); *see also* Pedroza v. Bryant, 101 Wash.2d 226, 677 P.2d 166 (1984) [hospital can be liable for granting privileges to physician who is not competent, but liability does not extend to treatment provided off the hospital's premises].

5. American Medical Association, BYLAWS: A GUIDE FOR HOSPITAL MEDICAL STAFFS (1984) [hereinafter cited as AMA Guide].

6. JCAH 1986, *supra* note 1 at 101–119.

7. 28 AM. MEDICAL NEWS, Mar. 22, 1985, 16.

8. *E.g.,* Weary v. Baylor Univ. Hosp., 360 S.W.2d 895 (Tex. 1962); *contra* St. John's Hosp. Medical Staff v. St. John's Regional Medical Center, 90 S.D. 674, 245 N.W.2d 472 (1976); AMA Guide, *supra* note 5 at 4.

9. American Medical Association and American Hospital Association, *The Report of the Joint Task Force on Hospital-Medical Staff Relationships,* Feb. 1985.

10. Jackson v. Metropolitan Edison Co., 419 U.S. 345 (1974).

11. *E.g.,* Modaber v. Culpeper Memorial Hosp., Inc., 674 F.2d 1023 (4th Cir. 1982).

12. *E.g.,* Downs v. Sawtelle, 574 F.2d 1 (1st Cir. 1978).

13. *E.g.,* Aasum v. Good Samaritan Hosp., 395 F. Supp. 363 (D. Or. 1975), *aff'd,* 542 F.2d 792 (9th Cir. 1976).

14. *E.g.,* Greco v. Orange Memorial Hosp., 513 F.2d 873 (5th Cir. 1975).

15. *E.g.,* Bricker v. Sceva Speare Memorial Hosp., 111 N.H. 276, 281 A.2d 589 (1971).

16. *E.g.,* Miller v. Indiana Hosp., 277 Pa. Super. 370, 419 A.2d 1191 (1980).

17. *E.g.,* Kaplan v. Carney, 404 F. Supp. 161 (E.D. Mo. 1975).

18. *E.g.,* Bello v. South Shore Hosp., 384 Mass. 770, 429 N.E.2d 1011 (1981).

19. N.Y. Public Health Law §2801-b (McKinney 1977).

20. *E.g.,* Guibor v. Manhattan Eye, Ear & Throat Hosp., Inc., 56 A.D.2d 359, 392 N.Y.S.2d 628 (1977).

21. Sussman v. Overlook Hosp. Ass'n, 95 N.J. Super. 418, 231 A.2d 389 (N.J. Super. Ct. App. Div. 1967); Anton v. San Antonio Community Hosp., 19 Cal.3d 802, 567 P.2d 1162 (1977); Silver v. Castle Memorial Hosp., 53 Haw. 475 and 563, 497 P.2d 564 (1972), *motion denied* 53 Haw. 675, 501 P.2d 60 (1972), *cert. denied,* 409 U.S. 1048 (1972).

22. Garrow v. Elizabeth General Hosp. and Dispensary, 79 N.J. 549, 401 A.2d 533 (1979).

23. Dunbar v. Hospital Auth., 227 Ga. 534, 182 S.E.2d 89 (1971) [misrepresentation of narcotics violation]; Unterthiner v. Desert Hosp. Dist., 33 Cal.3d 285, 656 P.2d 554, 188 Cal. Rptr. 590 (1983), *cert. denied,* 104 S.Ct. 973 (1984); Yeargin v. Hamilton Memorial Hosp., 225 Ga. 661, 171 S.E.2d 136 (1969), *cert. denied* 397 U.S. 963 (1970) [exception to agreement to abide by rules].

24. Many of these items are required by the JCAH. JCAH 1986, *supra* note 1 at 102.

25. 99 Wis.2d 708, 301 N.W.2d 156 (1981).

26. *E.g.*, Ferguson v. Gonyaw, 64 Mich. App. 68, 236 N.W.2d 543 (1975).

27. Sussman v. Overlook Hosp. Ass'n, 95 N.J. Super. 418, 231 A.2d 389 (N.J. Super. Ct. App. Div. 1967).

28. Miller v. Eisenhower Medical Center, 27 Cal.3d 614, 614 P.2d 258 (Cal. 1980); applied in Pick v. Santa Ana-Tustin Community Hosp., 130 Cal. App.3d 970, 182 Cal. Rptr. 85 (1982) [sufficient danger shown to justify denial].

29. McElhinney v. William Booth Memorial Hosp., 544 S.W.2d 216 (Ky. 1976).

30. *E.g.*, Kennedy v. St. Joseph's Memorial Hosp., 482 N.E.2d 268 (Ind. Ct. App. 1985); *but see* Quinn v. Kent General Hosp., Inc., 617 F. Supp. 1226 (D. Del. 1985) [factual issue of whether 15 mile rule was reasonable precluded summary judgment in antitrust case].

31. JCAH 1986, *supra* note 1 at 102.

32. *E.g.*, Sams v. Ohio Valley General Hosp. Ass'n, 413 F.2d 826 (4th Cir. 1969) [county boundary not a valid geographic limit]; *contra* Berman v. Valley Hosp., 196 N.J. Super. 359, 482 A.2d 944 (N.J. Super. App. Div. 1984) [can require office within two-county primary service area].

33. JCAH 1986, *supra* note 1 at 102.

34. *E.g.*, Pollock v. Methodist Hosp., 392 F. Supp. 393 (E.D. La. 1975); Holmes v. Hoemako Hosp., 117 Ariz. 403, 573 P.2d 477 (1977); Renforth v. Fayette Memorial Hosp. Ass'n, 178 Ind. App. 475, 383 N.E.2d 368 (1978); Wilkinson v. Madera Community Hosp., 144 Cal. App.3d 436, 192 Cal. Rptr. 593 (1983) [hospital can require insurance to be with company approved by the state].

35. *E.g.*, Holmes v. Hoemako Hosp., 117 Ariz. 403, 573, P.2d 477 (1977).

36. Hackett v. Metropolitan General Hosp., 456 So.2d 1246 (Fla. Dist. Ct. App. 1985); Berman v. Valley Hosp., 196 N.J. Super. 359, 482 A.2d 944 (A.D. 1984); Guerrero v. Burlington County Hosp., 70 N.J. 344, 360 A.2d 334 (N.J. 1976); Davis v. Morristown Memorial Hosp., 106 N.J. Super. 33, 254 A.2d 125 (Super. Ct. Ch. Div. 1969).

37. Walsky v. Pascack Valley Hosp., 45 N.J. Super. 393, 367 A.2d 1204 (N.J. Super. Ct. Ch. Div. 1976).

38. Claycomb v. HCA-Raleigh Community Hosp., 333 S.E.2d 333 (N.C. Ct. App. 1985).

39. JCAH 1986, *supra* note 1 at 102.

40. Brooks & Morrisey, *Credentialing: Say Good-bye to the "Rubber Stamp,"* 59 HOSPITALS, June 1, 1985, at 50, 52.

41. Chapman v. Peoples Community Hosp. Auth., 139 Mich. App. 696, 362 N.W.2d 755 (1984).

42. *E.g.*, Chowdhury v. Reading Hosp. and Medical Center, 677 F.2d 317 (3rd Cir. 1982).

43. *E.g.*, Griesman v. Newcomb Hosp., 40 N.J. 389, 192 A.2d 817 (1963).

44. *E.g.*, Natale v. Sisters of Mercy, 243 Iowa 582, 52 N.W.2d 701 (1952).

45. *E.g.*, Ascherman v. St. Francis Memorial Hosp., 45 Cal. App.3d 507, 113 Cal. Rptr. 507 (1975).

46. Martino v. Concord Community Hosp. Dist., 233 Cal. App.2d 51, 43 Cal. Rptr. 255 (1965).

47. JCAH 1986, *supra* note 1 at 110.

48. *Id.*

49. 42 C.F.R. §405.1023(e)(4) (1984).

50. *E.g.*, Khan v. Suburban Community Hosp., 45 Ohio St.2d 39, 349 N.E.2d 398 (1976).

51. *E.g.*, Armstrong v. Board of Directors of Fayette County General Hosp., 553 S.W.2d 77 (Tenn. Ct. App. 1976).

52. *E.g.*, Fahey v. Holy Family Hosp., 32 Ill. App.3d 537, 336 N.E.2d 309 (1975).

53. Johnson v. St. Bernard Hosp., 79 Ill. App.3d 709, 399 N.E.2d 198 (1979).

54. JCAH 1986, *supra* note 1 at 113–114; 42 C.F.R. §405.1023(d)(2) (1984).

55. 132 Cal. App.3d 332, 183 Cal. Rptr. 156 (1982).

56. JCAH 1986, *supra* note 1 at 103.

57. *E.g.*, Stearns & Joseph, *Passing JCAH Muster, or, Six Essential Ingredients for a Successful Quality Assurance Program*, 38 TRUSTEE, June 1985, at 15.

58. JCAH 1986, *supra* note 1 at 113 [no longer than two years].

59. 42 U.S.C. §§1320c–1320c-12 (1982 & Supp. I 1983), as amended by Pub. L. No. 98-369, 98 Stat. 1090, 1097 (1984).

60. Association of Am. Physicians and Surgeons v. Weinberger, 395 F. Supp. 125 (N.D. Ill. 1975), *aff'd*, 423 U.S. 975 (1975).

61. Peer Review Improvement Act of 1982, Pub. L. No. 97-248, §§141–150, 96 Stat. 382–395 (1982) (codified as 42 U.S.C. §§1320c–1320c-12).

62. Pub. L. No. 98-21, §602, 97 Stat. 167 (1983).

63. *E.g.*, Peterson v. Tucson General Hosp., 114 Ariz. 66, 559 P.2d 186 (1976).

64. Clair v. Centre Community Hosp., 317 Pa. Super. 25, 463 A.2d 1065 (1983).

65. Moore v. Board of Trustees of Carson-Tahoe Hosp., 88 Nev. 207, 495 P.2d 605 (1972), *cert. denied* 409 U.S. 879 (1972).

66. Pagliaro v. Point Pleasant Hosp., No. A-3932-75 (N.J. Super. Ct. App. Div. January 19, 1979).

67. Smith v. Cleburne County Hosp., 607 F. Supp. 919 (E.D. Ark. 1985).

68. Khan v. Suburban Community Hosp., 45 Ohio St.2d 39, 340 N.E.2d 398 (1976).

69. Fahey v. Holy Family Hosp., 32 Ill. App.3d 537, 336 N.E.2d. 309 (1975).

70. *E.g.*, Fla. Stat. §395.011(7) (1985).

71. Cuatico v. Idaho Falls Consol. Hosps., Inc., *without op.* 753 F.2d 1081 (9th Cir. 1985); 18 HOSP. LAW, Mar. 1985, at 6.

72. JCAH 1986, *supra* note 1 at 104.

73. *E.g.*, Hoberman v. Lock Haven Hosp., 377 F. Supp. 1178 (M.D. Pa. 1974) [hearing not required for censure]; *contra* Grodjesk v. Jersey City Medical Center, 135 N.J. Super. 393, 343 A.2d 489 (N.J. Super. Ct. Ch. Div. 1975) [censure requires notice and opportunity to respond].

74. Joint Commission on Accreditation of Hospitals, GUIDELINES FOR THE FORMULATION OF MEDICAL STAFF BYLAWS, RULES AND REGULATIONS (1971); JCAH MONOGRAPH: MEDICAL STAFF BYLAWS (1978); JCAH 1986, *supra* note 1 at 101-19.

75. Storrs v. Lutheran Hosps. and Homes Soc'y of Am., Inc., 609 P.2d 24 (Alaska 1980), *aff'd after remand* 661 P.2d 632 (Alaska 1983).

76. *E.g.*, Poe v. Charlotte Memorial Hosp., 374 F. Supp. 1302 (W.D. N. C. 1974) [two-year-old incidents were insufficient basis for summary action].

77. *E.g.*, Conley v. Brownsville Medical Center, 570 S.W.2d 583 (Tex. Civ. App. 1978) [injunction dissolved after mistreatment of patient].

78. *E.g.*, Woodbury v. McKinnon, 447 F.2d 839 (5th Cir. 1971).

79. Arizona Osteopathic Medical Ass'n v. Fridena, 10 Ariz. App. 232, 457 P.2d 945 (1969).

80. *E.g.*, Suckle v. Madison General Hosp., 499 F.2d 1364 (7th Cir. 1974).

81. Garrow v. Elizabeth General Hosp. and Dispensary, 79 N.J. 549, 401 A.2d 533 (1979).

82. Anton v. San Antonio Community Hosp., 19 Cal.3d 802, 567 P.2d 1162 (1977).

83. Applebaum v. Board of Directors of Barton Memorial Hosp., 104 Cal. App.3d 648, 163 Cal. Rptr. 831 (1980).

84. Laje v. R.E. Thomason General Hosp., 564 F.2d 1159 (5th Cir. 1977).

85. Ladenheim v. Union County Hosp. Dist., 76 Ill. App.3d 90, 394 N.E.2d 770 (1979).

86. In re Zaman, 329 S.E.2d 436 (S.C., 1985).

87. *E.g.*, Ezekiel v. Winkley, 20 Cal.3d 267, 572 P.2d 32 (1977).

88. *E.g.*, Woodbury v. McKinnon, 447 F.2d 839 (5th Cir. 1971).

89. *E.g.*, Poe v. Charlotte Memorial Hosp., 374 F. Supp. 1302 (W.D. N. C. 1974).

90. *E.g.*, Bradley v. Lakes Region Hosp. Ass'n, No. E-80-0060 (N.H. Super. Ct. Belknap County, July 2, 1980) [parents of patient cannot challenge denial]; Forster v. Fisherman's Hosp., Inc., 363 So.2d 840 (Fla. Dist. Ct. App. 1978), *cert. denied*, 376 So.2d 71 (Fla. 1979) [chief of hospital staff cannot challenge privileges granted after he recommended denial].

91. *E.g.*, Suckle v. Madison General Hosp., 499 F.2d 1364 (7th Cir. 1974); *but see* Quasem v. Kozarek, 716 F.2d 1172 (7th Cir. 1983) [failure to pursue hospital procedures does not bar suit seeking only payment of damages by credentials committee member].

92. *E.g.*, Christhilf v. Annapolis Emergency Hosp. Ass'n, Inc., 496 F.2d 174 (4th Cir. 1974).

93. Long v. Bates County Memorial Hosp., 667 S.W.2d 419 (Mo. Ct. App. 1983) [injunction of 21 day suspension for test without patient authorization].

94. *E.g.*, Westlake Community Hosp. v. Superior Ct., 17 Cal.3d 465, 551 P.2d 410 (1976); *but see* King v. Bartholomew County Hosp., 476 N.E.2d 877 (Ind. Ct. App. 1985) [immunity provision on application upheld].

95. Laje v. R.E. Thomason General Hosp., 665 F.2d 724 (5th Cir. 1982).

96. Visalli v. Mary's Help Hosp., No. 151707 (Cal. Super. Ct., San Mateo County, March 15, 1970).

97. *E.g.*, Spencer v. Community Hosp., 87 Ill. App.3d 214, 408 N.E.2d 981 (1980).

98. Baldwin v. McGrath, No. 76-5-336 (Pa. C. Pl. Ct., York County, Mar. 18, 1982).

99. *E.g.*, Malini v. Singleton and Assocs., 516 F. Supp. 440 (S.D. Tex. 1981).

100. 521 F. Supp. 842 (W.D. Pa. 1981), *aff'd*, 688 F.2d 824 (3rd Cir. 1982), *cert. denied*, 459 U.S. 971 (1982).

101. Harris v. Group Health Ass'n, Inc., 662 F.2d 869 (D.C. App. 1981).

102. *E.g.*, Ariz. Rev. Stat. Ann. §36-445.02 (West Supp. 1984–85).

103. Scappatura v. Baptist Hosp., 120 Ariz. 204, 584 P.2d 1195 (1978).

104. *E.g.*, Westlake Community Hosp. v. Superior Ct., 17 Cal.3d 465, 551 P.2d 410 (1976); *but see* King v. Bartholomew County Hosp., 476 N.E.2d 877 (Ind. Ct. App. 1985) [immunity provision on application upheld].

105. Rev. Proc. 82-15.

106. 42 U.S.C. §1395x(v)(1)(I) (1982), as amended by Pub. L. No. 98-369, §2354, 98 Stat. 1100 (1984); 42 C.F.R. §§420.300–420.304 (1984). The release cannot be conditioned on request of the hospital, Program Memorandum: Intermediaries, Transmittal No. A-85-9, Oct. 1985, MEDICARE & MEDICAID GUIDE (CCH) ¶ 34,933.

107. 453 Pa. 60, 311 A.2d 634 (1973), *cert. denied,* 414 U.S. 1131 (1974).

108. Hyde v. Jefferson Parish Hosp. Dist. No. 2, 687 F.2d 286 (5th Cir. 1982).

109. Jefferson Parish Hosp. Dist. No. 2 v. Hyde, 104 S.Ct. 1551 (U.S. 1984); on remand the appellate court rejected Dr. Hyde's other challenges to the denial of his application, 764 F.2d 1139 (5th Cir. 1985).

110. Marrese v. Interqual, 748 F.2d 373 (7th Cir. 1984), *cert. denied* 105 S.Ct. 3501 (U.S. 1985); *but see* Quinn v. Kent General Hosp., Inc., 617 F. Supp. 1226 (D. Del. 1985) [Delaware peer review statute does not provide antitrust protection under state action doctrine].

111. Coastal Neuro-Psychiatric Assocs., P.A. v. Onslow County Memorial Hosp., Inc., No. 84-51-CIV-4 (E.D. N. C. July 12, 1985).

112. Medical Center Hosp. v. Texas, No. 374,830 (Tex. Dist. Ct., Travis County, Oct. 17, 1985), *as discussed in* 18 HOSP. LAW, December 1985, at 4.

113. *E.g.,* Albes v. City of Parkersburg, No. 84-A106 (S.D. W. Va. Feb. 20, 1985) [refusal to dismiss challenge by nurse anesthetists to exclusive anesthesia contracts at two hospitals].

Chapter 8

Individual Licensure and Credentialing

A complex system of licensing and credentialing has developed in an attempt to assure that qualified people are engaged in health care practice. The primary purpose of this system is to protect the public health by helping the public identify qualified providers and by prohibiting unqualified providers from engaging in practices that require expertise. Those who place less weight on quality care criticize all licensing and credentialing as a barrier to others who want to enter the practice and, thus, a restriction on competition.

There are many public and private credentialing methods. The public method is individual licensure. The private methods include accreditation of educational programs, certification of individuals, and credentialing by institutions.

INDIVIDUAL LICENSURE

The public method of credentialing is licensure, which can be either mandatory or permissive. A mandatory licensing law requires that an individual obtain a license before practicing within the scope of practice reserved for those with a license, unless the individual is eligible under one of the exceptions provided in the law. A permissive licensing law usually regulates the use of titles; an individual cannot use the title without a license but can perform the functions. In the past some licensing laws, both mandatory and permissive, provided simply for registration, and no special qualifications were required. Today registration laws are rare. Nearly all licensing laws include certain educational qualifications and require that an examination be passed.

States have discretion to determine which professions to license. In 1889 the United States Supreme Court upheld mandatory licensure of physicians.[1] The discretion of the states concerning licensure is illustrated by the 1966 decision in which the Court ruled that a state may choose not to recognize naturopathy as a discipline distinct from orthodox medical practice.[2] Thus, naturopaths must qualify for a full medical license to practice legally unless the state chooses to license them separately.

In many states, physicians and dentists were the first health professionals to be licensed. All states now have mandatory licensing laws for them. Nursing was generally the next profession to be licensed, and all states now license nurses. Pharmacists are another professional group licensed in all states. Most other professionals are licensed in many states, including physical therapists, psychologists, speech pathologists, audiologists, occupational therapists, and podiatrists. Some technical personnel are licensed in some states, such as emergency medical technicians and radiologic technologists.

In some states, hospitals have the responsibility to determine that certain professional and technical personnel meet government-imposed qualifications, instead of having a government agency evaluate the qualifications and issue a license.

Hospitals must be familiar with the applicable licensing requirements and other governmentally established staff qualification requirements. Hospitals should have a system for determining that all staff have the required qualifications and licenses. Use of unqualified staff can potentially have many adverse consequences for a hospital. In some states, if a patient is harmed by a staff member who is practicing illegally, the hospital may be liable in situations where it would not be liable if the staff member were practicing legally. However, in liability cases involving unlicensed staff, most states focus on whether the employee was in fact competent, rather than on the lack of a license.[3] Hospitals can be subject to administrative and criminal penalties for using unlicensed staff. For example, a New Jersey hospital was ordered to pay an administrative fine for aiding and abetting the illegal practice of medicine because it employed an unlicensed physician in its emergency room.[4] The agency that licenses the hospital or some hospital activities, such as the pharmacy, could discipline the hospital by suspending the license or putting the hospital on probation. Even if no action is taken directly against the hospital, the unexpected staff vacancy and the adverse publicity can be damaging.

Courts generally understand that hospitals must take action against employees who fail to maintain necessary licenses. For example, a Pennsylvania court ruled in 1984 that a nurse who was terminated for failure to renew her license was not entitled to unemployment compensation.[5] The failure was considered "willful misconduct."

In some states, staff of hospitals or certain types of hospitals are exempt from some licensure requirements. Exemption gives those hospitals more flexibility in determining the necessary qualifications for their staffs.

Scope of Practice

Mandatory licensing laws reserve a certain scope of practice for those who obtain licenses. The definition and evolution of the scope of practice for physicians, nurses, and others have been controversial. The controversy has focused on two broad issues. First, who may make the judgment that certain procedures will be performed? Second, who may perform the procedures?

In general, medical diagnosis and the ordering of most diagnostic and therapeutic procedures are reserved for the physician. There is a trend toward permitting some other professionals to make some diagnoses and order some treatments. States vary concerning the procedures that may be ordered by a physician's assistant. Nursing diagnosis is gaining recognition. Generally, the nurse determines what nursing care the patient needs and when nursing care is insufficient so that medical attention or instructions must be sought. In some states, nurses are permitted to make some judgments traditionally reserved for physicians when the nurses act under standing orders or established protocols.[6]

Most medical procedures are restricted to physicians when they are first introduced. As experience with them grows and they become better defined, there is a tendency to permit nurses to perform the procedures and, in some situations, to permit technical personnel to perform them. This evolution has varied from state to state. The evolution has been officially recognized in several different ways. In some states, licensing statutes have been changed to list the new procedures permitted. In other states, the attorney general's office has issued an opinion stating that certain practices are permitted or prohibited. A third approach has been for the medical and/or nursing licensing board to issue either rules or statements concerning the permitted scope of practice. A fourth approach has been joint statements of private professional organizations, such as the state medical society and nurses' association. The fifth approach has been judicial decision. Thus, many sources must be examined to determine the accepted scope of practice in a particular state.

In evaluating the reliability of these determinations, the positions of interested agencies and organizations should be considered. If they disagree and can convince the courts that the announced position is not permitted by the statute, these announcements, opinions, and even agency determinations can be declared invalid. For example, in 1982 the Iowa Supreme Court affirmed an injunction prohibiting a chiropractor from performing acupuncture, withdrawing blood specimens, and giving advice on diet and nutrition, even though the Board of Chiropractic Examiners had issued a declaratory ruling that these practices were permitted.[7] The Board's authorization probably protected the individual from prosecution, but it did not protect him from a contrary court ruling and injunction.

The specific practices that have been addressed for nurses include administering anesthesia, giving injections, starting intravenous (IV) fluids and medications, and inserting various tubes. In nearly all states, these issues have been resolved for registered nurses. Some of these issues, especially starting IVs, are now being addressed for licensed practical nurses.

Some states have given physicians broad authority to delegate functions to nurses. For example, Michigan permits physicians to delegate tasks or functions under proper supervision if permitted by standards of acceptable and prevailing practice.[8] This has been interpreted by the Michigan Attorney General to permit physicians to delegate to nurses the authority to prescribe any drugs except controlled substances, as long as the supervising physician is identified on the prescription.[9] Other states have given licensing boards broad authority to expand the functions of nurses. For example, Iowa gives the Board of Nursing the authority to expand the role of nurses by rule when the expanded roles are recognized by the medical and nursing professions.[10]

It is important to be aware of scope of practice restrictions because licensed professionals who act outside their permitted scope of practice are unlicensed practitioners when performing those acts, with the potential adverse consequences for the hospital discussed above.

Rule Making

Some rules promulgated by licensing boards have been challenged on the basis that they are believed to be beyond the authority of the board. Licensing boards generally have broad authority to regulate the professions they license, but occasionally specific controversial rules have been found to exceed their authority.

In 1981 a New Jersey appellate court upheld a rule requiring licensed radiologists who provide diagnostic services for other physicians to provide them for licensed chiropractors.[11] Although this se.vice is inconsistent with the practice of most radiologists, the court ruled that it was reasonable, within the authority of the board, and promulgated in accord with applicable procedures.

In 1979 a Florida appellate court ruled that the licensing board did not have the authority to prohibit chelation therapy for arteriosclerosis unless the board found the therapy to be harmful or hazardous to patients.[12] The fact that it was used by a minority of physicians and had not been proved effective was not a sufficient basis. In 1969 an Illinois appellate court ruled that the licensing board could not enforce a rule requiring that those who took the dental licensing examination be graduates of a school approved by the American Dental Association or of a school with a curriculum equivalent to the University of Illinois College of Dentistry.[13] The statute required those taking the examination to be graduates of a "reputable" school, so the board could not arbitrarily determine that a school was not reputable; it had to evaluate the school. In 1985 a Florida appellate court ruled that a Board of Optometry rule authorizing optometrists to use certain drugs was beyond the authority of the board.[14]

The preceding cases illustrate some of the kinds of rules that licensing boards are promulgating. It is important to be familiar with the current positions of the boards that license hospital personnel. Some rules can be successfully challenged in some states. However, other state courts might rule differently on similar rules.

Discipline and Due Process

Licensing boards have broad authority to discipline licensed professionals when they violate the professional standards specified in the licensing law or the rules of the board. The discipline may be revocation or suspension of the license or a probationary period in which certain conditions must be met. Most licensing boards have been given authority to impose various conditions, including prohibiting certain types of practice or requiring substance abuse rehabilitation efforts, consultation or supervision of certain procedures, or satisfactory completion of special education programs.

Before imposing disciplinary sanctions, the licensing boards must provide ← due process to the licensed professional, which means notice of the wrongful conduct and an opportunity to present information. Many states impose stricter requirements that must be followed for the board's action to be valid. For example, the Colorado Supreme Court ordered a nurse's license to be reinstated, in part because the statute required the full licensing board to attend the hearing concerning the revocation of her license and the full board had not done so.[15] Most licensing laws do not require the full board to be present, but if the law does require it, the law must be followed.

Another element of due process is that the licensed professional must have adequate notice that the questioned conduct is prohibited. Usually the courts rule that a prohibition of "unprofessional conduct" gives adequate notice that a wide range of inappropriate behavior is prohibited. "Unprofessional conduct" is not considered too vague as long as it is applied to conduct widely recognized as unprofessional. In 1979 the Oregon Supreme Court upheld the revocation of a nurse's license for "conduct derogatory to the standards of professional nursing."[16] She had instructed, recommended, and permitted her daughter to serve as a registered nurse knowing that her daughter was not licensed as a nurse. However, "unprofessional conduct" is not adequate notice for all possible violations. In 1969 the Idaho Supreme Court ordered the reinstatement of a nursing license that had been suspended for six months for unprofessional conduct.[17] The Board of Nursing had found that the nurse had discussed laetrile treatment with a leukemia patient on chemotherapy in a hospital without the approval of the physician, interfering with the physician-patient relationship. The board considered this unprofessional conduct. The court ruled that the board could have prohibited this conduct by rule but that a prohibition of unprofessional conduct did not give nurses adequate warning that this conduct was prohibited.

Many licensing boards are now specifying by rule more detailed grounds for discipline. Hospitals and health professionals should monitor these efforts closely and participate in the rule-making process to assure that the rules do not inadvertently prohibit appropriate existing practices.

Competition

The state has broad authority to determine which professions it will license. Many professional and technical disciplines are seeking to be licensed. They claim that licensing is necessary to protect the public from unqualified practitioners. Licensure is also sought because of the status it provides and because it is one way to obtain authorization to expand the scope of practice into areas otherwise reserved for other previously licensed health professionals. Licensure can be an economic benefit to the licensee by reducing the number of people permitted to perform specific tasks. The educational and testing requirements necessary to protect the public reduce the number of people available to provide the service. They increase the time and expense of becoming qualified, both to society and to the individual. This can have a detrimental effect if the cost increase is too great. It can have a catastrophic effect if not enough people who can meet the requirements are available, since the public would then receive no service rather than just poor service. Another concern for the legislature is that licensure can be a barrier to innovation because of the difficulty in changing the statutes and rules that define what licensees may do. Thus, the state is confronted with a difficult cost-benefit analysis whenever it is requested to license a health discipline.

It is widely accepted that the barriers to entry imposed by licensing are justified for some health disciplines, especially for those health professionals who function independently in many settings, such as physicians, dentists, and nurses. More significant questions have been raised concerning the necessity or appropriateness of state licensure of dependent practitioners who function under the supervision of licensed independent practitioners. Some commentators believe that the public health could be adequately protected through placing responsibility on the institution and supervising independent health professionals, and that the public interest in innovative, cost-effective health services could be advanced by more flexibility to use dependent health personnel. However, the trend appears to continue toward licensure of more health disciplines.

PRIVATE CREDENTIALING

A wide variety of private credentialing methods have been developed. Educational programs are accredited; individuals are certified; and hospitals and other institutions investigate the credentials of prospective staff members before permitting them to practice in the institution.

Accreditation of Educational Programs

Private professional organizations sponsor programs that establish criteria to evaluate educational programs. Periodically, an individual or a team investigates educational programs that desire to be accredited. The organization then accredits the programs that meet the criteria. Although accreditation is voluntary, most educational programs make a significant effort to obtain and retain accreditation from established accrediting bodies because students prefer accredited programs. Graduates of accredited programs often find it easier to obtain permission to take licensing examinations or to be admitted for advanced study because their degrees are generally accepted without additional proof of the quality of their educational programs. Graduates of accredited programs also find it easier to convince employers that they are prepared for employment in the discipline. Others will usually have to provide more information concerning their training programs to demonstrate the adequacy of their training.

Not all accrediting bodies have earned the wide acceptance of the longer-standing bodies that accredit medicine and nursing programs. Hospitals should not automatically assume that accreditation assures high standards. If the hospital is not familiar with the accrediting body, it should make inquiries before relying on its accreditation. The Council on Postsecondary Accreditation recognizes, monitors, and coordinates accrediting bodies for both institutions and programs in health and other fields. The Secretary of Education, using published criteria, recognizes national accrediting bodies with the advice of the Advisory Committee on Accreditation and Institutional Eligibility.[18]

Certification

Private professional organizations sponsor programs to certify that individuals meet certain criteria and are considered prepared to practice in the discipline. Certification provides the same benefits to the certified individual as completion of an accredited educational program, plus the benefit of individual certification as having met additional criteria ordinarily related to performance, usually including passing a test. Some forms of certification, especially certification by medical specialty boards, have become so widely accepted that it may be difficult to practice without certification. However, as discussed in Chapter 7, hospitals should not adopt an absolute requirement of board certification for specialty clinical privileges because it violates Medicare conditions of participation and has been declared an impermissible criterion by some courts. Instead, hospitals should avail themselves of the value of certification, while avoiding the absolute requirement, by requiring "board certification or equivalent training and experience."

Certifying bodies have proliferated, resulting in a certifying body for virtually every professional and technical discipline practicing in the hospital. Not all of these bodies have earned the acceptance of the longer standing certification bodies. Hospitals must be familiar with the certifying body before giving it substantial weight in evaluating applications. One of the advantages of the private certification system is that the hospital generally has the discretion to use its own evaluation system.

Hospital Credentialing

As discussed in Chapter 7, hospitals have an elaborate system for evaluating the credentials of physicians and determining the appropriate clinical privileges to grant physicians. Hospitals also have a responsibility to evaluate the credentials of others working in the hospital and to delineate what they may do.

For most hospital staff, this responsibility is fulfilled through the hiring process, hospital or department rules concerning practice patterns, the ongoing supervisory system, performance evaluation, and verification of relicensure. In the hiring process, the qualifications of the individual should be checked, including verification of licensure or other credentials. This process is important not only to determine professional competence but also to make a reasonable effort to detect other problems that could interfere with proper patient care. In 1961 a Georgia appellate court ruled that a hospital could be liable for the molesting of an infant by an orderly because the hospital had not checked his past, which would have disclosed a criminal conviction for being a "peeping Tom."[19] In 1977 a Texas appellate court upheld the liability of a hospital to a patient who was injured when an orderly attempted to remove a catheter from a patient's bladder without first deflating a bulb that held it in place.[20] The court upheld an additional assessment against the hospital, called punitive or exemplary damages, because the hospital had failed to check the employment and personal references of the orderly before hiring him. A check would have indicated that the orderly had been expelled from Naval Medical Corps School with a serious drug problem and criminal record. After staff members are hired, their practice is delineated by hospital and departmental rules and the ongoing supervisory system. When licensure is required for particular positions, there should be a system for assuring that staff members maintain their licensure by appropriate renewals.

The more difficult problem for hospitals is the increasing number of professional groups that desire to be involved in patient care without being hospital employees. Traditionally, physicians, some dentists, and a few private duty nurses were the only nonemployees involved in patient care. Today many physicians and dentists seek authorization for their employees to assist in patient care. In addition, many professional groups are seeking authorization to practice in the hospital on an independent or quasi-independent basis. These groups include chiropractors, clinical psychologists, nurse anesthetists, other nurse practitioners, physical therapists, and podiatrists.

In nearly all states, hospitals have the authority to establish whether these services will be provided in the hospital and, if so, whether they will be provided by nonemployees. For example, in 1982 an Oregon appellate court ruled that hospitals do not have to admit any chiropractors or naturopaths to their staffs or provide a procedure for reviewing their applications.[21] However, in 1980 a federal appellate court ruled that a public hospital must provide a podiatrist who applies for clinical privileges with due process procedures, but does not have to admit any podiatrists to its staff.[22] The only apparent function of the due process procedures is to give the applicant an opportunity to urge that the hospital rules be changed, since the hospital may decide that no podiatrists will be admitted.

In some states, the hospital's discretion has been limited by statute or court decision. For example, in some states hospitals have been prohibited from discriminating against an applicant solely on the basis that the practitioner is a podiatrist or psychologist.[23] Hospitals are still permitted to deny admission on the basis of competence or other factors related to quality of care.

When a Maryland hospital challenged a requirement that it grant privileges to qualified podiatrists, a state appellate court ruled in 1984 that the statute was constitutional.[24] The court viewed the statute as a justified exercise of the state's police power, so that the hospital was not entitled to compensation for the state ordered use of its facilities.

Court decisions have limited the hospital's discretion in some states. For example, a New York court ordered a hospital to permit a "mohel," a Jewish official who performs ritual circumcisions, to perform a circumcision on the hospital premises because the parents' religion required that the procedure be performed on a certain day, no mohel had been granted clinical privileges, and it was not practical to remove the child from the hospital.[25]

If the hospital decides to permit or is required to permit these nonemployees to practice on hospital premises, there should be a procedure for verifying their qualifications, obtaining their commitment to abide by all applicable hospital and departmental rules, defining their scope of practice, assuring appropriate supervision and evaluation of their performance, and terminating their permission to practice. These nonemployees present a difficult matter that the administration should address. These procedures are necessary even when the person is an employee of a physician member of the medical staff. In 1973 a federal appellate court ruled that a hotel could be liable for the actions of a treating nurse employed by an independent contractor physician because the hotel did not check her qualifications and determine she was not licensed.[26] One aspect of the policies for employees of physicians should be different from the policies for other nonemployees. The permission for the physician's employee should be contingent on the continuation of the physician's clinical privileges. If the physician ceases to have clinical privileges, the permission for the physician's employee to practice should automatically cease.

NOTES

1. Dent v. West Virginia, 129 U.S. 114 (1889).
2. Beck. v. McLeod, 240 F. Supp. 708 (D. S. C. 1965), *aff'd*, 382 U.S. 454 (1966).

3. *E.g.*, Leahy v. Kenosha Memorial Hosp., 118 Wis.2d 441, 348 N.W.2d 607 (Wis. Ct. App. 1984).

4. State Bd. of Medical Examiners v. Warren Hosp., 102 N.J. Super. 407, 246 A.2d 78 (N.J. Dist. Ct. 1968).

5. Adams v. Commonwealth, Unemployment Comp. Bd. of Rev., 86 Pa. Commw. 238, 484 A.2d 232 (1984).

6. *E.g.*, Sermchief v. Gonzales, 600 S.W.2d 683 (Mo. 1983).

7. State, ex rel. Ia. Dep't of Health v. Van Wyk, 320 N.W.2d 599 (Iowa 1982).

8. Mich. Comp. Laws, §333.16215(1) (1980).

9. Opinion No. 5630, January 22, 1980.

10. Iowa Code Ann., §152.1(2)(d) (1985).

11. Brodie v. State Bd. of Medical Examiners, 177 N.J. Super. 523, 427 A.2d 104 (N.J. Super. Ct. App. Div. 1981).

12. Rogers v. State Bd. of Medical Examiners, 371 So.2d 1037 (Fla. Dist. Ct. App. 1979).

13. Garces v. Department of Registration and Educ., 118 Ill. App.2d 206, 254 N.E.2d 622 (1969).

14. Board of Optometry v. Florida Medical Ass'n, Inc., 463 So.2d 1213 (Fla. Dist. Ct. App. 1985).

15. Colorado State Bd. of Nursing v. Hohu, 129 Colo. 195, 268 P.2d 401 (1954).

16. Ward v. Oregon State Bd. of Nursing, 226 Or. 128, 510 P.2d 554 (1973).

17. Tuma v. Board of Nursing, 100 Id. 74, 593 P.2d 711 (1979).

18. 45 C.F.R. §§603.1–603.6 (1984).

19. Hipp v. Hospital Auth., 104 Ga. App. 174, 121 S.E.2d 273 (1961).

20. Wilson N. Jones Memorial Hosp. v. Davis, 553 S.W.2d 180 (Tex. Civ. App. 1977).

21. Samuel v. Curry County, 55 Or. App. 653, 639 P.2d 687 (1982), *petition review denied,* 292 Or. 863, 648 P.2d 850 (1982); *accord* Fort Hamilton Hughes Memorial Hosp. Center v. Southard, 12 Ohio St. 3d 263, 466 N.E.2d 903 (1984); *but see* Wilk v. American Medical Ass'n, 719 F.2d 207 (7th Cir. 1983).

22. Shaw v. Hospital Auth., 614 F.2d 946 (5th Cir. 1980).

23. *E.g.*, Nev. Rev. Stat. §§450.005 and 450.430 (1981) [podiatrists and psychologists]; Cal. Health & Safety Code §1316 (West 1979) [podiatrists].

24. State v. Good Samaritan Hosp., 299 Md. 310, 473 A.2d 892 (Md. Ct. App. 1984), *app. dismissed* 105 S. Ct. 56 (U.S. 1984).

25. Oliner v. Lenox Hill Hosp., 106 Misc.2d 107, 431 N.Y.S.2d 271 (N.Y. Sup. Ct. 1980).

26. Stahlin v. Hilton Hotels Corp., 484 F.2d 580 (7th Cir. 1973).

Chapter 9

Staff Relations

A hospital provides patient care through its staff. The quality and perform-ance of the staff and the relationship between the hospital and its staff determine whether good quality, compassionate care can be provided to patients in the hospital. Hospitals should carefully select, train, supervise, and discipline staff members. Many aspects of staff relations are now subject to detailed state and federal regulation, including equal employment opportunities, compensation and benefits, occupational safety, labor-man-agement relations, and other matters. The trend has been toward more federal regulation with reduced state regulation.

This chapter discusses some general concerns regarding staff relations and then reviews the primary federal laws. Some state laws are mentioned, but a detailed state-by-state analysis is not attempted. Three aspects of staff relations are not addressed here because they are covered in other chapters: (1) the relationship with the hospital administrator (Chapter 2); (2) the relationship with the medical staff (Chapter 7); and (3) the credentialing of other staff (Chapter 8).

GENERAL STAFF RELATIONS ISSUES

Selection

Hospitals must exercise care in selecting their employees. As discussed in Chapter 8, the hospital should verify any required licenses and should check references and other information provided by the applicant to confirm that it is reasonable to believe the applicant is qualified for the position. Selection must also be in compliance with applicable equal employment opportunity laws that are discussed later in this chapter.

Health Screening

Hospitals should screen employees to identify conditions, such as contagious diseases, that may constitute a risk to patients, and take appropriate steps to assure that persons who constitute risks do not have contact with patients or objects that could transmit their conditions. Hospitals that choose to perform health screening of applicants before hiring must require it for all applicants for covered positions. Selective screening of individual applications violates section 504 of the Rehabilitation Act of 1973.[1]

Training and Supervision

As discussed in Chapter 10, hospitals are liable for the injuries caused by the negligence of their employees. To optimize patient care and minimize liability exposure, hospitals must assure that employees receive necessary training and supervision. It is important for employees to participate in continuing education to maintain and improve their skills. While hospitals should facilitate continuing education, in most states there is no obligation to provide it without cost to employees or during compensated time.

Discipline and Dismissal

Hospitals have a responsibility to take appropriate steps to enforce institutional policies to maintain appropriate patient care and the integrity of the institution. It is important that proper procedures be followed and that action be based on legally permissible grounds. Generally, employees are considered to be employees at will unless they have contracts for a specified time period. Employers may terminate employees at will at any time without cause,[2] unless (1) the employer is bound by contract or statute to follow certain procedures or standards in terminations or (2) the termination violates public policy.

Many courts view some hospital procedures for discipline or dismissal as contracts with the employees that the hospital must follow.[3] However, courts have disagreed on what constitutes an enforceable policy or procedure. The Delaware Supreme Court ruled that statements in employee handbooks do not change an employee's at-will status unless they specify a definite term of employment.[4] A Florida appellate court ruled that hospital personnel policies might be enforceable and ordered a trial court to reconsider the matter.[5] Some public hospital employees are covered by civil service laws that require certain procedures. Absent statutory requirements, public employees are generally not entitled to a formal hearing. In 1985, the Supreme Court ruled that public employees must be given oral or written notice of the charges, an explanation of the employer's evidence, and a pretermination opportunity to present their side of the story, but a formal hearing was not required.[6]

When staff members are covered by individual employment contracts or collective bargaining agreements, procedures specified in the contract or agreement should be followed. Such contracts do not have to be in writing to be enforceable. A Louisiana court found a hospital liable for breaching an oral promise to five certified registered nurse anesthetists that they would be given a six-month notice of termination. The court awarded payment of salary for six months, less the amount they actually earned during the six months.[7] As this case illustrates, courts generally will not order employees reinstated unless authorized by statute; instead, former employees who are wrongfully discharged are awarded payment of lost wages and other damages.

One issue that is receiving increasing attention is the protection of employees from retaliatory discharge. Some statutes forbid retaliatory discharge for making certain reports to governmental agencies,[8] and some courts have extended such protection to employees who make other reports (such as worker's compensation claims[9]), who refuse to testify untruthfully in malpractice cases,[10] or who refuse to handle radioactive materials in violation of federal regulations.[11] However, the at-will doctrine is not dead even in the states in which courts have aggressively expanded protection from retaliatory discharge. For example, in 1985 the Illinois Supreme Court ruled that an employer did not violate public policy by discharging an at-will employee who filed a health insurance claim.[12]

There may be some protection for employees of public institutions who are discharged for exercising their rights of free speech,[13] but this protection does not extend to employees of private employers. For example, an Illinois appellate court ruled that, even if a nurse had been terminated solely in retaliation for reporting incidents to a newspaper, she would not be entitled to any more protection than other at-will employees of private employers.[14]

When an employer conducts an investigatory interview of an employee that the employee reasonably believes might result in discipline and the employee is part of a unit represented by a union, the employee has a right to have a representative present during the interview if the employee so requests.[15] The employer does not have to advise the employee of the right and the employer may decide not to conduct the interview if the right is invoked. In a collective bargaining agreement, a union can waive the right to representation in such interviews.[16] Non-union employees do not have a right to representatives.[17]

Some provisions of the National Labor Relations Act also apply when employees are not represented by a union. The equal employment opportunity laws apply to all aspects of employment, including discipline and dismissal, so the provisions of these laws also must be considered. Hospitals must also be aware of what grounds for dismissal will be considered "just cause" by the unemployment compensation agency in their states so that they are not required to pay unemployment compensation to a dismissed staff member. These regulatory aspects of dismissal decisions are discussed in more detail later in this chapter.

Communications about Former Staff

Many types of employers, including hospitals, have been sued for libel or slander by former staff members based on statements in unfavorable evaluations, termination notices, and responses to inquiries from prospective employers. Some supervisory personnel have been reluctant to communicate deficiencies accurately because of limited understanding of what they may legally communicate. It is essential that supervisors understand what they can communicate so that present and prospective employees can obtain accurate evaluations with minimum legal risk.

In general, no liability can be based on libel or slander for communicating the truth. However, since it is often difficult to prove the absolute truth of a statement, the law extends a "qualified privilege" to certain communications. This means that there is no liability as long as the communication was not made with malice. The qualified privilege applies to communications to certain persons who have a legitimate interest in the information given, as long as the communication is limited in scope commensurate with the legitimate interest and the communication is made in a proper manner so that others do not also learn of it inappropriately. Courts have recognized that an employer or prospective employer has a legitimate interest in employment-related information.[18] The best way to avoid exceeding the qualified privilege is to limit the communication to factual statements and avoid statements concerning personality or personal spite. Neutral factual statements can communicate the deficiences that need to be communicated without creating the appearance of malice.

Most former employers require a written authorization from the former employee before releasing information. This authorization provides some additional protection, but care must still be taken in drafting the response.

EQUAL EMPLOYMENT OPPORTUNITY LAWS

The federal government has enacted several laws to expand equal employment opportunities by prohibiting discrimination on various grounds. These laws include Title VII of the Civil Rights Act of 1964, the Equal Pay Act of 1963, the Age Discrimination in Employment Act, and sections 503 and 504 of the Rehabilitation Act of 1973. In addition, numerous state laws address equal employment opportunities.

Title VII of the Civil Rights Act of 1964

Title VII of the Civil Rights Act of 1964[19] prohibits disparate employment treatment based on race, color, religion, sex, national origin, or pregnancy. It applies to hiring, dismissal, promotion, discipline, terms and conditions of employment, and job advertising. It applies to nearly all employers; governmental agencies were included by the 1972 amendments. One of the few exemptions permits religious institutions to consider religion as a criterion in their employment practices.

The primary enforcement agency is the Equal Employment Opportunity Commission (EEOC). In some situations, the EEOC can defer to enforcement by local or state agencies or through individual suits. Three legal theories are used as the basis for finding employment discrimination. First, violations can be found on the basis of disparate treatment when work rules or employment practices are not applied in a consistent fashion due to a discriminatory motive. Second, violations can be found on the basis of disparate impact when an employment practice, such as a written employment test, has an adverse impact on minorities and cannot be justified as job related. Third, carryover from past discrimination can constitute a violation when minorities are in a disadvantageous position because of prior discriminatory practices.

Employers are prohibited from retaliating against employees who oppose discrimination by engaging in reasonable activities. In 1984 a federal appellate court found that a hospital had violated this provision when it fired a black registered nurse who had complained about black patient care.[20]

In some circumstances, sex or features related to religion or national origin are bona fide occupational qualifications reasonably necessary to the normal operation of a particular business. When hospitals can demonstrate this necessity, the use of the qualification is not a violation of the law. For example, in 1981 a federal district court ruled that it was not illegal sex discrimination for a hospital to employ only female nurses in its obstetrics-gynecology department.[21] The court noted that the policy was based on the privacy rights of the patients, not just patient preference. The Court of Appeals vacated the decision because the case became moot when the male nurse voluntarily quit his job.[22] In 1981 a federal appellate court ruled that it was not illegal discrimination based on national origin for a hospital to require all employees to have some facility in communication in the English language.[23] The court recognized that ability to communicate in English was a bona fide occupational qualification for virtually every position in a sophisticated medical center.

In 1978 Title VII was amended to prohibit discriminatory treatment of pregnant women for all employment-related purposes. No special considerations are required. However, for example, if leaves are offered for disability, similar leaves must be offered for disabling maternity. Mandatory maternity leaves not based on inability to work violate Title VII. Pregnancy itself is not considered a disability, but if a pregnant worker becomes unable to work, then disability benefits must be offered the pregnant worker. Some states require employers to offer a leave of absence for pregnancy. In 1984 a federal appellate court found a hospital that fired a pregnant radiology technician to have violated this Act.[24]

The EEOC has published guidelines on sexual harassment[25] that indicate the employer can be liable for sexual harassment by coworkers and nonemployees, as well as by supervisory and managerial staff. The employer may be liable for a supervisor's sexual harassment despite lack of knowledge of the behavior.[26] Thus, hospitals cannot conclude that a lack of reported incidents means there is no problem.

Some groups have sought to convince the courts that Title VII requires adoption of a comparable worth doctrine. This doctrine would require employers to revise wage scales so that pay is based on the comparable worth of the work done by persons in different job classifications when work categories that are predominantly filled with females have been assigned lower wage scales. This doctrine goes beyond the Equal Pay Act (discussed in the following section) that requires equal pay for essentially identical work. Nursing groups have been in the forefront of the effort to establish this doctrine. However, courts generally have ruled that Title VII does not require wage scales based on comparable worth.[27] The one exception, a 1983 federal court decision applying comparable worth principles to a broad range of public jobs in the state of Washington, was overturned by a federal appellate court in 1985.[28]

Title VII does not preempt the entire field of equal employment opportunity. While state law cannot permit something prohibited by Title VII, state law can assure more opportunities. Thus, many state laws that limit the types of work women may perform are superseded, but state laws requiring employers to offer pregnancy leaves are not suspended.

Equal Pay Act of 1963

The Equal Pay Act[29] is designed to prohibit discriminatory compensation policies based on sex. It requires equal pay for equal work. Equal work is defined as work requiring equal skill, equal effort, and equal responsibility and performed under similar working conditions. In 1985 a federal court in Georgia upheld paying physician's assistants more than nurse practitioners because of the greater training and skills required even though they provided substantially similar services.[30] The training and skills that state law requires for the positions may be relevant. The payment of higher wages to male orderlies than to female aides has been challenged in several cases.[31] In general, the courts have required equal pay except when the hospital has been able to prove actual differences in the work performed during a substantial portion of work time. The courts have adopted a case-by-case approach to the determination of whether work is equal.

Age Discrimination in Employment Act

The Age Discrimination in Employment Act[32] prohibits discriminatory treatment of persons from 40 to 69 years of age for all employment-related purposes. Mandatory retirement is prohibited for persons under 70, except for certain exempted executives. The law applies to governmental and private employers of 20 or more persons. There are exceptions for bona fide occupational qualifications, bona fide seniority systems, and reasonable factors other than age, such as physical fitness.

In 1984 a federal appellate court found a hospital guilty of age discrimination because its medical director had fired a 56-year-old secretary and replaced her with a 34 year old.[33] The replacement testified that the medical director told her she was selected for her appearance. Violations can also be found for discriminating in favor of those who are older. An Oregon appellate court found a retirement home guilty of age discrimination under a state nondiscrimination law because it had refused to hire a beautician, saying she was too young for its residents.[34]

Hospital administrators must be careful not to give the impression of age discrimination. After a 62-year-old day shift nurse supervisor resigned, she sued a hospital for age discrimination.[35] A federal appellate court ruled in 1985 that a jury should decide whether the administrator's statements concerning the need for "new blood" and her "advanced age" created intolerable working conditions in violation of the Act that forced her to resign.

Some hospitals have tried to settle age discrimination suits and have obtained from the employee a signed waiver of the right to sue for damages. These unsupervised waivers may not be effective. A federal appellate court ruled in 1985 that the right to sue could not be waived, so the waiver was not enforceable.[36] Thus, prior approval from the enforcement agency or a court may be necessary to make such waivers binding.

Rehabilitation Act of 1973

The Rehabilitation Act of 1973[37] prohibits discrimination on the basis of handicap. Section 503[38] prohibits discrimination by government contractors, while section 504[39] prohibits discrimination by entities that receive federal financial assistance. In 1984 the Supreme Court ruled that any entity receiving federal financial assistance may not discriminate in either services or employment.[40] Medicare and Medicaid reimbursement have been interpreted to be federal financial assistance.[41]

When the Rehabilitation Act applies, the institution is prohibited from discriminating against any qualified handicapped person who, with reasonable accommodation, can perform the essential functions on the job in question. Inquiries about handicaps prior to employment are prohibited, except that applicants can be asked if they are able to perform the job. Preemployment physical examinations may be required only if all applicants for similar positions must also undergo the same examination. In 1985 a federal appellate court ruled that chronic contagious diseases, such as tuberculosis, are handicaps that must be reasonably accommodated.[42] A hospital may refuse to hire a person on the basis of behavioral manifestations of the handicap, such as excessive absenteeism by an alcoholic. Hospitals may also refuse to hire or retain persons whose current use of alcohol or drugs prevents them from performing the duties of the job or constitutes a direct threat to property or the safety of others. Hospitals may strictly enforce rules prohibiting possession or use of alcohol or drugs in the workplace.

In 1985 the Supreme Court ruled that state agencies could not be sued for violating section 504 because of their Eleventh Amendment sovereign immunity from being sued.[43] Thus, sanctions for violations must be initiated by administrative agencies, not the courts.

LAWS CONCERNING COMPENSATION AND BENEFITS

The federal government has enacted several laws regulating compensation and benefits of employees, including the Fair Labor Standards Act, the Federal Wage Garnishment Law, and the Employee Retirement Income Security Act. In addition, numerous state laws address these issues.

Fair Labor Standards Act

The Fair Labor Standards Act[44] establishes minimum wages, overtime pay requirements, and maximum hours of employment. Employees of all nonprofit and for-profit hospitals are covered by this act, so hospitals must conform. Bona fide executive, administrative, and professional employees are exempt from the wage and hour provisions when the employees are salaried. While it is clear that these categories would include physicians and administrators, Department of Labor regulations must be consulted to determine the status of the other classifications of employees. The 1974 amendments to the Fair Labor Standards Act extended its minimum wage and overtime provisions to almost all employees of state and local governments. In 1976 the Supreme Court declared it unconstitutional to apply these provisions to states, but in 1985 the Supreme Court reversed itself and declared the amendment constitutional.[45]

Most employers are required to pay overtime rates for work that exceeds 40 hours in 7 days. However, the law permits hospitals to enter into agreements with employees, establishing an alternative work period of 14 consecutive days, rather than the usual 7-day week. If the alternative period is chosen, the hospital need pay the overtime rate only for all hours worked in excess of 80 hours during the 14-day period. If the alternate 14-day work period is established, the hospital is not relieved from paying overtime rates for hours worked in excess of 8 in any one day, even if no more than 80 hours are worked during such a period.

The Fair Labor Standards Act also addresses child labor by regulating the hours and conditions of employment of children. The Fair Labor Standards Act does not preempt more protective state or local laws that establish a higher minimum wage, a shorter minimum work week, or more protection for children.

Federal Wage Garnishment Law

One way to enforce a court judgment against another person is to impose garnishment of the debtor's wages. Garnishment is a court order to an employer to pay a portion of the debtor's paycheck to the creditor until the debt is paid. The Federal Wage Garnishment Law[46] and various state laws restrict how much of a paycheck may be garnisheed. When there are multiple garnishments, proper priorities must be observed not to exceed the limit on aggregate garnishments. State law may limit garnishment to a smaller amount than federal law. Federal law prohibits employers from discharging employees because of garnishment for one indebtedness. The limits on garnishment do not apply to certain bankruptcy court orders or debts due for state or federal taxes.

Employee Retirement Income Security Act of 1974

The Employee Retirement Income Security Act of 1974 (ERISA)[47] regulates nearly all pension and benefit plans for employees, including pension, profit-sharing, bonus, medical or hospital benefit, disability, death benefits, unemployment and other plans. The law applies to all employers except for government agencies and some plans of churches. The law regulates many features of the plans, including nondiscrimination, benefit accrual, vesting of benefits, coverage, responsibilities of plan managers, termination of the plan, descriptions of the plan, and required reports. The ERISA requirements should be considered before changing any pension or benefit plan that is not exempt.

Some health benefit plans have attempted to use ERISA to attack state laws that mandate certain benefits. In 1985 the Supreme Court ruled that neither ERISA nor the National Labor Relations Act preempts state laws that mandate that insured plans provide certain benefits, such as mental illness coverage.[48] However, states cannot require self-insured or uninsured health plans to provide the specific benefits because such plans are not covered by the savings clause in ERISA that allows state regulation of insurance.

Furnishing false information to a health or welfare fund subject to ERISA is a federal crime. The administrator of a provider of outpatient services was convicted of this crime because he did not report actual costs in a utilization report to a fund, but instead reported the estimated value of the services based on the higher Blue Shield charges.[49]

OCCUPATIONAL SAFETY AND HEALTH

Congress enacted the Occupational Safety and Health Act (OSHA) of 1970[50] to establish standards for occupational health and safety and to enforce the standards. Standards developed for various industries are mandatory for all covered employers. The statute provides that when no federal standard has been established, state safety rules remain in effect.

The Act mandates that each state enact legislation to implement the standards and procedures promulgated by the Department of Labor. Litigation has arisen over the issue of inspections by federal and state officials to enforce the OSHA standards. The courts have consistently held that an employer may refuse an inspection unless the inspector obtains the consent of a duly authorized agent of the employer (the night watchman might not be authorized) or the inspector has a search warrant validly issued in accordance with state law. The Supreme Court ruled unconstitutional an OSHA provision that permitted "spot checks" by OSHA inspectors without a warrant.[51]

OSHA regulations prohibit employers from discriminating against employees who refuse to expose themselves to conditions presenting a real danger of death or serious injury in urgent situations where there is insufficient time to pursue correction through OSHA.[52] This regulation was upheld by the Supreme Court in 1980.[53]

Under the law of some states, employers are charged by statute with the duty of furnishing employees with a safe place to work. Even in states that do not have such statutes, hospitals are liable for most injuries suffered by employees as a result of employment, unless the doctrine of governmental immunity is applicable. In most situations, the employee may pursue compensation only through the worker's compensation system, not through the courts.

In addition to provisions relating to unsafe conditions of the workplace, other state statutes require that specific facilities be provided to employees. These facilities, such as lavatories, must be provided for the convenience and safety of employees. Ordinances and laws of the city and county in which a hospital is located may also include requirements, such as sanitary and health codes, to promote and safeguard the health and safety of employees and others. In most instances, nonprofit status does not exempt an institution from these laws. However, in most states, state institutions are exempt from local regulation, unless state laws grant local governments the authority to encompass state institutions.

LABOR-MANAGEMENT RELATIONS

Unions are a significant factor in hospital-employee relations in many parts of the country. A number of different types of labor organizations are now recognized as collective bargaining representatives for groups of hospital employees. There are craft unions whose primary organizing efforts are devoted to skilled employees, such as carpenters and electricians; industrial unions and governmental employee unions that seek to represent large groups of relatively unskilled or semiskilled employees; and professional and occupational associations and societies, such as state nurse associations, that represent their members. The professional organizations are labor unions to the extent that they seek goals directly concerned with wages, hours, and other employment conditions and engage in bargaining activities on behalf of employees.

Labor-Management Relations Act

The Labor-Management Relations Act,[54] which defines certain conduct of employers and employees as unfair labor practices and provides for hearings upon complaints that such practices have occurred, explicitly exempts government hospitals from its coverage. This Act consists of the National Labor Relations Act of 1935,[55] the Taft-Hartley amendments of 1947,[56] and numerous other amendments, including the Labor-Management Reporting and Disclosure Act of 1959.[57] The Act is administered by the National

Labor Relations Board (NLRB). The NLRB (1) investigates and adjudicates complaints of unfair labor practices; and (2) conducts secret ballot elections among employees to determine whether they wish to be represented by a labor organization and, if so, to determine which organization.

The exemption for governmental hospitals has been interpreted by the NLRB to apply only to hospitals that are owned and operated by governmental agencies. For example, a municipal hospital operated under contract may be considered a private entity subject to the NLRB if overall daily control is by a private contractor. Exempt governmental hospitals are usually subject to state laws concerning governmental employees.

Nonprofit hospitals were exempt until the amendments of 1974[58] eliminated the exemption. The 1974 amendments attempted to deal with some of the unique aspects of health care by providing legislative direction about collective bargaining, mediation, conciliation, and strikes.

Some religious hospitals have challenged these laws. Federal appellate courts have found that it is not a violation of the First Amendment religious freedoms to apply these laws to religiously owned and operated hospitals.[59]

Hospitals are intended to receive special consideration from the NLRB because of their sensitive mission, but individual rulings by the NLRB will continue to be made on the basis of many factors in addition to the uniqueness of health care.

Exempt Staff

Several groups of staff members are excluded from the NLRB's jurisdiction, including independent contractors, supervisors, managerial employees, confidential employees, and some students. Each of these groups has been defined by numerous NLRB and court decisions, so familiarity with those decisions is necessary to determine whether a particular staff member is exempt.

Unfair Labor Practices

Section 7 of the National Labor Relations Act (NLRA) established four fundamental rights of employees: (1) the right to self-organize; (2) the right to engage in concerted activities for the purpose of collective bargaining or other mutual aid or protection; (3) the right to engage in collective bargaining; and (4) the right to refrain from union activities.

Employer Unfair Labor Practices

An employer commits an unfair labor practice through (1) interference with any of the four rights recognized in section 7; (2) domination of a labor organization; (3) discouragement or encouragement of union activity; (4)

discrimination against employees who file charges or testify in an NLRB proceeding; or (5) violation of the other obligations, including good faith bargaining, specified in section 8(a) of the NLRA.

The NLRA also applies to hospitals that do not have employees represented by a labor organization. The employee's right to engage in concerted activities for the purposes of mutual aid or protection can apply to isolated incidents, so hospitals should obtain legal advice before disciplining employees who may be engaged in protected activities. For example, in 1978 the NLRB ruled that a small group of unorganized staff was protected by the NLRA when the group left a work station to complain to hospital officials concerning work conditions.[60] Not all employee actions are protected. In 1982 the NLRB upheld the dismissal of two hospital employees for continual criticism of the program director.[61] The NLRB found this activity unprotected because it was aimed at influencing administration of the program rather than working conditions. Hospitals should also obtain legal advice before working with employee advisory committees. If their role is not appropriately limited, they may be considered labor organizations, and many of the hospital's interactions with them could be interpreted as unfair labor practices. For example, in 1977 the NLRB ruled that a hospital had engaged in the unfair labor practice of management domination of a labor organization because the hospital ran the election for an employee committee and wrote its bylaws.[62]

Labor Organization Unfair Labor Practices

A labor organization commits an unfair labor practice through (1) restraining or coercing interference with the exercise of the four rights recognized in section 7 or interfering in management's selection of its representatives; (2) attempting to cause the employer to discriminate to encourage or discourage membership in a labor organization; (3) failing to bargain in good faith; (4) engaging in prohibited secondary boycotts; (5) charging excessive union initiation fees; (6) causing employers to pay for services not performed; or (7) picketing solely to compel an employer to recognize a union (recognitional picketing) or to persuade employees to join the union (organizational picketing) without filing a petition for an election within the appropriate time limit.

In 1985 the Supreme Court ruled that a union committed an unfair labor practice by prohibiting members from resigning from the union during a strike or when a strike was imminent.[63]

Employee Representation

A labor organization seeking representation rights for employees may petition the NLRB for a secret ballot election. The petition must make a "showing of interest" supporting the petition. At least 30 percent of the workers who will ultimately make up the bargaining unit must support it and show their interest by signing union authorization cards.

Bargaining Unit Designation

The employer may take the position that certain persons (supervisors, confidential employees, temporary employees) should be excluded from the unit or that the unit would be inappropriate because of the hospital's organization. The NLRB will then conduct a representation hearing to determine the appropriate bargaining unit. The NLRB must implement the Congressional intent in the 1974 amendments to avoid "proliferation of bargaining units" in the health care industry.[64] In addition, section 9 of the NLRA forbids including professional employees in bargaining units with nonprofessionals unless a majority of the included professionals vote in favor of inclusion.

Until 1984 the NLRB determined whether the proposed unit was appropriate by applying a "community of interest" test. That is, a proposed unit was appropriate if its members had a community of interest. This resulted in the recognition of five basic units in health care institutions: (1) clerical; (2) service and maintenance; (3) technical; (4) professional; and (5) registered nurses.

In 1984 the NLRB abandoned the "community of interest" test, replacing it with a "disparity of interest" test.[65] Under this test, the NLRB begins with the broadest possible unit and excludes only those groups that are shown to have disparate interests. No unit is automatically assumed to be appropriate; all are examined on a case-by-case basis.

Solicitation and Distribution

Most hospitals have rules concerning solicitation of employees and distribution of materials in the hospital to avoid interference with patient care. These rules become especially important during campaigns to organize hospital employees, so they should be written to be enforceable under the NLRA. Each policy is examined on a case-by-case basis by the NLRB. Some general guidelines can be derived from past decisions. Nonemployees may generally be prohibited access to the facility for solicitation or distribution. Employees can be prohibited from solicitation or distribution during work time. However, in 1981 the NLRB ruled that work time does not include mealtimes or work breaks.[66] Solicitation or distribution can be limited to nonpatient care areas at all times. In 1979 the Supreme Court ruled that solicitation and distribution could be prohibited in areas devoted to patient care.[67] The NLRB is examining complaints concerning specific restricted areas on a case-by-case basis. In general, a genuine likelihood of patient disturbance is necessary, so areas where visitors have general access, such as cafeterias and lounges, usually cannot be prohibited. One important factor in determining the appropriateness of excluding certain areas is whether reasonable alternative space is designated for these activities.

Election

A labor organization can become the exclusive bargaining agent for a bargaining unit by winning a secret ballot election conducted by the NLRB. After an election, the employer or the labor organization can challenge the outcome by filing an objection alleging misconduct during the election. If the NLRB finds misconduct, it can set aside the election and order a new election.

Recognition without an Election

An employer can voluntarily recognize a labor organization as the exclusive bargaining agent without an election. If the employer participates in certain actions, such as checking the union authorization cards or polling the employees, the actions can sometimes constitute recognition of the labor organization. Recognition of a labor organization without an election can constitute an unfair labor practice in some circumstances, especially when other labor organizations are also seeking to represent the employees. Most employers avoid all actions that could be interpreted as voluntary recognition of a labor organization. A second way that a labor organization can be recognized without an election is by order of the NLRB. When the NLRB finds serious unfair labor practices, it has the authority to order the extraordinary remedy of recognition of the labor organization. A third way is accretion. If a labor organization has negotiated a contract for a bargaining unit at a hospital that later acquires a new facility, under some circumstances the new facility is considered to be accreted to the existing one, and new unit employees are automatically covered by the preexisting contract.

Collective Bargaining and Mediation

After a labor organization has been recognized as the exclusive bargaining agent, the employer and the labor organization have a duty to negotiate in good faith. They must bargain concerning mandatory subjects, including wages, hours, and other terms and conditions of employment. They may bargain concerning other permissive subjects but are not legally obligated to do so. It is unlawful to bring negotiations to an impasse, to strike, or to lock out employees over permissive subjects.

Several special notice, mediation, and conciliation safeguards were built into the law to help the health care industry avoid strikes when possible. For example, 90 days' notice is required if a party intends to terminate or modify a bargaining agreement, and the Federal Mediation and Conciliation Service (FMCS) must be given 60 days' notice. When notified, the FMCS is required to attempt to bring about an agreement, and all parties must participate fully and promptly in meetings called by the FMCS for the purpose of aiding settlement. If a strike is threatened, the FMCS can, under certain conditions, establish an impartial board of inquiry to investigate the issues and provide a cooling-off period of up to 30 days.

Strikes

Another special provision for health care institutions is a ten-day advance notice of intention to engage in concerted economic activities, including strikes, picketing, or any other concerted refusal to work. This provision is designed to allow a hospital to make plans for continuity of patient care in the face of work stoppage. Hospitals that use this opportunity to take "extraordinary steps" to stock up on ordinary supplies for an unduly extended period of time may, however, be engaging in an unfair labor practice that would permit the union to strike without notice or during the ten-day period.

Some courts have ruled that individual unorganized employees do not have to give a ten-day notice of work stoppage. In 1980 a federal appellate court ruled that two physicians who walked out of the hospital and joined the picket line of a lawful strike by other employees did not have to give the notice.[68] The court noted that the action was inconsiderate and ethically suspect, but protected.

In some circumstances, the "ally doctrine" allows a union to strike against a secondary employer not involved in original dispute. The strike is permitted when the secondary employer loses its neutrality by performing work during the course of the labor dispute that would have been performed by striking employees of the primary employer. The legislative history of the 1974 amendments modifies the "ally doctrine" by permitting a hospital to accept the critically ill patients of a struck hospital without losing its status as a neutral employer. In an advice memorandum issued by the NLRB in September 1977, a union was said to violate the act when it threatened to picket two neutral hospitals because they received critically ill patients and 46 pregnant women transferred from the struck hospital.[69]

Administering the Contract

After negotiating a labor agreement, the hospital and the labor organization should spend no less care on its administration. Managerial rights that have been established at the bargaining table, sometimes at a high price, can be eroded or entirely lost through inattention. The entire managerial team, especially first-line and second-line supervisors, should know the aspects of the contract applicable to their responsibilities. They must be trained to ensure that discipline is administered for the right reasons and by the appropriate procedures under the contract.

Reporting and Disclosure

The Labor-Management Reporting and Disclosure Act of 1959[70] places controls upon labor unions and the relationship between unions and their members. In addition, it requires employers to report payments and loans made to officials or other representatives of labor organizations. Payments to employees for the purpose of persuading them or causing them to persuade other employees to exercise or not to exercise their rights to organize and bargain collectively must also be reported. Many of these payments are illegal, and the reporting requirement does not make them legal. Expenditures to interfere with employee rights to organize and bargain collectively, as well as agreements with labor relations consultants under which such persons undertake to interfere with employee rights, must also be reported. Reports required under this law must be filed with the Secretary of Labor and are made public. Both nonprofit and for-profit hospitals making such payments or entering into such agreements must file the reports. Governmental hospitals are not subject to these provisions. There are substantial penalties for failure to make required reports or for making false reports.

STATE LAWS

State labor legislation is being increasingly preempted by federal programs; however, state laws still apply in at least two situations. First, if the federal law does not cover an area or activity, the state may regulate it. Second, if the courts have ruled that the state law does not conflict with the federal law on the same matter, the state law will be enforceable. Each existing state labor law will need to be examined for continuing application. Despite the broad sweep of the doctrine of federal preemption, states continue to possess the power to regulate labor relations activity that also falls within the jurisdiction of the NLRB where the regulated conduct touches interests deeply rooted in local feeling and responsibility. Thus, violence, threats of violence, mass picketing, and obstructing streets may be regulated by the states.

In some states, there are no labor relations statutes, but in others two types directly affect the rights of employees to organize and bargain collectively: (1) anti-injunction acts; and (2) laws regulating union security agreements. Other state labor legislation deals with equal employment opportunity, child labor, safety, worker's compensation, and unemployment compensation. Many states have laws concerning the relationship between public employees and governmental employers that apply to governmental hospitals.

Anti-Injunction Acts

The federal government and many states have enacted anti-injunction acts that establish special procedures and narrowly define the circumstances in which courts may issue injunctions concerning strikes, picketing, and related activities in labor disputes. The federal statute is the Norris-LaGuardia Act.[71] While some state statutes are similar to this federal act, others differ significantly. When valid state laws forbid strikes or lockouts, state anti-injunction statutes generally do not forbid injunctions to restrain violations of these statutes. However, federal law probably preempts most such state laws, except to the extent they apply to governmental employees and others not encompassed in the federal law. Anti-injunction acts generally apply to nonprofit hospitals.[72]

Union Security Contracts and Right To Work Laws

Labor organizations frequently seek to enter into union security contracts with employers. Such contracts are of two types: (1) the "closed shop" contract, which provides that only members of a particular union may be hired, and (2) the "union shop" contract, which makes continued employment dependent upon membership in the union, although the employee need not be a union member at the time of employment.

Many states have statutes making such contracts unlawful. These statutes are generally called "right to work" laws because employees may work without joining a union. Several other states have statutes or decisions that restrict union security contracts or provide for procedures to be completed before such agreements may be made. Some states permit forms of union security contracts if authorized by an employee election. Some states permit a union shop agreement but not a closed shop. State "right to work" laws are not preempted by the NLRA because section 14(b) of the NLRA explicitly authorizes them.

If such agreements are illegal in a state, any request for such a contract by a labor organization must be refused, and the hospital can obtain an injunction to stop a strike or picketing designed to induce the hospital to enter into a union security contract. In states that permit a union security contract, there is no legal obligation to enter into such a contract. It is one of the matters on which there may be bargaining.

Worker's Compensation

Every state has some form of worker's compensation legislation designed to assure that employees will be compensated for losses due to accidental on-the-job injuries. These acts replace the employee's common law remedy that required the employee to sue the employer for negligence, which was usually an unsuccessful process. Most employers are subject to the act, although some states provide exceptions. The majority of employers purchase worker's compensation insurance from an approved commercial insurance carrier, although self-insurance is an option. In cases not routinely paid by the insurance carrier, the matter will go to hearings before a state commission to determine questions of liability. State statutes define employee, injury, and other terms and have schedules of payment amounts for types of injuries. When the worker's compensation law applies, the employee is barred from suing the employer for the injury. Courts become involved only when there is an appeal concerning the decisions of the state official or agency administering the law.

Several issues are frequently litigated. One question is whether the injury occurred "out of and in the course of employment," a key phrase in qualifying for compensation. A related issue is whether the injury was caused by an "accident." Numerous exclusions are stated for preexisting or congenital physical conditions and injuries caused by horseplay or other causes not incidental to employment. Initially, an employee must give written notice of his or her injury to the employer. This report and the report of the medical treatment provided will ordinarily constitute the basis for compensation.

Usually an employee cannot receive compensation under worker's compensation laws (1) if the injury was caused by the intoxication of the injured worker; (2) if the injury was caused by the employee's willful intent to injure himself or another; or (3) in some states, if the injury was caused by the willful act of another directed against the employee for personal reasons.

Besides being an employer of persons eligible for worker's compensation benefits, the hospital will often be treating other employers' injured employees. The hospital will be relied upon to furnish information from the patient's medical records that is critical in determining eligibility and the amount of compensation. The issues concerning confidentiality and release of this information are discussed in Chapter 14.

Worker's compensation acts and other benefit programs under which injured workers may seek compensation are complex. Hospital administrators should be familiar with applicable state laws and seek appropriate consultation about matters relating to on-the-job employee injuries.

Unemployment Compensation

State law generally provides for payment of unemployment compensation to many unemployed individuals. Generally persons who have been discharged for misconduct forfeit all or part of the compensation they would have otherwise received. Thus, there is considerable litigation concerning what constitutes misconduct. For example, in 1981 the Pennsylvania Supreme Court found a nursing assistant guilty of misconduct for smoking in a patient's room contrary to hospital rules, so she was denied compensation.[73] In 1981 the Vermont Supreme Court ruled that a nurse who had been discharged for giving a patient medications by intravenous (IV) push instead of IV drip was entitled to unemployment compensation because her error had been in good faith.[74] In 1985 the Nebraska Supreme Court ruled that a change of hours from the 3:00 to 11:00 shift to the 11:00 to 7:00 shift was not good cause for a licensed practical nurse to resign, so she was not entitled to compensation.[75]

The amount of the employer's contribution to the state unemployment compensation fund often depends on the amount the state has paid to its former employees, so hospitals should be prepared to substantiate discharges for misconduct.

Public Employees

Since the NLRA does not apply to employees of state and local governmental agencies, the relations between these public employees and their governmental employers are controlled by state law. There is significant variation among the states. Some states prohibit collective bargaining by public employees, so that employees' rights are determined by state civil service laws and individual agency policies. Many states authorize representation by a labor organization and collective bargaining. A state agency similar to the NLRB is usually established to administer the law. State laws frequently limit the subjects that may be determined by collective bargaining, and they are different from the NLRA in other ways. Many states prohibit strikes by all or some public employees and require that an arbitration procedure be used to resolve impasses in bargaining.

NOTES

1. 29 U.S.C. §794 (1982).

2. *E.g.*, Lampe v. Presbyterian Medical Center, 590 P.2d 513 (Colo. Ct. App. 1978) [head nurse terminated for inability to follow staffing procedures and stay within budget].

3. *E.g.*, People ex rel. Miselis v. Health and Hosps. Governing Comm'n, 44 Ill. App. 3d 958, 3 Ill. Dec. 536, 358 N.E.2d 1221 (1976).

4. Heideck v. Kent General Hosp., 446 A.2d 1095 (Del. 1982) [dismissal for failure to heed patient's plea for privacy on bedside commode].

5. Falls v. Lawnwood Medical Center, 427 So.2d 361 (Fla. Ct. App. 1983) [alleged abuse of patient].

6. Cleveland Bd. of Ed. v. Loudermill, 105 S.Ct. 1487 (U.S. 1985).

7. Hebert v. Woman's Hosp. Found., 377 So.2d 1340 (La. Ct. App. 1979). However, if the oral contract is for a specified period of more than one year, instead of at-will, it will not be enforceable in most states because of the Statute of Frauds that requires such contracts to be in writing to be enforceable, 72 AM.JUR.2d *Statute of Frauds* (1974), *e.g.*, Santa Monica Hosp. v. Superior Court, 172 Cal. App. 3d 698, 218 Cal. Rptr. 543 (1985).

8. *E.g.*, Iowa Code Ann. §135C.46 (1985 Supp.) [reports by employees of health care facilities to the facility licensing agency].

9. Kelsay v. Motorola, Inc., 74 Ill. 2d 172, 23 Ill. Dec. 599, 384 N.E.2d 353 (1979); *contra* Meeks v. Opp Cotton Mills, Inc., 459 So.2d 814 (Ala. 1984).

10. Sides v. Duke Hosp., 72 N.C. App. 331, 328 S.E.2d 818 (1985).

11. Wheeler v. Caterpillar Tractor Co., 485 N.E.2d 372 (Ill. 1985).

12. Price v. Carmack Datsun, Inc., 485 N.E.2d 359 (Ill. 1985).

13. Hitt v. North Broward Hosp. Dist., 387 So.2d 482 (Fla. Dist. Ct. App. 1980) [private duty nurse put flyers concerning nursing group on public hospital bulletin board].

14. Rozier v. St. Mary's Hosp., 88 Ill. App. 3d 994, 44 Ill. Dec. 144, 411 N.E.2d 50 (1980); *see also* Maus v. National Living Centers, Inc., 633 S.W.2d 674 (Tex. Civ. App. 1982) [discharge of nurse's aide by nursing home for complaints to superiors concerning patient care].

15. NLRB v. J. Weingarten, Inc., 420 U.S. 251 (1975).

16. Prudential Ins. Co., 275 N.L.R.B. 30 (1985).

17. Sears Roebuck & Co., 274 N.L.R.B. 55 (1985). For a discussion of some of the issues concerning investigation and discipline of both union and nonunion employees, *see* Freeman & Freyer, *The Use of Polygraphs and Honesty Tests in the Workplace*, 1 TOPICS HOSP. LAW, Mar. 1986, at xxx; and Jacobs, *Discipline of Hospital Employees for Theft or Misappropriation of Hospital Property*, 1 TOPICS HOSP. LAW, Mar. 1986, at xxx.

18. *E.g.*, Gengler v. Phelps, 589 P.2d 1056 (N.M. Ct. App. 1978), *cert. denied*, 92 N.M. 353, 588 P.2d 554 (1979) [communication concerning nurse anesthetist].

19. 42 U.S.C. §§2000e–2000e-17 (1982).

20. Wrighten v. Metropolitan Hosp., Inc., 726 F.2d 1346 (9th Cir. 1984).

21. Backus v. Baptist Medical Center, 510 F. Supp. 1191 (E.D. Ark. 1981).

22. 671 F.2d 1100 (8th Cir. 1982).

23. Garcia v. Rush-Presbyterian Medical Center, 660 F.2d 1217 (7th Cir. 1981).

24. Hayes v. Shelby Memorial Hosp., 726 F.2d 1543 (11th Cir. 1984). Employer health plans that cover employees' spouses must cover pregnancy-related disabilities of spouses, Newport News Shipbuilding Co. v. EEOC, 462 U.S. 669 (1983).

25. 29 C.F.R. §1604.11 (1985).

26. Vinson v. Taylor, 753 F.2d 141 (D.C. Cir. 1985).

27. *E.g.*, Lemons v. City of Denver, 620 F.2d 228 (10th Cir. 1980); Briggs v. City of Madison, 536 F. Supp. 435 (W.D. Wis. 1982); American Nurses Ass'n v. Illinois, 606 F. Supp. 1313 (N.D. Ill. 1985).

28. A.F.S.C.M.E. v. Washington, 770 F.2d 1401 (9th Cir. 1985), *rev'g*, 578 F. Supp. 846 (W.D. Wash. 1983). The case was settled December 31, 1985 with the plaintiffs accepting prospective pay raises for some job classifications rather than appealing the court's decision, N.Y. Times, Jan. 2, 1986, at 7, col. 1; Feb. 10, 1986, at 10, col 6.

29. 29 U.S.C. §206(d) (1982).

30. Beall v. Curtis, 683 F. Supp. 1563 (M.D. Ga. 1985).

31. *E.g.*, Marshall v. Security Homes, 560 F.2d 12 (1st Cir. 1977) [no violation]; Brennan v. Prince Williams Hosp., 503 F.2d 282 (4th Cir. 1974) [violation].

32. 29 U.S.C. §§621–634 and 663(a) (1982), as amended by Pub. L. No. 98-369, 98 Stat. 1063 (1984) and Pub. L. No. 98-459, 98 Stat. 1792 (1984).

33. O'Donnell v. Georgia Osteopathic Hosp., Inc., 748 F.2d 1543 (11th Cir. 1984).

34. Ogden v. Bureau of Labor, 68 Or. App. 235, 682 P.2d 802 (1984), *aff'd*, 299 Or. 98, 699 P.2d 189 (1985).

35. Buckley v. Hospital Corp. of Am., 758 F.2d 1525 (11th Cir. 1985).

36. Runyon v. National Cash Register Corp., 759 F.2d 1253 (6th Cir. 1985).

37. 29 U.S.C. §§701–794 (1982), as amended by Pub. L. No. 98-221, 98 Stat. 17 (1984).

38. 29 U.S.C. §793 (1982).

39. 29 U.S.C. §794 (1982).

40. Consolidated Rail Corp. v. Darrone, 465 U.S. 624 (1984).

41. Baylor Univ. Medical Center v. United States, 736 F.2d 1039 (5th Cir. 1984), *cert. denied*, 105 S.Ct. 958 (U.S. 1985).

42. Arline v. School Bd., 772 F.2d 759 (11th Cir. 1985). Although there was no ruling as of Dec. 31, 1985, whether acquired immune deficiency syndrome (AIDS) was considered a handicap under the Act, there were a few rulings that it was a handicap under state nondiscrimination laws, e.g., Shuttleworth v. Broward County, No. 85-0624 (Fla. Comm. Human Relations, Dec. 11, 1985). For precautions for addressing hospital employees with AIDS or concerned about AIDS, *see* Stickler, *AIDS and the Hospital Employer*, 8 Health Law Vigil, Dec. 27, 1985, at 1.

43. Atascadero State Hosp. v. Scanlon, 105 S. Ct. 3142 (U.S. 1985).

44. 29 U.S.C. §§201–219 (1982).

45. Garcia v. San Antonio Metro. Transit Auth., 105 S.Ct. 1005 (U.S. 1985), *rev'g* National League of Cities v. Usery, 426 U.S. 833 (1976). The Fair Labor Standards Amendments of 1985, Pub. L. No. 99-150, 99 Stat. 787, mitigated the impact of *Garcia* by establishing some special rules and transitional provisions for public employers.

46. 29 U.S.C. §§1671–1677 (1982).

47. Pub. L. No. 93-406, 88 Stat. 829 (1974) (codified as amended in scattered sections of 5, 18, 26, 29, 31, and 42 U.S.C.); 29 C.F.R. pts. 2509 and 2601 (1985).

48. Metropolitan Life Ins. Co. v. Massachusetts, 105 S.Ct. 2380 (U.S. 1985).

49. United States v. Martorano, 767 F.2d 63 (3rd Cir. 1985).

50. Pub. L. No. 91-596, 84 Stat. 1590 (1970) (codified as amended in 29 U.S.C. §§651–678 and scattered sections of 5, 15, 29, 42, and 49 U.S.C.).

51. Marshall v. Barlow's, Inc., 436 U.S. 307 (1978).

52. 29 C.F.R. §1977.12(b)(2) (1985).

53. Whirlpool Corp. v. Marshall, 445 U.S.1 (1980).

54. 29 U.S.C. §§141–187 (1982).

55. Act of July 5, 1935, ch. 372, 49 Stat. 449.

56. Act of June 23, 1947, ch. 120, 61 Stat. 136.

57. Pub. L. No. 86-257, 73 Stat. 519 (1959).

58. 29 U.S.C. §§152(2), 158, and 169 (1982).

59. St. Elizabeth Community Hosp. v. NLRB, 708 F.2d 1436 (9th Cir. 1983); St. Elizabeth Hosp. v. NLRB, 715 F.2d 1193 (7th Cir. 1983).

60. Mercy Hosp. Ass'n, Inc., 235 N.L.R.B. 781 (1978).

61. Good Samaritan Hosp. and Health Center and Richey, 265 N.L.R.B. 92 (1982).

62. Rideout Memorial Hosp., 227 N.L.R.B. 1338 (1977).

63. Pattern Maker's League v. NLRB, 105 S.Ct. 3064 (U.S. 1985).

64. S. Rep. No. 93-766, 93rd Cong., 2d Sess. 5, *reprinted in* [1974] U.S. CODE CONG. & AD. NEWS 3946, 3950.

65. St. Francis Hosp. and Int'l Brotherhood of Electrical Workers, 271 N.L.R.B. 160 (Aug. 13, 1984). Direct versus indirect patient care is not a factor in this analysis, Health-Care Enters., 275 N.L.R.B. No. 194 (1985).

66. TRW Bearings, Div., 257 N.L.R.B. 442 (1981); *see also* One Way, Inc., 268 N.L.R.B. 61 (1983) [policy can refer to "worktime," but not to "work hours"].

67. NLRB v. Baptist Hosp., 442 U.S. 773 (1979).

68. Montefiore Hosp. and Medical Center v. NLRB, 621 F.2d 510 (2d Cir. 1980).

69. Memorandum from Dietz, Associate General Counsel, NLRB, to Siegel, Director, Region 31, September 2, 1977, concerning cases No. 31-CC-820, 821 and 31-CG-7, 8.

70. 29 U.S.C. §§401–531 (1982), as amended by Pub. L. No. 98-473, 98 Stat. 2133 (1984).

71. 29 U.S.C. §§101–111 (1982), as amended by Pub. L. No. 98-620, 98 Stat. 3359 (1984).

72. *E.g.*, District 1199E v. Johns Hopkins Hosp., 293 Md. 343, 444 A.2d 448 (1982).

73. Selan v. Unemployment Comp. Bd. of Rev., 495 Pa. 338, 433 A.2d 1337 (1981).

74. Porter v. Department of Employment Sec., 139 Vt. 405, 430 A.2d 450 (1981).

75. Montclair Nursing Center v. Wills, 371 N.W.2d 121 (Neb. 1985); *accord* Baptist Medical Center v. Stolte, 475 So.2d 959 (Fla. Dist. Ct. App. 1985) [nurse who refuses to accept offered 3:00–11:00 position is not "available for work" and, thus, ineligible for unemployment compensation].

Chapter 10

General Principles of Civil Liability

Everyone involved in the delivery of health care is acutely aware of the potential for patients or their families to make legal claims for money because of injuries they believed were caused by malpractice or other wrongful conduct. This chapter provides an outline of liability principles and the legal process. By developing a basic understanding of liability principles, hospitals and their staffs can help to minimize claims and to facilitate proper handling of claims that are made.

Civil liability is the liability imposed through mechanisms other than the criminal law. Civil liability can be divided into liability that is based on contract and liability that is not based on contract. The latter is called tort liability.

This chapter begins with an overview of contract law and then reviews tort law. The review of tort law includes (a) the three basic types of tort liability—strict liability, liability for intentional torts, and liability for negligent torts; (b) the basis for personal and institutional liability; and (c) the range of attempts to reform tort law.

Specific cases illustrating the tort liability of hospitals and various staff members are surveyed in Chapter 11.

CONTRACTS

A contract is a legally enforceable agreement. Hospitals have many contracts involving all areas of hospital operations, including employment contracts, contracts to purchase supplies and equipment, construction contracts, sales contracts, contracts to purchase services, leases, loans, and others. The primary purpose of a written contract is to set forth the agreement to facilitate compliance, not to prepare for litigation. It is essential that all elements of contracts be carefully thought through and clearly articu-

185

lated. This section outlines some of the legal problems associated with contracts, but the law of contracts is complex. Since there are exceptions to the general rules outlined, contracts should be reviewed with the assistance of legal counsel. Hospital administrators are expected to be sophisticated at business and will be bound by many disadvantageous contracts that might not be enforced for less sophisticated consumers.

Usually agreements to agree in the future are not enforceable. Generally, there is no contract until the agreement itself is reached.

Some agreements are not enforceable. In most situations, the courts require all participants in the agreement, usually called *parties,* to promise to do something or not to do something in order for a contract to exist. This promise is called the *consideration* for the contract. In some situations, when one party has not promised or provided any consideration, the courts will not enforce the contract, although this is unlikely in most written sales contracts because of state laws called the Uniform Commercial Code. The courts will not enforce many other contracts, such as illegal contracts, contracts that are viewed by the court as against public policy, oral contracts of the type the law requires to be written, and unconscionable contracts. Unconscionable contracts are contracts that shock the conscience of the courts, usually by being extortionate. Generally, courts apply the unconscionability doctrine only to consumer contracts, so it is doubtful that a hospital would be protected by the doctrine in the hospital's dealings with other businesses. However, some hospital contracts with patients, such as exculpatory contracts purporting to limit the patient's right to sue, could be found to be unconscionable and, thus, unenforceable.

In some situations, courts will refuse to enforce only a part of the agreement. For example, the courts will generally not enforce penalty provisions in contracts. Many contracts include a provision that, if a portion of the agreement is found invalid, the remainder is still enforceable. This provision can be disastrous when the invalid portion was actually considered to be of central importance.

Courts tend to limit their review of contracts to what is stated in the written contract by applying the "parol evidence rule," under which prior oral agreements merge in the written contract. Under this rule, an oral promise made during negotiations that is not included in the final written agreement is assumed to have been negotiated away. Thus, it is important not to rely on oral statements made prior to signing a written contract. If these statements are important to the agreement, they should be in the written contract.

In some circumstances, courts will amplify and add terms to contracts. First, when there is an ambiguity in a written contract or the contract is missing critical elements, courts will sometimes consider testimony concerning oral understandings. Courts try to avoid this, but sometimes oral understandings must be considered. The court then must sift through the usually conflicting recollections of the parties and decide what to believe. Second, sometimes it is clear that no agreement, written or oral, was reached concerning critical elements, such as a delivery date. A court will sometimes fill these gaps with a provision the court considers to be reasonable. However, courts will not always fill the gaps, which forces the parties to solve the problem on their own. Third, the law will routinely imply some elements in contracts if an issue is not otherwise addressed. For example, most states have passed laws called the Uniform Commercial Code that govern many sales. These statutes specify that certain contracts will be interpreted as having certain provisions unless the contract provides otherwise. For example, one provision is an implied warranty of merchantability, which means that the goods are fit for the ordinary purposes for which such goods are normally used. Another provision is an implied warranty of fitness for a particular use; meaning that the goods are fit for the specific use the seller has reason to know the buyer intends for the goods. There are many exceptions to these warranties. One of the clearest is when the contract explicitly disclaims the warranties. Not all of the implied elements are stated in statutes. The courts will sometimes imply additional elements, for example, that the person signing the contract has the authority to do so. Administrators should be very cautious about making promises or concessions, especially in writing. They should also carefully instruct other employees not to sign documents without proper authority and review.

The purpose of the contract is to document planning for completion of the agreement and for dealing with contingencies that preclude completion. As a last resort, litigation can be required to deal with breach of contract. The courts will compel performance of some contracts, such as contracts to transfer land or unique goods. Courts will also sometimes issue an injunction prohibiting another party from violating a restrictive covenant, such as an agreement not to compete or not to disclose a trade secret. However, in most situations, the only remedy the court will award is money, called *damages*. When it will be difficult to calculate the damages from breach of a contract, the parties sometimes agree in advance what the amount of damages will be, and this agreed amount is called *liquidated damages*. Although courts will usually not enforce contract provisions that are considered penalties, courts will frequently enforce liquidated damages provisions when the amounts are reasonable.

Contracts can address other issues concerning dispute resolution. They can specify which state's law will govern the contract and where litigation can be brought. Some contracts specify that disputes will be resolved by arbitration rather than court litigation.

There are several defenses to contract suits, including waiver and default. Sometimes courts interpret conduct of the parties, such as regular acceptance of late delivery without complaint, to imply a modification to the agreement, waiving rights under the agreement. The defense of default arises from the recognition that some promises are dependent on others and that some events must occur in a sequence. If one party fails to perform an earlier step in the sequence, it can be found to be in default, excusing the other parties from carrying out subsequent steps. Vendors sometimes claim that their delay is due to failure of the hospital to provide needed data or material. Sequences should be carefully structured, so this defense is available only when it is appropriate.

Promise To Cure or To Use a Certain Procedure

Most malpractice suits against physicians and hospitals are based on tort law, not on contract law. One type of malpractice case based on contract law is the claim that the physician promised a certain outcome that was not achieved. Absent a specific promise to cure, a physician is not a insurer of a particular outcome. However, if the physician is incautious enough to make a promise, the law will sometimes enforce it. One of the most publicized cases was *Guilmet v. Campbell*,[1] in which the Michigan Supreme Court upheld a jury finding that a physician had promised to cure a bleeding ulcer and on that basis imposed liability for the unsuccessful outcome even though the physician was not negligent in providing the care. The Michigan legislature later passed a law[2] making promises to cure unenforceable unless they are in writing, in effect overruling *Guilmet*.

Another type of breach of contract suit arises from the failure to use a promised procedure. In a 1957 Michigan case the patient had been promised that her child would be delivered by a Caesarean operation.[3] The physician failed to arrange for a Caesarean operation, and the baby was stillborn. The court upheld the jury's finding that the physician had breached his promise to arrange for a Caesarean operation.

These cases based on oral promises are unusual, but they demonstrate that physicians and hospital staff should be careful in what they say to patients so that their efforts to reassure do not become promises they cannot fulfill.

GENERAL PRINCIPLES OF TORT LIABILITY

A tort is a civil wrong that is not based on a violation of contract. Tort liability almost always is based on fault; that is, something was done incorrectly or something that should have been done was omitted. This act or omission can be intentional or can result from negligence. In some exceptional circumstances, there is strict liability for all consequences of certain activities regardless of fault.

Intentional Torts

Intentional torts include assault and battery, defamation, false imprisonment, invasion of privacy, intentional infliction of emotional distress, malicious prosecution, and abuse of process.

Assault and Battery

An *assault* is an action that puts another person in apprehension of being touched in a manner that is offensive, insulting, provoking, or physically injurious without lawful authority or consent. No actual touching is required; the assault is simply the credible threat of being touched in this manner. If actual touching occurs, then it is called *battery*. Liability for assault and battery compensates persons for violations of their right to be free from unconsented invasions of their person. Assault or battery can occur when medical treatment is attempted or performed without lawful authority or consent. Assault or battery can occur in other circumstances, such as in attempts to restrain patients who are competent and oriented without lawful authority.

Defamation

Defamation is wrongful injury to another person's reputation. Written defamation is called *libel*, and spoken defamation is called *slander*. The statement must be communicated to a third person; it is not defamation to make a statement only to the person whose reputation is impugned. A claim of defamation can arise from inappropriate release of inaccurate medical information or from untruthful statements about other members of the staff.

The two defenses to a claim of defamation are truth and privilege. A true statement is not defamatory even if it injures another's reputation. Some communications, although otherwise defamatory, are privileged because the law recognizes a higher duty to disclose the particular information to certain persons. Courts have recognized the importance of communications concerning a staff member's performance to supervisory staff and up through the organizational structure. Such communications are protected by a "qualified privilege" when they are made in good faith to the persons who need to know. This protection means the liability will not be imposed for defamation even if the communication is false as long as it was made without malice. For example, in 1979 a federal court found that a nurse's report to a supervisor concerning a disagreement over a physician order was protected by a qualified privilege.[4] The communication must be made within appropriate channels because discussions with others will not be protected by the qualified privilege.

Many courts have also recognized a qualified privilege for assessments provided by a former employer to a prospective employer. For example, in 1979 a Michigan court found the director of a department of health that had employed a nurse not liable for providing a prospective employer with information concerning the nurse's abilities.[5] The court ruled that the qualified privilege applied, and no malice had been shown. Most institutions do not release information regarding any former employee until they receive a written request signed by the former employee, so they do not need to rely on the court to decide that the qualified privilege applies. There still could be liability for untruthful information released with malice.

False Imprisonment

False imprisonment is the unlawful restriction of a person's freedom. Holding a person against his or her will by physical restraint, barriers, or even threats of harm can constitute false imprisonment if not legally justified. Claims of false imprisonment can arise from patients being detained inappropriately in hospitals or from patients challenging their commitments for being mentally ill. Hospitals do have the common law authority to detain patients who are disoriented. All states have a legal procedure to obtain authorization to detain some categories of persons who are mentally ill, are substance abusers, or have contagious diseases. When a patient is oriented, competent, and not legally committed, staff should avoid detaining the patient unless authorized by hospital policy or by a hospital administrator. There are few situations in which hospitals are justified in authorizing detention of such patients.

Invasion of Privacy

Claims for invasion of privacy can arise from unauthorized release of information concerning patients. However, not all releases of information violate the right of privacy. For example, in 1982 the Minnesota Supreme Court found that, even though the patient had requested that information not be released, it was not an invasion of privacy to disclose orally that the patient had been discharged from the hospital and that she had given birth, as long as the information was disclosed in response to a direct inquiry concerning that patient at a time near her stay in the hospital.[6] However, state law and regulations in some states may not permit this disclosure. The better practice would be to attempt to avoid release of discharge and birth information when the patient requests nondisclosure.

Sometimes information, such as a child abuse or contagious disease report, is required to be disclosed by law. These disclosures (discussed in Chapter 14) are not an invasion of privacy because they are legally authorized.

Institutional policies concerning confidentiality should be followed; some courts will impose liability for failure to follow institutional rules. One exception to the general rule permitting disclosure of admission and discharge information concerns information about substance abusers. Federal regulations[7] prohibit disclosure of information concerning patients being treated for substance abuse or related conditions unless one of the exceptions in the regulations applies. This prohibition extends to disclosing whether or not the patient is in the institution. Staff who are involved with substance abusers should be familiar with these regulations and know how to comply with them. They are discussed in more detail in Chapter 14.

Intentional Infliction of Emotional Distress

Intentional infliction of emotional distress is another intentional tort that includes outrageous conduct causing emotional trauma. This tort is easy to avoid by remembering to treat patients and their families in a civilized fashion but such treatment was apparently forgotten in the following two examples involving actions after the death of patients.

A 1975 Tennessee case concerned a mother who sought the body of her baby, who had died in the hospital.[8] A hospital staff member gave the body to her preserved in a jar of formaldehyde. The second example is a 1973 Ohio case that dealt with communications after death.[9] A woman died, and a month later her family physician's office sent a notice for her to come in for a periodic checkup. The court said that this first reminder was an excusable error. The husband sent the doctor a letter explaining she had died. The husband later sued the physician for malpractice in her death. After the suit was filed, the doctor's office sent two more reminders for the dead woman to come in for a checkup, one of which was addressed to the youngest daughter of the deceased. The court said that the second and third reminders could be the basis for liability.

Malicious Prosecution and Abuse of Process

Some unjustifiable or harassing litigation and other misuses of the legal system are intentional torts called *malicious prosecution* and *abuse of process*. The plaintiff alleging malicious prosecution must prove that (1) the other person filed a suit against the plaintiff; (2) the suit ended in favor of the plaintiff; (3) there was no probable cause for filing the suit; and (4) the other person filed the suit because of malice.

Some physicians who have successfully defended malpractice suits have in turn sued the patient and the patient's attorney for malicious prosecution. Generally, public policy favors giving people an opportunity to present their cases to the courts for redress of wrongs, so the law protects them when they act in good faith upon reasonable grounds in commencing either a civil or criminal suit. Thus, few countersuits have been successful.[10]

Negligent Torts

The most frequent basis for liability of health professionals and hospitals is the negligent tort. Fortunately, negligence by itself is not enough to establish liability. An injury caused by the negligence must also occur. Four elements must be proved to establish liability for negligent torts: (1) duty (what should have been done); (2) breach of duty (deviation from what should have been done); (3) injury; and (4) causation (the injury was the direct and legal cause of the deviation from what should have been done).

There is a "fifth element" that the courts do not discuss, but that hospitals and their staffs should remember: someone must be willing to make a claim. Health care providers who maintain good relations with their patients before and after incidents are less likely to be sued. If a hospital staff member suspects that an incident has occurred, the persons responsible for risk management in the institution should be notified promptly so steps can be taken to minimize the chance of a claim.

Duty

If a claim is made, the first element that must be proved in any negligence suit is the duty. Duty has two aspects. First, it must be proved that a duty was owed to the person harmed. Second, the scope of that duty, sometimes called the standard of care, must be proved.

In general, the common law does not impose a duty on individuals to come to the rescue of persons for whom they have no other responsibility. Under the common law rule, a person walking down the street has no legal obligation to come to the aid of a heart attack victim, unless (1) the victim is the person's dependent; (2) the person contributed to the cause of the heart attack; (3) the person owns or operates the premises where the attack occurred; or (4) the person has a contractual obligation to come to the victims aid—for example, by being on duty as a member of a public emergency care team. In most situations involving potential hospital liability, it is not difficult to establish a duty based on the admission of the patient to the hospital. Sometimes a question may arise concerning whether there was a duty to a patient who sought care but was not admitted. This issue is discussed in Chapter 12.

After the existence of a duty is established, the second aspect, the scope of the duty, must be established. This aspect is sometimes called the obligation to conform to the standard of care. The standard of care for hospitals is usually the degree of reasonable care the patient's known or apparent condition requires. Some states extend the standard to include the reasonable care required for conditions the hospital should have discovered through exercise of reasonable care. Usually, the standard for individual health care professionals is what a reasonably prudent health care professional engaged in a similar practice would have done under similar circumstances. A judge or jury will make the determination based on one or more of the following: (1) expert testimony; (2) common sense; or (3) published standards.

Expert Testimony. The technical aspects of care must be proved through expert testimony, usually by other health professionals. Sometimes the health care provider's out-of-court statements can be used against the provider as an admission, so care must be taken in what is said or written after an incident.

Common Sense. Nontechnical aspects of care can be proved by nonexperts. Some courts will permit juries to use their own knowledge and common sense when duty is considered common knowledge. For example, many courts consider one of the nontechnical aspects to be how a disoriented patient should be protected from falling out of bed.

Published Standards. Some courts will look to published standards, such as licensure regulations, accreditation standards, and institutional rules to determine the duty. Courts have permitted published standards to be used in two ways. In many cases, published standards are used in place of expert testimony, so the jury may consider them along with all other evidence to determine the standard of care. In other cases, published standards are presumed to establish the standard of care unless the defendant can prove otherwise.

Statutes or governmental regulations can be used to establish the standard of care when the plaintiff is a member of the class of people that the statute or regulation is intended to protect and the injury is of the general type that it is intended to prevent. For example, a Maryland court found a hospital liable for injuries that resulted from failure to comply with a hospital licensing regulation requiring segregation of sterile and nonsterile needles.[11] The patient had a liver biopsy with a needle that was suspected to be nonsterile, requiring postponement of other therapy and requiring immediate treatment with a series of painful gamma globulin injections to prevent infection from the needle. This clearly was the type of patient and harm the regulation was designed to address.

Accreditation standards have been used to establish the standard of care for accredited hospitals. For example, a Texas court found a hospital liable for injuries due to failure to employ a licensed pharmacist. JCAH standards that required a licensed pharmacist were used to establish the standard of care.[12]

Hospital rules and policies can also be used to establish the standard of care. For example, in 1975 the highest court of New York ruled that the hospital could be liable for injuries due to failure to raise the patient's bedrails when the hospital had a rule requiring bedrails to be raised for all patients over the age of 50.[13] Thus, it is important for staff members to be familiar with and act in compliance with the rules and policies of the hospital applicable to their areas of practice. If the rules are impossible to follow, steps should be taken to modify them instead of ignoring them.

Eliminating all rules is not a solution because failure to adopt necessary rules can be a violation of the standard of care for hospitals. In Michigan, a hospital was found liable for an infection transmitted by a transplanted cornea because it did not have a procedure to assure that the relevant medical records of the proposed donor were reviewed prior to the transplant.[14]

Respected Minority Rule. The proof of duty can become confused when there are two or more accepted approaches to a situation. The courts have attempted to resolve this through the "respected minority" or "two schools of thought" rule. If a health professional follows the approach used by a respected minority of the profession, then the duty is to follow that approach properly. The courts will not permit liability to be based simply on the decision not to follow the majority approach.[15] However, since part of the informed consent process is the disclosure of alternative treatments, it is important for the physician to disclose the alternative treatment to the patient before pursuing a minority approach. Failure to disclose the alternative approach followed by the majority could result in liability under the informed consent doctrine discussed in Chapter 13.

Locality Rule. In the past, some courts limited the standard of care of hospitals and health professionals to the practice in the same or similar communities. This was called the locality rule. Experts testifying on the standard of care had to be from the same or similar communities. This rule was designed to avoid finding rural hospitals and physicians liable for not following the practices of urban medical centers. In practice, the rule made it difficult to obtain expert testimony. The rule has been abandoned in nearly every state, so that experts from anywhere generally can testify if they are familiar with the relevant standard of care. In most states, the features of the locality are now just one of the circumstances that the jury considers in determining the standard of care.

Legally Imposed Standards. Courts occasionally will impose a new duty not previously recognized by the profession. A court may find the whole profession to be lagging in its standards, so it imposes a more stringent legal standard. For example, in 1974 the Washington Supreme Court established a legal standard that glaucoma tests must be given to all ophthalmology patients, although the universal practice of ophthalmologists was to administer such tests only to patients over age 40 and to patients with possible symptoms of glaucoma.[16] The court disregarded the evidence that so few cases would be discovered that expanded testing would not be cost effective. The court found the ophthalmologist liable for failing to administer the test to a patient under age 40 with no symptoms of glaucoma. In another case, after a woman was killed by a psychiatric patient, the California Supreme Court found liability for the psychiatrist's failure to warn the woman that his patient had threatened to kill her, even though other psychiatrists would have acted in the same manner.[17]

One of the most famous cases imposing a higher legal standard on hospitals is *Gonzales v. Nork*.[18] In this case, the hospital's system of peer review of physicians met all of the JCAH standards in effect at the time the patient was injured, but the California trial court found the hospital liable for injuries resulting from treatment provided by an independent staff physician because the hospital had failed to make use of available information that would have alerted it to Dr. Nork's propensity to commit malpractice. The court ruled that the hospital should have had a better system of becoming aware of available information and acting on it.

In Chapter 11, specific examples of duties of hospitals and individual staff members are discussed.

Breach of Duty

After the duty is proved, the second element that must be proved is the breach of this duty, that is, a deviation in some manner from the standard of care. Something was done that should not have been done or something was not done that should have been done.

Injury

The third element of the proof of negligence is injury. The person making the claim must demonstrate physical, financial, or emotional injury. In many malpractice cases, the existence of the injury is very clear by the time of the suit, although there still may be disagreement concerning the dollar value of the injuries.

With few exceptions, most courts will not allow suits based solely on negligently inflicted emotional injuries. Generally, they are compensated only when they accompany physical injuries. Intentional infliction of emotional injury is compensated without proof of physical injury. In some states, negligently inflicted emotional injuries are compensable without accompanying physical injuries in a few circumstances.

The most widely accepted circumstance is when the plaintiff was in the "zone of danger" created by the defendant's negligence; that is, when the plaintiff has actually been exposed to the risk of injury. A few states have extended this to when the plaintiff is not in the zone of danger but witnesses injury to a close relative. A California court permitted a father to sue for his emotional injuries from being present in the delivery room when his wife died, and placing his hands on her body after her death and feeling the unborn child die.[19] There is a trend toward compensating more negligently inflicted emotional injuries without requiring physical injury.

Causation

The fourth element is causation. The breach of duty must be proved to have legally caused the injury. For example, a treatment may be negligently administered (which is a breach of duty) and the patient may die (which is an injury), but the person suing must still prove a substantial likelihood that the patient would have lived if the treatment had been administered properly. Causation is often the most difficult element to prove.

Another example is a Texas case concerning a nurse who gave a patient solid food immediately after colon surgery (which is a breach of duty), and eight days later the ends of the sutured colon came apart (which is an injury).[20] Because of the time lag, the patient was not able to prove causation. Causation can be proved in many cases, as illustrated by an Iowa case involving a baby born with Rh blood incompatibility.[21] An outdated reagent was used for the tests of the bilirubin in the baby's blood, so the tests erroneously indicated a safe level. By the time the error was discovered, the baby had suffered severe permanent brain damage caused by the high bilirubin level in his blood. The hospital and the pathologists were liable because accurate tests would have led to timely therapy that probably would have prevented the brain damage.

Res Ipsa Loquitur

There is a major exception to the requirement that the four elements be proved. This is the doctrine of *res ipsa loquitur,* "the thing speaks for itself." In England, in the nineteenth century, a case arose from a barrel flying out of an upper story window and smashing into a pedestrian.[22] When the pedestrian tried to sue the owner of the building, the owner claimed that the four elements had to be proved. Of course, the person suing could not find out the specifics of what went wrong in the upper story room, so the case would have been lost. However, the court said the owner could not take advantage of the rules to escape liability in cases when someone clearly had done something wrong. Therefore, the court developed the *res ipsa loquitur* doctrine.

The courts have said all that must be proved is that (1) the accident is of a kind that does not happen without negligence; (2) the apparent cause is in the exclusive control of the defendants; (3) the person suing could not have contributed to the difficulties; (4) evidence of the true cause is inaccessible to the person suing; and (5) the fact of injury is evident.

Courts have frequently applied this rule to two types of malpractice cases: (1) sponges and other foreign objects unintentionally left in the body;[23] and (2) injuries to parts of the body distant from the site of treatment, such as nerve damage to a hand during a hysterectomy.[24] Some courts have extended the applicability of the rule to some other types of malpractice cases.[25]

Liability is not automatic in *res ipsa loquitur* cases. The persons being sued may attempt to explain why the injury was not the result of negligence. This can be successfully explained in some circumstances. For example, a physician could establish the absence of negligence by proving the sponge was left in the body because the patient had to be closed quickly on an emergency basis to save the patient's life and there was no time for a sponge count. The evidence necessary to avoid liability varies among states because of variation in the degree to which the burden of proof shifts to the defendant in *res ipsa loquitur* cases.

Defenses

Several defenses are sometimes available. One defense is the statute of limitations, which specifies the time period in which suits must be filed. Suits are barred after the time period has expired. The time period varies depending on the nature of the suit and the applicable state law. States have adopted different definitions of when the time period starts, including (1) the time of the incident; (2) the time the injury is discovered; (3) the time the cause of the injury is or should have been discovered; and (4) the time the patient ceases receiving care from the negligent provider.

The rules are complicated in many states. The time limit can be quite long, especially for injuries to children. In many states, minors may sue up to one year after becoming adults.[26] This means that suits arising out of care of newborns may be filed nearly 19 years later. Since few people have memories that long, it is important to document the care given to patients thoroughly. The records will be the only way to prove what was done. Judges and jurors may assume that if something is not written down, it was not done.

Another defense is release. As part of the process of settling a claim, the claimant is usually asked to sign a release of all future claims arising from the same incident. In most cases, if such a release has been signed, it will bar a future suit based on the same incident. An exculpatory contract is different from a release because it is signed before the care is provided and generally will not be a successful defense. Some providers have asked patients to sign an exculpatory contract agreeing not to sue or agreeing to limit the amount of the suit, but courts have refused to enforce these contracts on the grounds that they are against public policy.[27] However, in some states, a patient can sign a valid agreement to arbitrate any claims instead of taking them to court, as long as the agreement does not place other limits on the claim. If a patient has signed a valid agreement to arbitrate, courts will refuse to accept the case except for limited review of the completed arbitration process.

Contributory negligence is a defense to a claim of a negligent tort in some states. Contributory negligence occurs when the patient does something wrong that contributes so much to the injury that the health care provider is not responsible for the damage. Examples of contributory negligence include (1) the patient fails to follow clear orders and does not return for followup;[28] (2) the patient walks on a broken leg;[29] (3) the patient gets out of bed and falls;[30] (4) the patient lights a cigarette in bed when unattended;[31] or (5) the patient deliberately gives false information that leads to the wrong antidote being given for a drug overdose.[32] The success of this defense depends on the intelligence and degree of orientation of the patient. A patient who does not appear able to follow orders cannot be relied on to follow orders, so contributory negligence is not a successful defense against a claim by such a patient.

A majority of the states have abandoned the all-or-nothing contributory negligence rule. Instead, they apply comparative negligence, which means that the percentage of the cause due to the patient is determined and the patient does not collect that percentage of the total amount of the injury. Some states that have adopted the comparative negligence rule have retained one feature of the contributory negligence rule, so the patient cannot collect anything if the patient is determined to be responsible for 50 percent or more of the cause.[33]

Breach of Implied Warranties and Strict Liability

The major exception to the requirement that liability be based on fault occurs when liability is based on breach of implied warranties or on strict liability in tort. In this area of the law, liability based on contract and liability based on tort overlap. The implied warranties of merchantability and fitness for a particular use are based on contract and are discussed in the section of this chapter on contracts. These warranties form the basis for finding liability without fault for many of the injuries caused by use of goods and products. Normally, the seller is liable for the breach of the warranties, but in some situations persons who lease products to others have also been found liable.

Strict liability applies to injuries caused by the use of a product that is unreasonably dangerous to a consumer or user and that reaches the user without substantial change from the condition in which it was sold. Usually it is the manufacturer or seller of the product who is liable. Strict liability in tort does not require a contractual relationship between the seller and the person injured to establish the liability of the seller. Some courts have extended strict liability to persons who furnish goods or products without a sale.

Hospitals are generally considered to be providing services, not selling or furnishing products, so hospitals have seldom been found liable for breach of warranties or strict liability. However, plaintiffs have made numerous efforts to convince courts to apply these principles to make it easier to establish liability. These efforts have been based on services involving blood transfusions, drugs, radiation, and medical devices.

Blood Transfusions

One of the known risks of blood transfusions is the transmission of diseases such as serum hepatitis. In 1954 the New York courts ruled that blood transfusions were a service, not a sale, so that hospital liability could not be based on breach of warranty or strict liability.[34] However, in the late 1960s and early 1970s, courts in several other states began applying these product liability principles to blood transfusions.[35] Legislatures in nearly all states enacted statutes intended to reverse these court decisions.[36] Some of the statutes state that providing blood is a service, not a sale. Other statutes expressly forbid liability based on implied warranty or strict liability. The second type of statute provides somewhat more protection because a court that chose to ignore the public policy decisions of the legislature embodied in the first type of statute could still impose liability on the hospital by extending the applicability of strict liability to services. These immunity statutes have been found constitutional.[37] Of course, the hospital can still be liable for negligence in administering the blood transfusions. The immunity statutes in many states also apply to some other services, such as tissue transplantation.

Drugs

Efforts to use implied warranties or strict liability to impose liability on hospitals for administration of drugs have generally been unsuccessful. For example, a Texas appellate court refused to apply these product liability principles to the administration of a contaminated drug.[38]

Radiation

In 1979 the Illinois Supreme Court reversed a lower court's application of strict liability principles to X-ray treatment.[39] The court ruled that the issue in the case was the decision to use a certain dosage. The X-rays themselves were not a defective product, so strict liability in tort was not applicable.

Medical Devices

Most courts have not applied implied warranties or strict liability in tort to hospitals for injuries due to medical devices. For example, a California court ruled that the hospital was the user, not the supplier, of a surgical needle that broke during an operation.[40] However, this position is not unanimous. In 1984 the Alabama Supreme Court adopted the position that the hospital was liable based on the implied warranty of fitness for intended use when a suturing needle broke and remained in a patient's body.[41] The court viewed the hospital as a merchant, not a user. Even when the hospital is viewed as only a user, the hospital may still be liable based on negligence, and the manufacturer of the equipment may be liable based on implied warranties or strict liability in tort.

WHO IS LIABLE?

Liability can be divided into personal liability, liability for employees and agents, and institutional liability. Individual staff members are personally liable for the consequences of their own acts. Individual liability is nearly always based on the principle of fault. To be liable, the person must have done something wrong or must have failed to do something he or she should have done. Employers can be liable for the consequences of the job-related acts of their employees or agents even if the employer is not at fault personally. Institutions can also be liable for the consequences of breaches of duties owed directly to the patient and others, such as the maintenance of buildings and grounds, maintenance of equipment, and selection and supervision of employees and medical staff.

Respondeat Superior

Employers can be liable for the consequences of their employees' job-related acts whether or not the employer is at fault. This legal doctrine is called *respondeat superior,* which means "let the master answer." Under this doctrine, the employer can be liable for the consequences of employee activities within the course of employment for which the employee could be liable. The employer need not have done anything wrong. Thus, for example, if a nurse employed by a hospital injures a patient by giving the wrong medication, the hospital can be liable even if the nurse was properly selected, properly trained, and properly assigned the responsibility.

The supervisor is not the employer. Since the supervisor is an employee, *respondeat superior* does not impose liability on the supervisor. Supervisors are liable only for the consequences of their own acts or omissions. Of course, the employer can also be liable for those acts or omissions under *respondeat superior.*

The liability of the employer under *respondeat superior* is for the benefit of the injured person, not for the benefit of the employee. The employer's liability does not mean that the employee must be provided with liability protection. It means that the person who is injured can sue the employer, the employee, or both. If the employee is individually sued and found liable, the employee must pay. If, as usually occurs, the employee is not individually sued, then the employer must pay. Technically, the employer can sue the employee to get the money back. The repayment is called *indemnification.* Indemnification is almost never sought because of the negative effects on future recruiting efforts.

Many employers provide individual liability protection for their employees. Some governmental employers are required to provide employees with liability protection for acts committed in the scope of employment and are prohibited from suing employees to get the money back. This does not mean that the employer must buy commercial insurance. Many employers choose to provide liability protection through self-insurance. Before deciding what additional protection, if any, to obtain, an employee should determine the coverage provided by the employer. Most employers who provide liability protection cover only job-related activities, so some employees elect to purchase coverage for outside activities not covered by institutional insurance arrangements.

Borrowed Servant and Dual Servant

In some situations, hospitals may not be liable for the consequences of negligent acts of nurses and other employees because of the "borrowed servant" doctrine. In some states, when the hospital delegates its right to direct and control the activities of an employee to an independent staff physician who assumes responsibility, the employee becomes a borrowed servant. The physician, rather than the hospital, is then liable under *respondeat superior* for the acts of the employee. Courts in many states do not apply the doctrine when an employee continues to receive substantial direction from the hospital through its policies and rules. Thus, the trend appears to be toward abandoning the "borrowed servant" doctrine or replacing it with a dual servant doctrine under which both the physician and the hospital are liable under *respondeat superior* for the acts of the employee.[42]

Physician-Employees

Usually hospitals are not liable for the negligent acts of independent staff physicians.[43] When the physician is an employee of the hospital, the hospital can be liable under *respondeat superior* for the acts of the physicians in the course of employment. The trend is for courts to find more hospital-physician relationships to be employment relationships. The criteria for finding an employment relationship focus on whether the hospital has a right to control the time, manner, and method of the physician's work. Some courts require significant control to find an employment relationship. For example, a Georgia appellate court declined to find an emergency room physician to be an employee despite scheduling, billing, and other control features of the agreement between the physician and hospital.[44] The court focused on the contract provision that the hospital would exercise no control over the physician's methods of running the emergency room. However, other courts are more liberal in applying the criteria. For example, an Arizona court found the hospital to be the employer of a nonsalaried radiologist based on the hospital's legal right to control the professional performance of medical staff members, the exclusiveness of the contract, the hospital's role as billing agent, and the patient's lack of choice in selecting a radiologist.[45] The court declined to be bound by a statement on the hospital admission form, signed by the patient, acknowledging that the radiologist was an independent contractor and not a hospital employee.

Even when the courts find the physician not to be an employee, they may still find the hospital liable for the physician's acts on the basis of agency, apparent agency, or enterprise liability.

Agency

Hospitals can be liable for the consequences of the acts of their agents in a fashion similar to their liability for acts of their employees. For example, a federal court found a hospital liable for a radiologist's negligence in failing to relay promptly the results of an X-ray examination to the treating physician.[46] The court ruled that prompt reporting was an administrative responsibility and that the physician was functioning as an agent of the hospital when relaying the report.

Apparent or Ostensible Agency

Some courts refuse to examine the details of the relationship between the physician and the hospital. They rely instead on how the relationship appears to the patient. If the hospital appears to be offering particular physician services, the doctrine of apparent or ostensible agency is applied to find the hospital liable. For example, the Michigan Supreme Court found a physician to be the ostensible agent of a hospital because the patient did not have a patient-physician relationship with the physician independent of the hospital setting.[47] The physician, who was simply a member of the medical staff, had assisted in the patient's treatment. The court ruled that there was sufficient evidence that the hospital had appeared to provide the physician for the patient. The court noted that there was no evidence that the patient had been given any notice that the physician was an independent contractor. Thus, hospitals may find it helpful to give patients notice. However, even signed acknowledgments may not be sufficient in some states.[48]

Institutional Liability

Institutions can be liable for the consequences of breaches of duties owed directly to the patient. Two examples of these duties—the maintenance of building and grounds and the selection and maintenance of equipment—are discussed in Chapter 11. Proper selection and supervision of employees is a third duty, discussed in Chapters 8 and 9. Proper selection and monitoring of medical staff are increasingly being recognized as an institution's duty. They are discussed in Chapters 7 and 8.

In 1978 a Washington appellate court imposed another form of institutional liability. It found a hospital liable for the treatment provided in an emergency room by an independent professional corporation because the emergency services were an inherent function of the hospital's overall enterprise for which the hospital bears some responsibility.[49] Liability was not based on *respondeat superior,* ostensible agency, negligent selection, or negligent monitoring of the medical staff.

TORT REFORM

In the mid-1970s, the cumulative effect of the increasing number of malpractice cases and the increasing cost of individual cases led to a rapid increase in the cost of malpractice insurance and, in some areas of the country, reduced availability of malpractice insurance at any price. The malpractice insurance crisis led nearly every state to review and revise its laws concerning tort suits. Although some of these changes affected the situation in some states, in most states they were not a solution. The malpractice insurance problem recurred in the mid-1980's, leading to another round of efforts to reform the tort laws.

These tort reforms can be grouped into (1) changes in dispute resolution mechanisms; (2) changes in the amount of the award and how it is paid; (3) changes in the time in which the suit must be brought; and (4) other changes. These tort reforms have received a mixed reception in the courts. Courts have disagreed on whether they violate various state and federal constitutional provisions.

Dispute Resolution Mechanisms

The two primary changes in the mechanism for dispute resolution have been the introduction of screening panels and the authorization of binding agreements to arbitrate disputes.

Screening Panels

Several states have enacted laws that require all malpractice claims to be screened by a panel before a suit can be filed. These screening panels are designed to promote settlement of meritorious claims and abandonment of frivolous claims.

A few courts have held the panels unconstitutional as an infringement of state constitutional rights to access to the courts.[50] The Florida Supreme Court declared the state's medical mediation requirement unconstitutional on the ground that it violated due process by being arbitrary and capricious in operation because of its 10-month limitation on the mediation process.[51] The process was not completed for more than half of the cases because there was no procedure to extend the time limit, so the court ruled the law unconstitutional in its entirety.

Most courts have upheld the required use of screening panels, since the plaintiffs still have the right to sue after the screening process is completed.[52] However, state courts vary in how broadly they interpret the scope of cases subject to screening.[53] The federal courts require plaintiffs to complete any state-required screening process before pursuing a state malpractice claim in federal court.[54]

Arbitration

Several states authorize binding agreements to arbitrate future malpractice disputes. In many states, agreements to arbitrate were not valid unless signed after the dispute arose, so changes in the law were necessary to make agreements signed before the dispute enforceable. When there is a valid agreement to arbitrate, the dispute is submitted to an arbitrator who decides whether any payment should be made and, if so, how much. Many agreements provide for an arbitration panel rather than a single arbitrator. Several states specify that certain elements must be included in agreements to arbitrate, such as a right to withdraw from the agreement within 30 days after signing or 60 days after discharge. The laws differ on which health care providers are eligible to enter arbitration agreements. Generally, courts can set aside arbitration decisions only for limited reasons, such as failure to follow proper procedures or bias of the arbitrator. A valid arbitration decision has the same effect as a court judgment and can be enforced using the same mechanisms.

Arbitration is favored by some health care providers and patients because it is faster and less costly than litigation. It is a less formal process than litigation, avoiding adverse publicity and the complex rules of litigation that promote adversarial positions. Others are opposed to arbitration because they prefer having their disputes decided by a jury using procedures with which attorneys are more familiar. Some providers believe they have a better chance of avoiding any payment, while some patients believe that if they win they will be awarded a larger payment by a jury.

Arbitration agreements have been enforced in many cases. For example, in 1976 the California Supreme Court upheld the application to an individual employee of an arbitration agreement that had been included in a group medical contract negotiated between an employer and a health maintenance organization.[55] In 1985 a California appellate court ruled that an arbitration agreement in a group medical contract also applied to the spouse, children, and heirs of the employee.[56] In 1984 the Michigan Supreme Court declared the state's arbitration act to be constitutional, overruling several lower court decisions that had questioned several aspects of the process.[57] However, in some states, the status of arbitration is unclear.

Amount and Payment of the Award

The amount of the award has been limited in some states by means of a specified ceiling. Some states have abolished the "collateral source" rule, reducing the amount paid. State payment mechanisms that pay part of any malpractice award have been created. Award of periodic payments has been authorized.

Ceilings

Limitations on the amount that can be awarded in a malpractice suit have been one of the most controversial approaches to tort reform. Few states have enacted limits, and courts have disagreed on their constitutionality. In 1976 the Illinois Supreme Court declared ceilings to be an unconstitutional violation of equal protection because it could find no rational justification for treating those injured by medical malpractice different from those injured by other means.[58] In 1980 the Indiana Supreme Court declared ceilings to be constitutional because it found a rational justification in the need for a risk-spreading mechanism for malpractice liability at a reasonable cost to assure the continued availability of health services.[59]

Collateral Source Rule

In most states, the defendant must pay for the entire cost of the plaintiff's injuries even if the plaintiff has already been compensated for some of the injuries from other sources, such as insurance. This is called the *collateral source* rule. Several states abolished the collateral source rule, so the amount of compensation the plaintiff receives from other sources is deducted from the amount the defendant owes. This process has been declared constitutional by several courts.[60]

State Payment Mechanisms

Some states have created insurance mechanisms that pay part of any malpractice award. These laws have generally been upheld, including the requirement that all health care providers contribute to the fund.[61]

Periodic Payments

Under the common law, court judgments must be paid in a single lump sum. One of the advantages of settling cases involving large liabilities is that the parties can agree to periodic payments that are easier for the defendant to pay. Some states have passed laws authorizing courts to direct that large judgments be paid by periodic payments. The courts have not agreed on whether these laws are constitutional.[62]

Statute of Limitations

The statute of limitations specifies the time period in which suits must be filed or forever barred. One form of tort reform has been to shorten the time period. Prior to the malpractice crisis amendments, nearly all statutes of limitation permitted minors to wait to file suits until after they became adults. One type of amendment limits minors to a specific number of years after the right to sue accrues. Courts have not agreed on the constitutionality of these limits.[63]

Another way to shorten the time period for all patients has been to redefine when the time period begins. In most states, the time period begins when the patient discovers an injury that may be due to someone else's negligence. Courts have disagreed on whether limits that start on the date of the incident are enforceable. Such limits can bar the suit before the patient knows there is a basis to sue. In some cases, such as unwanted births after negligent sterilizations, the injury may not occur until many years after the incident.[64]

Other Tort Reforms

Other tort reform amendments (1) limited the grounds for suits based on lack of informed consent;[65] (2) restricted contingency fees for lawyers or gave courts the authority to modify them;[66] (3) prohibited asking for a specified amount of money in the suit;[67] and (4) restricted who could give expert testimony.[68]

What Law Applies?

State law may not always protect providers. Patients have tried increasingly to sue providers in other states under the laws of those states to avoid provider protections in the providers' home state laws. These efforts have generally been unsuccessful.[69] However, in a 1985 District of Columbia case, a health plan's Virginia facilities were found subject to District of

Columbia law because the health plan had contracted with the employer of the patient in the District of Columbia.[70] Thus, the plan's Virginia facilities were not protected by Virginia's cap on malpractice recoveries. Another federal appellate court allowed a hospital to be sued in a state in which the hospital had its telephone number listed and from which the hospital had received payment.[71]

NOTES

1. 385 Mich. 57, 188 N.W.2d 601 (1971).

2. Mich. Comp. Laws 566.132 (1985 Supp.).

3. Stewart v. Rudner and Bunyan, 349 Mich. 459, 84 N.W.2d 816 (1957).

4. Malone v. Longo, 463 F. Supp. 139 (E.D. N. Y. 1979).

5. Wynn v. Cole, 91 Mich. App. 517, 284 N.W.2d 144 (1979).

6. Koudski v. Hennepin County Medical Center, 317 N.W.2d 705 (Minn. 1982).

7. 42 C.F.R. pt. 2 (1985).

8. Johnson v. Woman's Hosp., 527 S.W.2d 133 (Tenn. Ct. App. 1975).

9. McCormick v. Haley, 37 Ohio App.2d 73, 307 N.E.2d 34 (1973).

10. Spencer v. Burglass, 288 So.2d 68 (La. Ct. App. 1974); *but see* Bull v. McCluskey, 96 Nev. 706, 615 P.2d 957 (1980) and Taub, *Malpractice Countersuits: Succeeding at Last?*, 9 LAW, MED. & HEALTH CARE, Dec. 1981, at 17.

11. Suburban Hosp. Ass'n v. Hadary, 22 Md. App. 186, 322 A.2d 258 (1974).

12. Sullivan v. Sisters of St. Francis, 374 S.W.2d 294 (Tex. Civ. App. 1963).

13. Haber v. Cross County Hosp., 37 N.Y.2d 888, 340 N.E.2d 734 (1975).

14. Ravenis v. Detroit General Hosp., 63 Mich. App. 79, 234 N.W.2d 411 (1975).

15. Furey v. Thomas Jefferson Univ. Hosp., 325 Pa. Super. 212, 472 A.2d 1083 (1984); Fraijo v. Hartland Hosp., 99 Cal. App.3d 331, 160 Cal. Rptr. 246 (1979) [applied to nursing decision].

16. Helling v. Carey, 83 Wash.2d 514, 519 P.2d 981 (1974).

17. Tarasoff v. Board of Regents, 17 Cal.3d 425, 551 P.2d 334 (Cal. 1976).

18. No. 228566 (Cal. Super. Ct. November 19, 1973), *rev'd on other grounds,* 20 Cal.3d 500, 573 P.2d 458 (1978).

19. Austin v. Regents of Univ. of Cal., 89 Cal. App.3d 354, 152 Cal. Rptr. 142 (1979).

20. Lenger v. Physician's General Hosp., 455 S.W.2d 703 (Tex. 1970).

21. Schnebly v. Baker, 217 N.W.2d 708 (Iowa 1974).

22. Byrne v. Boadle, 2 H. & C. 72 (Exch. 1863).

23. *E.g.,* Leonard v. Watsonville Community Hosp., 47 Cal.2d 509, 305 P.2d 36 (1956).

24. *E.g.,* Parks v. Perry, 314 S.E.2d 387 (N.C. Ct. App. 1984); Wiles v. Myerly, 210 N.W.2d 619 (Iowa 1973).

25. *E.g.,* Sanchez v. Bay General Hosp., 116 Cal. App.3d 678, 172 Cal. Rptr. 342 (1981); Reilly v. Straub, 282 N.W.2d 688 (Iowa 1979).

26. *E.g.,* Iowa Code, §614.8 (1983); *contra* Fla. Stat., §95.11(4)(b) (1985).

27. *E.g.,* Taham v. Hoke, 469 F. Supp. 914 (W.D. N.C. 1979) [agreement to limit all claims to $15,000 unenforceable].

28. *E.g.*, Roberts v. Wood, 206 F. Supp. 579 (D. Ala. 1962).

29. *E.g.*, Shirey v. Schlemmer, 140 Ind. App. 606, 223 N.E.2d 759 (1967).

30. *E.g.*, Jenkins v. Bogalusa Community Medical Center, 340 So.2d 1065 (La. Ct. App. 1976).

31. *E.g.*, Seymour v. Victory Memorial Hosp., 60 Ill. App.3d 366, 376 N.E.2d 754 (1978).

32. *E.g.*, Rochester v. Katalan, 320 A.2d 704 (Del. 1974).

33. *E.g.*, Jensen v. Intermountain Health Care, Inc., 679 P.2d 903 (Utah 1984); *contra* Hoffman v. Jones, 280 So.2d 431 (Fla. 1973).

34. Perlmutter v. Beth David Hosp., 308 N.Y. 100, 123 N.E.2d 792 (1954).

35. *E.g.*, Cunningham v. MacNeal Memorial Hosp., 47 Ill.2d 443, 266 N.E.2d 897 (1970).

36. *E.g.*, Iowa Code Ann. §142A.8 (1985 Supp.).

37. *E.g.*, McDaniel v. Baptist Memorial Hosp., 469 F.2d 230 (6th Cir. 1972).

38. Shivers v. Good Shepard Hosp., 427 S.W.2d 104 (Tex. Civ. App. 1968).

39. Dubin v. Michael Reese Hosp., 83 Ill.2d 277, 415 N.E.2d 350 (1980), *rev'g* 74 Ill. App.3d 932, 393 N.E.2d 588 (1979).

40. Silverhart v. Mount Zion Hosp., 20 Cal. App.3d 1022, 98 Cal. Rptr. 187 (1971).

41. Skelton v. Druid City Hosp. Bd., 459 So.2d 818 (Ala. 1984).

42. *E.g.*, City of Somerset v. Hart, 549 S.W.2d 814 (Ky. 1977) [surgeon and hospital both liable for nurse's instrument count].

43. *E.g.*, Reed v. Good Samaritan Hosp. Ass'n, 453 So.2d 229 (Fla. Dist. Ct. App. 1984).

44. Overstreet v. Doctor's Hosp., 227 S.E.2d 213 (Ga. Ct. App. 1977).

45. Beeck v. Tucson General Hosp., 18 Az. App. 165, 500 P.2d 1153 (1972).

46. Keene v. Methodist Hosp., 324 F. Supp. 233 (N.D. Ind. 1971).

47. Greve v. Mt. Clemens General Hosp., 404 Mich. 240, 273 N.W.2d 429 (1978).

48. Beeck v. Tucson General Hosp., 18 Az. App. 165, 500 P.2d 1153 (1972).

49. Adamski v. Tacoma General Hosp., 20 Wash. App. 98, 579 P.2d 970 (1978).

50. *E.g.*, State ex rel. Cardinal Glennon Memorial Hosp. v. Gaertner, 583 S.W.2d 107 (Mo. 1979).

51. Aldana v. Holub, 381 So.2d 231 (Fla. 1980).

52. *E.g.*, Paro v. Longwood Hosp., 373 Mass. 645, 369 N.E.2d 985 (1977); Johnson v. St. Vincent Hosp., Inc., 404 N.E.2d 585 (Ind. 1980); Cha v. Warnack, 476 N.E.2d 109 (Ind. 1985).

53. *E.g.*, Winoma Memorial Found. v. Lomax, 465 N.E.2d 731 (Ind. App. Ct. 1984) [screening not required for slip and fall case]; Brown v. Rabbitt, 300 Md. 171, 476 A.2d 1167 (1984) [screening required for express contract to cure].

54. *E.g.*, Feinstein v. Massachusetts General Hosp., 643 F.2d 880 (1st Cir. 1981).

55. Madden v. Kaiser Found. Hosps., 17 Cal.3d 699, 552 P.2d 1178 (1976).

56. Herbert v. Superior Ct., 169 Cal. App.3d 718, 215 Cal. Rptr. 477 (1985).

57. Morris v. Metriyakool, 418 Mich. 423, 344 N.W.2d 736 (1984).

58. Wright v. Central DuPage Hosp. Ass'n, 63 Ill. 2d 313, 347 N.E.2d 736 (1976); *accord* Baptist Hosp. of Southeast Tex., Inc. v. Baker, 672 S.W.2d 296 (Tex. Ct. App. 1984).

59. Johnson v. St. Vincent Hosp., Inc., 404 N.E.2d 585 (Ind. 1980); *see also* Fein v. Permanente Medical Group, 38 Cal.3d 137, 211 Cal. Rptr. 368, 695 P.2d 665 (1985), *appeal*

dismissed, 106 S. Ct. 83 (U.S. 1985) [$250,000 limit on noneconomic damages upheld]; Hoffman v. United States, 767 F.2d 1431 (9th Cir. 1985).

60. *E.g.,* Rudolph v. Iowa Methodist Medical Center, 293 N.W.2d 550 (Iowa 1980).

61. *E.g.,* Johnson v. St. Vincent Hosp., Inc. 404 N.E.2d 585 (Ind. 1980).

62. *E.g.,* American Bank and Trust Co. v. Community Hosp. of Los Gatos-Saratoga, Inc., 36 Cal.3d 359, 204 Cal. Rptr. 671, 683 P.2d 670 (1984) [constitutional].

63. *E.g.,* Baird v. Loeffler, 69 Ohio St.2d 533, 434 N.E.2d 194 (1982) [one-year limit upheld]; *contra* Barrio v. San Manuel Div. Hosp., 143 Az. 101, 692 P.2d 280 (1984) [unconstitutional to require minors injured when less than seven years old to sue by age ten].

64. *E.g.,* McDonald v. Haynes Medical Lab., Inc., 192 Conn. 327, 471 A.2d 646 (1984) [suit can be barred before injury occurs]; *contra* Shessel v. Stroup, 253 Ga. 56, 316 S.E.2d 155 (1984) [suit cannot be barred before injury occurs].

65. *E.g.,* Fla. Stat. §768.46 (1983), which was declared unconstitutional in Cunningham v. Parikh, 472 So.2d 746, (Fla. Dist. Ct. App. 1985) and amended in 1985 to create only a rebuttable presumption, Fla. Stat. §768.46 (1985).

66. *E.g.,* Iowa Code Ann. §147.138 (1985 Supp.).

67. *E.g.,* Iowa Code Ann. §619.18 (1985 Supp.); *contra* White v. Fisher, 689 P.2d 102 (Wyo. 1984) [unconstitutional].

68. *E.g.,* Fla. Stat. §768.45(2)(c).

69. *E.g.,* Etra v. Matta, 61 N.Y.2d 455, 474 N.Y.S.2d 687 (1984).

70. Kaiser-Georgetown Community Health Plan v. Stutsman, 491 A.2d 502 (D.C. 1985).

71. Wolf v. Richmond County Hosp. Auth., 745 F.2d 904 (4th Cir. 1985), *cert. denied* 106 S. Ct. 83 (U.S. 1985).

Chapter 11

Examples of Tort Liability

The previous chapter reviewed the general principles of civil liability. This chapter reviews the application of those principles in a variety of specific situations that have resulted in suits against hospitals and their staff members, illustrating the scope of the duty of hospitals and their staff members to patients and others.

HOSPITALS

Hospital liability can be based on (1) a violation by an employee of the employee's duties; or (2) a violation of the hospital's duties. The liability of the hospital for injuries caused by an employee's violation of the employee's duties is based on the doctrine of *respondeat superior* discussed in Chapter 10. The doctrine will not be discussed further here, but it must be kept in mind when considering the liability exposure of individual health professionals. Whenever they are functioning as employees or agents of the hospital, their liability exposure also constitutes liability exposure for the hospital.

Hospitals have duties to many persons that are independent of *respondeat superior*. To establish liability for injuries caused by breaches of these duties, it is not necessary to show that an individual staff member breached a duty; it is sufficient to show that the hospital's duty was breached. Areas in which hospitals have an independent duty include (1) physical condition of the buildings and grounds; (2) selection and maintenance of equipment; and (3) selection and supervision of staff.

Physical Condition of the Buildings and Grounds

The hospital must exercise reasonable care in maintaining its buildings and grounds in a reasonably safe condition. The occurrence of an accident alone is not enough to establish liability. In some localities, state or local regulations may establish standards, and injuries resulting from violations of those standards can lead to liability. When regulatory standards have not been violated, hospitals will generally be liable only when the plaintiff proves that the hospital's employees or agents created a condition likely to cause injury or that they knew or should have known of a condition likely to cause injury and failed to take action to provide warning or correct the condition.

The buildings and grounds of hospitals should meet the special needs of the unique population of infirm and disabled persons using the hospital facilities. When these patients are injured, it will not be a sufficient defense for the hospital to show its facilities were safe for people in ordinary physical condition. The hospital needs to provide handrails in lavatories, siderails in corridors, etc., where appropriate to maintain the safety of patients. The hospital also needs to provide maintenance for the facility to correct conditions that are likely to cause injury. For example, the hospital can be liable for injuries caused by wet or slippery floors, broken stairs, ripped carpets, unsafe accumulation of snow and ice, or even balconies or large windows not designed to prevent falls. The hospital may also be liable for injuries sustained by visitors and others because the hospital must exercise the same reasonable care as any other business that regularly invites the public onto its grounds and into its buildings. Of course, the hospital is not liable to either a patient or another person for injuries caused by a condition when the person was aware of the dangerous condition, was able to avoid the risk of injury and, nevertheless, chose to ignore the risk. For example, in a 1968 Texas case the antenna wire for a television in a patient's room was in a place where it could be tripped over.[1] The patient had been aware of the wire and had walked around the set to avoid the wire several times during her stay in the hospital. On the day of her discharge, she chose to step over the wire and tripped. The hospital won the suit because the danger was open and obvious and the patient had the ability to avoid it.

Selection and Maintenance of Equipment

A hospital has an obligation to furnish reasonably adequate equipment for use in diagnosis and treatment of patients. Problems can arise when the hospital does not own the necessary equipment, when the necessary equipment is not available, or when the equipment has not been properly inspected and maintained.

When a hospital does not have the equipment reasonably necessary for the treatment of certain conditions, patients with these conditions must be advised of the limitations of the hospital, and arrangements should be made for the transfer of the patient to another hospital with the necessary equipment unless the patient makes an informed decision to decline the transfer. In a 1977 federal case a woman delivered a stillborn baby because the 14-bed obstetrical clinic she entered for delivery did not have the facilities for a Caesarean delivery.[2] The court found the clinic liable because it undertook to care for the woman without having the necessary facilities or warning her during prenatal care of the limited nature of the facilities. In a 1963 California case, a hospital was found liable for injuries to a patient with third-degree burns who was kept for nearly two months in a hospital that did not have the equipment to care for the patient's burns.[3] The court ruled that the hospital had a duty to transfer the patient to another hospital with the necessary equipment. The court did not discuss whether an informed decision by the patient to decline transfer would have absolved the hospital. When the patient is reluctant to accept transfer, the most prudent practice is still to encourage the patient to accept transfer to an appropriate facility, rather than rely on refusal.

The hospital is not required to provide the latest equipment. For example, in a 1972 Louisiana case, a hospital was found not liable for having a freezing microtome process to cut sections of tissue for diagnosis instead of having a more modern cryostat that could cut thinner sections for a more accurate diagnosis.[4] Several experts testified that the freezing microtome was widely accepted and produces satisfactory results. A woman whose breast was removed due to a misdiagnosis of malignancy was not awarded compensation.

Even when the hospital owns equipment to provide the needed service, the equipment may not be available for use due to system design problems or hospital staff failure to plan to have the equipment in the area. For example, in a 1974 Texas case, the hospital was found liable for the death of a patient due to the unavailability of oxygen after she was transferred to a private room.[5] A wall plug in the room supplied oxygen, but the equipment accompanying the patient required a wall plug of a different shape. The design problem, lack of standardization of wall plugs, was the reason the oxygen was not available. Portable oxygen equipment could have supplied the necessary oxygen, but none had accompanied the patient during the transfer. Portable equipment was not brought to the area until after it was discovered that the wall plug shape did not match. Evidence that the patient would have survived if the oxygen had been available was sufficient to support a jury determination that the death was legally caused by lack of proper equipment.

A hospital must also exercise reasonable care in inspecting and maintaining equipment. The hospital obligation includes making reasonable periodic inspections of equipment and remedying the defects discovered in such inspections. Nearly all courts that have ruled on the issue have said that the hospital does not guarantee that the equipment will function properly during customary use. Liability for injuries due to defects in equipment generally depends on whether the defect is latent (hidden) or patent (visible). The user of equipment is generally liable for injuries due to use of equipment with patent defects. The owner of the equipment is generally liable for injuries due to equipment with latent defects detectable through reasonable inspections that were not performed. The manufacturer or seller of the equipment is generally liable when the equipment has a latent defect, such as a flaw in the metal, that the owner could not detect through reasonable inspection.

For example, a 1965 Alabama case addressed a patient who was injured because of a defect in an electrical-surgical instrument, a Stryker Dermatome, used in the removal of skin for grafting.[6] The defect, a bent spring that was not readily apparent, caused the removal of too thick a patch of skin. The bent spring could have been detected by dismantling the instrument for inspection. The court found the hospital, but not the surgeon who had used the instrument, liable for the injuries. If the bent spring had been visible to the surgeon without his dismantling the equipment, the surgeon would have been liable. In many circumstances the users of the equipment are hospital employees, so that the hospital can be liable under the doctrine of *respondeat superior* for their failure to detect patent defects. If hospital employees switch equipment that the physician has already inspected, the hospital can also be liable for resultant injuries. An Ohio case concerned a physician who examined a cauterizing machine to be used during surgery and then left the room for a few minutes.[7] While he was gone, a hospital employee substituted another machine that appeared so similar that the surgeon did not notice the switch. The patient was burned during the surgery due to a defect in the machine. The surgeon was found not to be liable.

When the hospital or physician knows that the equipment is defective, it is easier to establish liability because the defect is clearly patent. In an Oklahoma case, the employer of a technician was found liable for the technician's use of equipment that was clearly malfunctioning.[8] The technician knew the electrotherapy machine was malfunctioning, but instead of turning off the machine and seeking assistance, she continued to use the machine until the patient was burned. In an Iowa case, a surgeon was found liable for a patient's infection due to contaminated sutures because he knew they were contaminated when he used them.[9] An earlier patient had become infected through use of sutures from the same supply.

At least one state has adopted a minority position that hospitals may be liable for some defects that are not detectable. A 1975 New Jersey case involved a surgical device that broke, resulting in the lodging of a portion of the device in the patient's spine.[10] The break was due either to improper twisting by the surgeon or to a flaw in the metal that could not be detected by the inspections normally conducted by hospitals. The jury found that neither the physician nor the hospital had been negligent. The appellate court ordered a new trial at which either the physician or hospital must be found responsible.

Selection and Supervision of Staff

A hospital can be liable for failing to exercise reasonable care in selecting and supervising its staff. This liability applies to both professional and nonprofessional staff. Hospitals have a responsibility to evaluate the credentials of applicants for jobs. When a state license is required, the hospital must determine that the applicant has the license, but checking the license alone is not a sufficient check of the applicant's background and qualifications. The hospital must also provide appropriate training, supervision, and evaluation. These issues are discussed in more detail in the hospital credentialing section of Chapter 8 and the general staff relations issues section of Chapter 9.

The hospital also has a responsibility to exercise reasonable care in selecting and monitoring members of the medical staff, as discussed in Chapters 7 and 8. The potential for hospital liability for acts of physicians is discussed in the *respondeat superior,* agency, and institutional liability sections of Chapter 10.

GOVERNING BODY AND ADMINISTRATOR

Members of the governing body have seldom been found personally liable for the activities of the hospital or for their own activities related to the hospital. Their liability exposure is discussed in the liability of directors section of Chapter 2. Administrators have been found liable for negligent supervision of their subordinates, for entering contracts outside their authority, and for breaches of duties imposed by statute. This liability exposure is discussed in the liability of the administrator section of Chapter 2 and in the supervisor section of this chapter.

SUPERVISOR

Supervisors are not the employers of the staff they supervise. Thus, *respondeat superior* does not impose liability on supervisors for the acts or

omissions of staff they supervise. Supervisors are liable only for the consequences of their own acts or omissions. The supervisor is usually an
employee of the hospital, so the hospital can be liable under *respondeat
superior* for the acts or omissions of supervisors.

The liability of a supervising nurse for the actions of supervised nurses
was discussed in a California case involving a needle left in a patient's
abdomen during surgery.[11] The patient sued the physicians, the hospital,
and the supervising nurse. The court dismissed the suit against the supervising nurse because she had done nothing wrong. She had assigned two
competent nurses to assist with the surgery, and she had not been present.
Therefore, she had no opportunity to intervene. The court ruled that *respondeat superior* did not apply to the nursing supervisor because she was not
the employer.

The actions that can lead to liability of supervising health professionals
are discussed in more detail in a 1970 New Jersey court decision.[12] The
case involved a surgeon who had ordered a resident physician to remove a
tube being used to extract the patient's gastric contents. The patient's
esophagus was perforated in the process. The court ruled that the supervising surgeon was not liable for the acts of the resident. The court said that
the supervising surgeon could be liable only if (1) it was not accepted
medical or hospital practice to delegate the particular function to someone
with the resident's level of training; (2) he knew or should have known the
individual resident was not qualified to perform the task with the degree of
supervision provided; (3) he had been present and able to avoid the injury;
or (4) he had a special contract with the patient that he did not fulfill. Since
none of these circumstances were present, the supervising surgeon was not
liable. In some states the courts apply a different legal doctrine to supervising physicians, the "borrowed servant" doctrine. This doctrine applies only
to supervisors who are independently practicing professionals; the "borrowed servant" doctrine does not apply to supervisors who are also employees of the same employer. When the "borrowed servant" doctrine is
applied, the courts say that the supervising physician has borrowed the
employee from the regular employer. Therefore, the law will consider the
supervising physician to be the employer, and *respondeat superior* can be
applied to make the supervising physician liable for all acts of the borrowed
employee while working under the direction of the supervising physician.

Another case that illustrates the potential liability of supervising nurses
was decided in 1969 by a Canadian court.[13] The court found both the
supervising nurse and her hospital employer liable for injuries to a woman
who was not observed often enough in a post-anesthesia recovery room.
The patient had a cholecystectomy (excision of the gall bladder) without

complications and was transferred to the post-anesthesia recovery room. The hospital had provided two nurses for the area, which the court accepted as adequate staffing, but the supervising nurse permitted the other nurse to leave the area for a coffee break just before three patients were admitted to the area. One of the patients suffered a respiratory obstruction that was not observed until the lack of oxygen caused permanent brain damage. The court ruled that the supervising nurse was liable for permitting the other nurse to leave the area at a time when she knew that the operating schedule would result in several admissions to the unit. The court stated that even if she had not known the operating schedule, she would still be liable for not knowing the aspects of the schedule that applied to the staffing needs of the area she supervised. Since the supervising nurse also provided direct nursing care to the patients in the area, she was also liable for failing to observe the patient more frequently herself. The court ruled that the nurse who left the area would also have been liable if she had been included in the suit because she should have known the aspects of the operating schedule that applied to the staffing needs of the area in which she worked. The hospital was also liable for the acts of both nurses under the doctrine of *respondeat superior*.

The preceding case was followed two years later by a very similar case in the same province of Canada.[14] A ten-year-old boy who had undergone plastic surgery for overprominent ears suffered cardiac arrest resulting in a permanent coma of nearly four years until his death. The cardiac arrest occurred in a post-anesthesia area while three of the five nurses assigned to the area were on a coffee break. The hospital was found liable for the same reasons as in the previous case.

In a 1976 New York case, a patient who was disoriented had been found on a balcony outside a second-story window.[15] After the patient was returned to the hospital room, the physician told the staff to arrange to have the patient watched. The charge nurse called the patient's family to tell them to arrange to have someone watch the patient. The family said someone would be at the hospital in 10 to 15 minutes. When the family member arrived, the patient had fallen out of the window and was severely injured. The hospital was found liable for failing either to move the patient to a secure room, apply additional restraints, or find someone to watch the patient for 15 minutes. One charge nurse, one new registered nurse in orientation, one practical nurse, and one aide were working in a unit with 19 patients. The court found that all except the aide had been engaged in routine duties that could have been delayed for 15 minutes and that the aide had been permitted to leave for supper during the period. The court said this finding was evidence that staffing was sufficient to provide continuous supervision for a patient in known danger for 15 minutes. The failure of the supervising nurse to allocate the time of the available staff properly was one of the grounds for the hospital's liability.

The general principles discussed in this section also apply to other supervising health care professionals. In summary, a supervisor can be liable if

1. The supervisor assigns the subordinate to do something the supervisor knows or should know the subordinate is unable to do;
2. The supervisor does not provide the subordinate the degree of supervision the supervisor knows or should know the subordinate needs;
3. The supervisor is present and fails to take action when possible to avoid the injury; or
4. The supervisor does not properly allocate the time of available staff— for example, by permitting breaks from areas where there are critical needs at times when the supervisor knows or should know the staff will be needed.

NURSES

A professional nurse is held to the standard of care generally observed by other competent nurses under similar circumstances. The standard of care applicable to nursing students is not different from the standard for professional nurses. The standard of care applicable to professional nurses may be different in some circumstances. States vary in the standard of care expected of nurses in specialties that overlap with the scope of practice of physicians. In some states, such nurses are held to the standard of physicians. For example, a 1971 Louisiana decision ruled that when a person assisting a physician performs a task deemed to be medical in nature, such as removal of a cast with a Stryker saw, the person is held to the standard of care applicable to a physician.[16] Other states have recognized a distinct standard of care for such nurses. For example, a 1971 Texas ruling held nurse specialists to the standard of care observed by those in the same specialty under similar circumstances.[17] In 1985, the California Supreme Court ruled that nurse practitioners should not be held to the standard of care of a physician, even when performing functions that overlap with the physician's scope of practice.[18]

The standard of care is an essential element that must be proved to establish liability. As discussed in Chapter 10, to establish liability, it must be shown that the patient's injury was caused by the failure to meet the applicable standard of care.

Duty To Interpret and Carry Out Orders

Nurses have a duty to interpret and carry out orders properly. Nurses are expected to know basic information concerning the proper use of drugs and procedures they are likely to be ordered to use. When an order is ambiguous or apparently erroneous, the nurse has a responsibility to seek clarification from the ordering physician. This will almost always result in correction or explanation of the order. In the unusual situation when the explanation does not clarify the appropriateness of the order, the nurse has a responsibility to inform nursing, hospital, or medical staff officials designated by hospital policy who can initiate review of the order and, if necessary, other appropriate action. Pending review, if the drug or procedure appears dangerous to the patient, the nurse should decline to carry out the order, but should immediately notify the ordering physician. Hospitals should have established procedures for nurses to follow when they are not satisfied with the appropriateness of an order. Frequently, this procedure will involve notification of a nursing supervisor who will then contact appropriate medical staff officials. Hospital administration may occasionally need to become involved to resolve individual issues.

In a 1973 California case, a hospital was sued for the death of a patient.[19] The nurse had been ordered to check the patient's vital signs every 30 minutes, which she had failed to do. The hospital was found liable under *respondeat superior* for the nurse's failure to follow the physician's order and for her failure to notify the physician when the patient's condition became life threatening. In a 1976 New York case, a nurse and hospital were sued for the scalding of a young tonsillectomy patient by water that was served as part of his meal by a nurse, contrary to the dietary instructions ordered by the attending physician.[20] The nurse and hospital were held liable. A hospital was sued in a 1968 New York case for the blindness of an infant caused by too much oxygen when a nurse gave six liters per minute instead of the four liters per minute ordered by the physician.[21] The hospital presented evidence that six liters per minute was within the range of permissible dosages. The court found this evidence irrelevant because the nurse had not been given authority to deviate from the physician's order and, thus, had breached her duty to the patient. The court ordered a lower court to reconsider the case to determine whether the blindness had been caused by breach of duty.

Of course, in some situations, nurses are given authority to adjust the amounts of some drugs or other substances being given to patients within guidelines established by the physician. In such situations, the nurse has the added responsibility to exercise the appropriate judgment in making those adjustments. In many states, there are legal limits on the discretion that can be delegated concerning some drugs and substances, so familiarity with local law is important. In addition, as with all delegations, the physician should provide appropriate guidance and delegate this responsibility only to nurses who are able to make the required judgments. In 1979 a California court recognized the appropriateness of delegating to a nurse the decision concerning when a prescribed pain medication was needed.[22] The patient suffered cardiopulmonary arrest and died soon after pain medication was given. The court ruled that it was appropriate for the trial court to give the jury two special instructions usually used only for physicians because the case involved a nurse who was exercising independent judgment delegated by the physician. One instruction emphasized that perfection was not required, so liability could not be based on a mere error in judgment by a nurse who possessed the necessary learning and skill and exercised the care ordinarily exercised by reputable nurses under similar circumstances. Note that the standard applied was the conduct of nurses, not physicians. The other instruction emphasized that when there is more than one recognized method of treatment, it is not negligent to select one of the approved methods that later turns out to be wrong or not to be favored by certain other practitioners. The court upheld the jury verdict in favor of the nurse and hospital.

Nurses cannot assume that orders have remained unchanged from previous shifts. They have a duty to check for changes in orders. A 1962 Delaware case addressed a female patient who had been receiving a drug by injection.[23] The physician wrote an order on the patient's order sheet changing the mode of administration from injection to oral administration. When the nurse on the unit, who had been off duty for several days, was preparing to give the medication to the patient by injection, the patient objected and referred the nurse to the physician's new order. The nurse told the patient she was mistaken and gave the medication by injection. Either the nurse had not reviewed the order sheet after being told by the patient that the medication was to be given orally, or the nurse did so in a negligent manner and did not note the physician's entry. In either case, the nurse's conduct was held to be negligent. The court went on to state that the jury could find the nurse negligent by applying ordinary common sense, so expert testimony was not necessary to prove the applicable standard of care.

In a Louisiana case, the court focused attention on the responsibility of a nurse to obtain clarification of an apparently erroneous order from the patient's physician.[24] The order, as entered in the chart, was incomplete and subject to misinterpretation. Believing the medication order of the attending physician to be incorrect because of the dosage, the nurse asked two physicians present in the ward whether the medication should be given as ordered. The physicians did not interpret the order as the nurse did, so they did not share her concern and said the order did not appear out of line. The nurse did not contact the attending physician and administered the misinterpreted dosage of the medication. The court upheld the jury's finding that the nurse had been negligent in failing to contact the attending physician before giving the medication. The nurse was held liable, as was the physician who wrote the ambiguous order that led to the fatal dose.

This case illustrates the way in which a nurse's conduct is measured against the practice of competent and prudent nurses. There had been testimony at the trial that a prudent nurse, when confronted with an ambiguous or confusing medication order, will obtain clarification of the order from the prescribing physician. However, the nurse who administered the medication did not seek clarification from the physician who wrote the order, and that departure from the standard of competent nursing practice provided the basis for holding the nurse liable for negligence.

Duty To Monitor the Patient

Nurses have a duty to monitor the patient. Nurses are expected to distinguish abnormalities in the patient's condition and determine whether nursing care is a sufficient response or whether a physician or others may be required. The nurse has a responsibility to inform the physician promptly of abnormalities that may require physician attention. In a 1974 Kansas case, a nurse and hospital were sued because a woman was injured during delivery of a baby without attendance of a physician.[25] The nurse had refused to call the physician despite clear signs of imminent delivery. The nurse and hospital were found liable for the nurse's failure to give timely notification to the physician of impending delivery. In a 1965 West Virginia case, the court ruled that the hospital could be found liable for the death of a patient when the nurse failed to notify the physician of the patient's symptoms of heart failure for six hours.[26]

Observations should be properly documented. In a 1974 Illinois case, the hospital was sued for the loss of a patient's leg.[27] The patient had been admitted for treatment for a broken leg on May 7. The admitting physician entered an order on May 7 to "watch condition of toes" and testified at the trial that routine nursing care required frequent monitoring of a seriously injured patient's circulation, even in the absence of a physician's orders. The patient developed irreversible ischemia in his leg, requiring its amputation. The nursing notes for the seven-hour period prior to the discovery of the irreversibility of the ischemia did not reflect any observations of the patient's circulation. The court ruled that the jury could conclude that absence of entries indicated the absence of observations. Thus, the nurse and hospital could be liable even if the nurse had actually made the observations. In these circumstances, it is as important to document no change as it is to document changes.

A hospital and physician were sued in a 1963 California case for the damage to a patient's leg from infiltration of intravenous fluid into the tissue.[28] The nurse observed increasing swelling and redness in the area of the intravenous tube that indicated infiltration. She notified the physician several times of the swelling, but he ordered continuation of the intravenous infusions. There was conflicting testimony at the trial concerning (a) whether the nurse had communicated the seriousness of the swelling when it became markedly worse; and (b) whether the nurse had the authority to discontinue the intravenous infusion without a physician order. The court overturned the trial court decision in favor of the hospital and physician and ordered a new trial so a jury could determine these issues. This case illustrates the importance of clearly communicating changes in the patient's condition and clearly defining the authority of nurses to discontinue harmful therapy.

If the physician fails to respond appropriately when notified that a patient is in a dangerous situation, then the nurse is confronted with the same situation as when the physician has not adequately explained an apparently erroneous order. The nurse has a responsibility to inform nursing, hospital, or medical staff officials designated by hospital policy who can initiate review of the situation and, if necessary, take other appropriate action. This is the way a nurse confronted with the situation in the 1963 California case should respond today if the nurse believes the seriousness of the swelling has been communicated, the physician neither examines the patient nor orders discontinuance of the procedure, and the nurse does not have clear authority to discontinue the procedure without an order. In *Darling v. Charleston Community Memorial Hospital*,[29] one of the reasons for the hospital's liability for the amputation of the patient's leg was the failure of the nurses to inform hospital administration of the progressive gangrenous condition of the patient's leg and the inappropriate efforts of the attending physician to address the condition. No effective alternative channel had been established for direct nursing notification of the medical staff and for appropriate medical staff intervention. The court found that hospital administration should have been notified so that it could obtain appropriate medical staff intervention.

In most hospitals direct communication channels have been established between nursing administration and medical staff leadership, so direct hospital administration involvement is less frequent. These channels must be used when necessary. In a 1977 West Virginia case, the hospital was found liable for the failure of the nurses to comply with the hospital's nursing manual and report the patient's deteriorating condition to the department chairman when the attending physician failed to respond adequately to the patient's worsening condition.[30]

The fact that the nurse believes the physician will not respond does not justify failure to notify the physician and to take other action if the physician does not respond. A California court ruled in 1958 that two nurses and a hospital could be sued for the death of a woman from severe bleeding from an incision made to assist her in giving birth to a child.[31] Although the nurses believed the patient was bleeding heavily, the physician was not notified until nearly three hours later, when the patient went into shock. One nurse explained that she did not call the physician because she did not believe he would respond. The court concluded that she should have notified the attending physician and then notified her superiors if the attending physician did not respond rapidly enough.

Duty To Supervise the Patient

When nurses determine that a patient requires supervision, they have a duty to exercise appropriate judgment and provide appropriate supervision within the constraints of proper physician orders and available resources. The 1962 Louisiana case discussed in the section of this chapter on supervisors illustrates this duty.

The Iowa Supreme Court concluded in a 1971 case that hospitals have a direct duty to supervise patients in some situations.[32] A patient with a history of fainting spells had a seizure and fell during a shower, breaking her jaw and losing several teeth. An aide was outside the shower room but allowed the patient to enter the shower alone. The court ruled that decisions concerning supervision of patient showers are a matter of routine care, not professional care, so no expert testimony is necessary to establish the standard of care. The jury can apply its common sense to determine the reasonable care the patient's known condition requires. The court noted that absence of physician orders requiring close supervision does not insulate the hospital from liability. If subsequent circumstances show a need for change or action, the hospital should make the changes permitted without a physician order and, if further changes are necessary, seek appropriate orders. The court did not address the potential liability of the aide or the supervising nurses because they were not sued. This case illustrates that courts will find liability, without any expert testimony, in some cases concerning patient supervision.

Special Duty Nurses

Special duty nurses are held to the same standard of care as other nurses. Since they are not employees of the hospital, the hospital is usually not liable for their actions. Even when hospital rules require special duty nurses, they do not become hospital employees. However, in some situations, nurses who are called special duty nurses will be considered agents or employees of the hospital so that the hospital can be liable under *respondeat superior.*[33] Agency or employment is likely to be found when the special duty nurses are selected by the hospital, not by the patient or the patient's representatives. Collection of the nurse's bills by the hospital has also been interpreted by some courts to indicate agency.

PHARMACISTS

Courts vary in the terminology used to describe the standard of care applicable to pharmacists. They sometimes speak of ordinary care under the circumstances. However, because of the public health and safety involved in dealing with potent pharmacological agents, courts frequently describe the standard as the "highest degree of care." It is questionable whether these standards are substantively different in effect.

In a highly regulated profession like a pharmacy, the first place to look for standards of practice are federal or state statutes, agency regulations, and municipal or county ordinances. Generally, if the purpose of the law is to prevent the type of harm sustained by a plaintiff and if the plaintiff is a member of the class of persons the law is intended to protect, violation of the law can establish negligence. Otherwise, it may merely be evidence of possible negligence for the jury to consider along with other evidence.

JCAH and other accreditation standards may also establish duties, the breach of which may result in liability. For example, the JCAH standard concerning pharmaceutical services requires such services to be directed by a qualified pharmacist.[34] A pharmacist must have the primary responsibility for drugs throughout the institution. The hospital may be liable for drug-related injuries if it fails to employ a licensed and competent pharmacist.[35]

Court decisions concerning pharmacists also help to define their standard of care. Dispensing the wrong drug clearly can lead to liability. In a 1971 Michigan case, a tranquilizer was dispensed instead of the prescribed oral contraceptive.[36] The patient became pregnant, delivered a child, and sued the pharmacist for damages. Damages were awarded, including child support until the child reached the age of majority. In a 1972 California trial court decision, a patient with a serious cardiac condition received gout medication instead of the prescribed heart drug.[37] The dispensed medication did not harm the patient directly, but she had another heart attack because she did not receive the prescribed heart medication. The pharmacist was held liable. Before liability can be imposed, an improperly compounded prescription must be the legal cause of the patient's injury. In an unreported decision in which a pharmacist dispensed cortisone in a cream base rather than in a lotion, he was not found liable because the patient's injury was caused by the cortisone itself and not by the form in which it was dispensed.[38]

A hospital must take reasonable steps to assure that drugs are available when they are needed. In a 1969 New York case, the hospital was found liable for the death of a patient taking an investigational psychotropic drug.[39] One of the factors leading to liability was the unavailability of the drug during a long holiday weekend because it was stored in the research department, which was closed. If the drug had been stored in the pharmacy, which was open during the weekend, it would have been available, and the patient might not have committed suicide. Some investigational drugs are not available outside of approved research projects, so subjects can no longer receive the drug after they complete their involvement in the study. This is a necessary and appropriate practice, but the limited availability should be disclosed to the subject before the subject enters the study. In the above case, the patient was still in the study. At times, certain noninvestigational drugs are not available because of manufacturing, transport, or stocking problems. The hospital is not an insurer that drugs will continue to be available, but it should take reasonable steps to anticipate needs to minimize nonavailability.

Drugs should be properly stored to avoid deterioration and contamination. The skill with which this is ordinarily done is exemplified by the lack of reported cases arising from breaching this duty.

Pharmacists are increasingly assuming the responsibility to maintain profiles of the drugs patients are being administered, to advise physicians concerning drug selection, and to review the appropriateness of drug orders. Although pharmacists have avoided liability in some cases arising out of these new responsibilities,[40] it is likely pharmacists will soon be expected to meet a professional standard of care in fulfilling the responsibilities assumed. While physicians will remain primarily liable for injuries due to negligent prescriptions, it is likely that pharmacists will be codefendants when they assume the responsibility of review and carry it out negligently.

PHYSICAL THERAPISTS

The professional liability cases involving physical therapists have dealt with breaches of the following duties: (1) to follow the physician's instructions; (2) not to subject the patient to excessive therapy; and (3) to supervise the patient properly.

A physical therapist must follow the prescribing physician's instructions, unless they are apparently erroneous and dangerous to the patient. In a 1980

Florida case, a hospital was sued because of injuries to a patient who fell while undergoing physical therapy.[41] The physician had ordered the patient to be attended at all times. The therapist left the patient alone in a standing position while getting her a robe. A fall during that short time resulted in a fractured hip. The court affirmed an award of $135,000 to the patient. The court stated no expert testimony was necessary to establish the duty to follow the physician's instructions to attend the patient.

Physical therapists are expected to be familiar with the appropriate use of the procedures they use. If a physician's order is apparently erroneous, the therapist has a duty to seek modification or clarification from the prescribing physician. The therapist should not unilaterally initiate different treatment. If the orders are still apparently erroneous after discussion with the prescribing physician and if the ordered therapy is dangerous to the patient, the therapist should decline to provide the prescribed therapy and notify both the prescribing physician and the appropriate supervisory, medical staff, or administrative officials in accord with hospital policy.

The physician's orders often give the physical therapist latitude concerning the details of the therapy to be provided. The physical therapist is then generally held to the duty of acting as other physical therapists in good standing would act under the circumstances. In 1976 a Pennsylvania hospital was sued by a patient who fell in the physical therapy room and fractured her leg and arm.[42] The patient was receiving gait training after multiple hip surgeries. The patient was instructed to walk between the parallel bars. The patient fell either while between the parallel bars or while using her cane to take a few steps away from the parallel bars. The court ruled that the duty of the physical therapist must be established by expert testimony and that only ordinary care and skill was required, so the physical therapist was not liable for a mere mistake in judgment. The court affirmed a verdict for the hospital.

Physical therapists should be careful not to subject the patient to excessive therapy. The Kentucky Supreme Court applied *res ipsa loquitur* when bones were fractured during therapy that involved raising and lowering a patient's leg.[43] A femur was fractured during therapy to prepare the stump of the leg for an artificial leg. The court ruled that the hospital and the physical therapist could be liable under *res ipsa loquitur* because it did not believe bones would fracture while a leg was being lifted and lowered unless someone was negligent. Thus, it did not require expert testimony. The court ruled that the physician could also be liable for failing to provide an adequate explanation of the procedure to the therapist.

Falls are the most frequent cause of injuries involving patients receiving physical therapy. Some courts tend to apply *res ipsa loquitur* to cases involving falls, as illustrated by the Kentucky case, while other courts analyze the appropriateness of the attendance given from a professional perspective, as illustrated by the Pennsylvania case. Another example of a professional standard involved an Oregon patient undergoing therapy after hip surgery who became dizzy and fainted just after returning to a tilt table after walking between parallel bars.[44] His total hip replacement became dislocated when he fell. The patient's expert witness testified that he should have been given support, including being strapped to the tilt table, as soon as he became dizzy. The court found the hospital liable for the physical therapists' failure to fulfill this duty. In a 1972 Oregon case, a hospital and physical therapist were sued by a woman who injured her hip when she slid down a tilt table.[45] The circumstances were similar to the other Oregon case discussed above in that she was receiving therapy following hip surgery and became faint while walking. She was returned to the tilt table, where she slumped. The outcome of the case was different because the patient grabbed the handrails and pulled herself downward, thwarting the efforts of the therapist to prevent the fall. The court found the patient's act to be volitional and contributory negligence, so the patient lost the suit.

PATHOLOGY

Liability can arise from injuries due to negligent acts associated with laboratory tests and other pathology services. The error can be committed by a laboratory technician, a pathologist, or other staff members. The hospital can become liable under *respondeat superior* when the person who made the error is the hospital's employee or agent. As discussed in the *respondeat superior* and agency sections of Chapter 10, some courts hold hospitals responsible for the acts of physicians, particularly radiologists, pathologists, and emergency room physicians, by considering the physician to be the agent or apparent agent for the hospital.

Liability has arisen from mishandling specimens. In a 1975 Texas case, the court found the hospital liable for the mental anguish of a patient when an eyeball that had been removed because of a tumor was lost by a technician.[46] The technician was washing the eyeball and dropped it into the sink. The eyeball went down the drain and could not be removed, so the pathologist could not diagnose whether the tumor was malignant. In a 1974 Florida case, the patient was awarded $100,000 from the hospital and a surgeon because the identities of two specimens were confused, resulting in the unnecessary removal of one of the patient's breasts.[47] The surgeon had removed a biopsy specimen from each breast, and the two specimens were put in the same container without labels telling which breast each came from. The pathologist did not attempt to distinguish the two specimens. One specimen was malignant, and the other was not. Since it was impossible to determine which breast had the malignancy, both breasts were removed. The surgeon was liable for failing to instruct the nurses to label the specimens. The hospital was liable for the failure of the nurses to label the specimens and for the failure of its pathologist-employee to segregate the specimens.

Misreading a specimen can lead to liability for the pathologist and, if the pathologist is an employee or agent, for the hospital. In a 1963 Ohio case, a hospital was found liable because its pathologist-employee misdiagnosed a frozen section as indicating cervical cancer.[48] After a total hysterectomy (removal of the uterus and cervix) was performed, it was discovered the patient did not have cancer. Misdiagnosis alone is not enough to establish breach of duty. A diagnosing physician is not expected to be correct all of the time. It is recognized that most diagnoses are professional judgments. Thus, the misdiagnosis must be one that a physician in good standing in the same specialty would not have made in the same circumstances in order for there to be liability.

Using improper techniques or reagents to conduct a test can be a breach of duty. In 1971 a federal court found a hospital liable for a laboratory technician's use of sodium hydroxide instead of sodium chloride to perform a gastric cytology test.[49] In a 1974 Iowa case, a hospital was found liable for the use of a reagent that was too old.[50] A newborn baby had symptoms of Rh incompatibility. The pediatrician ordered appropriate blood tests, but the old reagent caused the results of the test to indicate normal blood levels of the critical substance rather than the extremely high levels that the baby actually had. By the time the high levels were discovered, it was too late to avoid the permanent severe brain damage that probably could have been avoided had therapy been initiated after the initial blood tests.

Genetic screening and prenatal genetic tests are frequently employed. Both parents and children have sued when negligently conducted tests have led parents to conceive or deliver children with genetic defects. For example, in 1978 a federal court ruled that the parents of an infant born with Tay-Sachs disease could recover damages because they had been informed, based on a negligently performed prenatal test, that the child could not have Tay-Sachs disease.[51] These wrongful conception, wrongful birth, and wrongful life cases are discussed further in Chapter 15.

Autopsies and other aspects of handling dead bodies are another area of potential liability arising from pathology services. Dead bodies are discussed in Chapter 16.

RADIOLOGY

Four of the common problem areas of radiology include radiation injuries, falls and other problems with positioning the patient, errors or delays in diagnosis, and pregnancy.

Radiation injuries from excessive radiation or radiation to the wrong part of the body have resulted in several suits. Even guide lights have occasionally caused injuries. In a 1970 Minnesota case, a hospital was found liable for the radiologic technician's misplacement of the machine that caused a guide light to contact the patient's skin, producing a burn.[52] Even though the radiologist was present, the radiologist was not liable because the alignment of the machine was within the scope of the routine activities of the technician and did not require personal physician supervision. The radiologist could not have intervened to prevent the burn after the misplacement occurred.

Most courts recognize that the application and effect of radiation is not within the knowledge of lay persons, so they require expert proof of negligence in administering the radiation to establish liability. If the injury is to a part of the body that was not intended to receive radiation, most courts will apply *res ipsa loquitur.* However, some courts apply *res ipsa loquitur* in all cases involving severe radiation injuries. These courts require the defendant to show the patient was hypersensitive or otherwise explain the injuries to avoid liability.

Several cases have addressed the duty to disclose the risk of radiation injuries from therapeutic radiologic procedures. One of the earliest cases to apply the modern requirement of informed consent ruled in 1960 that a Kansas physician had a duty to inform the patient of the probable consequences of the dose of radioactive cobalt he administered for breast cancer.[53] In a 1976 federal case, the court ruled that the physician had to disclose the probable consequences and the experimental nature of the therapy he proposed when he planned to give extremely large doses that exceeded the accepted range and were justified only by research papers read at conferences.[54] The responsibility to obtain informed consent is discussed in Chapter 13.

When radiologic technologists fail to check the status of the patient adequately, sometimes necessary precautions are not taken to protect the patient. When this results in injuries to the patient, liability is likely. In a 1972 Louisiana case, the court ruled the hospital could be liable for a patient's broken ankle that was discovered after the patient slumped on an X-ray table.[55] The radiologic technologist had not noticed that the patient was sedated, and the requisition for the X-rays had not included the brief history required by hospital policy, so the technologist had not strapped the patient to the table before raising it. The technologist had a duty to strap the sedated patient. In a 1972 federal case, the court ruled that the hospital could be sued for a radiologic technologist's handling of a patient.[56] Although the patient was to be X-rayed for suspected neck and spinal injuries from an automobile accident, the radiologic technologist told the patient to scoot onto the table and then twisted the patient's neck to position her, resulting in permanent spinal cord damage. Experts testified the patient should not have been moved to the table before her neck was immobilized and, after she was on the table, the machine, not the patient's head, should have been moved to achieve the desired angles.

Misdiagnosis by the physician reading X-ray film or another radiologic test has also led to suits. The radiologist is held to the standard of other physicians. Thus, the misdiagnosis must be more than a mere judgmental error to establish breach of duty. The misdiagnosis must be outside the accepted range of determinations by qualified radiologists under similar circumstances. Even when there is misdiagnosis, liability may be avoided if the misdiagnosis did not cause the injury. In a 1963 Iowa case, the court ruled in favor of the radiologists in a suit arising from the loss of a patient's eyesight.[57] The radiologist had not detected a piece of steel in the patient's eye. A second set of X-rays led to the discovery of the piece. The patient was unable to prove that the delay in diagnosis had caused the loss of eyesight.

Delay in reporting a proper diagnosis can also result in liability. In a 1971 federal court decision, an Indiana hospital was found liable for the death of a patient due to delay in forwarding a radiologist's report.[58] The patient was brought to the hospital emergency room early Christmas morning because of head injuries received in a fight. Four skull X-rays were taken, and the patient was examined by a physician and released. After the patient was released, a radiologist read the X-rays and found a skull fracture. He did not call the physician who had ordered the X-rays. He dictated his report, which was transcribed two days later. The patient was found unconscious later on Christmas day, after the X-rays had been read. The patient was taken to a hospital, where emergency surgery was performed, but he died that evening. The court ruled that the forwarding of reports was an administrative responsibility of the hospital and that the physician was a hospital agent when performing that function. Although it is not clear that other courts will adopt this basis for finding liability, there is a risk that other courts will find hospitals liable when no system exists for promptly reading emergency X-rays and reporting critical X-ray findings.

Radiologists may also be liable for not informing the treating physician that the X-rays ordered are too limited in scope, so the diagnosis cannot be relied on.[59]

Radiation is known to cause damage to fetuses, especially during the early stages of pregnancy. It is important to avoid exposing the abdomen of a woman of childbearing age to radiation, unless the radiation exposure is of critical importance. When exposure is necessary, the woman should be asked if she is pregnant. In a 1977 Florida case, a woman sued a radiologist for failing to ask her whether she was pregnant before X-raying her abdomen to determine the extent of her injuries from an accident.[60] Two days later, her obstetrician discovered she was pregnant. When the obstetrician learned of the X-rays, he advised an abortion, which was performed. The court ruled that it had been negligent not to ask. However, since she would have said that she was not pregnant, there was no liability because the breach of duty had not caused the injury. It is clear there could have been liability if she had known she was pregnant. However, an abortion would no longer be automatically suggested after most diagnostic radiation because the risk of significant injury from low-level radiation is known to be small.

INFECTION CONTROL

Hospitals have been found liable for some infections that patients acquire in the hospital. This liability has been based on the hospital's independent duty concerning the physical condition of the buildings and grounds and selection and maintenance of equipment, plus the hospital's liability under *respondeat superior* for the acts of its employees and agents.

In the past, courts found liability for infections when the patient proved that there were unsanitary conditions in the hospital. With improvements in infection control and in the determination of sources of infections, courts have increasingly recognized that hospitals cannot guarantee the absence of infection and that infections do occur in hospitals for many reasons other than negligence. Thus, most courts require proof of a causal relationship between the alleged injury and a deviation from proper practices. In a 1963 Washington case, the hospital was found liable for the staphylococcus infection of a patient who showed that nurses failed to take the necessary precautions, such as handwashing, to avoid cross-infection from the other patient in the semiprivate room who was infected with the same staphylococcus organism.[61]

Some hospital licensing rules specify infection control steps that must be taken, particularly isolation and sterilization procedures. These rules can be used to prove the standard of care. In a 1974 Maryland case, the hospital was found liable for injuries due to failure to comply with a regulation requiring the segregation of sterile and nonsterile needles.[62] A hospital may be held to a higher standard of care than specified in the regulation if other hospitals follow a higher standard. However, a hospital should not ignore outdated licensing regulations unless advised to do so by competent legal counsel. The hospital should usually either comply with both the regulations and proper practice or seek changes in the regulations.

When hospital employees fail to sterilize equipment properly, the hospital can be liable. In a 1955 California case, the hospital was found liable for a nurse's failure to sterilize a needle before using it to give a patient an injection.[63] The use of presterilized supplies has reduced both the risk to the patient and the hospital's liability exposure in these situations. If a patient is infected by a presterilized item, the manufacturer will usually bear the liability, unless the items were contaminated by negligent conduct of hospital staff or there was a pattern of infection that should have led the hospital to discontinue the supplies. The Iowa case discussed in the equipment section of this chapter is an example of a pattern of infection from presterilized supplies.

Another aspect of infection control is preemployment and periodic screening of hospital personnel. In a 1966 federal case, liability was found for failing to give an employee a preemployment examination before she was assigned to a newborn nursery in a military hospital.[64] The employee had a staphylococcus infection of the same type that was transmitted to a baby for whom she cared. If the hospital becomes aware that a staff member may be infected, it must remove the person from direct and indirect patient contact until the condition is diagnosed and, if the condition is infectious, until the condition is no longer infectious. Other aspects of health screening are discussed in Chapter 9.

Hospitals are increasingly expected to have a system to monitor their facilities, discover infections, and take appropriate remedial action. JCAH standards require such a system.[65] Failure to have an appropriate system could result in liability if a patient's infection could have been prevented by the type of system other hospitals have.

EMERGENCY SERVICES

Emergency services are a source of substantial liability exposure for hospitals and their staff members. The possible bases of liability of the hospital for acts of a physician in the emergency room are discussed in the *respondeat superior,* agency, and institutional liability sections of Chapter 10. The hospital's duty to provide assistance to patients who come to the emergency room and the proper handling of transfers are discussed in Chapter 12. Consent issues are discussed in Chapter 13. This section focuses on issues concerning the examination of the patient.

The responsibility for diagnosis rests with the physician. Physicians should not diagnose severely injured patients over the telephone because of the risk of communication errors. It is best for all patients who come to the emergency room to be seen by a physician. However, this is not practical in some small hospitals. They have substantial liability exposure whenever a patient is sent home without seeing a physician. Thus, even these hospitals should require the on-call physician to examine the patient personally whenever there is doubt concerning the patient's condition. A 1972 Maryland case illustrates the problem.[66] The patient had been drinking some beer. When he left the bar, he was hit by a car and thrown through the air. He was brought to the emergency room, and the on-call surgeon was telephoned. The surgeon told the nurse to admit the patient and X-ray him in the morning. Since the hospital was full, the patient was placed in the hall outside the nursing station. His condition deteriorated, and he died within three hours of entering the hospital. The autopsy found a lacerated liver and a badly fractured leg and pelvic area, with bone fragments penetrating the peritoneal cavity. The physician and nurses contradicted each other concerning the information exchanged over the telephone. The physician was found liable because he failed to examine the patient personally, and the hospital was found liable because the nurses failed to notify the physician of the deterioration of the patient's condition.

Emergencies are not always apparent. All patients should be treated as having emergencies until they are determined not to have emergency problems. The most obvious aspect of the patient's condition frequently is not the most critical. Several cases have arisen from emergency personnel assuming that drunkenness is the only problem and overlooking more serious problems. This assumption may have been part of the reason for the actions leading to the Maryland case discussed above. Another example is a Florida case involving a young man who was brought unconscious to an emergency room.[67] A superficial examination indicated he was drunk, so he was turned over to the police. He was later found dead in his cell with his thoracic cavity pierced by broken ribs. The trial court dismissed the suit, but the Florida Supreme Court ordered a new trial. It ruled that a jury could have found a responsibility to make a thorough examination of an unconscious patient and to take a history from those accompanying such a patient. A history would have uncovered the information that the patient was found lying on a lawn after a suspected fall of 23 feet.

In addition to securing a history, it is important to examine existing records as time permits. This is illustrated by a 1974 Louisiana case involving a man who had chest pains in the early morning and called his physician, who advised him to go to the emergency room.[68] The physician alerted the emergency room, ordered an electrocardiogram (EKG), and told the emergency room staff to advise him of the outcome. The physician on duty in the emergency room was not notified of the call, so he ordered an EKG and, without comparing it to prior EKGs, decided there was no heart attack. He sent the patient home with medication and instructions to call if he got worse. The personal physician was not called. The patient got worse and was later admitted for cardiac care. The court said the emergency room physician could be sued for his misdiagnosis due to failure to compare the EKG to prior EKGs. This case illustrates the importance of involving a physician, when available, who knows the patient.

Another reason to examine prior records is that distraught patients may forget information, such as allergies. However, reliance can generally be placed on a history from a competent patient. A 1975 Michigan case illustrates this in a nonemergency context.[69] The patient had a fatal allergic reaction to morphine. He had denied allergies to any painkilling drugs. Although records of a prior unrelated stay noted the allergy, the court found the hospital not liable.

When laboratory and radiologic diagnostic tests are performed on emergency patients, the patients should be advised to wait in the emergency room until the tests are completed. This point is illustrated by the 1971 federal case discussed in the radiology section of this chapter.

Another problem is falls by patients who are left unattended during examinations. Patients should not be left unattended when they are known to be at risk of falling. The risk of falling is removed for some patients by having them lie down or by restraining them. Appropriate precautions should be taken to reduce the risk of falls.

RESIDENTS AND OTHER STUDENTS

Hospitals are generally liable under *respondeat superior* for the acts of residents and other students because they are considered employees or agents of the hospital. In states where they are not considered employees, they are nevertheless considered agents for purposes of hospital liability under *respondeat superior.*

Residents are persons who have graduated from medical school and are pursuing further training in the hospital. Trainees in the first year of training after medical school used to be called interns. Since residency programs have been reorganized to begin immediately after medical school, first-year trainees are now called residents. The term *intern* is no longer in official use, although it is still used unofficially. Residents are generally not considered employees of the hospital.

Residents are generally expected to exercise the same degree of skill and knowledge possessed by members of the medical profession. In 1972 a federal appellate court ruled that the trial court must reconsider its decision against the patient because the decision was based on applying a standard of care that accounted for the resident's personal level of knowledge and experience.[70] The court ruled that if the resident could not reasonably be expected to discern subtle abnormalities in electrocardiogram tracings, then he should not have been permitted to make unaided electrocardiogram analyses. However, a few courts have instructed juries that residents should only be held to the standard of others with the same amount of training.[71]

NOTES

1. Charrin v. Methodist Hosp., 432 S.W.2d 572 (Tex. Civ. App. 1968).

2. Hernandez v. Smith, 552 F.2d 142 (5th Cir. 1977).

3. Carrasco v. Bankoff, 220 Cal. App.2d 230, 33 Cal. Rptr. 673 (1963).

4. Lauro v. Travelers Ins. Co., 261 So.2d 261 (La. Ct. App. 1972).

5. Bellaire General Hosp. v. Campbell, 510 S.W.2d 94 (Tex. Civ. App. 1974).

6. South Highlands Infirmary v. Camp. 279 Ala. 1, 180 So.2d 904 (1965).

7. Clary v. Christiansen, 54 Ohio Abs. 254, 83 N.E.2d 644 (Ohio Ct. App. 1948).

8. Orthopedic Clinic v. Hanson, 415 P.2d 991 (Okla. 1966).

9. Shepard v. McGinnis, 251 Iowa 35, 131 N.W.2d 475 (1964).

10. Anderson v. Somberg, 67 N.J. 291, 338 A.2d 1 (1975).

11. Bowers v. Olch, 120 Cal. App.2d 108, 260 P.2d 997 (1953).

12. Stumper v. Kimel, 108 N.J. Super. 209, 260 A.2d 526 (N.J. Super. Ct. App. Div. 1970).

13. Laidlaw v. Lions Gate Hosp., 8 D.L.R.3d 730 (B.C. Sup. Ct. 1969).

14. Krujelis v. Esdale, [1972] 2 W.W.R. 495 (B.C. Sup. Ct. 1971).

15. Horton v. Niagara Falls Memorial Medical Center, 51 A.D.2d 152, 380 N.Y.S.2d 116 (1976).

16. Thompson v. Brent, 245 So.2d 751 (La. Ct. App. 1971); for a more detailed discussion of professional liability cases involving nurses, see *Tort Liability and Nurses* in A. Rhodes & R. Miller, Nursing & the Law, 141–183 (1984).

17. Webb v. Jorns, 473 S.W.2d 328 (Tex. Civ. App. 1971), *rev'd on other grounds,* 488 S.W.2d 407 (Tex. 1972).

18. Fein v. Permanente Medical Group, 38 Cal.3d 137, 211 Cal. Rptr. 368, 695 P.2d 665 (1985), *appeal dismissed* 106 S.Ct. 214 (U.S. 1985).

19. Cline v. Lund, 31 Cal. App.3d 755, 107 Cal. Rptr. 629 (1973).

20. Striano v. Deepdale General Hosp., 54 A.D.2d 730, 387 N.Y.S.2d 678 (1976).

21. Toth v. Community Hosp., 22 N.Y.2d 255, 239 N.E.2d 368 (1968).

22. Fraijo v. Hartland Hosp., 99 Cal. App.3d 331, 160 Cal. Rptr. 246 (1979).

23. Larrimore v. Homeopathic Hosp. Ass'n, 54 Del. 449, 181 A.2d 573 (1962).

24. Norton v. Argonaut Ins. Co., 144 So.2d 249 (La. Ct. App. 1962).

25. Hiatt v. Groce, 215 Kan. 14, 523 P.2d 320 (1974).

26. Duling v. Bluefield Sanitarium, Inc., 149 W.Va. 567, 142 S.E.2d 754 (1965).

27. Collins v. Westlake Community Hosp., 57 Ill.2d 388, 312 N.E.2d 614 (1974).

28. Mundt v. Alta Bates Hosp., 223 Cal. App.2d 413, 35 Cal. Rptr. 848 (1963).

29. 33 Ill.2d 326, 211 N.E.2d 253 (1965), cert. denied, 383 U.S. 496 (1966).

30. Utter v. United Hosp. Center, Inc., 236 S.E.2d 213 (W.Va. 1977).

31. Goff v. Doctors General Hosp., 166 Cal. App.2d 314, 333 P.2d 29 (1958).

32. Kastler v. Iowa Methodist Hosp., 193 N.W.2d 98 (Iowa 1971).

33. Emory Univ. v. Shadburn, 180 Ga. 595, 180 S.E. 137 (1935).

34. Joint Commission on Accreditation of Hospitals, ACCREDITATION MANUAL FOR HOSPI-
TALS (1986 ed.), 165 [hereinafter cited as JCAH 1986].

35. Sullivan v. Sisters of St. Francis, 374 S.W.2d 294 (Tex. Civ. App. 1963).

36. Troppi v. Scarf, 31 Mich. App. 240, 187 N.W.2d 511 (1971).

37. Warren, PROBLEMS IN HOSPITAL LAW (3rd ed. 1978), 219.

38. 32 ILLINOIS PHARMACIST 401 (Dec. 1970).

39. McCord v. State, Nos. 43405, 43406, and 43407 (N.Y. Ct. Cl. 1969).

40. E.g., Mielke v. Condell Memorial Hosp., 124 Ill. App.3d 42, 463 N.E.2d 216 (1984)
[no liability for not notifying physician of drug interaction discovered by monitoring system].

41. South Miami Hosp. v. Sanchez, 386 So.2d 39 (Fla. Dist. Ct. App. 1980).

42. McAvenue v. Bryn Mawr Hosp., 245 Pa. Super. 507, 369 A.2d 743 (Pa. Super. Ct.
1976).

43. Meiman v. Rehabilitation Center, Inc., 444 S.W.2d 78 (Ky. 1969).

44. Forsyth v. Sisters of Charity, 39 Or. App. 851, 593 P.2d 1270 (1979).

45. Gilles v. Rehabilitation Inst., 262 Or. 472, 498 P.2d 777 (1972).

46. Mokry v. University of Tex. Health Science Center, 529 S.W.2d 802 (Tex. Civ. App.
1975).

47. Variety Children's Hosp. v. Osle, 292 So.2d 382 (Fla. Dist. Ct. App. 1974).

48. Lundberg v. Bay View Hosp., 175 Ohio St. 133, 191 N.E.2d 821 (1963).

49. Insurance Co. of N. Am. v. Prieto, 442 F.2d 1033 (6th Cir. 1971).

50. Schnebly v. Baker, 217 N.W.2d 708 (Iowa 1974).

51. Gildiner v. Thomas Jefferson Univ. Hosp., 451 F. Supp. 692 (E.D. Pa. 1978).

52. Synott v. Midway Hosp., 287 Minn. 270, 178 N.W.2d 211 (1970).

53. Natanson v. Kline, 187 Kan. 186, 354 P.2d 670 (1960).

54. Ahern v. Veterans Admin., 537 F.2d 1098 (10th Cir. 1976).

55. Albritton v. Bossier City Hosp. Comm'n, 271 So.2d 353 (La. Ct. App. 1972).

56. Modave v. Long Island Jewish Medical Center, 501 F.2d 1065 (2nd Cir. 1974).

57. Barnes v. Bovenmeyer, 255 Iowa 220, 122 N.W.2d 312 (1963).

58. Keene v. Methodist Hosp., 324 F. Supp. 233 (N.D. Ind. 1971); see also Davidson v.
Mobile Infirmary, 456 So.2d 14 (Ala. 1984) [failure to inform treating physician of X-rays
showing large number of pills in stomach].

59. E.g., Shuffler v. Blue Ridge Radiology Assocs., 73 N.C. App. 232, 326 S.E.2d 96
(1985).

60. Salinetro v. Nystrom, 341 So.2d 1059 (Fla. Dist. Ct. App. 1977).

61. Helman v. Sacred Heart Hosp., 62 Wash.2d 136, 381 P.2d 605 (1963).

62. Suburban Hosp. Ass'n v. Hadary, 22 Md. App. 186, 322 A.2d 258 (Md. Ct. Sp. App. 1974).

63. Kalmas v. Cedars of Lebanon Hosp., 132 Cal. App.2d 243, 281 P.2d 872 (1955).

64. Kapuschinsky v. United States, 248 F. Supp. 732 (D. S.C. 1966).

65. JCAH 1986, *supra* note 34 at 69.

66. Thomas v. Corsco, 265 Md. 84, 288 A.2d 379 (1972).

67. Bourgeois v. Dade County, 99 So.2d 575 (Fla. 1957).

68. Fox v. Argonaut Sw. Ins. Co., 288 So.2d 102 (La. Ct. App. 1974).

69. Howell v. Outer Drive Hosp., 66 Mich. App. 142, 238 N.W.2d 553 (1975).

70. McBride v. United States, 462 F.2d 72 (9th Cir. 1972).

71. Hilyer v. Hole, 114 Mich. App. 38, 318 N.W.2d 598 (1982).

Chapter 12

Beginning and Ending the Relationship with the Patient

There is some overlap between the physician-patient relationship and the hospital-patient relationship, but they are not identical. Some physician-patient relationships are entirely outside the hospital. Even when hospital care is required, the physician may not be able to initiate a hospital-patient relationship with a particular hospital because the hospital does not have space available or the physician does not have admitting privileges. In some emergency situations, the relationship with the hospital may begin before the relationship with the physician. Sometimes a patient changes physicians while in the hospital, establishing a new physician-patient relationship. In most situations, after the relationship with the hospital ends, the physician-patient relationship continues.

This chapter discusses the ways that a physician-patient or hospital-patient relationship begins and ends.

PHYSICIAN-PATIENT RELATIONSHIP

Beginning the Relationship

Generally a physician has the right to accept or decline to establish a professional relationship with any person. A physician does not have a legal responsibility to diagnose or treat anyone, unless there is an express or implied agreement to do so. Likewise, an individual does not have an obligation to accept diagnosis or treatment from any particular physician, unless the situation is one in which the law authorizes the person to be cared for involuntarily.

There are three ways that a physician can establish a physician-patient relationship: (1) by contracting to care for a certain population and to have one of that population seek care; (2) by entering an express contract with

239

the patient or the patient's legal representative by mutual agreement; or (3) by engaging in conduct from which a contract can be implied.

Contracts To Care for a Certain Population

A physician who enters a contract to care for members of a certain population must provide care for them to the extent required by the contract. For example, physicians enter contracts with hospitals to care for emergency patients or to provide certain services such as radiology or pathology. Usually these contracts do not permit the physician to refuse to care for individual hospital patients requiring those services. Physicians frequently enter contracts with other institutions and organizations, such as athletic teams, schools, companies, prisons, jails, nursing homes, and health maintenance organizations, that include an agreement to provide certain kinds of care to all members of certain populations who seek care.

Express Contract

The most frequent way that the physician-patient relationship is begun is by mutual agreement of the physician and the patient or the patient's representative, such as the parent or guardian of a minor or the guardian or next-of-kin of an incompetent adult. The physician may limit the scope of the contract and not assume responsibility for all the patient's medical needs. For example, the services can be limited to a particular specialty, so an internist can refuse to perform surgery.[1] An obstetrician can refuse to participate in home deliveries.[2] Physicians may limit the geographic area in which they practice. A California court ruled that a patient who became ill while visiting out of town could not sue her physician for refusing to come to the other town to see her.[3] A consulting physician who examines a patient at the request of the primary physician can limit involvement with the patient to the consultation and refuse continuing responsibility as long as this limitation is made clear to the patient and primary physician.

Some limitations on the scope of the contract are not permissible. For example, an admitting physician assumes the responsibility to examine the patient and offer appropriate treatment until the physician-patient relationship is terminated. In a 1975 Florida case a physician who was at home recovering from an illness had agreed to admit a patient to the hospital as a favor to a friend but attempted to limit his contract solely to the act of admission by making it clear that he could not treat the patient.[4] The patient died of an undiagnosed brain abscess within a few days. The physician never saw her. The court ruled that there was a physician-patient relationship that included a duty to see the patient, so the father of the patient could sue the physician for malpractice.

Implied Contract

Sometimes a physician-patient relationship with all of its attendant responsibilities is inferred from the physician's conduct. If the physician commences treatment of a person, the courts will generally find a physician-patient relationship. However, some courts have found a relationship from lesser contact. The Iowa Supreme Court ruled that a relationship was established when a physician told a patient he would perform surgery.[5] A New York court based an implied contract on the fact that the physician had listened to a recital of the patient's symptoms over the telephone.[6] Thus, physicians who do not wish to assume the responsibility of a relationship should limit telephone calls to advising the caller to seek medical assistance elsewhere.

In some situations, very limited conversations may not be interpreted as creating a relationship. For example, a Georgia hospital employee sued the hospital medical director for giving her erroneous medical advice when he responded with a few suggestions to her questions while stopped in the hospital hallway.[7] The court found that this incident was not enough to conclude that the physician had agreed to treat her or advise her as a physician.

Although some specialists, such as pathologists and diagnostic radiologists, seldom see their patients, a physician-patient relationship is still established. This relationship does not usually include the responsibility for continuing care that is one of the elements of most relationships, but it does include responsibility for the consequences of intentional or negligence errors in providing pathology or radiology services.

Ending the Relationship

A physician has a duty to continue to provide medical care until the relationship is legally terminated. A physician who discontinues care before the relationship is legally terminated can be liable for abandonment.[8]

The physician-patient relationship can be ended if (1) medical care is no longer needed; (2) the patient withdraws from the relationship; (3) the care of the patient is transferred to another physician; (4) ample notice of withdrawal is given by the physician to the patient; or (5) the physician is unable to provide care.

If the patient withdraws from the relationship, the physician has a duty to attempt to warn the patient if further care is needed. Upon request, the physician should advise the successor physician, if any, of information necessary to continue treatment. If care is still needed, the physician should usually request written confirmation of the withdrawal from the patient, realizing that in many situations the patient will decline to provide it.

The care of the patient can be transferred to another physician. It is recognized that physicians attend meetings, take vacations, and have other valid reasons they cannot be available. A physician can fulfill the duties of the physician-patient relationship by providing a qualified substitute.[9] A physician can withdraw from the relationship without providing a substitute by giving the patient reasonable notice in writing with sufficient time for the patient to locate another physician willing to accept the patient if continuing care is required. Some of the reasons for withdrawal are noncooperation or failure to pay bills when able to do so.

A physician can be excused from the responsibilities of the relationship when unable to provide care. A physician who is ill should not accept additional responsibilities and should attempt to arrange for a substitute.[10] However, it is recognized that sometimes physicians become too ill to be able to arrange a substitute. It is also recognized that a physician cannot be with two patients simultaneously. Thus, the necessity of attending another patient may provide a valid excuse as long as the physician has exercised prudence in determining the priority.[11] The physician cannot entirely give up one patient to attend another. The frequency of attendance to each patient will be an important factor in assessing whether one patient has been abandoned.

A physician who fails to see a patient with whom there is a physician-patient relationship without an acceptable reason may face liability for breach of contract or, if the patient is injured as a result, malpractice.

Physicians do not have to be with the patient continuously to satisfy their responsibility. Physicians can leave orders for others to administer medications or other care, as long as they return at intervals appropriate to the patient's condition. When admission to a hospital is not indicated, the patient can usually be sent home with instructions to call if further care is needed. The patient has the responsibility to call. The major exception to this is when the patient and those responsible for the patient are unable to provide the needed care in the home. The physician should then have arrangements made for other assistance or placement. Finally, the patient or representative can be told to follow certain instructions or to return at a certain time. It is not abandonment if the patient fails to return or follow instructions. However, if the patient has a known debility, it may be necessary to follow up if the patient does not return.

HOSPITAL-PATIENT RELATIONSHIP

This section addresses the hospital's responsibilities to persons who are not in need of emergency care; the hospital's responsibilities to persons who need emergency care; and issues concerning discharge.

Nonemergency Patients

Under common law, a person who does not need emergency care usually does not have a right to be admitted to a hospital. The hospital can legally refuse to admit any person unless one of three broad categories of exceptions applies: (1) the common law; (2) contractual exceptions; and (3) statutory exceptions. Several statutes forbid discriminatory admission policies but do not grant a right to be admitted. Rights to be admitted are contingent on necessity for hospitalization, appropriateness of the hospital for the patient's needs, and availability of space.

Common Law Right to Admission

A person generally has a right to be admitted when the hospital is responsible for the original injury that caused the need for hospitalization. In some circumstances, a person who becomes ill or injured in the hospital buildings or on the hospital grounds may have a right to be admitted even if the hospital is not otherwise responsible for the illness or injury. If a hospital begins to exercise control of a person by examining or beginning to provide care, a hospital-patient relationship may be started, entitling the patient to be admitted.

Contractual Right to Admission

If a hospital has a contract to accept members of a certain population, then they have a right to be admitted when they need care the hospital is able to provide. Some hospitals have contracts with employers to provide services to their employees or with health care insurers, such as Blue Cross or health maintenance organizations, agreeing to accept patients covered by the insurer. An Alabama court found a hospital liable for breach of a contract to furnish hospital services to the employees of a company because the jury concluded that a decision that hospitalization was unnecessary was not made in good faith.[12] When entering such contracts, hospitals should assure that the contract clearly provides that patients will be entitled to admission only when admitted by a physician with clinical privileges in the hospital.

Hospitals that accepted Hill-Burton construction grants or loans agreed to a "community service" obligation. The regulations defining this obligation specify that no person residing in the area serviced by the hospital will be denied admission to the portion of the hospital financed by Hill-Burton funds on any grounds other than the individual's lack of need for services, the availability of the needed services in the hospital, or the individual's ability to pay.[13] Inability to pay cannot be a basis for denial when the person needs emergency services or when the facility still has a Hill-Burton uncompensated care obligation. Emergency patients who are unable to pay and for whom services are not available under the uncompensated care obligation may be discharged or transferred to another facility that is able to provide necessary services. However, there must be a medical determination that the discharge or transfer does not substantially risk deterioration in the patient's medical condition. Advance deposits can be required if the hospital permits alternative arrangements when patients who are able to pay do not have the necessary cash. Hospitals may require admission by a physician with clinical privileges only if sufficient physicians on the staff are willing to admit the patients who must be admitted under the community service obligation. If insufficient physicians on the medical staff will admit certain types of patients, such as Medicaid patients, the hospital must either hire physicians who will admit them, condition appointments to the medical staff on an agreement to admit some of them,[14] or grant temporary admitting privileges to the patient's personal physician. Any hospital that received construction funds after the 1974 amendments must provide this access to persons who work in the area served by the facility, in addition to those who reside in the area.

Statutory Right to Admission

Some hospitals, especially governmental hospitals, are obligated by statute to accept all patients from a certain population that may be defined by geographic area of residence, inability to pay for care, or a combination of both. For example, county hospitals in Iowa are required to provide care and treatment to any resident of the county who is sick or injured and observes the rules of conduct adopted by the governing body.[15]

Nondiscrimination Statutes

Several statutes forbid discrimination in admission but do not grant a right to be admitted. Title VI of the Civil Rights Act[16] forbids discrimination on the basis of race, color, or national origin in any institution that receives federal financial assistance. A hospital must comply with this statute and its implementing regulations[17] if it receives Medicare or Medicaid reimbursement. The Rehabilitation Act of 1973[18] forbids discrimination on the basis of handicap in any institution that receives federal financial assistance. A hospital that receives Medicare and Medicaid reimbursement must comply with this statute and its implementing regulations.[19] Most substance abusers are considered handicapped under this law, so hospitals cannot discriminate against alcoholics and drug abusers in the providing of services.

Reasons for Nonadmission

Even when a person otherwise has a right to be admitted to a hospital, several reasons are generally recognized as justifying nonadmission. First, if hospitalization is not medically necessary, there is no right to admission. A hospital is not a hotel; it is an institution for the provision of necessary medical services. Second, if the hospital does not provide the services the patient needs, it does not have to admit the patient. If the patient needs emergency care to prepare for transfer to an appropriate facility, the hospital usually will be expected to provide such care.

Generally, when space is not available, the hospital may refuse to admit the patient, but still must provide the emergency care necessary to prepare for transfer.[20] This rule usually applies even when a court orders admission. For example, the South Dakota Supreme Court ruled that the lower court had exceeded its jurisdiction when it ordered a state training school to accept a juvenile when no space was available.[21] Therefore, the superintendent's disobedience was not punishable as contempt. However, not all courts adopt this realistic position, so such court orders should not be violated except upon advice of legal counsel. In 1982 the Washington Supreme Court interpreted state law to require a mental hospital to accept all patients presented to the hospital by mental health professionals within its allocated area, even though they would exceed the institutional capacity.[22] It based its analysis in part on the need of these patients for immediate treatment, so perhaps this case should be viewed as an example of the hospital's responsibility for emergency patients.

Emergency Patients

In the past, the general rule was that persons did not have a right to emergency hospital care except under the circumstances discussed earlier in this chapter in which they would be entitled to any necessary hospital services. In most states, persons now have a special right to hospital care in actual emergencies. In states that have not yet formally adopted the rule, hospitals that maintain an emergency room should still provide necessary emergency care because it is unlikely that many courts will rule today that emergency care may be denied.

In some states, some or all hospitals are required by statute or regulation to provide necessary emergency services to anyone who arrives at the hospital. For example, in Texas it is a crime for any officer or employee of a general hospital supported with public funds to deny a person emergency services available in the hospital on the basis of inability to pay if a physician has diagnosed that the patient is seriously ill or injured.[23]

Many courts have recognized a common law right to emergency services in states that do not have statutes. In a Delaware case, the hospital had refused to accept a baby as a patient because the family's personal physician was not available.[24] The emergency room staff asked the parents to return the next day with the baby, but the baby died at home that afternoon. The court ruled that in an unmistakable emergency patients have a right to care in a hospital that maintains an emergency room, so the hospital was liable for the child's death. Courts in several other states have reached the same conclusion.[25] Often they base the right on an implied invitation to the public by operating an emergency room. However, even when the hospital is clearly operated only for a limited population, some courts still impose an obligation to provide emergency care.[26]

When care is provided under the emergency care obligation to patients the hospital would not otherwise accept, the hospital generally does not have a duty to provide continuing care if arrangements can be made to transfer the patient to an appropriate hospital without substantial danger to the patient. This is recognized by the Hill-Burton community service regulations discussed earlier in this chapter. For example, the Alabama Supreme Court ruled that a hospital has no obligation to admit a patient after providing proper emergency care.[27] The patient in this case had no right to stay in the hospital. The hospital fulfilled its responsibility by arranging for transfer to a charitable hospital. However, if the emergency care had created a dangerous condition requiring further care, the hospital would have had a duty to admit the patient under the general common law responsibility that everyone has to assist persons they have put in peril. In some states, financial transfers are permitted in a smaller range of circumstances.[28]

If the hospital cannot provide the care the patient needs, it has a duty to attempt to arrange a transfer. A California court found a hospital and treating physician liable for the negligent care of a severely burned patient, in part because the hospital did not have the facilities to care for severe burns.[29]

If a transfer is required, the hospital has a duty to prepare the patient properly for the move and to make arrangements for it. Preparation of the patient includes appropriate examination and stabilization. In a Mississippi case, a veteran who came to a community hospital emergency room bleeding profusely had been transferred to a Veterans Administration hospital by the emergency nurse without the nurse's making any effort to stop the bleeding.[30] The first hospital was found liable for the patient's death because the nurse did not obtain information concerning his condition from the people who brought him to the hospital, did not tell the physician on call of the extent of the bleeding, and did not do anything to stop the bleeding. Transfer arrangements include appropriate attendants and speed. When ambulances and helicopters staffed with emergency medical technicians, emergency nurses, or physicians are available, it will be difficult to convince a court of the appropriateness of an interhospital transfer of a critically ill patient in an unequipped vehicle that is not staffed with specially trained personnel.

Emergency room staff can take actions based on the reasonably available information. They do not have to be able to foresee the future in the absence of information. For example, a Florida hospital was sued by the wife of a man who had been stabbed by a person briefly seen in the emergency room.[31] A grandmother had taken her grandson to the emergency room because she suspected he had taken LSD, but the hospital did not have the testing facilities to determine the presence of the drug. While the grandmother was driving the grandson to another hospital, he jumped out of the car, ran into a building, and fatally stabbed the plaintiff's husband. The court found that the hospital was not liable because the patient exhibited no behavior that would have led the personnel at the first hospital to suspect a risk of this outcome. If there had been reasons to suspect this, other arrangements would have had to be made for transport.

DISCHARGE

There is a fundamental tension between the liability that can result from holding a patient too long and the liability that can result from releasing a patient too soon. This section discusses the liability for false imprisonment and for discharge of patients in need of additional care. Refusal to leave, temporary releases, and escapes are also discussed.

False Imprisonment

False imprisonment is holding a person against his or her will without lawful authority. Physical restraint or a physical barrier is not necessary. Threats leading to a reasonable apprehension of harm can provide enough restraint to establish false imprisonment.

In the past, a few cases of false imprisonment arose when hospitals attempted to hold patients until their bills were paid.[32] There have been no reported decisions concerning this situation in more than 20 years, which indicates that hospitals now understand this practice is unacceptable.

In some cases, hospitals inappropriately restrain patients as part of treatment leading to liability. An unreported 1970 Michigan Circuit Court decision from Wayne County, *Smith v. Henry Ford Hospital,* is an example. A patient who had been transferred from the coronary care unit to a semiprivate room decided to leave the hospital because he did not like the room. When the patient tried to leave, several staff members returned the patient to the hospital room and restrained him in the bed. He escaped from the restraints and exited through the window. He was injured in his fall to the ground. Since there was no evidence that the patient was disoriented or mentally unsound, the court found the hospital liable.

In many situations, it is not only appropriate but also a duty of the hospital to detain or restrain a patient. All states have laws providing procedures for the commitment of persons who are seriously mentally ill, are substance abusers, or are a danger to the public health due to contagious disease. They also have laws that provide procedures for taking custody of minors who are neglected or abused. Generally, a hospital can hold these persons while reporting them to authorities and obtaining commitment or custody orders. When these laws do not apply, the hospital still has a common law duty to protect temporarily disoriented patients.

Physicians and hospitals have authority under the common law to temporarily detain and even restrain temporarily disoriented medical patients without court involvement. This authority is inferred from the cases in which hospitals have been found liable for injuries to patients because they are not restrained during temporary disorientation. This common law authority does not apply when the patient is being detained for treatment for mental illness or substance abuse. The applicable statutory procedures should be followed in those cases. This common law authority does not apply when the patient is fully oriented, as in the *Henry Ford Hospital* case, but the hospital can usually maintain custody long enough for the patient's status to be determined if there is reasonable doubt.

If parents try to take children out of the hospital when removal presents an imminent danger to the child's life or health, most states either authorize the health care provider to retain custody of the child or provide an expeditious procedure for obtaining court authorization to retain custody. However, many parents will agree to an acceptable treatment or at least postpone precipitous withdrawal when advised that these procedures will be invoked.

If an adult patient is neither disoriented nor committable, the patient generally has a right to leave, unless it is one of the unusual situations when courts will order treatment, as discussed in Chapter 13. Interfering with this right can lead to liability, as illustrated by the *Henry Ford Hospital* case. Those involved with hospital care should understand that honoring the patient's wishes to leave can cause the patient care staff great distress. For example, nearly all physicians or nurses are distressed when an oriented patient with a spinal fracture insists on leaving the hospital, risking paralysis or even death that could probably be prevented by appropriate care in the hospital. This distress does not change the patient's right to leave. It will affect the staff's efforts to convince the patient to stay and to explain the risks of leaving.

Patients who decide to leave against medical advice should be advised of the risks of leaving, if possible, and should be urged to reconsider if further care is needed. The explanation should be documented. Patients should be asked to sign a form that they are leaving against medical advice and that the risks have been explained to them. However, patients cannot be forced to sign. If patients refuse to sign, the explanation and refusal should be documented in the medical record by the involved staff.

Discharge of Patients Needing Additional Care

A patient should be discharged only with (1) a written order of a physician familiar with the patient's condition or (2) the patient's decision to leave against medical advice. This procedure helps to protect the patient from injury and the hospital from liability for premature discharge.

Most premature discharge cases arise from misdiagnosis, but sometimes they arise from discharging patients who are ready to leave but for whom adequate arrangements have not been made. It is essential for children, the infirm aged, and others who are unable to care for themselves to be discharged only to the custody of someone who can take care of them. A California physician was found liable for discharging an abused 11-month-old child to the abusing parents without first giving the state an opportunity to intervene.[33]

Patients do not have to be kept in the hospital until cured. When they no longer need the level of care provided in a hospital, they can be transferred to a nursing home or discharged to home care. When they no longer need the level of hospital care in a referral center or begin to need the more specialized level of care in a referral center, interhospital transfer is appropriate and sometimes necessary.

If a patient becomes sufficiently difficult or disruptive, it is permissible in some situations for the hospital to discontinue providing care. In 1982 a California court refused to order a physician and several hospitals to continue to provide chronic hemodialysis to a noncooperative, disruptive patient who had even refused to comply with the conditions of a court order that provided for continued treatment during the litigation.[34] The physician had given her due notice of his withdrawal from the physician-patient relationship with ample time for her to make other arrangements. The court was clearly troubled by the possibility that she would not be able to receive necessary care but concluded that several alternatives were available.

Courts are more comfortable with involuntary discharges when the patient's condition is not so severe. For example, an Arizona court ruled that a physician and hospital were not liable for discharging a difficult patient who had been admitted for treatment of lesions on his lips.[35] The court observed that the patient was uncomfortable but not helpless, and the hospital staff had done nothing actively to retard his treatment or worsen his condition. Any discharge of a patient in need of continued care could be controversial, so it should usually be limited to situations that interfere with the care of other patients or threaten the safety of staff members. It is prudent to have hospital administration review each case to minimize legal liability and other adverse effects on the hospital. When the attending physician desires an inappropriate discharge, it may be necessary to transfer the care of the patient to another physician or to discuss with the physician the compatibility of the proposed discharge with the hospital's standards for continued membership on the medical staff.

The need for a treating physician's discharge order is especially important to remember when the utilization review committee or a third party reviewer decides that a patient should be discharged, but the treating physician believes the patient should stay in the hospital. While the decision of a physician reviewer may be given some weight, it will not insulate the physician or hospital from liability. An independent judgment must be made by the treating physician. In some cases, the reviewer may face liability. For example, a state physician reviewer in California was found liable for the complications a patient suffered when the reviewer authorized only half the additional hospital days requested by the treating physician.[36]

Refusal To Leave

Patients and patient representatives do not have the right to insist on unnecessary hospitalization. If the patient refuses to leave or the patient's representatives refuse to remove the patient after the physician's discharge order, the patient is a trespasser, and the hospital can take appropriate steps to have the patient removed. If the situation is a delay in discharge due to difficulties in arranging placement, the hospital will usually take reasonable steps to assist in making arrangements. However, if the patient and the patient's representatives will not cooperate, it may be necessary to use reasonable force to remove the patient or to obtain a court order.[37] In a few states it is a crime to refuse to leave a hospital after discharge.[38] As with the discharge of noncooperative and disruptive patients discussed in the previous section, hospital administration should make decisions concerning forceable removal after appropriate review.

Temporary Releases

Sometimes children, incompetent adults, cooperative committed patients, or competent adults who need continuing supervision or care ask to leave the hospital for a short time. This is permissible in many situations and may assist in the care of the patient. Since there is a possibility of liability, certain precautions should be taken. A written physician authorization should indicate that the temporary release is not medically contraindicated. Written authorization from competent adult patients or from the parent or guardian of other patients should acknowledge that the hospital is not responsible for the care of the patient while the patient is out of the custody of the hospital. Except for adult patients who are able to take care of themselves and are not a danger to others, patients should only be released to appropriate adults who have been instructed concerning the needs of the patient during the release, such as medications and wheelchair use, and the way to contact the hospital for information or assistance if needed. If the necessary arrangements are then made for patient needs, such as medications or wheelchairs, the risks associated with temporary releases are minimized.

If patients who are a danger to themselves or others are temporarily released and are harmed or harm others, the hospital could be liable. A Florida court ruled that a hospital could be sued by a person who was injured in an automobile accident caused by a patient on a temporary release because the hospital should have known she would attempt to operate an automobile and could not do so safely.[39] This case illustrates the significance of careful review by the physician before authorizing release.

A Minnesota hospital's policy concerning passes for the mentally ill was challenged as a violation of the state's commitment law.[40] In 1984 the Minnesota Supreme Court upheld the policy by ruling that the passes were not discharges. The court reviewed the precautions that were taken, including monitoring and giving interested individuals an opportunity to comment before the pass was issued, and concluded they were appropriate. These precautions may not be required in other states.

Escape

Hospitals are frequently sued when patients who have escaped either commit suicide, are injured or killed in accidents, or injure or kill others. The courts usually focus on (1) how much those involved in the care of the patient knew or should have known about the dangerousness of the patient to self or others; and (2) the appropriateness of the precautions taken to prevent escape in light of that knowledge. Generally, if the injury was not foreseeable, there is little likelihood of liability for failure to take additional precautions. If the injury was foreseeable, courts will examine the reasonableness of the precautions, and liability will be more likely. However, many courts have recognized the therapeutic benefits of more open patient care units and have found them to be reasonable even for some patients at risk. In other cases, the precautions have been found to be inadequate, and liability has been imposed.

NOTES

1. *E.g.,* Skodje v. Hardy, 47 Wash.2d 557, 288 P.2d 471 (1955).

2. *E.g.,* Vidrine v. Mayes, 127 So.2d 809 (La. Ct. App. 1961).

3. McNamara v. Emmons, 36 Cal. App.2d 199, 97 P.2d 503 (1939).

4. Giallanza v. Sands, 316 So.2d 77 (Fla. Dist. Ct. App. 1975).

5. McGulpin v. Bessmer, 241 Iowa 1119, 43 N.W.2d 121 (1950).

6. O'Neil v. Montefiore Hosp., 11 App. Div. 2d 132, 202 N.Y.S.2d 436 (1960).

7. Buttersworth v. Swint, 53 Ga. App. 602, 186 S.E. 770 (1936).

8. *See Liability of Physician Who Abandons Case,* 37 A.L.R.2d 432 (1958).

9. *E.g.,* Kearns v. Ellis, 18 Mass. App. 23, 465 N.E.2d 294 (1984), *review denied,* 393 Mass. 1102, 469 N.E.2d 830 (1984).

10. *E.g.,* Kenny v. Piedmont Hosp., 136 Ga. App. 660, 222 S.E.2d 162 (1975) [not abandonment for ill surgeon to permit associate to operate].

11. *E.g.,* Young v. Jordan, 106 W.Va. 139, 145 S.E. 41 (1928) [another patient not excuse when physician induced labor in first patient].

12. Norwood Hosp. v. Howton, 32 Ala. App. 375, 26 So.2d 427 (1946).

13. 42 C.F.R §§124.601-124.607 (1984).

14. *E.g.,* Clair v. Center Community Hosp., 317 Pa. Super. 25, 463 A.2d 1065 (1983) [hospital can suspend physician who does not comply with rule requiring indigent care].

15. Iowa Code Ann. §347.16 (1985 Supp.).

16. 42 U.S.C. §§2000d-2000d-6 (1982).

17. 45 C.F.R. pt. 80 (1985).

18. 29 U.S.C. §794 (1982).

19. 45 C.F.R. pt. 84 (1985).

20. People v. Flushing Hosp. and Medical Center, 471 N.Y.S.2d 745 (N.Y. Crim. Ct. 1983) [hospital found guilty of misdemeanor and fined when a patient died after emergency care was refused because the hospital was full].

21. People ex rel. M.B., 312 N.W.2d 714 (S.D. 1981).

22. Pierce County Office of Involuntary Commitment v. Western State Hosp., 97 Wash. 2d 264, 644 P.2d 131 (1982).

23. Tex. Rev. Civ. Stat. Ann. Art. 4438a (Vernon 1985); the first criminal prosecution of an administrator under this statute resulted in a mistrial. *See Admitting and Discharge,* HOSPITAL LAW MANUAL, 17 (1980).

24. Wilmington General Hosp. v. Manlove, 54 Del. 15, 174 A.2d 135 (1962).

25. *E.g.,* Stanturf v. Sipes, 447 S.W.2d 558 (Mo. 1969).

26. Guerrero v. Copper Queen Hosp., 112 Az. 104, 537 P.2d 1329 (1975) [privately owned hospital operated solely for employees of one company must provide emergency care, even to illegal aliens].

27. Harper v. Baptist Medical Center-Princeton, 341 So.2d 133 (Ala. 1976).

28. *E.g.*, Thompson v. Sun City Community Hosp., Inc., 141 Az. 597, 688 P.2d 605 (1984).

29. Carrasco v. Bankoff, 220 Cal. App.2d 230, 33 Cal. Rptr. 673 (1963).

30. New Biloxi Hosp. v. Frazier, 245 Miss. 185, 146 So.2d 882 (1962).

31. Nance v. James Archer Smith Hosp., 326 So.2d 377 (Fla. Dist. Ct. App. 1976).

32. *E.g.*, Gadsden General Hosp. v. Hamilton, 212 Ala. 531, 103 So. 533 (1925).

33. Landeros v. Flood, 17 Cal.3d 399, 551 P.2d 389 (1976).

34. Payton v. Weaver, 131 Cal. App.3d 38, 182 Cal. Rptr. 225 (1982).

35. Modla v. Parker, 17 Ariz. App. 54, 495 P.2d 494 (1972), *cert. denied*, 409 U.S. 1038 (1972).

36. Wickline v. State, 27 Cal. Cir. No. NWC 60672 (Cal. Super. Ct. 1982).

37. *E.g.*, Jersey City Medical Center v. Halstead, 169 N.J. Super. 22, 404 A.2d 44 (N.J. Super. Ct. Ch. Div. 1979); Lucy Webb Hayes Nat'l Training School v. Geoghegan, 281 F. Supp. 116 (D. D.C. 1967).

38. *E.g.*, N.C. Stat. §§131–137 (1981).

39. Burroughs v. Board of Trustees of Alachua General Hosp., 328 So.2d 538 (Fla. Dist. Ct. App. 1976).

40. Hennepin County v. Levine, 345 N.W.2d 217 (Minn. 1984).

Chapter 13

Authorization for Treatment

Health care providers must obtain appropriate authorization before examining a patient or performing diagnostic or therapeutic procedures. In most circumstances, authorization is obtained by the patient or the patient's representative giving express or implied consent. The law requires that the patient or the patient's representative be given sufficient information concerning the available choices so that the consent is informed consent. If the decision is not to consent, usually the examination or procedure cannot be performed. However, in several circumstances the law overrides the decision and provides authorization for involuntary treatment, such as for some mental illness and for substance abuse. Consent is not sufficient authorization for a procedure in circumstances where it is illegal.

Physicians and other independent practitioners have the primary responsibility for obtaining informed consent or other authorization for treatment. Hospitals are generally not liable for the physician's failure to obtain authorization unless (1) the physician is an employee or agent of the hospital or (2) the hospital is aware of the lack of consent and fails to take appropriate action. However, the hospital is frequently involved in advising members of the medical staff and helping to obtain authorization when informed consent cannot be obtained. Thus, both hospital administrators and individual health care providers should be familiar with the principles discussed in this chapter.

The requirements of consent and informed consent, the decision-making roles of patients and their representatives, and the exceptions to the consent requirement are discussed in this chapter. Decisions concerning reproductive issues are discussed in Chapter 15. Withholding and withdrawing treatment from dying patients are discussed in Chapter 16.

THE DISTINCTION BETWEEN CONSENT AND INFORMED CONSENT

The common law has long recognized the right of persons to be free from harmful or offensive touching. The intentional harmful or offensive touching of another person without authorization is called *battery* (as discussed in Chapter 10). The earliest medical consent lawsuits arose when surgery was done without consent or other authorization, so the courts found the surgeons liable for battery. When there is no consent or other authorization, the physician or other practitioner doing the medical procedure can be liable for battery, even if the procedure is properly performed, is beneficial, and has no negative effects. The touching alone leads to liability.

Courts began to be presented with cases in which the patient consented to the procedure but did not have sufficient information for an informed decision. The courts held that the physician had a legal duty to disclose sufficient information. In some early cases, the courts ruled that providing incorrect or insufficient information invalidated the consent, making the physician liable for battery. Courts have now adopted the position that failure to disclose the necessary information does not invalidate consent, so the procedure is not a battery. However, failure to disclose is a separate wrong for which there can be liability based on principles applicable to negligent torts, discussed in Chapter 10. Thus, uninformed consent protects from liability for battery, but informed consent is necessary to protect from liability for negligence.

Some courts have extended the informed consent doctrine to require informed refusal. In 1980 the California Supreme Court ruled that a physician could be liable for a patient's death from cancer of the cervix based on the physician's failure to inform the patient of the risks of not consenting to a recommended Pap smear.[1] The Pap smear probably would have discovered her cancer in time to begin life-extending treatment.

CONSENT

Consent may be either express or implied. Express consent is consent given by direct words, either oral or written. A few procedures, especially procedures involving reproduction, require written consent in some circumstances. With the exception of these few procedures, either oral or written consent can be legally sufficient authorization.[2] However, it is often difficult to prove oral consent, so most providers seek written consent.

Implied consent can be divided into consent that is inferred from the patient's conduct and consent that is presumed in certain emergencies. When a patient voluntarily submits to a procedure with apparent knowledge of its nature, the courts will usually find implied consent. For example, the highest court of Massachusetts found that a woman had given her implied consent to being vaccinated by extending her arm and accepting the vaccination without objection.[3] Implied consent is the basis for the practice of not seeking explicit consent for physical examinations or minor procedures performed on competent adults.

Consent is presumed to exist in medical emergencies unless the provider has reason to believe that consent would be refused. An immediate threat to life or health is clearly a sufficient emergency. The Iowa Supreme Court found implied consent to the removal of a mangled limb that had been run over in a train accident.[4] The court accepted the physician's determination that the amputation was necessary to save the patient's life. Courts have disagreed on whether pain is enough justification to find implied consent.[5]

Some courts have found implied consent to extensions or modifications of surgical procedures beyond the scope specifically authorized when unexpected conditions arise, especially when the additional action is necessary to preserve the patient's life.[6] Many surgical consent forms include explicit authorization of extensions or modifications to preserve life or health. This inclusion minimizes disagreements over the scope of the authorization by providing an opportunity for patients to specify extensions or modifications that they forbid.

Express consent or consent implied from the patient's conduct must be voluntary. While no reported cases deal with this issue outside of the research context, in an unusual situation consent might be challenged for being obtained through coercion or undue inducement.

Exceptions to the requirement of consent, in which the law authorizes treatment despite refusal, are discussed later in the chapter.

INFORMED CONSENT

The courts have developed two standards for determining the adequacy of disclosure—the professional (reasonable physician) standard and the reasonable patient standard. Courts in many states use the professional standard of accepted medical practice. In those states, the physician or other independent practitioner has a duty to make the disclosure that a reasonable medical practitioner would make under the same or similar circumstances.[7] Expert testimony is necessary to prove the required disclosure.

The reasonable patient standard has been adopted by an increasing number of states. This standard provides that the duty to disclose is determined by the informational needs of the patient, not by professional practice. Information that is "material" to the decision must be disclosed. One federal court defined a risk to be material "when a reasonable person, in what the physician knows or should know to be the patient's position, would be likely to attach significance to the risk or cluster of risks in deciding whether or not to forego the proposed therapy."[8] No expert testimony is required on the scope of disclosure, although expert testimony may be necessary to establish what the risks and alternatives are.

A few states have adopted hybrid standards. For example, in Iowa the reasonable patient standard applies to elective procedures, and the professional judgment standard applies to necessary procedures.[9]

The usual elements of the explanation are the patient's medical condition, the nature and purpose of the proposed procedure, its consequences and risks, and the feasible accepted alternatives,[10] including the consequences of no treatment. Only risks that are known or should be known by the physician to occur without negligence are required to be disclosed. Nearly all courts recognize that not all risks can be disclosed. One useful guideline is to disclose the risks of the most severe consequences and the risks that have a large probability of occurring.

When the patient indicates the need for additional information, there can be a duty to provide it. For example, a patient told the physician that his ability to work was crucial, so the Arizona Supreme Court ruled that the physician should have informed the patient of the risks that could affect ability to work.[11]

The most difficult element for the patient to prove in an informed consent case is causation. Since informed consent suits are based on the principles of liability for negligent torts, the plaintiff must prove that the deviation from the standard caused the injury. Thus, the plaintiff must prove that consent would not have been given if the risk that occurred had been disclosed.

The courts have developed two standards. Some jurisdictions apply an "objective" standard of what a prudent person in the patient's position would have decided if informed of the risk or alternative.[12] Other courts apply a "subjective" standard, so that it must be proved that the patient would have refused to consent if informed of the risk or alternative.[13] Either of these standards provides substantial protection for the conscientious health care professional who discloses the major risks and then has a more remote risk occur. A patient who consents to a procedure knowing of the risk of death and paralysis will find it difficult to convince a court that knowledge of a minor risk would have led to refusal. However, courts may be more easily convinced when there are undisclosed alternatives.

Exceptions to the Disclosure Requirement

The courts have recognized four exceptions to the disclosure requirement in the circumstances where consent still must be obtained: emergencies, the therapeutic privilege, patient waiver, and prior patient knowledge.

In emergencies when consent is implied, there is a corollary modification of the disclosure requirement. When there is no time to obtain consent, there clearly is no time to make disclosures. Courts have recognized that even when there is time, emergency situations may still leave time for only an abbreviated disclosure.[14]

Most courts recognize a therapeutic privilege when disclosure poses a significant threat of detriment to the patient. Courts have tried to limit the privilege carefully so it is not applicable when the physician solely fears that the information might lead the patient to forgo needed therapy. Thus, physicians should rely on the privilege only when they can document that a patient's anxiety is significantly above the norm. Some courts have ruled that when the therapeutic privilege is applied to keep information from the patient, the information must be disclosed to a relative and that relative must concur with the patient's consent before the procedure can be performed.[15] Most courts that have addressed the issue have adopted this position. However, at least one court has ruled that no disclosure needed to be made to relatives.[16]

A patient can waive the right to be informed.[17] However, it is doubtful that courts will accept a waiver initiated by the physician, so a prudent physician should not suggest a waiver but instead should encourage reluctant patients to be informed.

There is no liability for nondisclosure of risks that are common knowledge or that the patient has previously experienced.

One state eliminated the requirement of disclosure of risks by statute. The Georgia Code states that the physician need only disclose "in general terms the treatment or course of treatment" to obtain an informed consent.[18] The Georgia courts have interpreted this statement as an elimination of the requirement that risks be disclosed, so they no longer base liability on failure to disclose risks.[19]

RESPONSIBILITY FOR OBTAINING CONSENT

It is the physician's responsibility to provide the necessary information and to obtain informed consent; it is not the hospital's responsibility. Other independent practitioners who order procedures have the same responsibility concerning the procedures they order. The hospital is generally not liable for the failure of the physician or other independent practitioners to obtain informed consent, unless the professional is an employee or agent of the hospital. This principle has been applied in several court decisions, and some states have enacted it in their statutes.[20] There have been increasing efforts to convince courts to require hospitals to intercede in the professional relationship with the patient by imposing liability on the institution for inadequate disclosures by independent physicians. These efforts have not been successful except in a few cases, such as one Illinois appellate court decision.[21]

One of the earliest court decisions addressing physician liability for operating without consent observed that while the hospital generally is not liable for nonconsensual operations by physicians who are independent contractors, the hospital may be liable for failing to intervene when it has actual knowledge the procedure is being performed without authorization.[22] Some attorneys believe that this liability could be extended to situations in which the hospital should have known there was no authorization. It is generally recognized that it is not feasible for the hospital to be responsible for the content of the physician's disclosure underlying the consent because the necessary monitoring could destroy the physician-patient relationship. However, the hospital could be liable if it failed to intervene when it knew the disclosure was not proper.

There is a disagreement concerning the appropriate role of hospital staff members in obtaining consent.[23] Some hospitals permit nurses to obtain the signature of the patient or the patient's representative on the consent form. Some hospitals permit nurses to provide some or all of the information necessary for an informed consent. Both of these practices may impair the physician-patient relationship by reducing the opportunity for adequate communication and negotiation. These practices could shift the liability for disclosure inadequacies to the hospital as the employer of the nurse. To avoid these adverse consequences, many hospitals do not permit nurses to obtain consents. In hospitals where this rule is not practical, nurses who obtain signatures on consent forms should not attempt to answer patient questions concerning the procedure unless authorized to do so by the hospital and the physician. The physician may legally delegate the provision of information and the obtaining of documentation, but the physician remains legally responsible for the adequacy of the disclosure and validity of the consent. Hospitals should make appropriate arrangements to assure that the physician acknowledges responsibility and liability before it permits its employees to accept the delegation. Absent hospital and physician approval, if the patient seeks additional information or expresses reluctance, the nurse should contact the physician instead of attempting to convince the patient to sign the form.

To help reduce the hospital's exposure to liability for lack of consent, most hospitals require the use of a standard form before major procedures. The battery consent form described in the next section will fulfill this purpose. The role of hospital staff usually should be limited to (1) screening for completion of the form or alternative authorization; and (2) conveying information to the physician. For procedures for which the hospital requires consent, hospital staff members should be assigned the responsibility to ascertain whether consent is appropriately documented or another type of authorization has been obtained before permitting the procedure to be performed. A hospital staff member who becomes aware of a patient's confusion or change of opinion regarding a procedure should notify the responsible physician. If the physician does not respond, appropriate medical staff and hospital officials should be notified so they can determine whether intervention is necessary.

One area receiving increasing attention is the identity of the surgeon. It is the responsibility of the physician who performs the surgery to obtain consent, not the responsibility of referring physicians or consultants.[24] Even when informed consent to the procedure is otherwise obtained, some patients have sued when a physician other than the one they expected performed the procedure. The highest court of Massachusetts ruled in 1984 that it was not a battery for another physician to perform a myelography when the patient had not directed that the procedure be postponed in the absence of the requested physician.[25] However, when the patient directs that a specific physician not perform a procedure and that physician performs the procedure, both the physician and those who let the physician perform the procedure can be liable.[26]

DOCUMENTATION

Most attorneys who represent physicians and hospitals agree that the best way to document consent is to obtain the signature of the patient or the patient's representative on an appropriate form. Usually, if a proper form is signed by the appropriate person, most courts accept it as proof of consent, unless the plaintiff can prove the form should be ignored because of special circumstances. A few attorneys disagree with this position and recommend that the physician write a note in the medical record concerning the discussion with the patient or the patient's representative. These attorneys are concerned that courts will consider a consent form to contain all the information given to the patient and not believe testimony that additional information was provided. Those who recommend the use of forms write them to indicate that the form does not contain all information provided by the physician.

JCAH accreditation standards concerning medical records require "evidence of appropriate informed consent" for procedures or treatments for which informed consent is required by hospital policy.[27] The JCAH requires a hospital policy that is consistent with legal standards. The JCAH does not specify the procedures or treatments and does not require the consent to be documented by the signature of the patient or the patient's representative. Several hospitals that do not require the use of signed consent forms are accredited. A better practice is for the hospital or medical staff to adopt a policy concerning which procedures or treatments should usually be preceded by signed consent. One list of procedures to use as a starting point for developing a policy includes (1) major or minor surgery that involves an entry into the body; (2) all procedures that involve more than a slight risk of harm or that cause a change in the patient's body structure; (3) all forms of radiological therapy; (4) electroconvulsive therapy; and (5) all experimental procedures.

When developing or applying a policy concerning the use of consent forms, it is essential to remember that the actual process of providing information to the person giving consent and of determining the person's decision is more important than the consent form. The form is evidence of the consent process, not a substitute for the consent process. Someone should have the authority to determine that there is actual consent even when the form has been lost or inadvertently not signed prior to sedation of the patient or when other circumstances make it difficult to obtain the necessary signature.

Consent Forms

There are three basic types of consent forms: (1) the blanket consent form; (2) the battery consent form; and (3) the detailed consent form.

Blanket Consent Form

In the past, many hospitals provided consent forms that authorized any procedure the physician wished to perform. Courts have ruled that these blanket consent forms are not evidence of consent to major procedures because the procedure is not specified on the form.[28] Many attorneys recommend the continued use of a blanket admission consent form to cover the procedures for which individual special consent is not sought. There is a disagreement whether these admission forms provide more protection than the implied consent inferred from admission and submission to minor procedures. Of course, admission forms can serve many other purposes unrelated to consent, such as assigning insurance benefits.[29]

Battery Consent Forms

For major procedures, most hospitals now provide consent forms that include space for the name and a description of the specific procedure. In addition, the form states that (1) the person signing has been told about the medical condition, consequences, risks, and alternatives; and (2) all the person's questions have been answered to his or her satisfaction. This type of consent form will almost always preclude a successful claim of battery as long as the proper person signs the form and the procedure described in the form is performed. This form also provides strong support for the reasonableness of the hospital's lack of suspicion that the person who signed was uninformed, while providing some support for the physician's assertion that the patient was informed. However, it is still possible for the person who signed to convince a court that the information concerning consequences, risks, and alternatives was not actually given.

Detailed Consent Forms

Some physicians use forms that detail the medical condition, procedure, consequences, risks, and alternatives. Such forms have been mandated for federally funded sterilizations and research.[30] It is much more difficult for the patient to prove that the information included in the form was not disclosed. The primary difficulty with detailed consent forms is that it is costly and time consuming to prepare them for each individual procedure. Thus, some physicians who use detailed consent forms use them only for procedures, such as cosmetic surgery, that carry a higher risk of misunderstanding and unsatisfactory results.

Challenges to Consent Forms

Although consent forms are strong evidence of informed consent, they are usually not conclusive.[31] The person challenging the adequacy of the consent process will usually be permitted an opportunity to convince the court that informed consent was not actually obtained. This can be done by proving that the person who signed the form was not competent—for example, due to transient impairment by medication. Thus, it is important that the explanation be given and the signature be obtained at a time when the person is able to understand.

Another basis for challenging a consent form is that its wording was too technical or that it was written in a language the person did not understand. In general, persons are presumed to have read and understood documents they have signed. However, sometimes courts will not apply this rule when the document is either too technical or in a language foreign to the patient. Thus, it is important that forms be written so that the person signing can understand them. There has been increasing criticism that many forms require too high a level of reading ability. Several journal articles have been published that describe how to simplify the wording of forms.[32] If the person has difficulty understanding English, then someone should translate the form. It is usually not necessary to have forms in other languages unless a substantial portion of the patients served by the hospital speak a primary language other than English. Otherwise, it is usually sufficient to have the form orally translated and have the translator certify that the form and discussion of the procedure have been orally translated for the person signing the form. Another basis for challenging a consent form is that the signature was not voluntary. The person signing would have to demonstrate that there had been some threat or undue inducement to prove the signature was not voluntary, so it is unlikely that this basis will apply in hospital situations.

Exculpatory Clauses

Some providers have included in their consent forms a paragraph that states that the person signing waives the right to sue for injuries or agrees to limit any claims to not more than a specified amount. These paragraphs are called exculpatory clauses. Courts will not enforce them in suits on behalf of patients against health care providers. For example, in 1979 a federal court refused to enforce a $15,000 limit on liability in an agreement the patient signed before surgery.[33]

Period of Validity of Consent Forms

There is no absolute limit on the period of validity of a consent or the documentation of that consent by a signature on a consent form. If the patient's condition or the available treatments change significantly, the earlier consent is no longer informed, and a new consent should be obtained. Otherwise, the consent is valid until it is withdrawn. A claim that consent was withdrawn becomes more credible as time passes, so the guideline some hospitals follow is to recommend a new consent each time the patient is admitted. The consent may be obtained in the physician's office before the admission. Some hospitals use a guideline that consent forms should be signed no more than 30 days before the procedure. Hospitals are not legally required to have guidelines, but generally are required to follow their own rules. Thus, when a hospital adopts guidelines, they should clearly state that they are not a requirement, or, if they are a hospital requirement, someone should have authority to make exceptions to the requirement in dealing with repetitive treatments for chronic disease, situations when the person who gave consent is no longer competent or available, and other unusual circumstances.

Impact of Statutes

Some states have passed statutes concerning consent forms. The statutes should be considered when developing consent forms for use in those states. Several of the states provide that, if the consent form contains certain information and is signed by the appropriate person, it is conclusive evidence of informed consent or creates a presumption of informed consent. For example, in Nevada, if certain information is on the form, it is conclusive evidence of informed consent.[34] In Iowa, if certain information is on the form, informed consent is presumed.[35] Such statutes address how the courts shall consider forms that contain certain information. They do not address forms that do not contain the information. Thus, it is not a violation of these statutes to use a form that contains different information or to forgo the use of a form. However, especially in states that make certain forms conclusive evidence, serious consideration should be given to using forms that qualify. However, these statutes do not guarantee protection. A Florida appellate court declared a conclusive statute to be unconstitutional in 1985.[36]

Supplements to Documentation

Some physicians are now supplementing their explanations to patients with other educational materials, such as booklets and movies. Some physicians are making audio and visual recordings of the consent process to supplement or even substitute for written consent. Some physicians are giving their patients tests of knowledge or are having their patients write their own consent forms to determine and document the level of understanding. None of these steps is legally required today, but they should be given serious consideration whenever controversial procedures are being used.

THE DECISION MAKER

The person who makes the decision concerning the treatment or procedure must be legally and actually competent to make the decision and must be informed, unless one of the exceptions applies. Competent adults and some mature minors make the decisions regarding their own care. Someone else must make the decisions for incompetent adults and other minors.

Competent Adults

The age of majority is established by the legislature of each state. In most states, it is now 18 years of age, but there is still some variation. In some states, a person can become an adult before the established age by certain actions, such as marriage.

An adult is competent if (1) not declared incompetent and (2) generally capable of understanding the consequences of alternatives, weighing the alternatives by the degree they promote his or her desires, and choosing and acting accordingly. There is a strong legal presumption of continued competence. For example, a Pennsylvania court found a woman competent to refuse a breast biopsy even though she was committed to a mental institution with a diagnosis of chronic schizophrenia and two of her three reasons for refusal were delusional.[37] In 1978 a Massachusetts court found a woman competent to refuse the amputation of her gangrenous leg even though her train of thought sometimes wandered, her conception of time was distorted, and she was confused on some matters.[38] The fact that her decision was medically irrational and would lead to her death did not demonstrate incompetence. The court believed she understood the alternatives and the consequences of her decision.

The determination of competence is not necessarily the function of psychiatrists. It is usually a practical assessment that should be made by the physician who obtains the consent or accepts the refusal. When it is difficult to assess competence, consultation is advisable. If there is suspicion of underlying mental retardation, mental illness, or disorders that affect brain functions, the consultant should be a psychiatrist or appropriate specialist.

Incompetent Adults

The guardian or, if there is no guardian, the representative of the incompetent adult patient makes decisions concerning the patient's care. Because of the obligations of representatives to the patients, they have a narrower range of permissible choices than they would have concerning their own care. In addition, the known wishes of the patient should be considered.[39]

When a court rules that a person is incompetent, the court designates a person as guardian, who then has the legal authority to make most of the decisions regarding the incompetent person's care.

Some patients who are actually incompetent have never been determined to be incompetent by a court, so they do not have guardians. When decisions must be made concerning the care of these patients, it is common practice to seek a decision from the next of kin or others who have assumed supervision of the patient. In many states, laws or court decisions support this practice.[40]

If the incompetence is temporary, the procedure should be postponed until the patient is competent and can make his or her own decision, unless the postponement presents a substantial risk to the patient's life or health.

When patients express their wishes concerning treatment before becoming incompetent, the wishes should be seriously considered in deciding how to treat the patients. When patients know their condition and available treatment when their wishes are expressed, the wishes should usually be followed. When there is a significant unanticipated change in the patient's condition or in available treatments, the patient's representative or guardian has more latitude to reach a decision different from the patient's wishes. The living will and other directives concerning the care of the terminally ill are discussed in Chapter 16.

When a hospital has determined that a patient is incompetent, it should treat the patient consistently as incompetent until it determines that competence is restored and begins treating the patient consistently as competent. In a 1984 federal case, the court ruled that when the Veterans Administration issues a "statement of incapacity" and designates the patient's wife or another person to be the one to whom it will turn for decisions on the patient's behalf, the patient's consent is no longer sufficient authorization for treatment; the consent of the person designated must be sought.[41]

Minors

Parental or guardian consent should be obtained before treatment is given to a minor, unless it is (1) an emergency; (2) one of the situations where the consent of the minor is sufficient; or (3) a situation where a court order or other legal authorization is obtained.

Emergency Care

As with adults, consent is implied in medical emergencies when there is an immediate threat to life or health, unless the provider has reason to believe that consent would be refused by the parent or guardian. When there is reason to believe that treatment would be refused, the procedure for seeking court authorization should be followed when treatment is necessary.

Emancipated Minors

Emancipated minors may consent to their own medical care. Minors are emancipated when they are no longer subject to parental control or regulation and are not supported by their parents. The specific factors necessary to establish emancipation vary from state to state. Some states require that the parent and child agree on the emancipation, so that a minor cannot become emancipated in those states simply by running away from home.

Mature Minors

Mature minors may consent to some medical care under common law and constitutional principles and under the statutes of some states. Many states have minor treatment statutes empowering older minors to consent to medical treatment. The age limits and scope of treatments vary from state to state. In many states, special laws concerning minor consent to venereal disease and substance abuse treatment have no age limits. In states that do not have an applicable minor consent statute, the risk associated with providing necessary treatment to mature minors with only their consent is minimal. The oldest minor who underwent a medical procedure with his personal consent and won a reported lawsuit based on lack of parental consent was 15.[42] That 1941 case involved a procedure that was not necessary for the minor. It was the removal of some skin for donation to another person for a skin graft operation.

The constitutional right of privacy restricts state authority to mandate parental involvement in certain reproductive decisions, such as abortions. Reproductive issues are discussed in Chapter 15.

When treating any minor, the minor should be urged to involve the parents. When a mature minor refuses to permit parental involvement, the provider can provide necessary care without substantial risk, unless (1) there is likelihood of harm to the minor or others that requires parental involvement to avoid or (2) institutional policy requires parental involvement. When such harm is likely, parents should usually be involved, unless state law forbids notification of the parents.

Parental or Guardian Consent

Either parent can give legally effective consent, except when there is legal separation or divorce. While it is not necessary to determine the wishes of the other parent, when it is known that the other parent objects, either the procedure should not be done or court authorization should be obtained.[43] When the parents are legally separated or divorced, usually the consent of the custodial parent must be obtained.

Limits on the Authority to Consent

There are limits to what an adult or mature minor can authorize a provider to do. Persons making decisions on behalf of incompetent adults and other minors have a narrower range of permissible choices than persons making decisions for themselves because of their duty to act in the best interest of the incompetent adult or minor.

Mayhem

Intentional maiming or disfiguring of a person without justification, such as intended medical benefit, is the ancient crime of mayhem, which now is sometimes called *willful injury*. Consent or even request of the victim is not a defense when there is no medical justification. For example, in 1961 a North Carolina physician was convicted of aiding and abetting mayhem because, at the victim's request, he anesthetized the victim's fingers so they could later be removed by the victim's brother.[44]

Suicide

Aiding and abetting suicide is a crime in most states. Consent and even request of the victim are not a defense. However, as discussed in Chapter 16, courts have recognized that withholding and withdrawing treatment from the terminally ill is not aiding and abetting suicide.

Statutory Prohibitions

The federal government, through the Food and Drug Administration (FDA), has restricted the use of new drugs and devices until their safety and efficacy are proven. The drugs and devices cannot be used outside approved testing projects until they are approved by the FDA, regardless of the patient's desires. Even after drugs are approved for general distribution, many can be distributed only by prescription. A physician or other authorized health professional can write a prescription only for appropriate medical uses. Inappropriate prescriptions can subject the professional to discipline by the licensure board and to criminal prosecution. Consent of the patient to the prescription is irrelevant.

Insistence on Other Inappropriate Treatment

Physicians have a professional obligation to refuse to provide clearly inappropriate treatment despite the patient's insistence. Some courts in the 19th century ruled that the patient's insistence after being informed of the inappropriateness insulated the physician from liability.[45] It is unlikely that courts would rule in favor of physicians in such circumstances today.

Limits on Consent for Incompetent Adults or Minors

Any person acting on behalf of an incompetent adult or a minor has a responsibility to act in the best interest of the adult or minor. Decision makers cannot authorize two procedures—organ donation and sterilization—for incompetent adults or minors without prior court approval. Courts in a few states will not approve kidney donations by minors and incompetents,[46] but courts in other states have authorized them.[47] The courts that have approved kidney donations have usually based their approval on the close relationship between the donor and the proposed recipient and the emotional injury to the donor if the recipient were to die. The issue of sterilization of minors and incompetent adults is discussed in Chapter 15.

THE RIGHT TO REFUSE

Generally, the right to consent implies a right to refuse. Most courts have found that since a competent adult has the right to refuse, those making decisions on behalf of incompetent adults and minors must have the right to refuse on their behalf in appropriate situations. However, in certain situations courts have found that the state's interests outweigh the patient's interests and have ordered treatment. When the patient's right to refuse is honored, the patient may have to forgo other benefits.

There are three legal bases for the right to refuse treatment: (1) the common law right to freedom from nonconsensual invasion of bodily integrity, embodied in the informed consent doctrine and the law of battery; (2) the constitutional right of privacy; and (3) the constitutional right to freedom of religion.

Common Law Bodily Integrity

The common law has long recognized the strong interest of all people to be free from nonconsensual invasion of their bodily integrity.[48] One element of this freedom is the right to make decisions concerning medical care. Medical care without express or implied authority is a battery. The common law requirement of informed consent has developed to assure that adequate information is made available to provide an opportunity for a knowledgeable decision even when there is not a battery. Courts have recognized that the right to make decisions concerning medical care includes the right to decline medical care. This right is illustrated by the 1981 decision by the highest court in New York recognizing the right of Brother Fox, through his guardian, to decline respiratory support based on these principles.[49]

Right of Privacy

The second basis for the right to refuse medical care is the constitutional right of privacy. Unwanted infringements of bodily integrity have been recognized as violations of the right to privacy, unless state interests outweigh the right. For example, in 1980 the Florida Supreme Court recognized the constitutional right of a competent 73-year-old man with amyotrophic lateral sclerosis (Lou Gehrig's disease) to discontinue the use of a respirator.[50] The right of privacy was also recognized as a basis for refusal in *In re Quinlan*,[51] even though Karen Ann Quinlan was unable to express her wishes because she was in a permanent vegetative state. The right of privacy has been the basis for accepting refusals in situations where the patient is neither terminally ill nor comatose. For example, in 1978 a Massachusetts court honored a 77-year-old woman's refusal to have her gangrenous leg amputated based on the right of privacy.[52]

Freedom of Religion

Freedom of religion is another basis for refusal in a few situations. However, freedom of religion applies primarily to freedom of belief, not freedom of action, so the state may restrain religious conduct. A second reason that freedom of religion seldom has an important role in medical decisions is that few religions command adherents to refuse treatments. Most religions merely permit refusal, so legally required treatment does not violate their religious tenets. The only cases in which freedom of religion has been significant have involved Jehovah's Witnesses refusing blood transfusions or Christian Scientists refusing all treatment. Many courts have upheld the right of adherents to these religions to refuse care that violates their religion. For example, in 1972 a District of Columbia court refused to authorize involuntary transfusion of a 34-year-old man who was a Jehovah's Witness.[53]

Refusals on Behalf of Minors and Incompetents

The courts have tended to find that, since a competent adult has the right to refuse, those making decisions on behalf of minors and incompetent adults have a right to refuse on their behalf in some situations. However, because the decision makers have an obligation to act in the best interest of the minor or incompetent adult, they must provide necessary treatment. Their discretion to decline treatment is limited to situations where the treatment is elective or not likely to be beneficial. The duty to provide necessary treatment to minors is reinforced in all states by legislation concerning abused or neglected minors that facilitates state intervention to provide needed assistance. Legislation concerning abused or neglected adults has been enacted in a few states.

Courts have generally permitted the refusal of extraordinary care for terminally ill or irreversibly comatose minors and incompetent adults. For example, *In re Quinlan*[54] permitted the father of an adult daughter in a permanent vegetative state to authorize the withdrawal of respiratory support. In 1982 the highest court of Massachusetts approved a decision not to attempt resuscitative efforts if a terminally ill child less than one year of age experienced cardiac or respiratory arrest.[55]

Courts have declined to override parental refusals in several situations where the benefit did not clearly outweigh the risk. For example, the Washington Supreme Court refused to authorize the amputation of an 11-year-old girl's arm, which was so abnormally large that it was useless and interfered with her association with other people.[56] In 1972 the Pennsylvania Supreme Court refused to authorize blood transfusions for the 16-year-old son of a Jehovah's Witness so that an operation could be conducted to correct severe spinal curvature.[57]

Courts will generally decline to intervene when the parents or guardian are following the advice of a licensed physician in good standing, even if the advice is unorthodox. In 1979 the highest court of New York refused to authorize chemotherapy for a child with leukemia because the parents were following the advice of a physician who had prescribed laetrile, even though laetrile was not proven to be effective.[58]

Another factor that has sometimes led courts not to intervene has been the wishes of the minor or incompetent. For example, the highest court of New York declined to authorize surgery to repair the harelip and cleft palate of a 14-year-old boy because both the father and son opposed the surgery.[59] In 1985 the Washington Supreme Court refused to order surgery for an incompetent patient with malignant cancer of the larynx.[60] The guardian desired the surgery, but the incompetent patient preferred radiation, even though it was less effective, because surgery would result in the loss of the ability to speak.

Consequences of Refusal

Patients who refuse often must accept consequences beyond the health consequences. Worker's compensation, disability, and other benefit payments may be denied or reduced in claims concerning the underlying illness if the refused procedure would help diagnose or reduce the injury. For example, the Iowa Supreme Court affirmed the denial of payment to a policeman for his continuing medical expenses because he refused to submit to coronary arteriography that was necessary to diagnose his condition.[61]

LIMITS ON REFUSAL

State Interest

The state asserts five interests as bases for overriding the patient's right to refuse: (1) preservation of life when the patient's condition is curable; (2) protection of the patient's dependents, especially minor children; (3) prevention of irrational self-destruction; (4) preservation of the ethical integrity of health care providers; and (5) protection of the public health and other interests. In cases involving minors and incompetent adults, the state asserts its general interest in protecting their welfare.

Preservation of Life

The preservation of life is the most basic of the state interests that have been asserted to outweigh the right to refuse medical care. Courts have uniformly ruled that this interest does not outweigh the right of the terminally ill patient to refuse treatment. The *Quinlan* decision ruled that the state's interest in preserving life decreases as the prognosis dims and the degree of bodily invasion of the proposed procedure increases. In *Superintendent of Belchertown v. Saikewicz*,[62] which authorized withholding chemotherapy from a patient with leukemia, the court concluded: "The value of life as so perceived is lessened not by a decision to refuse treatment, but by the failure to allow a competent human being the right of choice." Even when the patient is not terminally ill, courts have declined to order treatment when the intervention is major, such as the amputation of a gangrenous limb.

When the patient is a minor or is incompetent, courts tend to authorize even major interventions that are necessary to save the patient's life, unless the patient is terminally ill or irreversibly comatose.

Courts will authorize some treatments for pregnant women to preserve the life of the fetus, especially immediately before and during birth. In 1964 the New Jersey Supreme Court authorized transfusions for a woman if necessary to save the life of either the fetus or herself.[63] However, other courts have limited their authorizations to transfusions necessary to save the life of the fetus.[64] In 1981 the Georgia Supreme Court authorized a Caesarean section operation because it was informed of a near certainty the fetus would not survive a vaginal delivery.[65] In 1983 the highest court of Massachusetts refused to order a pregnant women to submit to an operation to help postpone premature delivery.[66]

Dependents

The state also asserts an interest in protecting minor children and other dependents from the emotional and financial damage of the patient's refusal. This interest has been discussed in cases in which Jehovah's Witness patients refuse blood transfusions. For example, in 1964 a federal appellate court in the District of Columbia authorized transfusions for a woman in part because she was the mother of a seven-month-old child.[67] However, in 1972 another District of Columbia court refused to authorize a transfusion for a father of two minor children because adequate arrangements had been made for their future well-being.[68] These cases involved patients who could probably be restored to normal functioning by appropriate therapy. It is doubtful whether dependents will be a determinative issue in cases involving the terminally ill or irreversibly comatose because emotional and financial damage will seldom be increased by discontinuing treatment.

Irrational Self-Destruction

The prevention of irrational self-destruction is the third state interest. In 1975 a Pennsylvania court authorized transfusions to prevent self-destruction of a male 25-year-old Jehovah's Witness with a bleeding ulcer.[69] Many other courts have refused to consider refusal by Jehovah's Witness adults to be irrational self-destruction. Courts have also generally recognized that there can be a competent, rational decision to refuse treatment when the treatment involves substantial risks or death is imminent.

Some courts have declined to intervene when terminal patients have taken active steps to hasten death. For example, in 1984 a Florida court addressed the situation of a 55-year-old patient, terminally ill with cancer and in intense pain. After attempting suicide by stabbing herself, she refused surgery for her stab wounds, and her husband concurred. Even though the wounds were due to a suicide attempt, the court refused to order the surgery.[70]

Ethical Integrity of Health Care Providers

Several courts have discussed whether they should recognize a state interest in maintaining the ethical integrity of the medical profession and allowing hospitals the opportunity to care for patients who have been admitted. The courts have concluded that it is not a countervailing interest. Some courts have found that the right of privacy is superior to these professional and institutional considerations. Other courts have concluded that honoring the wishes of the patient or patient's representative is consistent with medical ethics, at least in the cases in which the issue has been raised, so there is no conflict.

Public Health and Other Interests

The power of the state to require individuals to submit to medical care when the refusal presents a threat to the community at large has been recognized by the courts longer than the other state interests. In 1905 the Supreme Court upheld the right of the state to require an adult to submit to vaccination to help prevent the spread of disease.[71] In 1973 a federal appellate court upheld a Denver ordinance that required prostitutes to accept treatment for venereal disease.[72]

In unusual individual cases, courts have based authorization of medical procedures on other state interests. For example, in 1979 the highest court of Massachusetts authorized dialysis for a prisoner because he attempted to manipulate his placement by refusing dialysis until he was moved.[73] Although prisoners ordinarily have the same rights as others to decline treatment, the state's interest in orderly prison administration was found to outweigh those rights.

Some interventions have been authorized on the basis of the state's interest in securing evidence of crimes. These interventions are discussed later in this chapter in the section on law enforcement.

Competent Adults

Applying these interests, the state has required competent adult patients to accept treatment despite their refusal in the following groups of cases: (1) public health cases; (2) pregnancy cases; (3) religious refusal cases; (4) civil commitment cases involving treatment for mental illness or substance abuse; and (5) law enforcement and prison cases. The first two groups have already been discussed, and the last two groups are discussed later in the chapter. The third group has been discussed but will be discussed further here. Disoriented patients will also be addressed.

Religious Refusals

Jehovah's Witnesses refuse blood transfusions based on a literal interpretation of the Biblical prohibition against eating blood. In many of the court cases, courts have refused to authorize treatment of competent adults. In a few cases, involuntary transfusions have been authorized for adults with a minor dependent or fetus. Some courts refuse to authorize transfusions even when there are minor children. Nearly all the other court authorizations involving Jehovah's Witness adults have applied to patients who said they would not resist the transfusion if ordered. Thus, the authorization was designed to protect the patient from fellow adherents, not to override the patient's wishes. Changes in the position of the church have eliminated the protective effect of court authorization, so these cases are much less frequent.

Artificial blood substitutes are being studied and are available in only a few medical centers.[74] Until they are approved for wider distribution or proved to be ineffective, it will be necessary in some cases involving Jehovah's Witnesses to arrange transfer to a participating center or rule out the possibility of transfer before a court will authorize a transfusion.

Until 1985 it was thought that health care providers could rely on documents signed by Jehovah's Witnesses releasing the hospital from all liability for not providing blood transfusions. The Washington Supreme Court cast doubt on that reliance in the case of *Shorter v. Drury*.[75] After a Jehovah's Witness patient and her husband signed releases, the patient underwent a dilation and curettage procedure. The surgeon negligently perforated her uterus during the procedure, causing bleeding. The patient would have survived if blood could have been given. However, in accord with her wishes, blood was not given and she died. Her husband sued the surgeon. The court ruled that the release form did not provide protection from liability for the surgeon's negligence. The jury found the surgeon liable for the patient's death, but allocated 75 percent of the liability to the patient and her husband for refusing blood. Thus, the surgeon had to pay 25 percent of the $412,000 verdict. The dissenting state supreme court judges felt the surgeon should have paid the full amount.

Disoriented Patients

A situation involving a temporarily disoriented patient is different from situations involving oriented patients. Disoriented patients are frequently restrained temporarily. Physicians and hospitals have the authority under common law to detain temporarily and even restrain temporarily disoriented medical and surgical patients without court involvement. This authority derives from the hospital's duty to use such reasonable care as the patient's known mental and physical condition requires. Hospitals have been found liable for injuries to patients because they were not restrained during temporary disorientation. This common law authority usually does not apply when the patient is being detained for treatment for mental illness or substance abuse. The statutory commitment procedures should be followed for those patients. This common law authority also does not apply when the patient is fully oriented, although custody can be maintained temporarily while the patient's status is adequately determined.

Incompetent Adults and Minors

In addition to the group of cases listed for competent adults, various other types of treatment have been authorized for incompetent adults and minors, including major surgery and chemotherapy. Courts have also taken a different view of religious refusals involving minors than they have of cases involving adults.

Religious Refusals

Courts have taken the position that the state should give minors an opportunity to mature and make their own decisions concerning their religious beliefs. Thus, courts have authorized blood transfusions for minors in every reported case in which the minors had life-threatening conditions and were not terminally ill.[76] In nearly all cases where the condition was not life threatening, the courts have also authorized transfusions.[77] One of the few exceptions was the 1972 Pennsylvania case, described earlier in this chapter, in which the court declined to order transfusions to permit surgery for spinal curvature.[78]

Major Surgery

Courts have authorized the amputation of gangrenous limbs of incompetent adults. For example, a 1978 Tennessee case addressed a patient who was not terminally ill but who would have died if her leg was not amputated.[79] She was unable to understand that her life was endangered by her refusal, so the court authorized the amputation. Courts have authorized major surgery for minors when it is likely to be beneficial. In 1981 an Oregon court authorized surgical treatment of an infant's hydrocephalus to prevent mental retardation even though her life was not in immediate danger.[80]

Chemotherapy and Other Medication

When parents are not following reputable medical advice, courts authorize treatment that is likely to be beneficial for life-threatening conditions. In 1979 the highest court of Massachusetts authorized chemotherapy for a child with leukemia despite parental insistence on laetrile treatment.[81] The federal courts refused to intervene.[82] Courts will also authorize necessary medications for incompetent adults.[83]

Hospitalization

Some states have laws that authorize certain health care providers to hold and treat minors in emergencies. For example, Iowa authorizes a physician to take custody of a child without a court order when there is imminent danger to the child's life or health and not enough time to obtain a court order.[84] However, the statute does not authorize treatment of the child, so application must be made to the court to treat. If there is no time to obtain court authorization, apparently the common law emergency exception to the consent requirement must be relied on, notwithstanding the parent's refusal. North Carolina authorizes the physician, with the concurrence of another physician, to provide necessary care when the parents refuse and there is no time to obtain a court order.[85] Familiarity with local law is essential, so proper procedures can be followed promptly when these situations arise.

CIVIL COMMITMENT

Most states have laws that establish procedures for involuntarily committing persons to institutions for treatment for mental illness or substance abuse. In 1975 the Supreme Court held that the Constitution was not violated when mentally ill persons were involuntarily confined, but that they must be treated if their confinement is not based on dangerousness.[86] The procedures for obtaining a commitment order vary from state to state. For adults, a judicial hearing is generally required, after which the judicial officer decides whether evidence is sufficient to justify commitment. Many states do not permit involuntary commitment unless the person is found to be dangerous to self or others. Most states permit adults to be held temporarily on an emergency basis until the judicial officer can act. In 1979 the Supreme Court ruled that states could permit parents to admit their minor children involuntarily for mental treatment without court authorization if there is a requirement that the admission be approved as necessary by a qualified physician after adequate inquiry.[87] However, many states require judicial involvement in commitment of minors.

Commitment is not the same as a court determination of incompetency. A person who has been involuntarily committed is still competent to be involved in some or all medical decisions, unless a court has determined otherwise. Generally, commitment laws authorize involuntary treatment that is necessary to preserve the patient's life or to avoid permanent injury to the patient or others. However, there is variation in the extent to which commitment laws authorize the use of antipsychotic drugs or electroconvulsive therapy for purposes of nonemergency treatment of mental illness. Thus, familiarity with local law is important. However, several courts have ruled that the constitutional rights to privacy and due process are violated if medications or electroconvulsive therapy are given involuntarily without a judicial finding of incompetency.[88] Some states have resolved this issue by requiring that the judicial officer find the person unable to make treatment decisions as part of the commitment process.[89] In states that authorize involuntary treatment of committed patients without a judicial determination of inability to make treatment decisions, hospitals should give consideration to this evolving standard in developing their treatment policies.

A few courts have required a judicial determination of the need for antipsychotic medications when a patient who has been adjudicated incompetent refuses the medications in a nonemergency situation.[90]

LAW ENFORCEMENT

Law enforcement officers call upon medical personnel, particularly those based in hospitals, to perform procedures on criminal suspects for the purpose of gathering evidence. These procedures include examining the patient, taking blood samples, pumping stomachs, removing bullets, and performing other interventions. Tests performed at the request of law enforcement authorities without the consent of the subject raise two legal questions. The first is whether the medical personnel performing the test or the institution in which the test is performed are subject to civil liability for battery or violation of the subject's civil rights. The second is whether the information obtained is admissible as evidence in a criminal action involving the subject. The second issue leads to the most litigation but is of less interest to the health care provider.

In 1951 the Supreme Court ruled, when police ordered the pumping of a suspect's stomach, that it "shocks the conscience," so the contents of the stomach could not be admitted into evidence.[91] In 1957 the Court ruled that blood drawn from an unconscious person following a traffic accident could be admitted into evidence if the blood was drawn after the person was properly arrested with probable cause to believe the person was intoxicated while driving.[92] In 1966 the Court ruled that blood drawn from an objecting defendant without a search warrant can be admitted into evidence if five conditions are satisfied: (1) the defendant is formally arrested; (2) it is likely the blood will produce evidence for the criminal prosecution; (3) delay would lead to destruction of the evidence; (4) the test is reasonable and not medically contraindicated; and (5) the test is performed in a reasonable manner.[93] If these conditions are present and properly documented, hospital personnel can safely cooperate in drawing blood for law enforcement officers to the extent authorized by state law. To maximize the applicability of immunity provisions under state law, hospital staff should comply with all additional state requirements concerning by whom, how, and when blood may be withdrawn involuntarily. However, in most states the hospital or health professional has no legal duty to perform the test requested by the law enforcement officer. In jurisdictions where the providers who perform the tests are frequently required to testify at the criminal trial of the subjects, many health care professionals decline to become involved in order to avoid the disruption of their clinical schedules. When the subject physically resists the test, it is also prudent to decline in order to avoid injury to the subject and the involved health personnel.

Several cases have involved requests for court authorization of the removal of a bullet from a suspect. In 1985 the Supreme Court ruled that the reasonableness and, thus, the constitutionality of court-ordered surgery to remove a bullet for evidence is to be decided on a case-by-case basis, weighing the individual's interest in privacy and security against the societal interest in gathering evidence.[94] The Court indicated that the privacy interest was very strong when general anesthesia would be required for the surgery or other inherent dangers to life and health were present. The Court also indicated that there were few situations in which the state's interest would prevail; when the other evidence was sufficiently strong to assure that the surgery was likely to produce helpful evidence, the other evidence would be sufficient without the addition of the bullet.

RESEARCH

Ordinarily, patients expect physicians to use the drugs and procedures customarily used for their condition. When experimental methods are used, or established procedures are used for purposes of research, the investigator must disclose this to the subject and obtain the consent of the subject or the subject's representative. Governmental regulations specify the review procedures for many types of research and specify the disclosures that must be made to obtain informed consent to such research.

All research supported by HHS must comply with regulations for the protection of human subjects.[95] These regulations require that an institutional review board (IRB) approve the research before HHS may support the research. The IRB must determine that the following requirements are met before approving research:

1. Risks to subjects are minimized. . . .
2. Risks to subjects are reasonable in relation to anticipated benefits, if any, to subjects, and the importance of the knowledge that may reasonably be expected to result. . . .

3. Selection of subjects is equitable. . . .
4. Informed consent will be sought from each prospective subject or the subject's legally authorized representative. . . .
5. Informed consent will be appropriately documented. . . .
6. Where appropriate, the research plan makes adequate provision for monitoring the data collected to ensure the safety of the subjects.
7. Where appropriate, there are adequate provisions to protect the privacy of subjects and to maintain the confidentiality of data.
8. Where some or all of the subjects are likely to be vulnerable to coercion or undue influence, such as persons with acute or severe physical or mental illness, or persons who are economically or educationally disadvantaged, appropriate additional safeguards have been included in the study to protect the rights and welfare of these subjects.[96]

The general requirements for informed consent require that consent be sought "only under circumstances that provide the prospective subject or the representative sufficient opportunity to consider whether or not to participate and that minimize the possibility of coercion or undue influence." The information must be in a language understandable to the subject or representative. Exculpatory wording cannot be included in the information given. The basic elements of information that must be included are

1. A statement that the study involves research, an explanation of the purposes of the research and the expected duration of the subject's participation, a description of the procedures to be followed, identification of any procedures which are experimental;
2. A description of any reasonably foreseeable risks or discomforts to the subject;
3. A description of any benefits to the subject or to others which may reasonably be expected from the research;
4. A disclosure of appropriate alternative procedures or courses of treatment, if any, that may be advantageous to the subject;
5. A statement describing the extent, if any, to which confidentiality of records identifying the subject will be maintained;
6. For research involving more than minimal risk, an explanation as to whether any compensation and an explanation as to whether any medical treatments are available if injury occurs and, if so, what they consist of, or where further information may be obtained;
7. An explanation of whom to contact for answers to pertinent questions about the research and research subjects' rights, and whom to contact in the event of a research-related injury to the subject; and

8. A statement that participation is voluntary, refusal to participate will involve no penalty or loss of benefits to which the subject is otherwise entitled, and the subject may discontinue participation at any time without penalty or loss of benefits to which the subject is otherwise entitled.[97]

Additional elements that should be included as appropriate include (1) the potential for unforeseeable risks; (2) circumstances under which the subject's participation may be terminated; (3) additional costs to the subject; (4) consequences of a decision to withdraw from the study; (5) a statement that significant new findings will be disclosed to the subject; and (6) the number of subjects involved in the study.

Several kinds of studies are exempted from these regulations, such as the "collection or study of existing data, documents, records, pathological specimens, or diagnostic specimens, if these sources are publicly available or if the information is recorded by the investigator in such a manner that subjects cannot be identified. . . ."[98] Expedited review is authorized for categories of research that the Secretary of HHS determines involve no more than minimal risk.[99] Examples of the expeditable categories of research are collection of small amounts of blood by venipuncture from certain adults and moderate exercise by healthy volunteers.

Each institution must submit an acceptable institutional assurance to HHS that it will fulfill its responsibilities under the regulations before HHS will accept the decisions of its IRB. HHS has suggested that the instituional assurance promise that all research sponsored by or conducted in the institution will comply with the regulations. It is prudent to subject all research in the institution to the same review. However, it is unnecessary to promise HHS that exactly the same standards will be applied. The institution may want to preserve the flexibility to permit research not supported by HHS to be conducted in a way HHS would not permit for research it is funding. HHS states that, in making funding decisions, it will take into account whether the applicant has "materially failed to discharge responsibility for the protection of the rights and welfare of human subjects (whether or not Department funds are involved)."[100] Thus, the flexibility to differ from HHS standards must be exercised with discretion by institutions that do not want to risk losing future HHS funding.

The HHS regulations do not preempt other applicable federal, state, or local laws or regulations. Thus, proposals involving investigational new drugs or devices must also satisfy the regulations of the Food and Drug Administration.[101] State and local law must also be reviewed because several states have enacted laws regulating research with human subjects.[102]

Hospitals should take appropriate steps to review research involving human subjects, regardless of the sponsorship of the research, to protect their patients and avoid liability.

NOTES

1. Truman v. Thomas, 27 Cal.3d 285, 611 P.2d 902 (1980).

2. *E.g.,* Kelly v. Gershoff, 112 R.I. 507, 312 A.2d 211 (1973) [jury can find informed consent without documentary evidence].

3. O'Brien v. Cunard S.S. Co., 154 Mass. 272, 28 N.E. 266 (1891).

4. Jacovach v. Yocum, 212 Iowa 914, 237 N.W. 444 (1931); *accord* Stafford v. Louisiana State Univ., 448 So.2d 852 (La. Ct. App. 1984) [no liability for emergency amputation after good faith attempt to contact family].

5. *E.g.,* Sullivan v. Montgomery, 155 Misc. 448, 279 N.Y.S. 575 (N.Y. City Ct. 1935) [pain is a sufficient emergency]; Cunningham v. Yankton Clinic, 262 N.W.2d 508 (S.D. 1978) [pain is not sufficient].

6. *E.g.,* Kennedy v. Parrott, 243 N.C. 355, 90 S.E.2d 754 (1956).

7. Natanson v. Kline, 186 Kan. 393, 350 P.2d 1093 (1960).

8. Canterbury v. Spence, 464 F.2d 772, 787 (D.C. Cir. 1972).

9. Cowman v. Hornaday, 329 N.W.2d 422 (Iowa 1983).

10. *E.g.,* Smith v. Reisig, 686 P.2d 285 (Okla. 1984); Marino v. Ballestras, 799 F.2d 162 (3d Cir. 1984) [parents must be told alternatives to surgery for child]; Logan v. Greenwich Hosp. Ass'n, 191 Conn. 282, 465 A.2d 294 (1983) [feasible alternatives involving greater risks must also be disclosed].

11. Hales v. Pitman, 118 Ariz. 305, 576 P.2d 493 (1978).

12. *E.g.,* Canterbury v. Spence, 464 F.2d 772 (D.C. Cir. 1972).

13. *E.g.,* Wilkinson v. Vesey, 110 R.I. 606, 295 A.2d 676 (1972).

14. Crouch v. Most, 78 N.M. 406, 432 P.2d 250 (1967).

15. Lester v. Aetna Casualty and Surety Co., 240 F.2d 676 (5th Cir. 1957), *cert. denied,* 354 U.S. 923 (1957).

16. Nishi v. Hartwell, 52 Hawaii 188, 52 Hawaii 296, 473 P.2d 116 (1970).

17. Putenson v. Clay Adams, Inc., 12 Cal. App.3d 1062, 91 Cal. Rptr. 319 (1970).

18. Ga. Code §31-9-6(d) (1982).

19. *E.g.,* Young v. Yarn, 136 Ga. App. 737, 222 S.E.2d 113 (1975).

20. *E.g.,* Fiorentino v. Wenger, 19 N.Y.2d 407, 227 N.E.2d 296 (1967) and Ohio Rev. Code Ann. §2317.54 (Page 1981).

21. Magana v. Elie, 108 Ill. App.3d 1028, 439 N.E.2d 1319 (1982).

22. Schloendorff v. Society of N.Y. Hosp., 211 N.Y. 125, 105 N.E. 92 (1914).

23. For a more detailed discussion of the nurse's role, see A. Rhodes & R. Miller, NURSING AND THE LAW (4th ed., 1984), 205–206.

24. *E.g.,* Hill v. Seward, 122 Misc.2d 375, 470 N.Y.S.2d 971 (N.Y. Sup. Ct. 1983).

25. Forland v. Hughes, 393 Mass. 502, 471 N.E.2d 1315 (1984).

26. *E.g.,* Johnson v. McMurray, 461 So.2d 775 (Ala. 1984).

27. Joint Commission on Accreditation of Hospitals, ACCREDITATION MANUAL FOR HOSPITALS (1986 ed.) 60 (ambulatory services), 91 (general) and 218 (radiological services).

28. *E.g.*, Rogers v. Lumbermen's Mutual Casualty Co., 119 So.2d 649 (La. Ct. App. 1960).

29. *E.g.*, State Central Collection Unit v. Columbia Medical Plan, 300 Md. 318, 478 A.2d 303 (Md. Ct. App. 1984) [valid assignment in registration form].

30. 42 C.F.R. §§441.250–441.259 (1985) [sterilization]; 45 C.F.R. pt. 46 (1985) [research].

31. *E.g.*, Gordon v. Neviaser, 478 A.2d 292 (D.C. 1984); Siegel v. Mt. Sinai Hosp., 62 Ohio App.2d 12, 403 N.E.2d 202 (1978).

32. *E.g.*, Kaufer, Steinberg, & Toney, *Revising Medical Consent Forms: An Empirical Model and Test,* 11 LAW, MED. & HEALTH CARE 155 (1983).

33. Tatham v. Hoke, 469 F. Supp. 914 (W.D. N.C. 1979); *see also* Emory Univ. v. Porubiansky, 248 Ga. 391, 282 S.E.2d 903 (1981) [dental school exculpatory clause invalid].

34. Nev. Rev. Stat. §41A.110 (1981).

35. Iowa Code Ann. §147.137 (1985 Supp.).

36. Cunningham v. Parikh, 472 So.2d 746 (Fla. Dist. Ct. App. 1985); the statute was later amended to convert the conclusive presumption to a rebuttable presumption, H.B. 1352, §21, Fla. Laws, 1985.

37. In re Yetter, 62 Pa. D. & C.2d 619 (Pa. C. Pl. Ct., Northampton County 1973).

38. Lane v. Candura, 6 Mass. App. 377, 376 N.E.2d 1232 (1978).

39. *E.g.*, In re Ingram, 102 Wash.2d 827, 689 P.2d 1363 (1984) [court refused to override incompetent patient's preference to treat cancer with radiation rather than surgery].

40. *E.g.*, Farber v. Olkon, 40 Cal.2d 503, 254 P.2d 520 (1953) [consent by next of kin]; Ritz v. Florida Patient's Compensation Fund, 436 So.2d 987 (Fla. Dist. Ct. App. 1983) [consent by parents]; In re Barbara C., 101 A.D.2d 137, 474 N.Y.S.2d 799 (1984) [consent by parents]; Miss. Code Ann. §§41-41-3 and 41-41-5 (1972 & 1984 Supp.).

41. Aponte v. United States, 582 F. Supp. 65 (D. P. R. 1984).

42. Bonner v. Moran, 126 F.2d 121 (D.C. Cir. 1941).

43. *E.g.*, In re Rotkowitz, 25 N.Y.S.2d 624 (N.Y. Dom. Rel. Ct. 1941) [surgical correction of deformity ordered when parents disagreed].

44. State v. Bass, 255 N.C. 42, 120 S.E.2d 580 (1961).

45. *E.g.*, Gramm v. Boener, 56 Ind. 497 (1877).

46. *E.g.*, In re Pescinski, 67 Wis.2d 4, 266 N.W.2d 180 (1975) [incompetent adult]; In re Richardson, 284 So.2d 185 (La. Ct. App. 1973) [minor].

47. *E.g.*, Strunk v. Strunk, 445 S.W.2d 145 (Ky. 1969) [incompetent adult]; Hart v. Brown, 29 Conn. Super. 368, 289 A.2d 386 (1972) [minor].

48. *E.g.*, Schloendorff v. Society of N.Y. Hosp., 211 N.Y. 125, 105 N.E. 92 (1914).

49. In re Storar, 52 N.Y.2d 363, 420 N.E.2d 64 (1981).

50. Satz v. Perlmutter, 379 So.2d 359 (Fla. 1980), *approving* 362 So.2d 160 (Fla. Dist. Ct. App. 1978).

51. 70 N.J. 10, 355 A.2d 647 (1976); *accord* John F. Kennedy Memorial Hosp. v. Bludworth, 452 So.2d 921 (Fla. 1984).

52. Lane v. Candura, 6 Mass. App. 377, 376 N.E.2d 1232 (1978).

53. In re Osborne, 294 A.2d 372 (D.C. 1972); *see also* In re Brown, 478 So.2d 1033 (Miss. 1985) [state interest in preserving life of only eyewitness to murder not sufficient to overcome right of adult Jehovah's Witness to refuse blood transfusion].

54. 70 N.J. 10, 355 A.2d 647 (1976).

55. Custody of a Minor, 434 N.E.2d 601 (Mass. 1982).

56. In re Hudson, 13 Wash.2d 673, 126 P.2d 765 (1942).

57. In re Green, 448 Pa. 338, 292 A.2d 387 (1972).

58. In re Hofbauer, 47 N.Y.2d 648, 393 N.E.2d 1009 (1979).

59. In re Seifert, 309 N.Y. 80, 127 N.E.2d 820 (1955).

60. In re Ingram, 102 Wash.2d 827, 689 P.2d 1363 (1984).

61. McQuillan v. City of Sioux City, 306 N.W.2d 789 (Iowa 1981); *see also Duty of Injured Person to Submit to Surgery to Minimize Tort Damages,* 62 A.L.R.3d 9 (1975) and *Duty of Injured Person to Submit to Nonsurgical Medical Treatment to Minimize Tort Damages,* 62 A.L.R.3d 70 (1975).

62. 373 Mass. 728, 370 N.E.2d 417, 426 (1977).

63. Raleigh Fitkin–Paul Morgan Memorial Hosp. v. Anderson, 42 N.J. 421, 201 A.2d 537 (1964), *cert. denied* 377 U.S. 985 (1964); *accord* Crouse Irving Memorial Hosp., Inc. v. Paddock, 485 N.Y.S. 2d 443 (N.Y. Sup. Ct. 1985).

64. *E.g.,* In re Bentley, Misc. No. 65-74 (D.C. Super. Ct. April 25, 1974); Mercy Hosp., Inc. v. Jackson, 62 Md. App. 409, 489 A.2d 1130 (Md. Ct. Sp. App. 1985), *cert. granted* 497 A.2d 484 (Md. Ct. App. 1985).

65. Jefferson v. Griffin Spalding County Hosp. Auth., 247 Ga. 86, 274 S.E.2d 457 (1981).

66. Taft v. Taft, 388 Mass. 331, 446 N.E.2d 395 (1983).

67. Application of President and Directors of Georgetown College, Inc., 331 F.2d 1000 (D.C. Cir. 1964), *reh'g denied,* 331 F.2d 1010 (D.C. Cir. 1964), *cert. denied,* 377 U.S. 978 (1964).

68. In re Osborne, *supra* note 53.

69. In re Dell, 1 Pa.D&C.3d 655 (Pa. C. Pl. Ct., Allegheny County 1975).

70. MIAMI HERALD, Oct. 23, 1984, at 1A; Oct. 24, 1984, at 17A; January 26, 1985 at 1B; NEW YORK TIMES, Oct. 24, 1984, at 11, col. 6.

71. Jacobson v. Massachusetts, 197 U.S. 11 (1905).

72. Reynolds v. McNichols, 488 F.2d 1378 (10th Cir. 1973).

73. Commissioner of Corrections v. Myers, 379 Mass. 255, 399 N.E.2d 452 (1979).

74. *FDA Committee Questions Fluosol Efficacy; U.S. Approval Not Imminent,* 250 J.A.M.A. 2585 (1983); Hunt et al., *Synthesis and Evaluation of a Prototypal Artificial Red Cell,* 230 SCIENCE 1165 (1985).

75. Shorter v. Drury, 103 Wash.2d 645, 695 P.2d 116 (1985), *cert. denied,* 106 S. Ct. 86 (U.S. 1985).

76. *E.g.,* In re Ivey, 319 So.2d 53 (Fla. Dist. Ct. App. 1975).

77. *E.g.,* In re Sampson, 29 N.Y.2d 900, 278 N.E.2d 918, 328 N.Y.S.2d 686 (1972) [transfusions needed to permit surgical correction of deformed face and neck].

78. In re Green, 448 Pa. 338, 292 A.2d 387 (1972).

79. State Dep't of Human Servs. v. Northern, 573 S.W.2d 197 (Tenn. Ct. App. 1978).

80. In re Jensen, 54 Or. App.1, 633 P.2d 1302 (1981).

81. Custody of a Minor, 393 N.E.2d 836 (Mass. 1979).

82. Green v. Truman, 459 F. Supp. 342 (D. Mass. 1978).

83. *E.g.,* In re Edmundson, 15 Lebanon Co. J. 34 (Pa. C. Pl. Ct. 1973) [diabetes medication authorized].

84. Iowa Code Ann. §233.79 (1985).

85. N.C. Gen. Stat. §§90-21.1–90-21.3 (1981).

86. O'Conner v. Donaldson, 422 U.S. 563 (1975).

87. Parham v. J.L. and J.R., 442 U.S. 640 (1979).

88. *E.g.,* In re K.K.B., 609 P.2d 747 (Okla. 1980).

89. *E.g.,* Iowa Code Ann. §229.1(2) (1985).

90. *E.g.,* In re Roe, 383 Mass. 415, 421 N.E.2d 40 (1981); Rogers v. Commissioner of Dep't of Mental Health, 390 Mass. 489, 458 N.E.2d 308 (1983).

91. Rochin v. California, 342 U.S. 1165 (1951).

92. Breithaupt v. Adams, 352 U.S. 432 (1957).

93. Schmerber v. California, 384 U.S. 757 (1966).

94. Winston v. Lee, 105 S.Ct. 1611 (U.S. 1985).

95. 45 C.F.R. pt. 46 (1984).

96. 45 C.F.R. §46.111 (1984).

97. 45 C.F.R. §46.116(a) (1984).

98. 45 C.F.R. §46.101(b) (1984).

99. 45 C.F.R. §46.110 (1984); see 46 FED. REG. 8392 (1981) for the initial list of approved categories.

100. 45 C.F.R. §46.123(b) (1984).

101. 21 C.F.R. pts. 50, 56, 312, 314, and 812 (1985).

102. *E.g.,* N.Y. Public Health Law §§2440–2446 (1984–85 Supp.).

Chapter 14

Collection and Disclosure of Patient Information

Hospitals and health professionals must collect a large amount of sensitive information about patients to provide appropriate diagnosis, treatment, and care. This chapter discusses the recording of patient information and its uses, the law concerning confidentiality of patient information, and the circumstances in which disclosure of the information is prohibited, permitted, or mandated.

MEDICAL RECORDS

Accurate and complete medical records and a functioning medical records library are required by both governmental and nongovernmental agencies. The licensing laws and regulations of many states include specific requirements with which hospitals must comply. In addition, nongovernmental agencies, such as the Joint Commission on Accreditation of Hospitals (JCAH), establish standards for the maintenance of medical records.

The primary purpose of medical records is diagnosis, treatment, and care of the patient. The recording of data provides a communications link among the team members caring for the patient. Records are also documentation of what was found and what was done so that patient care can be evaluated, billing and collections can be made, and other administrative and legal matters can be addressed. Medical records are also of value in hospital educational and research programs.

Contents

Many statutes and regulations require hospitals to maintain medical records. Hospitals that participate in the Medicare program must comply with minimum content requirements.[1] State hospital licensing laws and regulations addressing medical records can be divided into three groups: (1) those detailing the information required; (2) those specifying the broad areas of information required; and (3) those stating simply that the medical record shall be adequate, accurate, or complete. Some local governments require additional information to be kept.

To be accredited, hospitals must meet JCAH medical records standards, including a long list of items that must be in the medical record.[2] The list is designed to assure that the patient is identified, the diagnosis is supported, the treatment is justified, and the results are accurately documented. While many of the specific items apply only to inpatients, the general standards apply to all patients, including ambulatory care patients, emergency patients, and patients in hospital-administered home care programs.

Certain basic information should usually be recorded concerning each patient. The medical record consists of three types of data: (1) personal; (2) financial; and (3) medical. Personal information, usually obtained upon admission, includes name, date of birth, sex, marital status, occupation, other items of identification, and the next of kin or other person to contact in the event the need to do so arises. Financial data usually include the name of the patient's employer, the patient's health insurance program, type of insurance and policy or identification number, and other information that will enable the hospital to bill for its services. Medical data form the clinical record, a continuously maintained history of the patient's condition and treatment provided. These data include physical examinations, medical history, treatment administered, progress reports, physicians' orders, clini-.cal laboratory reports, radiological reports, consultation reports, anesthesia records, operation records, signed consent forms, nurses' notes, and discharge summaries. The medical record should be a complete, current record of the history, condition, and treatment of the patient. Some hospitals also collect social data concerning family status, community activities, and other information related to the patient's position in society.

Accuracy and Timely Completion of Medical Records

Accurate and timely completion of medical records is essential to comply with governmental and accreditation requirements and to minimize liability exposure.

State hospital licensing statutes and regulations and JCAH standards require accurate records. An inaccurate record may increase the hospital's exposure to liability by destroying the credibility of the entire record. In a 1974 Kansas case, the court found that a discrepancy between what was stated in the medical record in one place and what actually happened to the patient could justify a jury's finding that the record could also be erroneous in other parts and considered generally invalid.[3]

Complete records include notations of observations that the patient's condition has not changed, as well as observations of change. If there is no notation of an observation, many courts permit the jury to infer that no observation was made. In 1974 the Illinois Supreme Court was presented with a case involving a patient who had been admitted to the hospital with a broken leg.[4] The leg suffered irreversible ischemia while in traction and required amputation. The physician had ordered the nurse to observe the patient's toes, and the medical record indicated hourly observations during the first day of hospitalization. There was no documentation of observations during the seven hours prior to finding the foot cold and without sensation. Though the nurse may have observed the foot during that period, the court ruled that the jury could infer from the lack of documentation that no observations were made, indicating a breach of the nurse's duty. The hospital, as employer, could be liable for the resulting injuries.

Complete records can protect the hospital and staff in many situations. A Kentucky hospital was found not liable for the death of a patient approximately 13 hours after surgery because the medical record included documentation of proper periodic observation of the patient by the nursing staff, contacts with the physician concerning management of the patient, and compliance with the physician's directions.[5] As discussed in Chapter 11, compliance with the physician's directions does not protect the hospital and its staff when the directions are clearly improper. However, when the directions are within the ambit of acceptable professional practice, compliance that is properly documented provides substantial protection from liability.

Medical records entries should usually be made when the treatment is given or the observations are made. Entries made several days or weeks later have less credibility than those made during or immediately after the patient's hospitalization. Medicare conditions of participation require completion of hospital records within 15 days following the patient's discharge.[6] JCAH accreditation standards require each hospital's medical staff regulations to state a time limit for completion of the record that cannot exceed 30 days after discharge.[7] Persistent failure to conform to this medical staff rule is an adequate basis for suspension of the staff member.[8]

Corrections and Alterations

Proper methods should be used to correct errors in medical records. Improper alterations can reduce the credibility of the record, exposing the hospital to an increased risk of liability.

There are two types of errors in medical records: (1) minor errors in transcription, spelling, and the like; and (2) more significant errors involving important test data, medication orders, inadvertently omitted progress notes, and similar substantive entries. Persons authorized by hospital policy to make record entries may correct minor errors in their own entries when discovered soon after the original entry is made. Only a physician or administrative or nursing staff supervisor should correct substantive errors and errors that are discovered some time after the original entry was made. If the original entry is likely to have been read by others who could be misled by the error, the physicians, nurses, and others likely to be relying on the original entry should be notified of the change.

The person correcting the error should place a single line through the incorrect entry, enter the correct information, initial or sign the correction, and enter the time and date the correction was made. Mistakes should not be erased or obliterated, since such changes may lead jurors to suspect the original entry.

After a claim has been made or a lawsuit filed against the hospital or a staff member, changes should not be made in the record without first consulting defense counsel. After a group of New York physicians had won a malpractice suit, it was discovered that a page of the medical record had been replaced not long before the beginning of the suit.[9] Therefore, the court ordered a new trial.

Altering or falsifying a medical record to obtain reimbursement wrongfully is a crime. In some states a practitioner who improperly alters a medical record is subject to license revocation or other discipline for unprofessional conduct. In some states improper alteration of a medical record is itself a crime.

Some patients request modification of medical records. Since the records are the evidence of what occurred in the hospital and were relied on in making patient care decisions, hospitals should usually not modify records except to update the identity of patients whose names are changed. If a patient disagrees with an entry, some hospitals permit the physician or nurse supervisor to make amendments in the same manner as corrections of substantive errors if the physician concurs in the appropriateness of the amendment. Such an amendment should include a note that it is being made at the request of the patient, so that the patient will be responsible for explaining the change if it is questioned later. Instead of changing the original entry, some hospitals permit the patient to add a letter of explanation to the record. If the staff concurs with the statement, the concurrence can be noted on the letter. This approach clearly documents the source of the change.

Occasionally courts will order modification of records, especially in cases involving involuntary evaluation or treatment for mental illness.[10]

Retention of Records

Since hospital records are maintained primarily for the use of the hospital and the medical staff in providing patient care, decisions concerning record retention periods should be based on sound hospital and medical practice, as well as applicable regulations. In several states, regulations specify the minimum retention period for all records; in others, retention periods are specified only for selected records: for example, X-rays and clinical lab test records. The Medicare program requires records to be kept for the longer of five years after the filing of the hospital's cost report or the period in which suits may be filed.[11] Medicare providers must include in contracts with subcontractors a provision requiring the subcontractor to retain records for at least four years after services are provided and to permit HHS to inspect them.[12] Several state regulations provide that the record must be kept permanently, but more are now requiring that the records be kept for the period in which suits may be filed for breach of contract or personal injuries. Several states provide that records cannot be destroyed without the approval of a regulatory agency.

Where there are no controlling regulations, the length of time medical records should be retained after they are not needed for medical and administrative purposes should be determined by the hospital administration with the advice of legal counsel. Hospitals should consider storage space, feasibility of microfilming, the future need for such records, and the need for record availability if a patient sues the hospital or a third party. In hospitals where extensive medical research is conducted, a longer retention period may be appropriate to facilitate retrospective studies.

The importance of retaining records until the time has passed for lawsuits is illustrated by a 1984 Florida appellate court decision.[13] The anesthesia records concerning a patient were lost, so the proof necessary to sue the anesthesiologist was not available. The court ruled that the hospital could be sued for negligently maintaining its records and that the hospital could avoid liability only by showing that the treatment recorded in the missing records was performed nonnegligently, which would be difficult to do without the records.

Destruction of Records

The issue of destruction of records can arise when the retention period specified by hospital policy has passed or when the patient requests destruction prior to expiration of the retention period.

Some state hospital licensing regulations specify the method by which records may be destroyed. Although several states permit burning, the Environmental Protection Agency has recommended shredding and recycling. Regardless of the method used, procedures should be followed to protect confidentiality of record information. The records should be completely destroyed. The hospital should retain certificates of destruction permanently as evidence of record disposal. Some states require hospitals to create a permanent abstract of records prior to destruction.

Some patients request premature destruction of medical records, and some state statutes forbid destruction of records on an individual basis.[14] In states without specific statutes, it is still prudent not to destroy individual records unless ordered to do so by a court. Courts have generally refused to order the destruction of records. For example, in 1978 the highest court of New York ruled that records could be ordered sealed but not destroyed.[15] One exception is a 1978 case in which the Pennsylvania Supreme Court ordered the destruction of the records of a mental patient who had been illegally hospitalized.[16]

Ownership

The hospital owns the hospital medical record, which is its business record. The hospital's ownership is explicitly stated in the statutes and regulations of some states, and courts have recognized the hospital's ownership.[17] If the physician maintains separate records, they are the property of the physician. However, when separate records are maintained, the physician still has a responsibility to maintain complete hospital records.

The medical record is an unusual type of property because, physically, it belongs to the hospital and the hospital must exercise considerable control over access, but the patient and others have an interest in the information in the record. One way of viewing this situation is that the hospital owns the paper or other material on which the information is recorded, but it is just a custodian of the information. The patient and others have a right of access to the information in many circumstances, but they do not have a right to possession of the original records.[18] Courts have also ruled that the patient does not have a right to X-ray negatives.[19] The patient does not purchase a picture; the patient purchases the professional service of interpreting the X-ray. Thus, the patient could not use the physician's retention of the X-ray as a defense to a suit to collect professional fees.

Computers

Taking advantage of automated data processing techniques, some hospitals are developing new methods for handling medical record information. Several legal questions are raised by these new techniques. In states that require authentication of physicians' entries and orders by the physicians' signatures, some accommodation will be necessary since in some completely automated systems there may be no conventional written record for the physician to sign or initial. In states requiring retention of the original medical record for a period of time, the record produced in an automated system may not suffice. In some states, there may be a question of admissibility in court of information generated by the system. Questions of confidentiality may arise in automated systems because of the potential accessibility to a larger number of people. However, a properly designed computer access security system may provide more protection of confidentiality than traditional medical records because (1) there are few points of access to the computer; (2) it is possible to restrict each person's access to a limited scope of information; and (3) it is possible to monitor continuously or selectively the information being sought through individual access codes, making misuse easier to detect. The security system depends in part on educating staff that disclosure of their personal access codes is equivalent to disclosure of confidential medical information and subject to the same sanctions by the hospital.

At the outset, each hospital contemplating the introduction of these new techniques must evaluate any proposed system to ensure it will serve the medical and health needs of the hospital, facilitate the appropriate quality of patient care, and conform to legal standards. Some state standards may have to be modified to allow for the application of these new techniques. If the new techniques aid hospitals in providing cost-effective, quality care, the legal standards will be modified to allow for the application of these new techniques. In many states the hospital licensing agency has the authority to grant a waiver of some of the requirements to permit individual hospitals to proceed with implementation.

CONFIDENTIALITY

The primary rationale for confidentiality of patient information is to encourage candor by patients and their associates to optimize diagnosis and treatment. Confidentiality also respects the patient's privacy; people should not have to broadcast details of their bodily condition to obtain medical care. Confidentiality can also promote candor by those caring for the patient.

People outside the hospital often seek to obtain patient information. There is much interest in the condition and care of individuals. Family members are interested in their relatives. Some individuals can have a significant effect on affairs of business and state, and their conditions are valuable information. The general interest in unusual health conditions and the conditions of those involved in public events focuses media attention on health information. The health condition of individuals is an important element of many insurance coverage determinations and legal proceedings, both criminal and civil.

The tension between access and secrecy has existed since the beginning of medicine. Most health professions have addressed the issue, incorporating confidentiality mandates in their ethical standards. For example, the Hippocratic Oath of physicians states: "And whatsoever I shall see or hear in the course of my profession, as well as outside my profession in my intercourse with men, if it be what should not be published abroad, I will never divulge, holding such things to be holy secrets."[20] These ethical standards led to tensions as legal disclosure requirements evolved. For example, some physicians challenged early laws requiring reporting of births and deaths. However, most modern codes recognize the obligation of professionals to make legally mandated disclosures. The American Medical Association code, adopted in 1980, states: "A physician . . . shall safeguard patient confidences within the constraints of the law."[21]

ACCESS FOR INTRAHOSPITAL USES

There are many needs for access to information within the hospital, including direct patient care, administrative uses, and research uses.

Patient Care

Those who are involved in patient care must have timely access to records, or the communication function of the record is defeated to the detriment of good patient care. Records must be located where they are readily accessible for present and future patient care, even when accessibility increases the risk of unauthorized access by others. Although confidentiality is an important goal that hospitals and health professionals should strive to achieve, unauthorized access results in less liability exposure than improper patient care due to unavailable records.

Administrative Uses

Medical records are also hospital business records. Many hospital staff members must have access to them to operate the hospital. Hospitals have the authority to permit internal access by professional, technical, and administrative personnel who need access. Examples of uses requiring access include auditing, filing, billing, replying to inquiries, and defending potential litigation.

These administrative uses are so widely understood that they have seldom been addressed in reported court decisions. The few cases have been decided in favor of administrative access. In 1965 the highest court of New York authorized a trustee to examine medical records of patients involved in a controversial research project.[22] The court observed, "Actually, the supposed strict secrecy does not really exist as to qualified persons since these records have been seen, read and copied by numerous staff members and employees of the hospital and co-operating institutions." In 1975 a Missouri court upheld the authority of hospitals to review records for quality assurance purposes.[23] In 1979 a Canadian court ruled that the hospital's insurers and lawyers may have access to prepare to deal with patient claims.[24]

Research

Research is another major purpose of intrahospital access. Some important medical discoveries made through researching medical records are surveyed in an article by Gordis and Gold entitled *Privacy, Confidentiality, and the Use of Medical Records in Research.*[25] A few commentators still question records research without patient consent, but the practice is generally recognized as appropriate and permissible. The general practice is to permit staff members to use the medical records for bona fide research. Research by non–staff members should be subject to a review and approval process, including obtaining assurances against redisclosure of individually identifiable information. The Department of Health and Human Services recognizes this practice in its human studies regulations by making some federally funded research involving only records eligible for exemption from institutional review or eligible for expedited review.[26]

ACCESS BY AUTHORIZATION OF THE PATIENT

One source of authority to release information to nonhospital personnel is the competent patient.

Patient Access

Competent patients can generally authorize their own access to medical records concerning their care. Some states have statutes that establish the right of patients to obtain access to records regarding their own care and establish the procedure they are to follow.[27] A common law right of access has been recognized by several courts. In cases over the past 25 years, patients have generally been held to have a right of access.[28] Courts have also ruled that the hospital may require the patient to pay a reasonable charge for the copy.[29] However, courts have disagreed on how much is reasonable.[30] Copying charges should be based on the hospital's costs, including the cost of clerical and medical records personnel time. In setting copying charges, it is prudent to check the charges of local courts and their libraries because it will be difficult for courts to find comparable charges unreasonable.

Access by Others

When patients may authorize their own access, they may authorize access by others. A federal court in Oklahoma ruled that insurers of the patient have a right to copy the hospital's records upon proper authorization of the patient.[31] The court found the hospital's refusal to provide a copy to be unlawful interference with the insurer's business.

There is implied consent to keep the immediate family informed of the patient's progress unless the patient directs that no information be released or a statutory prohibition applies, such as the federal substance abuse confidentiality rules discussed later in this chapter. In 1963 a Louisiana court ruled that a husband has a right of access to information concerning his wife's care even though they were separated and he is pursuing divorce.[32] It is doubtful whether many courts would extend the right of access that far today. The most prudent practice is to require patient consent or court authorization before releasing information when estrangement is known.

Release of psychiatric information is subject to special restrictions in some states. In 1982 a New York court stated that a spouse should not be given psychiatric information, even when there is no estrangement, unless the patient authorizes the disclosure or a danger to the patient, spouse, or another person can be reduced by disclosure.[33] Some states authorize the disclosure of psychiatric information to the spouse in more circumstances.[34]

Hospitals can refuse to release records until presented with a release form that complies with its reasonable policies. A Missouri court upheld a hospital's refusal to release records to an attorney who presented a form with an altered date.[35]

Exceptions

Some courts have recognized exceptions to the general rule in favor of access. They recognize that there may be situations when the release of information is against the best interests of the patient's health. However, the courts have generally insisted that medically contraindicated information be made available to the patient's representative, who is frequently an outside professional acting on behalf of the patient. For example, in 1979 a federal appellate court addressed the withholding of information from patients preparing for hearings challenging their transfer to a lower level of care.[36] The court ruled that it was not enough for the state to offer to release the information to a representative when the patient did not have a representative. The state was permitted to withhold medically contraindicated information from the patient only when the patient actually had a representative, provided by the state if necessary. In a 1983 case, a New York mental hospital attempted to enforce its policy of releasing records only to a physician, even when the patient authorized other releases.[37] The court ruled that the records could be protected from disclosure only if the hospital proved the release would cause detriment (1) to the patient, (2) to involved third parties, or (3) to an important program of the hospital. Since none of these was proved, the court ordered disclosure. In a 1965 case, a federal court stated that records containing information that would be adverse to the patient's health could be withheld from insurance companies.[38] It is doubtful whether this rule would be applied today, since there is widespread recognition of the need for third party payers to have access to records.

Suggested Hospital Policies

It is recommended that hospitals give patients and their representatives access to medical records when authorized to do so by the patient. In some situations, when the patient is unable to authorize access, approval of the representative should be accepted, as discussed in the next section of this chapter. Since records contain technical information and many abbreviations and specialized terms, the hospital protocol should offer the patient and representative an opportunity to review the record with someone who can explain it.

The American Hospital Association has recommended that the attending physician be notified before medical records are released, and many hospitals follow the practice. Some medical staffs rely on the hospital to determine which releases can be made without notification, which require notification, and which require physician review before release. Other medical staffs and hospitals agree on guidelines concerning which releases fall in each category. The medical staff should understand and accept the approach followed.

However, physicians should not be given a veto over release of medical records. If the physician has substantial reasons for believing release to the patient is contraindicated, arrangements should be made for release to someone acting on the patient's behalf. In some situations, especially in the case of psychiatric records that contain sensitive information about other members of the patient's family, the person acting on the patient's behalf may need to be from outside the patient's family.

The American Hospital Association's Patient's Bill of Rights focuses on release of information by the physician rather than by the hospital. It states that patients should be able to obtain complete information from their physicians, except when disclosure is not medically advisable. In that case, information should be given to an appropriate person on the patient's behalf. When patients will accept information from their physicians, this approach is preferable to having the patient read the medical record. Physicians should be encouraged to provide information to their patients.

However, some patients still wish to see their medical records. Medical record access is recommended because in many situations the curiosity and concerns of the patient will be satisfied, avoiding any appearance of a cover-up and avoiding the need for the patient to hire an attorney or file suit to obtain the records. A 1980 study that analyzed patient reactions found

1. Approximately one-third of the patients who read their charts had self-induced or factitious illness and were angry to have been uncovered.
2. One-third believed their physicians to be unsympathetic to their symptoms, and some found their suspicions confirmed, while others gained renewed confidence.
3. One-third were worried about their prognosis, fearing the physician was not telling them the true severity of their illness, and all these patients were reassured.[39]

Another good reason to provide prompt access to the medical record is that some courts have ruled that any unreasonably long period from the request until the release does not count toward exhausting the statute of limitations period in which suits must be brought.[40] Thus, resistance to disclosure can reduce the protection of the statute of limitations.

ACCESS BY AUTHORIZATION OF THE PATIENT'S REPRESENTATIVE

When the patient is unable to authorize access because of incompetency, minority, or death, someone else must be able to authorize access.

Mentally Incompetent Patients

In general, guardians of mentally incompetent patients are entitled to access in circumstances when competent patients can obtain access. However, some courts have stated they will suppress portions of the record that contain family confidences or information that may upset the patient severely.[41]

When a mentally incompetent patient does not have a guardian, the hospital generally may rely on the authorization of the next of kin or other responsible person who is authorizing medical treatment, especially for access by the responsible person or by others for continuity of patient care or payment of charges. When the mental incompetence is temporary and the release of the information can reasonably wait, it usually is prudent to wait for the patient's authorization.

Minors

The scope of parent and guardian access to records of minors is less clear. Some state statutes specify that information regarding certain types of treatment, such as treatment for venereal disease and substance abuse, may not be disclosed without the minor's consent. Some statutes specify that parents must be informed before minors may obtain certain kinds of services. For example, Utah requires parents to be informed of abortions. In 1981 the Supreme Court found the Utah reporting law constitutional, but declined to rule on whether the law would be constitutional if it were applied to mature minors.[42]

When state law permits minors to consent to their own care, it is likely that parents do not have a right to information concerning the care. If the minor fails to make other arrangements to pay for the care and relies on the parents to pay, the parents may be entitled to more information. However, providers can release information concerning immature minors to their parents without substantial risk of liability, unless state statutes expressly prohibit the release. When a mature minor wishes information withheld from parents, the provider must make a professional judgment concerning information release to the parents, except in the few circumstances where the law is settled, such as when a constitutional statute requires or forbids notification. Disclosure is generally permitted when there is likelihood of harm, such as contagious disease, to the minor or others that requires parental involvement to avoid.

Deceased Patients

After the death of the patient, if there is an executor of the estate, the authorization of the executor should usually be sought before releasing information. If there is no executor, authorization should be obtained from the next of kin, such as a surviving spouse[43] or child.[44] If there is known conflict among next of kin, it is most prudent to obtain the authorization of all the nearest kin available. Thus, a surviving spouse could authorize release alone, but, if there is no spouse, the authorization of all of the available children should be obtained.

In a few states the legal responsibility to maintain confidentiality ends with the death of the patient. However, it is still prudent to insist on appropriate authorization to avoid compromising the interests of the surviving family.

ACCESS BY LAW

Even if the patient or representative opposes release of the information, the law requires hospitals and health care professionals to permit access to medical information in many circumstances. The law grants parties in lawsuits access through subpoenas and other mechanisms to discover evidence. The law requires health care providers (1) to report a variety of patient conditions to law enforcement or public health authorities and (2) to provide certain persons access to information when requested.

Subpoenas and Other Discovery Mechanisms

In lawsuits and many administrative proceedings, the court or administrative agency has the authority to issue orders to assist one side in the suit or proceeding in gaining access to information in the control of others. Lawyers call this the "discovery" process. The most frequent discovery order is called a *subpoena*. A subpoena is an order for a person to appear at a certain place on or before a certain time, and it frequently requires the person to bring certain documents. Other discovery orders can require a person to submit to a physical or mental examination or to permit someone to inspect land, buildings, or other property.

Medical Records

A subpoena may order that medical records (or copies) be provided to the court or to the other side in the suit. A subpoena may order a person to submit to formal questioning under oath prior to the trial. This question and answer session is called a *deposition* and often is used as testimony if the person cannot be at the trial. If the person is at the trial and gives different testimony, the deposition can be used to cast doubt on what is said at trial.

Under the current liberal discovery practices, medical records of parties to the suit can nearly always be subpoenaed if the mental or physical condition of the party is relevant to the suit. In some states, the physician-patient privilege, discussed later in this chapter, is not automatically waived by the patient's filing of a personal injury claim, and the medical records custodian, therefore, has a duty to refuse to provide the records in response to some subpoenas. When records can be subpoenaed, those who provided the health care usually can be ordered to give depositions.

In most circumstances, courts will not permit the discovery of information concerning the health care of persons who are not parties. Some attorneys have sought such information to establish what happened when similar treatment was given to other patients. Providers have resisted these attempts on the basis that they invade patients' privacy, violate the physician-patient privilege discussed later in this chapter, and are not relevant because of the uniqueness of the condition and reaction of each patient.

The only widely accepted exceptions to the general rule of not permitting discovery have been in cases involving billing fraud by or professional discipline of health care providers. However, in recent years some courts have permitted access to medical records of nonparties in malpractice suits but have required all "identifiers" to be deleted.[45] There is no clear trend because several courts have reaffirmed the traditional rule and declined to order access.[46]

Patient's Names

Some attorneys have attempted to bypass the rule on nondisclosure of nonparty medical records by seeking the names of the nonparty patients and obtaining their permission to get the records. Providers have resisted these attempts for reasons similar to those for resisting discovery of their records. Most courts have not permitted the discovery of the names of nonparties. For example, in 1964 the Michigan Supreme Court ruled that the names of patients are protected by the physician-patient privilege.[47] However, in 1976 the Arizona Supreme Court ruled that the physician-patient privilege does not protect patients' names in Arizona but still refused to order release of other names because it did not consider them relevant to the case.[48] Thus, there is a risk that records obtained without identifiers could be linked later to patient names through another exception.

Committee Reports

Many states have enacted statutes protecting quality assurance-related activities and committee reports from discovery or admission into evidence. These laws are designed to permit the candor necessary for effective peer review to improve quality and reduce morbidity and mortality. Courts have found these laws constitutional.[49]

Some courts have strictly interpreted statutory protections, reducing their effectiveness. For example, in a 1975 New Jersey case, the court refused to apply the statutory protection for "utilization review committees" to related committees, such as the medical records and audit, tissue, and infection control committees.[50] Some courts have interpreted statutory protections broadly. For example, the Minnesota Supreme Court found that a complications conference report was protected under a statute that protected "the proceedings and records of a review organization."[51]

Some courts have recognized a common law qualified privilege on the basis of the public interest in these peer review activities. In 1970 a District of Columbia court refused to order release of information concerning a peer review committee's activities.[52] However, other courts have refused to recognize a common law privilege for peer review.[53]

Because the status of many committee reports is still an open question in many states, these reports should be carefully written so that, if they must be released, they will not inappropriately increase the exposure to liability.

Responses to Subpoenas and Other Discovery Orders

In most situations, the proper response to a valid subpoena or other discovery order is compliance. However, prompt legal assistance should be sought whenever a discovery order is received because some orders are not valid and others should be resisted. A discovery order should never be ignored.

Subpoenas from state courts in other states are usually not valid unless they are given to the person being subpoenaed while that person is in the state of the issuing court. However, subpoenas from federal courts in other states usually are valid. Courts in some states have authority to issue subpoenas to persons only in a limited area. Most states have a procedure for obtaining a valid subpoena from a local court to require releasing information for a trial in a distant court that does not have the authority to issue a valid subpoena.

Sometimes challenges to subpoenas are successful. In a New Jersey case, the court refused to order a woman or her psychiatrist to answer questions concerning nonfinancial matters in a marriage separation case because the husband had failed to demonstrate relevance or good cause for the order.[54] When judges are not certain whether to order a release, they sometimes will order that the information be presented to them for their review before ruling on the matter. An Illinois court ruled that this review should be by a judge, not an administrative hearing officer.[55]

In some situations, the only way to obtain prompt appellate review of an apparently inappropriate discovery order is to risk being found in contempt of court. In one case a physician challenged a grand jury subpoena of the records of 63 women he had treated in an abortion clinic.[56] The trial court found him to be in contempt of court for failing to comply. The Illinois Supreme Court held that he must release the records of the one patient who had waived her physician-patient privilege, but reversed the contempt finding on the other 62 records. The court ruled that they were protected by the physician-patient privilege in Illinois until a showing that a criminal action relating to malpractice or abortion was involved. Valid subpoenas should never be ignored and should never be challenged except on the advice of an attorney. In 1978 an Illinois court affirmed a $1,000 fine for contempt of court assessed against an orthopedic surgeon for ignoring a subpoena and refusing to appear at a trial involving a patient he had treated.[57] In a Kansas case the court affirmed the commitment to jail of a treating physician who refused to testify until he was paid an expert witness fee.[58] However, in 1983 the Iowa Supreme Court ruled that an expert witness who is a stranger to the litigation may not be compelled to give opinion testimony absent a demonstration of compelling necessity.[59]

Statutory Duty To Disclose: Reporting Laws

The law compels disclosure of medical information in many contexts other than discovery or testimony. A variety of reporting laws have been enacted that require many kinds of medical information to be reported to governmental agencies. The most common examples are vital statistics, communicable disease, child abuse, and wound reporting laws. Familiarity with these and other reporting laws is important to assure compliance and to avoid reporting to the wrong agency. Reports to the wrong agency many not be legally protected, resulting in potential liability for breach of confidentiality.

Vital Statistics

All states require the reporting of births and deaths. Courts have ruled that these laws are a valid exercise of the state's police power.[60] Many states also require the reporting of some fetal deaths and abortions. In a 1976 Missouri case, the Supreme Court upheld some abortion reporting requirements.[61]

Public Health

Most states require the reporting of venereal disease and other communicable diseases. In a 1975 California case, the court observed that, in addition to the criminal penalties for not reporting, civil liability is possible in a suit by persons who become diseased but might have avoided the disease if it had been properly reported.[62] Some states have expanded the reporting requirement to encompass cancer and selected other diseases. A few states require reports to the state driver licensing agency of conditions such as seizures that could lead to loss of license.

Child Abuse

Most states require the reporting of suspected cases of child abuse or neglect. Some professionals, such as physicians and nurses, are required to make reports and, thus, are often called mandatory reporters. Usually, anyone who is not a mandatory reporter may make a report as a permissive reporter. Any report arising out of diagnosis or treatment of a child in an institution usually must be made through the administration of the institution. Most child abuse reporting laws extend some degree of immunity from liability for mandatory or permissive reporters who make their reports through proper channels.[63] There are usually criminal penalties for mandatory reporters who do not make required reports, but there have been few prosecutions. A mandatory reporter who fails to report child abuse is at risk of civil liability. Some states specify in the statute that a mandatory reporter who fails to make a required report is civilly liable for future injuries to the child that could have been avoided if a report had been made.[64] In 1976 the California Supreme Court ruled that there could be civil liability under the common law even when the statute did not address whether there should be civil liability.[65] Some states have enacted adult abuse laws that are similar to the child abuse reporting laws.

Wounds

Many states require the reporting of certain wounds. Some states specify that all wounds of certain types must be reported. For example, New York requires the reporting of wounds inflicted by sharp instruments that may result in death and all gunshot wounds.[66] Other states limit the reporting requirement to wounds caused under certain circumstances. For example, Iowa requires reporting of wounds that apparently resulted from criminal acts.[67] Thus, wounds that are clearly accidental or self-inflicted do not have to be reported in Iowa.

Other Reporting Laws

Some states require the reporting of other types of information, such as industrial accidents, so it is important to be familiar with the requirements of local law. Several national reporting laws apply to hospitals that are involved in manufacturing, testing, or using certain substances and devices. For example, fatalities due to blood transfusions must be reported to the FDA.[68] A report must be filed with the FDA by the sponsor of an investigational medical device when unanticipated adverse effects result from the use of the device.[69] Device manufacturers have a continuing duty before and after the device is approved to report to the FDA any information that death or serious injury has occurred or may occur in connection with the device.[70]

Statutory Duty To Disclose: Access Laws

A second kind of statute does not mandate reporting but authorizes access on request to certain individuals or organizations or to the general public without the patient's permission.

Worker's Compensation

Some state statutes specify that all parties to a worker's compensation claim have access to all relevant medical information after a claim has been made.[71] In states that do not authorize access by statute, the medical records should not be released until the patient or the patient's representative authorizes the release or the records are legally subpoenaed by an administrative agency or court. One exception is in states where the courts have ruled that filing a worker's compensation claim is a waiver under the common law of the right to confidentiality of relevant medical information.[72]

Federal Freedom of Information Act

The federal Freedom of Information Act (FOIA) applies only to federal agencies.[73] A hospital does not become a federal agency by receiving federal funds, so the FOIA applies to few hospitals outside of the Veterans Administration and Defense Department hospital systems. When the FOIA applies, medical information is exempted from disclosure only when the disclosure would "constitute a clearly unwarranted invasion of personal privacy." Thus, the Act provides only limited protection of the confidentiality of medical information in the possession of federal agencies.

State Public Records Laws

Many states have public records laws that apply to public hospitals. Some state statutes explicitly exempt hospital and medical records from disclosure.[74] In a 1974 case Colorado's law was interpreted not to permit a publisher to obtain all birth and death reports routinely.[75] In 1983 the Iowa Supreme Court addressed the effort of a leukemia patient to force the disclosure of an unrelated potential bone marrow donor whose name was in the records of a public hospital.[76] The court ruled that names of patients could be withheld from disclosure and that, although the potential donor had never sought treatment at the hospital, the potential donor was a patient for purposes of the exemption from the public records law because the medical procedure of tissue typing had been performed. However, in a 1978 Ohio case, the state law was interpreted to require access to the names and the dates of admission and discharge of all persons admitted to a public hospital.[77] In states that follow the Ohio rule, it is especially important to resist discovery of nonparty records because removal of "identifiers" does not offer much protection since dates in the records may make it possible to identify the patient from the admission list. It is important for those associated with public hospitals to be familiar with local law concerning access to public records.

Other Access Laws

Some federal and state statutes give specified governmental agencies access to certain medical records on request or through administrative subpoena. For example, Peer Review Organizations (PROs) have access to all medical records pertinent to their federal review functions on request. A federal court has ruled that Medicare surveyors have a right of access to records of non-Medicare patients as well as Medicare patients.[78] Hospital licensing laws in many states grant state licensing inspectors access without subpoena for audit and inspection purposes.

Common Law Duty To Disclose

In addition to these statutory requirements, the common law has recognized a duty to disclose medical information in several circumstances. Persons who could have avoided injury if the information had been disclosed have won civil suits against providers who failed to disclose the information.

Contagious Diseases

There is a duty to warn persons at risk of the presence of contagious disease. Hospital staff, family members, and others caring for the patient should be warned. In a 1928 case a court ruled that a physician could be liable for the death of a neighbor who contracted smallpox while assisting in the care of the physician's patient with smallpox because the physician failed to warn the neighbor of the contagious nature of the disease.[79] However, there is no duty to warn all members of the public individually, although in a California case the court observed that liability to the general public might result from failure to make a required report to public health authorities.[80]

Threats to an Identified Person

The courts of a few states have ruled that there is a duty to warn an identified person that a patient has made a credible threat to kill him or her. The first decision to impose this duty was in *Tarasoff v. Board of Regents.*[81] When the Tarasoffs sued for the death of their daughter, the California Supreme Court found the employer of a psychiatrist liable for his failure to warn the daughter that his patient had threatened to kill her. The court ruled that he should have either warned the victim or advised others likely to apprise the victim of the danger. In a 1980 case, the same court clarified the scope of this duty by ruling that only threats to readily identified individuals create a duty to warn.[82] There is no duty to warn a threatened group. In 1983 the Washington Supreme Court ruled that the duty to warn extended to unidentifiable victims.[83] In 1985 the Vermont Supreme Court extended the duty to warn to include property damage, imposing liability on a counseling service when a patient burned his parents' barn.[84] Some courts have declined to establish a duty to warn even readily identified individuals.[85] The more prudent practice today is to follow the California rule and warn identified individuals of credible threats when the patient is not detained.

Other Duties

Courts have recognized other situations when there is a duty to disclose. One example is the duty of referral specialists to communicate their findings to the referring physician.[86] A competent patient can waive this duty by directing the referral specialist not to communicate with the referring physician.

LIMITATIONS ON DISCLOSURE

Several statutory and common law limitations on disclosure have evolved that assist in preserving confidentiality and impose sanctions for some violations of confidentiality.

Physician-Patient Privilege

The physician-patient privilege is the rule that a physician is not permitted to testify as a witness concerning certain information gained in the physician-patient relationship. There was no physician-patient privilege from testimonial disclosure under the English common law. Nearly all American courts also have adopted this position, so with few exceptions the privilege exists only in states that have enacted privilege statutes. One exception is Alaska, which established a common law psychotherapist-patient privilege for criminal cases.[87]

Approximately two-thirds of the states have enacted a statutory physician-patient privilege. Privilege statutes address only situations where the physician is being compelled to testify, such as in a deposition, an administrative hearing, or a trial. There is a widespread misperception that privilege statutes apply to other disclosures, but in most states this is not true. The duty to maintain confidentiality outside of testimonial contexts is grounded on other legal principles discussed later in this chapter. Thus, privilege statutes are usually of concern to hospitals only when the hospitals are responding to legal compulsion.

The privilege only applies when a bona fide physician-patient relationship exists. Thus, for example, the privilege usually does not apply to court-ordered examinations or other examinations solely for the benefit of third parties, such as insurance companies.

The scope of the privilege varies among the states. For example, Pennsylvania limits the privilege to communications that tend to blacken the character of the patient,[88] while Kansas extends the privilege to all communications and observations.[89] Michigan limits the privilege to physicians,[90] while New York extends the privilege to dentists and nurses.[91] When a nurse is present during a confidential communication between physician and patient, some states extend the privilege to the nurse, while other states rule that the communication is no longer privileged for the physician. Generally the privilege extends to otherwise privileged information recorded in the hospital record.[92] However, information that is required to be reported to public authorities has generally been held not to be privileged, unless the public authorities are also privileged not to disclose it.

Waiver

The patient may waive the privilege, permitting the physician to testify. In nearly all states the privilege can be waived by contract. Waiver is often called for in applications for insurance and in medical and disability insurance policies. A variety of other actions constitute implied waiver. Patients who introduce evidence disclosing details of their medical conditions or who fail to object to testimony by the physician are generally found to have waived the privilege by their actions. Most courts have ruled that authorization of disclosure outside the testimonial context does not waive the privilege.[93] Thus, the patient could authorize other parties to have access to medical records outside of court and still successfully object to having them introduced into evidence, unless other actions have waived the privilege. A few courts have adopted the opposite position, so in those states authorization of any disclosure to opposing parties waives the privilege.[94]

Waiver of the privilege usually permits only formal discovery and testimony, not informal interviews. This rule requires express patient consent before informal interviews are permitted.[95] However, other courts have permitted informal interviews based on waiver of the privilege.[96] The most prudent practice is for providers to limit disclosures to formal channels unless express patient consent is obtained.

Other Statutory Limitations on Disclosure

Some federal and state statutes, such as federal substance abuse confidentiality laws and state licensing and confidentiality laws, limit access to medical information.

Substance Abuse Confidentiality

Special federal rules deal with confidentiality of information concerning patients treated or referred for treatment for alcoholism or drug abuse.[97] The rules apply to any facility receiving federal funds for any purpose, including Medicare or Medicaid reimbursement. The regulations explicitly preempt any state law that purports to authorize disclosures contrary to the regulations, but they permit states to impose tighter confidentiality requirements. The rules apply to any disclosure, even acknowledgment of the patient's presence in the facility. Information may be released with the patient's consent if the consent is in writing and contains all of the following elements: (1) the name of the program to make the disclosure; (2) the name or title of the person or organization to receive the information; (3) the name of the patient; (4) the purpose or need for the disclosure; (5) the extent or nature of the information to be disclosed; (6) a statement that the consent may be revoked and when the consent will automatically expire; (7) the date signed; and (8) the patient's signature.

A court order, including a subpoena, does not permit release of information unless the requirements of the regulations have all been met. The regulations require a court hearing and a court finding that the purpose for which the order is sought is more important than the purpose for which Congress mandated confidentiality. Fortunately, the regulations have been interpreted to permit hospitals to tell the court why they cannot comply with the order until after a hearing. After a hearing, courts have ordered disclosures to assist probation revocation and child abuse proceedings. In 1981 a federal court ordered disclosure to assist an Internal Revenue Service investigation of a surgeon.[98] Courts have declined to order disclosure when the information was sought to challenge the credibility of witnesses or to assist in determining the rehabilitation potential of a convicted person for purposes of sentencing.

Numerous written opinions interpreting these rules have been issued by HHS. The opinions have been collected into booklets by the Alcohol, Drug Abuse, and Mental Health Administration of HHS. In 1983 substantial revisions in the regulations were proposed,[99] but they were not adopted.

It is important that staff members be oriented to these rules. In one case a nurse successfully challenged her discharge for failure to report a fellow employee's theft of patient files by establishing the reasonableness of her belief (which was actually erroneous) that these federal regulations prohibited the report.[100]

Professional and Hospital Licensing Laws

Professional licensing laws or regulations frequently specify that breach of confidentiality is unprofessional conduct and grounds for discipline by the licensing board. Examples are the Iowa rules pertaining to physicians and nurses.[101] Hospital licensing laws and regulations frequently require that confidentiality of records be maintained.[102]

Other State Confidentiality Laws

Some states have statutes that establish a general responsibility to maintain confidentiality of medical records.[103] Some states have statutes that address only records regarding treatment for certain conditions, such as venereal disease.[104] Thus, it is important for each hospital to be familiar with local statutes and regulations.

Accreditation Standards

The JCAH medical records standards specify that hospitals have the responsibility of protecting the medical record and the information in the medical record "against loss, defacement, and tampering and from use by unauthorized individuals."[105] If a hospital accepts this responsibility through its hospital rules to become accredited, many courts will require the hospital to follow its own rules and impose liability for injuries that result from violations.

Common Law Limitations

As discussed in the section on the physician-patient privilege, the common law does not provide for any protection from disclosure in testimonial contexts, except in a few states, such as Alaska. Courts have uniformly refused to impose liability for testimonial disclosures.[106] Physicians and hospitals are not obligated to risk contempt of court to protect confidences (except for substance abuse records), although they may choose to do so.

In nontestimonial contexts, courts have found limitations on permissible disclosure based on the implied promise of confidentiality in the physician-patient relationship, violation of the right of privacy, and violation of professional licensing standards. For example, in 1977 a New York court permanently enjoined a psychoanalyst from circulating a book that included detailed information concerning a patient.[107] The patient was identifiable to close friends despite the psychoanalyst's efforts to disguise her identity. The court ruled that the book violated the implied covenant of confidentiality and the right of privacy. The court awarded $20,000 to the plaintiff for the 220 copies that were sold before the injunction. In 1985 the Oregon Supreme Court held that a physician could be liable for revealing his patient's identity to the patient's natural child, who had been adopted.[108] The court ruled that, while it was not a violation of the patient's right of privacy, it was a breach of the professional duty to maintain secrets.

Courts have ruled in favor of physicians and health care employees in cases where the disclosure was intended to prevent the spread of contagious disease.[109] As discussed in the section on the common law duty to disclose information, there could be liability in some circumstances for failing to disclose a contagious disease.

Disclosures to the patient's employer or insurance company have resulted in several suits. In 1973 the Alabama Supreme Court ruled that disclosures to an employer without authorization violated the implied promise of confidentiality and could result in liability.[110] The employer who induces the disclosure can also be liable.[111] However, in 1960 a New York court ruled that when a patient authorized incomplete disclosure to his employer, the physician was not liable for giving a complete disclosure.[112] It is questionable whether other courts would rule this way, so the prudent practice is to refuse to release any information when only a misleading partial release is authorized.

Some courts have found implied authorization to release information to an insurance company based on actions of the patient. In a 1973 Colorado case submission to a medical examination at the insurance company's request was considered implied authorization.[113] However, the prudent practice is to obtain a written authorization from the patient. Most insurance companies do so. In some cases, courts have ruled that insurance companies may be sued for inducing a physician to divulge confidential information.[114]

A frequent basis for suits for disclosures of confidential information has been defamation. In most cases involving physicians, the courts have found a qualified privilege to make the specific disclosures. The few cases where liability has been found involved misdiagnosis and disclosure of an embarrassing condition (such as venereal disease) that the patient did not actually have, in a manner that sufficiently demonstrated malice, so that the qualified privilege provided no protection.[115]

PHOTOGRAPHY

In general, physicians may take and use photographs of patients for the medical record or for professional educational purposes, unless the patient expressly forbids photographs. In 1969 the highest court of Massachusetts enjoined public showing of a film of inmates of an institution for insane persons charged with crimes or delinquency but permitted continued showings to audiences of a specialized or professional character with a serious interest in rehabilitation.[116] The court observed that the public interest in having these people informed outweighs the rights of the inmates to privacy. In 1976 the Maine Supreme Court ruled that, when the patient had expressly objected to being photographed, there could be liability for photographing the patient even if the photograph was solely for the medical records.[117] The most prudent approach is to obtain express consent for taking and using photographs, but there is little likelihood of liability for photographs taken without express consent if the patient does not object and uses are appropriately restricted. Of course, public or commercial showing without consent can lead to liability.[118] In 1985 a New York appellate court ruled that representatives of an incompetent patient do not have a right to photograph the patient in the hospital.[119] The petitioners failed to show a sufficient need to justify a court order that they be permitted to film an eight-hour videotape of their comatose daughter in an intensive care unit for use in a suit.

DISCIPLINE OF STAFF MEMBERS

Hospital staff members have been discharged for unauthorized disclosure of medical records. However, courts and arbitration panels tend to reinstate them unless there has been a consistent pattern of enforcement. For example, a Royal Commission that investigated the confidentiality of medical records in Ontario found many unauthorized disclosures. One of the persons responsible for the unauthorized disclosures was a nurse who had given records to her husband, an attorney representing patients' opponents in legal proceedings. She was fired, but the arbitration board ordered her reinstated with the sanction of suspension without pay up to the time of the ruling.[120] The board accepted her position that, since no one else had been disciplined, she was the scapegoat for the hospital's embarrassment concerning the Royal Commission's findings. In 1983 a Minnesota court addressed a nurse who had been dismissed for a breach of confidentiality.[121] The court found that she was not guilty of misconduct and, thus, should receive unemployment compensation because the hospital's policy had not been adequately enunciated to the staff. Thus, a consistent pattern of enforcing a well-communicated policy is important both to emphasize the importance of confidentiality to the staff and to increase the likelihood that disciplinary actions will be sustained if challenged.

NOTES

1. 42 C.F.R. §405.1026(g) (1984).

2. Joint Commission on Accreditation of Hospitals, ACCREDITATION MANUAL FOR HOSPITALS (1986 ed.), 87–99 [hereinafter cited as JCAH 1986].

3. Hiatt v. Groce, 215 Kan. 14, 523 P.2d 320 (1974).

4. Collins v. Westlake Community Hosp., 57 Ill.2d 388, 312 N.E.2d 614 (1974).

5. Engle v. Clarke, 346 S.W.2d 13 (Ky. 1961).

6. 42 C.F.R. §405.1026(j) (1984).

7. JCAH 1986, *supra* note 1 at 95.

8. *E.g.*, Board of Trustees of Memorial Hosp. v. Pratt, 72 Wyo. 120, 262 P.2d 682 (1953). Note that some hospitals place more emphasis on financial incentives than on penalties, e.g., *Incentives Spur Physicians To Complete Record-Keeping*, 15 MOD. HEALTHCARE, Dec. 6, 1985, at 64.

9. Kaplan v. Central Medical Group, 71 A.D.2d 912, 419 N.Y.S.2d 750 (1979).

10. *E.g.*, In re Morris, 482 A.2d 369 (D.C. 1984).

11. 42 C.F.R. §405.1026(b) (1984); MEDICARE & MEDICAID GUIDE (CCH), ¶6420.85.

12. 42 U.S.C. §1861(v)(i) (1982).

13. Bondu v. Gurvich, 473 So.2d 1307 (Fla. Dist. Ct. App. 1984).

14. *E.g.*, Tenn. Code Ann. §68-11-305(c) (1983).

15. Palmer v. New York State Dep't of Mental Hygiene, 44 N.Y.2d 958, 380 N.E.2d 154 (1978).

16. Wolfe v. Beal, 477 Pa. 447, 384 A.2d 1187 (1978).

17. *E.g.*, Pyramid Life Ins. Co. v. Masonic Hosp. Ass'n, 191 F. Supp. 51 (W.D. Okla. 1961).

18. *E.g.*, Cannell v. Medical and Surgical Clinic, 21 Ill. App.3d 383, 315 N.E.2d 278 (1974).

19. *E.g.*, McGarry v. J. A. Mercier Co., 272 Mich. 501, 262 N.W. 296 (1935).

20. S. Reiser, A. Dyck, & W. Curran, ETHICS IN MEDICINE 5 (1977).

21. American Medical Association, PRINCIPLES OF MEDICAL ETHICS (August 1980).

22. Hyman v. Jewish Chronic Disease Hosp., 15 N.Y.2d 317, 258 N.Y.S.2d 397, 399 (1965).

23. Klinge v. Lutheran Medical Center, 518 S.W.2d 157 (Mo. Ct. App. 1975).

24. In re General Accident Assurance Company of Canada and Sunnybrook Hospital (1979) 23 O.R.(2d) 513 (Ont. High Ct. of Justice).

25. 207 SCIENCE 153 (1980).

26. 45 C.F.R. §46.101(b)(5) (1985); 46 FED. REG. 8392 (1981).

27. E.g., Ill. Rev. Stat. Ch. 110 §§8-2001–8-2004 (1984 & 1985 Supp.).

28. E.g., Wallace v. University Hosps., 84 Ohio Abs. 224, 170 N.E.2d 261 (Ohio Ct. App. 1960), appeal dismissed 171 Ohio St. 487, 172 N.E.2d 459 (1960); Hutchins v. Texas Rehabilitation Comm'n, 544 S.W.2d 802 (Tex. Ct. App. 1976).

29. E.g., Rabens v. Jackson Park Found., 40 Ill. App.3d 113, 351 N.E.2d 276 (1976).

30. E.g., Hernandez v. Lutheran Medical Center, 104 A.D.2d 368, 478 N.Y.S.2d 697 (1984) [$1 per page is reasonable]; contra Mauer v. Mount Sinai Hosp., 193 N.Y.L.J. No. 22 (N.Y. Sup. Ct. Feb. 1, 1985) [$1 per page not reasonable, reduced to 25 cents].

31. Pyramid Life Ins. Co. v. Masonic Hosp. Ass'n, 191 F. Supp. 51 (W.D. Okla. 1961).

32. Pennison v. Provident Life and Accident Ins. Co., Inc., 154 So.2d 617 (La. Ct. App. 1963), writ refused 156 So.2d 226 (La. 1963).

33. MacDonald v. Clinger, 84 A.D.2d 482, 446 N.Y.S.2d 801 (1982).

34. E.g., Iowa Code Ann. §229.25 (1985).

35. Thurman v. Crawford, 652 S.W.2d 240 (Mo. Ct. App. 1983).

36. Yaretsky v. Blum, 592 F.2d 65 (2nd Cir. 1979).

37. Cynthia B. v. New Rochelle Hosp. Medical Center, 91 A.D.2d 1111, 458 N.Y.S.2d 363 (1983).

38. Bishop Clarkson Memorial Hosp. v. Reserve Life Ins. Co., 350 F.2d 1006 (8th Cir. 1965).

39. Altman, Patients Who Read Their Hospital Charts, 302 NEW ENG. J. MED. 169 (1980).

40. E.g., Emmett v. Eastern Dispensary and Casualty Hosp., 396 F.2d 931 (D.C. Cir. 1967).

41. E.g., Gaertner v. State, 385 Mich. 49, 187 N.W.2d 429 (1971).

42. H.L. v. Matheson, 450 U.S. 398 (1981).

43. E.g., Claim of Gurkin, 434 N.Y.S.2d 607 (N.Y. Sup. Ct. 1980).

44. E.g., Emmett v. Eastern Dispensary and Casualty Hosp., 396 F.2d 931 (D.C. Cir. 1967).

45. E.g., Community Hosp. Ass'n v. District Ct., 194 Colo. 98, 570 P.2d 243 (1977); State ex rel. Lester E. Cox Medical Center v. Keet, 678 S.W.2d 813 (Mo. banc 1984).

46. E.g., Teperson v. Donato, 371 So.2d 703 (Fla. Dist. Ct. App. 1979).

47. Schechet v. Kesten, 372 Mich. 346, 126 N.W.2d 718 (1964).

48. Banta v. Superior Ct., 112 Az.544, 544 P.2d 653 (1976).

49. E.g., City of Edmund v. Parr, 587 P.2d 56 (Okla. 1978); Jenkins v. Wu, 102 Ill.2d 468, 468 N.E.2d 1162 (1984). For a review of the cases on discovery of peer review records, see Holdenreid, Discovery of Hospital Information, 1 TOPICS HOSP. LAW, Dec. 1985, at 14, 15–21.

50. Young v. King, 136 N.J. Super. 127, 344 A.2d 792 (N.J. Super. Ct. 1975).

51. Warrick v. Giron, 290 N.W.2d 166 (Minn. 1980).

52. Bredice v. Doctors Hosp., Inc., 50 F.R.D. 249 (D.D.C. 1970).

53. Davison v. St. Paul Fire and Marine Ins. Co., 75 Wis.2d 190, 248 N.W.2d 433 (1977).

54. Ritt v. Ritt, 52 N.J. 177, 244 A.2d 497 (1968).

55. Laurent v. Brelji, 74 Ill. App.3d 214, 392 N.E.2d 929 (1979).

56. People v. Bickham, 89 Ill.2d 1, 431 N.E.2d 365 (1982).

57. Schmoll v. Bray, 61 Ill. App.3d 64, 377 N.E.2d 1172, (1978).

58. Swope v. State, 145 Kan. 928, 67 P.2d 416 (1937).

59. Mason v. Robinson, 340 N.W.2d 236 (Iowa 1983).

60. *E.g.*, Robinson v. Hamilton, 60 Iowa 134, 14 N.W. 202 (1882).

61. Planned Parenthood v. Danforth, 428 U.S. 52 (1976).

62. Derrick v. Ontario Community Hosp., 47 Cal. App.3d 154, 120 Cal. Rptr. 566 (1975).

63. *E.g.*, Awkerman v. Tri-County Orthopedic Group, P.C., 373 N.W.2d 204 (Mich. Ct. App. 1985).

64. *E.g.*, Iowa Code Ann. §232.75 (1985).

65. Landeros v. Flood, 17 Cal.3d 399, 551 P.2d 389 (1976).

66. N.Y. Penal Law §265.25 (McKinney 1980).

67. Iowa Code Ann. §147.111 (1972).

68. 21 C.F.R. §606.170(b) (1985).

69. 21 C.F.R. §812.150 (1985).

70. 49 FED. REG. 36326–51 (1984); *Medical Device Hazard Reports Required,* 59 HOSPITALS, Mar. 16, 1985, at 76.

71. *E.g.*, Iowa Code Ann. §85.27 (1984).

72. *E.g.*, Acosta v. Cary, 365 So.2d 4 (La. Ct. App. 1978).

73. 5 U.S.C. §552 (1982), as amended by Pub. L. No. 98-620, 98 Stat. 3357 (1984).

74. *E.g.*, Iowa Code Ann. §22.7(2) (1985 Supp.).

75. Eugene Cervi & Co. v. Russell, 184 Colo. 282, 519 P.2d 1189 (1974).

76. Head v. Colloton, 331 N.W.2d 870 (Iowa 1983).

77. Wooster Republican Printing Co. v. City of Wooster, 56 Ohio St.2d 126, 383 N.E.2d 124 (1978).

78. O'Hare v. Harris, MEDICARE & MEDICAID GUIDE (CCH), ¶31,054 (D.N.H. Mar. 12, 1981).

79. Jones v. Stanko, 118 Ohio St. 147, 160 N.E. 456 (1928).

80. Derrick v. Ontario Community Hosp., 47 Cal. App.3d 154, 120 Cal. Rptr. 566 (1975).

81. 17 Cal.3d 425, 551 P.2d 334 (1976).

82. Thompson v. County of Alameda, 27 Cal.3d 741, 614 P.2d 728 (1980).

83. Peterson v. State, 100 Wash.2d 421, 671 P.2d 230 (1983).

84. Peck v. Counseling Serv., 499 A.2d 422 (Vt. 1985).

85. *E.g.*, Shaw v. Glickman, 45 Md. App. 718, 415 A.2d 625 (1980).

86. *E.g.*, Thornburg v. Long, 178 N.C. 589, 101 S.E. 99 (1919).

87. Allred v. State, 554 P.2d 411 (Alaska 1976).

88. Pa. Stat. Ann., tit. 42, §5929 (Purdon 1982).

89. Kan. Stat. Ann. §60-427 (1983).

90. Mich. Comp. Laws §600.2157 (1968).

91. N.Y. Civil Practice §4504 (McKinney Supp. 1984-1985).

92. *E.g.,* In re New York City Council v. Goldwater, 284 N.Y. 296, 31 N.E.2d 31 (1940).

93. *E.g.,* Cartwright v. Maccabees Mutual Life Ins. Co., 65 Mich. App. 670, 238 N.W.2d 368 (1975).

94. *E.g.,* Willis v. Order of R.R. Telegraphers, 139 Neb. 46, 296 N.W. 443 (Neb. 1941).

95. Wenniger v. Muesing, 307 Minn. 405, 240 N.W.2d 333 (1976).

96. *E.g.,* Transworld Investments v. Drobny, 554 P.2d 1148 (Alaska 1976).

97. 42 C.F.R. pt. 2 (1985); *see e.g.,* Heartview Foundation v. Glaser, 361 N.W.2d 232 (N.D. 1985).

98. United States v. Providence Hosp., 507 F. Supp. 519 (E.D. Mich. 1981).

99. 48 Fed. Reg. 38758-79 (1983).

100. Heng v. Foster, 63 Ill. App.3d 30, 379 N.E.2d 68 (1978).

101. Iowa Admin. Code §§470-135.401(10) (1979) [physicians] and 590-1.2(d)(6) (1980) [nurses].

102. *E.g.,* Kan. Admin. Regs. §28-34-9(b) (1974).

103. *E.g.,* Cal. Civil Code §§56-56.37 (West 1982 & 1985 Supp.).

104. *E.g.,* Iowa Code Ann. Ch. 140 (1972 & 1985 Supp.) [venereal disease].

105. JCAH 1986, *supra* note 2 at 93.

106. *E.g.,* Boyd v. Wynn, 150 S.W.2d 648 (Ky. 1941).

107. Doe v. Roe, 93 Misc.2d 201, 400 N.Y.S.2d 668 (N.Y. Sup. Ct. 1977).

108. Humphers v. First Interstate Bank, 68 Or. App. 573, 684 P.2d 581 (1984), *aff'd,* 298 Or. 706, 696 P.2d 527 (1985).

109. *E.g.,* Simonsen v. Swenson, 104 Neb. 224, 177 N.W. 831 (1920) [physician]; Knecht v. Vandalia Medical Center, Inc., 14 Ohio App.3d 129, 470 N.E.2d 230 (1984) [receptionist].

110. Horne v. Patton, 291 Ala. 701, 287 So.2d 824 (1973).

111. Alberts v. Devine, 395 Mass. 59, 479 N.E.2d 113 (1985).

112. Clark v. Geraci, 29 Misc.2d 791, 208 N.Y.S.2d 564 (N.Y. Sup. Ct. 1960).

113. Conyers v. Massa, 512 P.2d 283 (Colo. Ct. App. 1973).

114. *E.g.,* Hammonds v. Aetna Casualty and Surety Co., 243 F. Supp. 793 (N.D. Ohio 1965).

115. *E.g.,* Beatty v. Baston, 130 Ohio L. Abs. 481 (Ohio Ct. App. 1932).

116. Commonwealth v. Wiseman, 356 Mass. 251, 249 N.W.2d 610 (Mass. 1969).

117. Estate of Berthiaume v. Pratt, 365 A.2d 792 (Me. 1976).

118. Feeney v. Young, 191 A.D. 501, 181 N.Y.S. 481 (1920) [public showing of a film of a Caesarean section delivery]; Vassiliades v. Garfinkels, 492 A.2d 580 (D.C. 1985) [public use of before and after photos of cosmetic surgery in department store and on television].

119. In re Simmons, 112 A.D.2d 806, 492 N.Y.S.2d 308 (1985).

120. Metropolitan General Hosp. v. Ont. Nurses' Ass'n, 22 L.A.C.(2d) 243 (Ont. Lab. Arb. 1979).

121. Group Health Plan, Inc. v. Lopez, 341 N.W.2d 294 (Minn. Ct. App. 1983).

Chapter 15

Reproductive Issues

This chapter discusses the sensitive reproductive issues of contraception, conception, and abortion. These areas are sensitive both because of their effect on the individuals involved and because of the intense political and social controversy concerning them. They have been recognized by the courts as a fundamental aspect of the right to privacy of the individuals involved. However, the divergence of moral and religious views concerning the propriety of the procedures related to these issues has led to social controversy. Some believe that their views should be public policy and should be enforced through the legal system, so there is also political controversy. This chapter also discusses prenatal testing, genetic screening, and liability for the birth of children after negligent sterilizations or failure to inform of genetic risks.

CONTRACEPTION

Contraception includes the various drugs, devices, and procedures designed to avoid pregnancy.

Contraceptive Drugs and Devices

Numerous drugs and devices are available to reduce the probability of pregnancy. In the past, some states passed laws restricting the sale or use of these drugs and devices. In 1965 the Supreme Court declared a Connecticut law forbidding the use of contraceptives by married persons to be an unconstitutional violation of the right of privacy.[1] In 1972 the Court declared a Massachusetts law forbidding the sale or use of contraceptives by unmarried persons to be unconstitutional.[2] In striking down the law, the

Court ruled that whatever the rights of adults to access to contraceptives may be, the rights are the same for married and unmarried persons alike.

These two cases establish that a state may not prohibit the use of contraceptives by adults, although states may regulate sales of contraceptives. In 1977 the Supreme Court limited the permissible scope of state regulation of the sale and distribution of contraceptives.[3] The Court invalidated a New York statute prohibiting the distribution of nonprescription contraceptives to persons over 16 by anyone other than licensed pharmacists, finding it an undue burden on an individual's right to decide whether to bear a child. The Court also invalidated the prohibition on advertising and display of both prescription and nonprescription contraceptives by persons licensed to sell such products.

Thus, few legal barriers confront an adult who seeks to obtain contraceptives. For safety reasons, prescription contraceptives or those requiring fitted insertion must be obtained through a physician or other authorized individual. Other birth control devices may be purchased without medical involvement.

Minors

Minors still face obstacles to obtaining contraceptives in some states. The Supreme Court's first comment on a minor's right of access to birth control came in the 1977 case discussed above.[4] The Court struck down a portion of a New York law that prohibited the sale or distribution of nonprescription contraceptives to minors under 16. However, the justices disagreed on the rationale for the decision. Only four of the nine justices based their decisions on extending the right of privacy in decisions affecting procreation to minors.

In 1979 one federal court ruled that federally funded family planning centers could not require parental notice or consent as a condition to providing services.[5] The court based its ruling on its interpretation of the federal statute authorizing the program, not on constitutional principles. In 1980 a federal court ruled that minors have a right to obtain contraceptive devices from a county-run family planning center without parental notification or consent.[6]

A 1981 federal law added a requirement that federally funded family planning projects "encourage family participation" in counseling and decisions about services.[7] HHS proposed rules interpreting this to require parental notification after services were initially provided to any minor under age 18 unless (1) the minor was emancipated under state law; or (2) the project director determined that notification would result in physical harm to the minor by a parent or guardian. The proposed rules also required compliance with all state laws concerning notification or consent.[8] The rules never took effect because they were blocked by a federal court order.[9] The courts ruled that Congress intended to encourage, not require, parental involvement, so the rules exceeded statutory authority. In 1983 a federal court declared unconstitutional a Utah law requiring parental notification before furnishing contraceptives to minors.[10] Many questions are still unanswered. States may still be able to regulate a minor's access to contraceptives more strictly than would be allowed for adult access to the same materials.

While the most prudent practice is to encourage minors to involve their parents in the decision making, many minors cannot or will not accept parental involvement. Physicians must then decide whether to prescribe contraceptives in the absence of parental involvement. Physicians who choose to prescribe contraceptives to unemancipated minors face a theoretical possibility of civil liability for battery or malpractice in some states. Several states explicitly authorize minors to consent to these services. Even in states without a minor consent statute, the legal risk is small, especially when the minor is mature. The most likely difficulty for the physician will be in collecting payment because the parents will probably not be responsible for payment.

Liability for the Side Effects of Contraceptives

Both oral contraceptives and intrauterine devices are known to have harmful side effects in a few instances. Litigation has resulted from the most serious of these situations. Much of this litigation has been against the manufacturer and has been based on product liability or inadequate warnings of the risks involved in taking birth control pills or using certain devices. It appears that physicians will not be held liable in the absence of negligence or intentional misconduct. They will be held liable for injuries to their patients if they (1) negligently prescribe a contraceptive, (2) negligently insert a contraceptive device, (3) fail to give adequate information concerning potential side effects, or (4) fail to monitor a patient who is at risk or develops adverse reactions.

VOLUNTARY STERILIZATION

Sterilization involves the termination of the ability to produce children. Sterilization may be the desired result of a surgical operation or the incidental consequence of an operation to remove a diseased reproductive organ or to cure a malfunction of such an organ. When the reproductive organs are not diseased, most sterilizations are effected by vasectomy for males and tubal ligation for females.

In the past, there were concerns about the legality of voluntary sterilizations of competent adults. States recognized a distinction between (1) therapeutic sterilizations to protect women who were at risk of impairment of life or health from pregnancy and (2) contraceptive sterilizations for which there was no therapeutic reason. Some states permitted therapeutic sterilization but not contraceptive sterilizations. However, these restrictions have been eliminated, so that no state prohibits voluntary consensual sterilization of a competent adult, regardless of the purpose.

Federal regulations require the signing of a special consent form at least 30 days prior to sterilizations funded by Medicaid.[11] Exceptions are made for some therapeutic cases. Some states, such as California, impose similar requirements on all sterilizations performed in the state.[12] A California court upheld the constitutionality of these state requirements in a 1981 case.[13]

The specific wording of the federal consent forms and the 30-day waiting requirement do not apply to other patients unless required by state law. However, the consent of the person who is to be sterilized or subject to an operation that may incidentally destroy the reproductive function should be obtained before the operation is performed. In the absence of consent, even if an operation is medically necessary, a sterilization almost always constitutes a battery. Courts are less likely to find implied consent to sterilization than to other extensions of surgical procedures. When it may be predicted that an operation necessary to treat a condition will incidentally destroy the ability to procreate, the consequences of the operation to the reproductive function should be clearly brought to the attention of the patient. When sterilization is to be performed in conjunction with another procedure, specific reference should be made to the sterilization. The use of a specific consent form that clearly indicates the effect upon the reproductive process is recommended. The form should disclose that reproduction probably will not be possible, but that a risk that the sterilization will be unsuccessful remains. Failure to inform of the small risk of future reproductive ability can expose the provider to liability for wrongful conception or wrongful birth as discussed later in this chapter.

Ordinarily, the patient's consent alone is sufficient authorization for any operation. But since sterilization affects the sensitive procreative function, some hospitals and physicians have a policy of requiring that the spouse's consent also be obtained when the patient is married. It is doubtful whether public hospitals can enforce such policies. In several cases, courts have declared such a policy by a public hospital to be an unconstitutional violation of the right of privacy.[14] In 1973 a federal court ruled that a governmental hospital may not impose greater restrictions upon sterilization procedures than upon other procedures that are medically indistinguishable in the risk to the patient or demand on staff or facilities.[15] The hospital was enjoined from enforcing its policy against all contraceptive sterilization procedures. However, private hospitals can forbid contraceptive sterilizations or require spousal consent.[16]

In the past, several states had laws requiring spousal consent to sterilizations, but when these laws have been challenged, federal courts have consistently declared them unconstitutional and enjoined their enforcement.[17]

It is prudent to encourage spousal involvement in the decision to sterilize, especially when the spouses are not estranged. Individual physicians may have a personal practice of not performing sterilizations without spousal consent in any hospital if the practice is not required by institutional policy. The broad latitude to establish personal policies is illustrated by the following case. In 1977 a federal court found no violation of the United States Constitution in a physician's personal policy to condition treatment of pregnant indigent patients on their voluntary submission to sterilization following the delivery of their third living child.[18] The fact that the doctor served Medicaid patients did not make his actions "state action." He applied his policy to all his patients and notified them of his practice early in their relationship so that they were free to go elsewhere for care.

Performing a sterilization procedure without spousal consent presents little legal risk. For example, when a husband sued an Oklahoma physician for performing a sterilization procedure without his consent, the court dismissed the suit because his marital rights did not include a child-bearing wife, so he had not been legally harmed by the procedure.[19]

Voluntary contraceptive sterilization of unmarried minor patients presents special problems, so local laws concerning minor consent should be carefully observed. Some states' statutes authorize such sterilizations if the parent or guardian also consents.[20] Other state statutes forbid sterilization of an unmarried person who is a minor.[21] As discussed in the following section of this chapter, it is well established that parents or guardians alone cannot authorize sterilizations. The consent of the patient is essential unless court authorization is obtained. Unless there is a medical reason for the sterilization and the consent of the minor and the parent is clearly voluntary, informed, and unequivocal, prudent providers should be reluctant to sterilize a minor without a court order. Federal funds can be used to pay for sterilizations only if the person is competent and at least 21 years old.[22]

Some states have enacted legislation stating that hospitals are not required to permit the performance of sterilization procedures and that physicians and hospital personnel may not be required to participate in the performance of such procedures or be discriminated against for refusal to participate.[23] Such legislation, more frequently found with regard to abortion procedures, is often referred to by the term *conscience clause* and was not found objectionable by the Supreme Court in its decisions striking down most state abortion laws. In 1979 a nurse-anesthetist was awarded payment from a hospital that violated the Montana conscience clause by dismissing her for refusing to participate in a tubal ligation.[24] However, it is doubtful that this legislation could constitutionally be interpreted to authorize governmental hospitals to forbid sterilization by willing physicians and staff.

INVOLUNTARY STERILIZATION

Statutes and courts in some states have authorized involuntary sterilization of two groups of people. The first to be addressed were those believed to transmit hereditary defects to succeeding generations. In the first half of this century, many states enacted eugenic sterilization laws authorizing the sterilization of these people against their will. The Supreme Court upheld such laws in a 1927 case.[25] However, many states have repealed their eugenic sterilization laws. The second group to be addressed consists of those who are severely retarded, sexually active, unable to use other forms of contraception, and unable to care properly for their offspring. Several states have enacted involuntary sterilization laws authorizing the sterilization of individuals a court determines to meet all of these criteria. The primary focus of these laws is the best interests of the patient and potential future offspring, rather than genetics.

These modern laws have been upheld by the courts. For example, North Carolina's statute[26] was upheld by the North Carolina Supreme Court and by the federal courts.[27] The statute does not allow the patient's next of kin or guardian to initiate sterilization proceedings, restricting the duty to the director of a state institution or the county director of social services. The key elements of a constitutional statute appear to be (1) identification of an appropriate class of persons subject to the statute without discrimination or arbitrary bias; and (2) guarantees of procedural due process, including notice, hearing, right to appeal, and assurance that decisions will be supported by qualified medical opinion.

Parents or guardians do not have the authority to consent to sterilization of retarded children or wards without a valid court authorization.[28]

Several courts have been presented with applications for court orders authorizing involuntary sterilizations in states that do not have statutes specifically giving the court authority to issue such orders. Thus, the courts have had to decide whether they have authority to issue such orders under their general jurisdiction concerning the welfare of incompetents.

Prior to 1978 most state courts ruled that they did not have the authority and refused to issue orders authorizing sterilization. The primary causes of this position were the decisions in two federal court cases that judicial immunity did not protect judges who issued sterilization orders without specific statutory authority because they were not acting within their jurisdictions.[29] These decisions permitted civil rights suits against the judge and the involved health care providers. However, the Supreme Court reversed the decision in the second case in 1978, ruling that a court of broad general jurisdiction has the jurisdiction to consider a petition for sterilization of a minor unless statutes or case law in the state circumscribe the jurisdiction to foreclose consideration of such petitions.[30] Thus, the judge was protected by judicial immunity. The Court directed a lower federal court to decide the liability of the private individuals who had sought the petition and carried out the order. The lower court ruled they could not be sued for federal civil rights violations because there was no showing of conspiracy between the private individuals and state officials.[31]

Since the Supreme Court's 1978 decision, several state courts have ruled that they have authority to authorize involuntary sterilization of incompetents in appropriate cases. The decisions have set forth procedures to be followed and criteria that must be met, which are generally similar to those specified in modern involuntary sterilization statutes.[32] However, the Alabama Supreme Court ruled that its state courts do not have such authority.[33] In 1981 the Wisconsin Supreme Court adopted the unusual position that its state courts have the authority but should not exercise it.[34] Under its power to regulate the lower state courts, the court ordered them not to issue authorizations. The court called upon the legislature to pass appropriate legislation and said that, if it did not do so, the court might in the future permit lower courts to issue authorizations.

In 1985 the California Supreme Court declared that a law that prohibited sterilization of incompetents violated the federal and state constitutions.[35] The court found that the developmentally disabled have a constitutional right to procreative choice and that the state had not demonstrated a compelling state interest to overcome that right. However, the court declined to authorize sterilization in the particular case because there was no evidence of the necessity of contraception or of the lack of less intrusive means.

Hospitals and physicians should participate in involuntary sterilizations only when court authorization has been obtained following procedures and criteria established by statute or by the highest state court. The procedures should include notice, a hearing, and an opportunity to appeal.

ASSISTED CONCEPTION

When couples who desire children cannot achieve pregnancy, they often seek medical assistance. Techniques such as artificial insemination, surrogate mothers, and in vitro fertilization have been attempted when other approaches fail.

Artificial Insemination

When the woman can conceive but the man either cannot deliver the semen or cannot produce effective semen, artificial insemination may be attempted. In the former situation, the artificial insemination is achieved through injection of the husband's semen, while in the latter situation donor semen is used. There are few legal problems in artificial insemination with the husband's semen (A.I.H.).

Artificial insemination with donor semen (A.I.D.) presents several legal issues, including whether the resulting child is legitimate and who is responsible for child support. Over a third of the states have passed statutes concerning artificial insemination. Typical statutes specify (1) the child is legitimate when the husband consents to the A.I.D.; and (2) the donor is not responsible for child support.[36] In states without statutes, some courts have ruled that the child is legitimate and the consenting husband is responsible for child support.[37] However, courts disagree on whether the child is legitimate under the common law.[38] Sound hospital policy would be to allow performance of A.I.D. procedures only for married women and only with the written consent of the woman and her husband, including an acknowledgment of paternity and an acceptance of child support responsibilities. Some writers question whether public hospitals may prohibit A.I.D. procedures for single women. Since it is unclear in most states whether the woman can waive the child's support claims, all hospitals should insist on a statutory or judicial determination before expanding the practice. If a statute or a decision of the highest state court protects the donor, the hospital, and its staff from child support responsibilities, then consideration can prudently be given to performing A.I.D. procedures in the protected situations.

Most state statutes require the procedure to be performed by a licensed physician.[39] Although the procedure can be performed by untrained persons and even be self-administered,[40] the most prudent practice is to permit only physicians to perform it.

Surrogate Mothers

When a man has viable semen but the woman cannot conceive, some couples seek a surrogate mother to bear a child after artificial insemination with the man's semen. The artificial insemination is legal in most states, but the agreement by the surrogate mother to give the child to the couple is probably not enforceable and may be illegal in some states.[41] The Michigan courts have ruled against enforceability.[42] The most prudent policy for hospitals is not to permit artificial insemination of surrogate mothers on hospital premises. If the hospital decides to permit the practice, it should not become involved in the agreement to give the child to the couple.

In Vitro Fertilization

Some couples produce viable reproductive cells, but conception is not possible naturally or through artificial insemination. A procedure called *in vitro fertilization* is available for some of these couples. The reproductive cells of the couple are combined outside the woman's body, are allowed to begin growing there, and are later implanted in the woman's womb. In 1979 the Department of Health, Education and Welfare Ethics Advisory Board approved experimental use of in vitro fertilization.[43] It is estimated that by the end of 1984 more than 1000 "test tube" babies had been born as a result of this procedure.[44]

In one lawsuit arising from in vitro fertilization, John and Doris Del Zio were awarded $50,000 by a federal jury in New York in 1978 for their emotional distress following intentional destruction of a cell culture containing their reproductive cells.[45] This award illustrates the importance of establishing clear procedures that are understood by all involved, including the parents, before attempting in vitro fertilization.

It is now possible to store frozen embryos for later implantation. In 1983 a California couple died in a plane crash in Chile after leaving two frozen embryos in Australia. A scholarly committee in Australia recommended that the embryos be destroyed, but in 1984 the Victoria legislature passed a law requiring that an attempt be made to implant the embryos in a surrogate mother and then place them for adoption if they were born.[46]

A few states have passed laws that affect the use of this procedure. A physician who wished to start using the procedure in Illinois was concerned that the state abortion law could be interpreted to hold him liable for the care and custody of any child that resulted from the procedure, so he challenged the law.[47] In 1983 the court dismissed the suit because the state attorney general informed the court that he did not intend to prosecute under the law for the use of the procedure.

ABORTION

Medically, an abortion may be defined as the premature expulsion of the products of conception from the uterus. An abortion may be classified as spontaneous or induced. An abortion can be induced for the purpose of saving the life of the fetus, saving the life or health of the mother, or terminating the pregnancy to preclude the birth of a child. The attention of the law has focused on the induced abortions that are not intended to result in a live birth.

Historically, the common law did not prohibit induced abortions prior to the first fetal movements. By statute, many states made induced abortions a crime, whether before or after fetal movements began, unless performed to preserve the life of the mother. The laws were amended in the 1960s and early 1970s to permit induced abortions when there were threats to the physical or mental health of the mother, the child was at risk of severe congenital defects, or the pregnancy resulted from rape or incest. A few states, such as New York, permitted induced abortions on request up to a designated state of pregnancy if performed by a licensed physician in a licensed hospital.

Roe v. Wade and Doe v. Bolton

In January 1973 the Supreme Court held in *Roe v. Wade*[48] that the Texas criminal abortion law was unconstitutional, stating "A state criminal abortion statute . . . that excepts from criminality only a *life saving* procedure on behalf of the mother, without regard to pregnancy stage and without recognition of other interests involved is violative of the Due Process Clause of the Fourteenth Amendment."[49]

The Court discussed three stages of pregnancy, concluding that the right of privacy of the patient and her physician precluded most state regulation during the first trimester but that the state's interest in protecting the patient's health and the potential life of the fetus permitted some forms of regulation. In the companion decision, *Doe v. Bolton*,[50] the Court declared a Georgia abortion statute unconstitutional and further defined the types of state regulations that are not permitted.

In a 1983 decision that reaffirmed the analysis based on the three stages, *City of Akron v. Akron Center for Reproductive Health, Inc.*,[51] three justices dissented, expressing their belief that the trimester analysis was unworkable.

The First Stage

During the first stage or trimester of pregnancy, the state is virtually without power to restrict or regulate the abortion procedure; the decision to perform an abortion is between the woman and her physician. A state may require only that abortions be performed by a physician licensed pursuant to its laws. However, a woman does not possess an unqualified right to an abortion since the decision to perform the procedure must be left to the medical judgment of her attending physician. Any woman has the right in the first three months to seek out a physician willing to perform an abortion and to have that physician perform the abortion free from state intervention. The state has no "compelling interest" at this stage of pregnancy to justify legislation to override the woman's right to privacy. The state may require that all abortions be performed by licensed physicians but cannot require them to be performed in a hospital.

The Second Stage

In *Roe v. Wade* the Supreme Court stated that, "For the stage subsequent to approximately the end of the first trimester, the State, in promoting its interest in the health of the mother, may, if it chooses, regulate the abortion procedure in ways that are reasonably related to maternal health."[52] Thus, during approximately the fourth to the sixth month of pregnancy, the state may regulate the medical conditions under which the procedure is performed. The test of any legislation concerning abortion during this period is its relevance to protecting maternal health.

The Third Stage

By the time the final stage of pregnancy has been reached, the Court reasoned, the state had acquired a compelling interest in the fetus that could override the woman's right to privacy and justify stringent regulation, even to the extent of prohibiting abortions. The court stated:

> For the stage subsequent to viability the State, in promoting its interests in the potentiality of human life may, if it chooses, regulate, and even proscribe abortion except where it is necessary, in appropriate medical judgment, for the preservation of the life or health of the mother.[53]

Thus, during the final stage of pregnancy, a state may prohibit all abortions except those necessary to protect maternal life or health. The state's legislative powers increase as the pregnancy progresses toward term.

Specific Requirements

In *Doe v. Bolton* further restrictions were placed on state regulation of abortions. The court applied the test of the relationship to maternal needs and found the following preabortion requirements invalid: (1) period of residency in the state; (2) performance only in an accredited hospital;

(3) approval by a medical staff committee; and (4) consultations with other physicians.

Status of State and Local Regulation

The effect of the Supreme Court's decisions was to invalidate all or parts of virtually all state abortion statutes in existence prior to 1973. State and local governments have enacted a variety of new laws designed to regulate abortions. Court decisions resulting from challenges to the constitutionality of these laws have helped to define the limits within which state and local governments may regulate abortions. Some of the requirements addressed have concerned informed consent, paternal approval and notification when the woman is married, parental approval and notification when the woman is a minor, instances when the procedure must be performed in a hospital, the type of procedure, reporting of abortions, and zoning restrictions.

Informed Consent

Reasonable requirements concerning informed consent were upheld by the Supreme Court in 1976.[54] The Supreme Court addressed several issues involving informed consent in the *Akron* case.[55] That case challenged several city ordinances that required physicians to make specific statements to the patient as part of the consent process and required patients to wait 24 hours between signing the consent form and having the procedure performed. The ordinances required the patient to be told of the status of her pregnancy, development of fetus, date of viability, the possible physical and emotional consequences, and the availability of agencies to provide information and assistance with birth control, childbirth, and adoption. The woman also had to be told that "the unborn child is a human life from the moment of conception."

The Court ruled that informed consent can be required based on the state's interest in protecting the health of the woman, but that this interest does not justify attempts to influence her choice. The Court noted that many of the required statements were designed to persuade the woman not to consent rather than to promote informed consent. The Court found the requirement of specific statements to be a prohibited intrusion on the discretion of the physician in the consent process. The 24-hour waiting period and the requirement that the physician personally provide all information and counseling were also invalidated. In 1985 a federal court ruled that the 24-hour waiting period could not be required for minors.[56]

Paternal Approval and Notification

In 1976 the Supreme Court ruled that states could not require paternal approval of abortions.[57] However, one federal circuit court ruled that the state may require a married woman to notify her husband prior to the abortion when the pregnancy was jointly conceived.[58] It returned the case to the District Court to make findings concerning notifications for pregnancies not jointly conceived. The lower court concluded that there was no valid justification for requiring notification when the husband was not the father, so the statute was invalid for being too broad.[59] In 1984 a Maryland court denied a husband's petition to enjoin his wife's first trimester abortion.[60]

Parental Approval and Notification

In 1979 the Supreme Court ruled that states could require parental approval before a minor has an abortion if the state provides an appropriate and timely alternate procedure for (1) mature, informed minors; and (2) other minors whose best interests indicate that parents should not be involved.[61] In 1981 the Supreme Court reaffirmed that a state could require the notification of a parent before a minor has an abortion but declined to rule on the constitutionality of enforcing the law when the minor is mature or when the disclosure would not be in the best interest of the minor.[62] Parental approval or notification is not required unless the state has enacted a requirement. However, it is prudent for providers to encourage minors to involve their parents or other adult relatives in the decision-making process.

In 1984 a Massachusetts court ruled that when a court finds a minor sufficiently mature to consent to an abortion, the court's role is completed and it cannot go further and require that a certain type of procedure be used.[63]

In 1972 a Maryland court ruled that parents do not have authority to give consent for an abortion unless the minor also consents.[64] However, in 1984 a New York court ruled that a father could consent for an incompetent adult child.[65] Prudent providers will insist that a court order be obtained in each case that the woman is unable or unwilling to consent.

Hospitalization

In 1977 the Supreme Court declared requirements that first trimester abortions be performed in a hospital to be unconstitutional.[66] In the *Akron* case, the Court also struck down a requirement that all abortions after the first trimester be performed in a hospital.[67] The state failed to show how the requirement was reasonably related to the preservation and protection of maternal health. In 1983 the Court upheld a requirement that all abortions after the first trimester be performed either in a hospital or in a licensed outpatient clinic.[68]

Procedure

In 1976 the Court invalidated a Missouri law that prohibited the saline method of abortion.[69]

Definitions of Viability

Since the state's power to prohibit abortions begins at viability, several states have attempted to define viability by statute. In *Roe v. Wade,* the Court ruled that fetuses are viable when they are potentially able to live outside their mothers' wombs, even with artificial aid.[70] The Court has upheld statutory definitions that comport with this definition, but has emphasized that viability is ultimately a matter of medical judgment and skill.[71] However, efforts to require a determination of viability by duration of pregnancy or by whether the fetus "may be" viable have been invalidated.[72]

Reporting

In 1976 the Supreme Court ruled that states could require record keeping and reporting reasonably directed to preservation of maternal health if it respects the patient's confidentiality and privacy.[73] In 1983 the Supreme Court upheld a state requirement of a pathological examination and report on all abortions.[74]

Zoning

Courts have enjoined zoning rules that preclude abortion clinics from locating in a community.[75] Courts have refused to enjoin zoning rules that prohibit abortion clinics in some areas but not the entire community.[76] However, an ordinance that prohibited abortion services in all local retail business districts was enjoined.[77]

Funding of Abortions

Under the United States Constitution, there is no obligation to provide public funding for abortions, but several state constitutions have been interpreted to require public funding. In 1980 the Supreme Court ruled that the Congress could constitutionally forbid the use of federal funds to pay for abortions.[78] The Court said that the prohibition

. . . places no governmental obstacle in the path of a woman who chooses to terminate her pregnancy, but rather, by means of unequal subsidization of abortion and other medical services, encourages alternative activity deemed in the public interest . . . although government may not place obstacles in the path of a woman's exercise of her freedom of choice, it need not remove those not of its own creation. Indigency falls in the latter category.[79]

In a companion case, the Court ruled that similar state funding restrictions do not violate the United States Constitution.[80] However, several state courts have ruled that state constitutional provisions restrict the state's latitude. For example, in 1981 the highest court of Massachusetts ruled that the state constitution prohibits restricting Medicaid payments for abortions to cases where the mother's life is endangered.[81]

Hospital Restrictions on Abortions

The *Wade* and *Bolton* decisions left open the question of what restrictions and prerequisites hospitals may place on those seeking abortions. Both decisions focused on state regulation.

Lower federal courts have ruled that public hospitals may not forbid the use of their facilities for the performing of abortions.[82] In 1977 the Supreme Court ruled that St. Louis did not have to provide publicly funded abortions in a city hospital.[83] However, the court did not address the use of the city hospital facilities for privately funded abortions.

Lower federal courts have ruled that there is no state action when private hospitals forbid or restrict the use of their facilities for abortions, so there is no violation of the Constitution.[84] Lower federal courts found state action in a few cases in the 1970s, but it is doubtful whether these decisions will be followed in future cases because, as discussed in the medical staff chapter, courts now apply stricter standards in determining whether there is state action.

State courts in some states will limit the discretion of some private hospitals based on state law. In 1976 the New Jersey Supreme Court decided that a private, nonprofit, nonsectarian hospital may not deny the use of its facilities for elective first trimester abortions when it permits therapeutic abortions, has staff and facilities available, and is the only general hospital in its community.[85] The opinion was based on the common law responsibilities of "quasi-public" hospitals in New Jersey.

Conscience Clause

Several states have enacted conscience clauses that prohibit discrimination against physicians and hospital personnel who refuse to participate in abortions. These clauses were found to be constitutional in *Doe v. Bolton*.[86] In 1980 a New Jersey court ruled that it was not discrimination to transfer a refusing nurse from the maternity to the medical-surgical nursing staff with no change in seniority, pay, or shift.[87] Thus, in some jurisdictions staff may be transferred to areas where they are not involved with the procedure without violating their right to refuse.

Trespass

Some opponents have tried to disrupt the operation of abortion facilities. When their actions have gone beyond picketing to actual harassment and disruption, the courts have issued injunctions and enforced trespass convictions.[88] Of course, these sanctions can apply to anyone who enters a restricted area of a health care facility or disrupts the operations of the facility. For example, in 1979 the Florida Supreme Court upheld the trespass convictions of a group of women who violated hospital rules concerning entrance to the postpartum area even though they said they were conducting a "consumer inspection."[89]

PRENATAL TESTING AND GENETIC SCREENING

It is possible through certain tests during pregnancy and soon after birth to detect numerous disorders.

One of the most common genetic tests during pregnancy is amniocentesis. It involves withdrawing through a long needle a small amount of amniotic fluid that surrounds the fetus. The fetal cells in the fluid are cultured and studied for genetic defects. Over 100 genetic conditions can be detected. These tests can help parents decide whether to have the child. However, the tests actually reduce the number of abortions. By family genetic history, it is often possible to identify parents at risk of having children with genetic defects. Many of these parents elected abortions even when the risk was one-fourth or lower. Most frequently, amniocentesis shows that the fetus does not have the feared genetic disorder, so that the parents decide to have the child.

The major legal issues concerning amniocentesis involve consent and disclosure. In 1982 the Utah Supreme Court ruled that the consent of the mother to amniocentesis was sufficient.[90] There was no obligation to obtain the father's consent. Risks must be disclosed when obtaining consent. There is a small risk that the fetus will be injured or die. Thus, amniocentesis is usually not performed unless there is known risk of genetic defect due to family history or maternal age. It is important to offer the option of amniocentesis to any woman known to be at increased risk of a child with genetic defects that could be detected by amniocentesis. Failure to offer the procedure can lead to the liability discussed in the next section of this chapter.

A second major type of genetic screening is the blood test within a few days after birth to detect metabolic disorders, such as phenylketonuria (PKU). Some states have encouraged or required these tests to be performed on all newborns. If these conditions are detected early, special diets and other treatment can be given to preclude the severe mental retardation that is caused if the condition is not treated. Even when the test is not required by local law, it is still important to offer the tests to every family and explain the consequences of refusal. If the test is not offered, liability is possible for the complications that detection could have precluded.

WRONGFUL CONCEPTION, WRONGFUL BIRTH, AND WRONGFUL LIFE SUITS

Parents have sued physicians and hospitals for wrongful conception or wrongful birth of children they did not want or deformed children they would have aborted had they known of the deformity. Deformed children have sued for their alleged wrongful life, claiming they were injured by being born. Courts have struggled with these suits to determine when there should be liability and what the basis for calculating the payment by the defendants should be.

Wrongful Conception and Wrongful Birth

The term *wrongful conception* is used, whether or not birth results, when (1) an unwanted pregnancy results from medical negligence; or (2) a fetus with a genetic defect is conceived after the parents were not informed or were misinformed of the risk of the genetic condition. The term *wrongful birth* is used when (1) a birth results from a wrongful conception; or (2) a birth follows medical negligence after conception that denies the mother the opportunity to make a timely informed decision whether to have an abortion. Parents have made six basic types of wrongful conception or wrongful birth claims. Three types concern unsuccessful sterilization and abortion procedures, and the other three types concern genetic counseling and testing.

The three types that arise from unsuccessful sterilization and abortion procedures include parental claims that (1) they were not informed of the risk that the procedure might be unsuccessful; (2) they were promised the procedure would be successful; or (3) the procedure was performed negligently. The first type is based on lack of informed consent, the second on breach of contract, and the third on malpractice.

Since there is a known risk of pregnancy after a properly performed procedure, the mere fact pregnancy occurs is not sufficient to establish that the procedure was performed negligently. Since it is usually difficult to establish negligence in performing the procedure, claims tend to be of the first two types. However, a well-written consent form can make the first two types of claims difficult to pursue. For example, in 1975 a Colorado court affirmed the dismissal of the suit by the parents because the consent form included a statement that no guarantee had been made concerning the result of the treatment.[91]

The other three types of claims arise when an abnormal child is born whom the parents would have aborted if they had known of the abnormality. The parents' claims parallel the claims that arise from negligent sterilizations. The parents claim that (1) they were not advised of the possibility of the condition and the availability of tests; (2) they were told there was no risk of the particular abnormality; or (3) the tests were performed negligently, and the abnormality was not discovered. Thus, when there is reason to suspect that an abnormality is likely, it is prudent to advise the parents and offer them available tests.

Courts have generally awarded parents some payment when they are able to prove one or more of the six claims. There is some disagreement on what the basis for the payment should be. The most significant difference concerns whether the defendants must pay for the cost of raising the child to adulthood. A few courts have permitted parents to collect the entire cost of raising the child.[92] Several courts have permitted parents to collect the cost of rearing the child, reduced by the amount the jury believes the parents benefit from the joy and other advantages of parenthood.[93] Most courts have refused to permit the parents to collect the cost of rearing the child, especially if the child is healthy.[94] The courts have based their refusal on public policy considerations. They have been reluctant to label as an injury the presence of an additional child in a family. They have been concerned about the implications of the general rule that those who are injured must take steps to reduce their injuries, which could mean the parents would be required to seek an abortion or put the child up for adoption to reduce their injuries. Several of the courts that generally do not permit collection of the costs of child rearing do allow collection of the special additional expenses of raising a defective child to adulthood.[95]

Wrongful Life

Some deformed children have sued physicians and hospitals, claiming they were injured by being born. They have based their suits on the same claims that their parents have made. Most courts have refused to allow suits by these children. In one of the earliest cases addressing this issue, the New Jersey Supreme Court observed that compensation is ordinarily computed by "comparing the condition plaintiff would have been in, had the defendants not been negligent, with plaintiff's impaired condition as a result of the negligence."[96] The condition of the child had the defendants not been negligent would have been the "utter void of nonexistence." The court said that courts could not affix a price tag on nonlife, so it would be impossible to compute the amount to award.

In 1982 the California Supreme Court adopted the unusual position of permitting a child to collect for the extraordinary expenses of living with deafness due to a genetic defect, even though there was no way the child could have been born without the deafness.[97] From the perspective of the defendant's actual liability, the decision does not appear unusual. The court permitted the child to collect the same amount the parents could have collected in several other states if the suit had been in their names. A few other states have adopted this position.[98]

NOTES

1. Griswold v. Connecticut, 381 U.S. 479 (1965).

2. Eisenstadt v. Baird, 405 U.S. 438 (1972).

3. Carey v. Population Servs. Int'l, 431 U.S. 678 (1977).

4. *Id.*

5. Doe v. Pickett, 480 F. Supp. 1218 (S.D. W.Va. 1979); *accord* Jane Does v. Utah Dep't of Health, 776 P.2d 253 (10th Cir. 1985).

6. Doe v. Irving, 615 F.2d 1162 (6th Cir. 1980).

7. 42 U.S.C. §300(a) (1982).

8. 48 FED. REG. 3600–14 (1983).

9. Planned Parenthood Fed'n, Inc. v. Schweiker, 559 F. Supp. 658 (D. D.C. 1983), *aff'd* 712 F.2d 650 (D. C. Cir. 1983); New York v. Heckler, 719 F.2d 1191 (2d Cir. 1983).

10. Planned Parenthood Ass'n v. Matheson, 582 F. Supp. 1001 (D. Utah 1983).

11. 42 C.F.R. §§441.250–441.259 (1985).

12. Cal. Admin. Code, tit. 22, §§70707.1–70707.8 (1977).

13. California Medical Ass'n v. Lachner, 124 Cal. App.3d 28, 177 Cal. Rptr. 188 (1981).

14. *E.g.,* Sims v. University of Ark. Medical Center, No. LR 76-C67 (E.D. Ark. Mar. 4, 1977).

15. Hathaway v. Worcester City Hosp., 475 F.2d 701 (1st Cir. 1973).

16. *E.g.*, Taylor v. St. Vincent Hosp., 523 F.2d 75 (9th Cir. 1975), *cert. denied,* 424 U.S. 948 (1976).

17. *E.g.*, Coe v. Bolton, No. C-87-785A (N.D. Ga. Sept. 30, 1976).

18. Walker v. Pierce, 560 F.2d 609 (4th Cir. 1977).

19. Murray v. Vandevander, 522 P.2d 302 (Okla. Ct. App. 1974).

20. *E.g.*, Colo. Rev. Stat. Ann. §§25-6-101–25-6-102 (1982).

21. *E.g.*, Ga. Code Ann. §31-20-2 (1982).

22. 42 C.F.R. §50.203 (1985); 42 C.F.R. §441.253 (1985).

23. *E.g.*, Kan. Stat. Ann. §§65-446 and 65-447 (1980).

24. Swanson v. St. John's Lutheran Hosp., 597 P.2d 702 (Mont. 1979), *judgment after remand aff'd,* 615 P.2d 883 (Mont. 1980).

25. Buck v. Bell, 275 U.S. 200 (1927).

26. N.C. Gen. Stat. §§35-36–35-50 (1981 & Supp. 1983).

27. In re Sterilization of Moore, 289 N.C. 95, 221 S.E.2d 307 (1976); North Carolina Ass'n of Retarded Children v. North Carolina, 420 F. Supp. 451 (M.D. N.C. 1976).

28. *E.g.*, In re Grady, 85 N.J. 235, 426 A.2d 467 (1981); In re Mary Moe, 385 Mass. App. 555, 432 N.E.2d 712 (1982).

29. Wade v. Bethesda Hosp., 337 F. Supp. 671 (S.D. Ohio 1971) and 356 F. Supp. 380 (S.D. Ohio 1973); Sparkman v. McFarlin, 552 F.2d 172 (7th Cir. 1977).

30. Stump v. Sparkman, 435 U.S. 349 (1978).

31. Sparkman v. McFarlin, 601 F.2d 261 (7th Cir. 1979).

32. *E.g.*, In re Hayes, 93 Wash.2d 228, 608 P.2d 635 (1980).

33. Hudson v. Hudson, 373 So.2d 310 (Ala. 1979).

34. In re Eberhardy, 102 Wis.2d 539, 307 N.W.2d 881 (1981).

35. Conservatorship of Valerie N., 40 Cal.3d 143, 219 Cal. Rptr. 387, 707 P.2d 760 (1985).

36. *E.g.*, Okla. Stat., tit. 10, §§551-553 (West Supp. 1982–1983).

37. *E.g.*, People v. Sorenson, 68 Cal.2d 280, 437 P.2d 495 (1968).

38. *E.g.*, Gursky v. Gursky, 39 Misc.2d 1083, 242 N.Y.S.2d 406 (1963).

39. *E.g.*, Ore. Rev. Stat. §677.360 (1983).

40. *E.g.*, C.M. v. C.C., 152 N.J. Super. 160, 377 A.2d 821 (1977).

41. *E.g.*, Cal. Penal Code §§273(a) and 181 (1970 & 1985 Supp.).

42. Doe v. Kelly, 6 Fam. L. Rptr. 3011 (Mich. Cir. Ct. Jan. 28, 1980), *aff'd sub nom.* Doe v. Attorney General, 160 Mich. App. 169, 307 N.W.2d 438 (1981), *lv. denied,* 414 Mich. 875 (1982), *cert. denied,* 459 U.S. 1183 (U.S. 1983); *but see* Syrkowski v. Appleyard, 420 Mich. 367, 362 N.W.2d 211(1985); note also that an English court took custody of a baby born to a surrogate mother, N.Y. TIMES, Jan. 10, 1985, at 7, col. 6.

43. Ethics Advisory Board, *Report and Conclusions: HEW Support of Research Involving Human In Vitro Fertilization and Embryo Transfer,* 44 FED. REG. 35033–58 (1979).

44. Henahan, *Fertilization, Embryo Transfer Procedures Raise Many Questions,* 252 J.A.M.A. 877 (1984).

45. Del Zio v. Presbyterian Hosp., 74 Civ. 3588 (S.D.N.Y. Apr. 12, 1978).

46. N.Y. TIMES, June 23, 1984, at 9, col. 1; Oct. 24, 1984, at 9, col. 1.

47. Smith v. Hartigan, 556 F. Supp. 157 (N.D. Ill. 1983).

48. 410 U.S. 113 (1973).

49. *Id.* at 164.

50. 410 U.S. 179 (1973).

51. 462 U.S. 416 (1983).

52. Roe v. Wade, *supra* note 48, at 164.

53. *Id.*

54. Planned Parenthood Ass'n v. Fitzpatrick, 401 F. Supp. 554 (E.D. Pa. 1975), *aff'd without opinion sub nom.*, Franklin v. Fitzpatrick, 428 U.S. 901 (1976).

55. City of Akron v. Akron Center for Reproductive Health, Inc., 462 U.S. 416 (1983).

56. Zbaraz v. Hartigan, 763 F.2d 1532 (7th Cir. 1985).

57. Planned Parenthood v. Danforth, 428 U.S. 52 (1976).

58. Scheinberg v. Smith, 659 F.2d 476 (5th Cir. 1981).

59. Scheinberg v. Smith, 550 F. Supp. 1112 (S.D. Fla. 1982).

60. Coleman v. Coleman, 298 Md. 353, 469 A.2d 1274 (1984), *cert. denied,* 57 Md.App. 755, 471 A.2d 1115 (Md. Ct. Sp. App. 1984).

61. Bellotti v. Baird, 443 U.S. 622 (1979).

62. H.L. v. Matheson, 450 U.S. 398 (1981).

63. In re Moe, 18 Mass. App. 727, 469 N.E.2d 1312 (1984).

64. In re Smith, 16 Md. App. 209, 295 A.2d 238 (1972).

65. In re Barbara C., 101 A.D.2d 137, 474 N.Y.S.2d 799 (1984).

66. Arnold v. Sendak, 416 F. Supp. 22 (S.D. Ind. 1976), *aff'd sub nom.* Sendak v. Arnold, 429 U.S. 968 (1977).

67. City of Akron v. Akron Center for Reproductive Health, Inc., 462 U.S. 416 (1983).

68. Simopoulos v. Virginia, 462 U.S. 506 (1983).

69. Planned Parenthood v. Danforth, 428 U.S. 52 (1976).

70. Roe v. Wade, 410 U.S. at 160.

71. Planned Parenthood v. Danforth, 428 U.S. at 59–60, 63.

72. Colautti v. Franklin, 489 U.S. 379 (1979) ["may be" viable is too vague]; Hodgson v. Anderson, 378 F. Supp. 1008 (D. Minn. 1974), *appeal dismissed,* 420 U.S. 903 (1975).

73. Planned Parenthood v. Danforth, 428 U.S. 52 (1976).

74. Planned Parenthood Ass'n v. Ashcroft, 462 U.S. 476 (1983).

75. *E.g.,* Framingham Clinic, Inc. v. Board of Selectmen, 373 Mass. 279, 367 N.E.2d 606 (1977); Planned Parenthood of Minn., Inc. v. Citizens for Community Action, 558 F.2d 861 (8th Cir. 1977).

76. *E.g.,* West Side Women's Servs., Inc. v. City of Cleveland, 450 F. Supp. 1976 (N.D. Ohio 1978), *aff'd without opinion,* 582 F.2d 1281 (6th Cir. 1978), *cert. denied,* 439 U.S. 983 (1978).

77. *Id.*

78. Harris v. McRae, 448 U.S. 297 (1980).

79. *Id.,* at 315–16.

80. Williams v. Zbaraz, 448 U.S. 358 (1980).

81. Moe v. Secretary of Admin. of Finance, 382 Mass. 629, 417 N.E.2d 388 (1981).

82. *E.g.,* Nyberg v. City of Virginia, 667 F.2d 754 (8th Cir. 1982) [city hospital could not prohibit non-therapeutic abortions].

83. Poelker v. Doe, 432 U.S. 519 (1977).

84. *E.g.*, Doe v. Bellin Memorial Hosp., 479 F.2d 756 (7th Cir. 1973).

85. Bridgeton Hosp. Ass'n v. Doe, 71 N.J. 478, 366 A.2d 641 (1976), *cert. denied*, 433 U.S. 914 (1977).

86. Doe v. Bolton, 410 U.S. 179 (1973).

87. Jeczalik v. Valley Hosp., No. C-2312-78 (N.J. Super. Ct., Bergen County, Jan. 8, 1980).

88. *E.g.*, Northern Va. Women's Medical Center v. Balch, 617 F.2d 1045 (4th Cir. 1980) [injunction against harassment by demonstrators]; Cleveland v. Municipality of Anchorage, 631 P.2d 1073 (Alaska 1981) [trespass convictions for sit-in]; Sigma Reproductive Health Center v. State, 297 Md. 660, 467 A.2d 483 (Md. Ct. App. 1983) [no defense of necessity to charge of trespassing in abortion facility]. For a more detailed discussion of these issues, *see* Kenefick, *Controlling Access to Health Care Facilities,* 1 TOPICS HOSP. LAW, Mar. 1986, at xxx.

89. Donner v. State, 375 So.2d 840 (Fla. 1979).

90. Reisner v. Lohner, 641 P.2d 93 (Utah 1982).

91. Herrara v. Roessing, 533 P.2d 60 (Colo. Ct. App. 1975).

92. *E.g.*, Ochs v. Borelli, 187 Conn. 253, 445 A.2d 883 (1982).

93. *E.g.*, Sherlock v. Stillwater Clinic, 260 N.W.2d 169 (Minn. 1977); Jones v. Malinowski, 229 Md. 257, 473 A.2d 429 (Md. Ct. App. 1984).

94. *E.g.*, Kingsbury v. Smith, 122 N.H. 237, 442 A.2d 1003 (1982).

95. *E.g.*, Fassoulas v. Ramey, 450 So.2d 822 (Fla. 1984).

96. Gleitman v. Cosgrove, 49 N.J. 22, 227 A.2d 689 (1967).

97. Turpin v. Sortini, 31 Cal.3d 220, 643 P.2d 954 (1982).

98. *E.g.*, Procanik by Procanik v. Cillo, 97 N.J. 339, 478 A.2d 755 (1984); *contra* Nelson v. Krusen, 687 S.W.2d 918 (Tex. 1984).

Chapter 16

Dying, Death, and Dead Bodies

Hospital staffs must regularly consider the dying process, the determination of death, and the handling of dead bodies. Increasing attention is being focused on the dying process, due to medical care developments that make it possible to sustain life, many widely publicized legal cases, and the increasing openness of discussions concerning death. An understanding of the legal aspects of the dying process is essential to deal humanely with this crisis in the life of the patient and the patient's family and friends while complying with the law. The definition of death is once again relatively settled, but its application requires care. The law regarding the handling of dead bodies is also relatively settled and must be followed strictly because of the important societal and individual interests affected.

THE DYING PATIENT: WITHHOLDING AND WITHDRAWING MEDICAL TREATMENT

Physicians, other involved professionals, and the hospital have legally recognized duties to all patients. The legal duties have always been shaped by (a) the needs and wishes of the patient and the patient's representatives; (b) professional practices; (c) the capacities of medical science and the individual professionals and hospital involved; and (d) societal expectations and norms. Professional practice has long reflected the different needs of terminally and irreversibly comatose patients. The *Quinlan* case states the difference as follows:

> We glean from the record that physicians distinguish between curing the ill and comforting and easing the dying; that they refuse to treat the curable as if they were dying or ought to be; and that

they have sometimes refused to treat the hopeless and dying as if they were curable.[1]

The law has recognized this difference.

Classification of Patients

Physicians must identify which patients are to be treated differently because they are dying. Some institutions have developed formal classification systems. Although these formal systems can be helpful, they are not required.

There is no widely accepted definition of terminal illness; it remains a diagnosis based on medical judgment. Clearly, one element is that no available course of therapy offers a reasonable expectation of remission or cure of the condition. Another element is that death is imminent, but there is nonconsensus on the time period, largely because it is not possible to predict time of death precisely. Some courts have accepted patients as terminally ill with predicted lives of one to five years.[2] Thus, the range of medical opinion concerning terminal illness appears to be legally acceptable. It is prudent to avoid establishing a specific time period. The most widely publicized institutional classification systems have not included a definition of terminal illness, but instead have focused on the nature of the appropriate therapeutic effort.[3]

The institutional classification systems have focused on the decision-making process and documentation of decisions concerning withholding resuscitative efforts and other extraordinary care.

Do Not Resuscitate Orders

The term *cardiopulmonary resuscitation* (CPR) describes a series of steps developed over the past two decades to reestablish breathing and heartbeat after cardiac or respiratory arrest. Some of the procedures are highly intrusive and even violent in nature. The interventions are medically justified for patients whose condition is not yet diagnosed or for those who have a hopeful prognosis. The purpose of CPR is the prevention of sudden, unexpected death. CPR is not indicated in cases of terminal irreversible illness where death is not unexpected.

To ensure that CPR is not initiated when it is not indicated, hospitals should require a written "Do not resuscitate" (DNR) or "No CPR" order before nurses and other staff members become involved in not initiating CPR. A written DNR order documents the fact that a decision has been made and by whom it was made; it ensures that the decision is communicated to the staff so that inappropriate CPR is not initiated. When CPR is clearly not part of the planned care, staff members can act in accordance with the decisions without concern that they misunderstood the decision or will later be thought to have neglected the patient. Written orders reflect that these decisions are an appropriate part of medical practice and have been made after careful deliberation.

Until recently, some physicians were reluctant to write DNR orders because they feared legal liability. Numerous courts have recognized the practice of writing such orders. For example, in a 1978 Massachusetts case, the court ruled that court authorization is not necessary for a DNR order.[4] Hospitals have been investigated by licensing agencies and grand juries for permitting unwritten DNR orders or written orders by other than licensed physicians.[5] The risk of legal liability from a failure to resuscitate is much less when there is a written order than when no order is in the record.

The patient or the patient's representative should be involved in the decision and concur in the DNR order. The nature of the care to be withheld should be explained before obtaining the concurrence. A DNR order was challenged in a 1981 Minnesota case.[6] The court was not convinced the patient's parents knew what they were declining, so it ordered the cancellation of the DNR order until the parents gave "knowledgeable approval" to reinstate the order.

No Extraordinary Care

Theologians and ethicists have long recognized a distinction between ordinary and extraordinary medical care. They have maintained that humans have a moral and ethical responsibility to seek and accept ordinary medical care to save their lives but that extraordinary medical care may be declined. The law has generally recognized a legal right to refuse even ordinary care. Most physicians, while deeply troubled by refusals of ordinary care by nonterminal patients, have accepted this legal principle. They find it easier to concur with the wishes of the terminally ill patients and their families who decline extraordinary care, and may sometimes recommend that such treatment not be pursued.

A precise definition of which care is ordinary and which is extraordinary is not possible. One of the most widely quoted definitions is by a Roman Catholic ethicist, Gerald Kelly:

> Ordinary means all medicines, treatments, and operations which offer a reasonable hope of benefit and which can be obtained and used without excessive pain, or other inconvenience. Extraordinary means are all medicines, treatments, and operations which cannot

> be obtained or used without excessive expense, pain, or other
> inconvenience, or if used, would not offer a reasonable hope of
> benefit.[7]

It is not possible to create a list of "extraordinary" procedures. The circumstances of the individual situation and the judgment of those involved determine whether a procedure is extraordinary.

Numerous courts have recognized and accepted the decision to withhold or withdraw extraordinary care. The majority of decisions have addressed the use of respirators. The court in *Quinlan,* for example, discussed the distinction between ordinary and extraordinary care, citing religious and medical sources. The court concluded that it would be extraordinary care to use a respirator for a comatose young woman in a chronic, persistent, vegetative state with no reasonable possibility of emerging to a cognitive, sapient state. Therefore, the court authorized discontinuance.

Other cases have addressed several other treatments. In *Superintendent of Belchertown v. Saikewicz,*[8] the highest court of Massachusetts discussed the distinction between extraordinary and ordinary care and stated that its decision was intended to be consistent with this "medical ethos." Thus, it implicitly concluded that chemotherapy could be extraordinary care when it approved withholding chemotherapy from a profoundly mentally retarded 67-year-old man with leukemia. The same court in *In re Spring*[9] did not use the extraordinary-ordinary terminology but reached a similar differentiation based on the "magnitude of the invasion." It concluded that it is appropriate to discontinue dialysis for a 78-year-old man with irreversible kidney failure and chronic organic brain syndrome, but it was not appropriate to discontinue "supportive oral or intravenous medications." In the 1980 case of *In re Severns*[10] a Delaware court discussed the ordinary-extraordinary distinction and concluded that nearly all treatment is extraordinary for a 55-year-old woman in an irreversible coma, since none can return her to a sentient and sapient state. Thus, the court authorized withholding respirators, antibiotics, feeding tubes, CPR, and all other drugs and medicines except for those normally used to preserve bodily hygiene, particularly those related to constipation or diarrhea. Many physicians would consider some of these treatments ordinary care despite their inability to restore the patient's mental functioning. For example, in a 1979 District of Columbia case a neurosurgeon testified that he discontinued "heroic measures," including the respirator and drugs to reduce the pressure in the comatose patient's head, but would have continued feeding the patient and preventing pneumonia if the patient had lived.[11]

Although some courts and commentators have questioned whether the ordinary-extraordinary distinction provides an adequate basis for determining which treatments are withheld,[12] the distinction remains an integral part of the analysis of most courts.

Maintenance of Supportive Care

Even when terminally ill patients are not receiving extraordinary care, physicians and hospitals have duties to them. While some patients, such as Karen Ann Quinlan, can appropriately be transferred to nursing homes, others require continued hospitalization. Ordinary supportive care must be continued—the "comforting and easing the dying" to which the *Quinlan* decision referred—including medications for pain.

There is a difference of opinion concerning the supportive care required—for example, whether special mechanisms for feeding are required. The trend appears to be toward accepting decisions not to use artificial feeding mechanisms in selected cases. A committee of physicians in 1984 issued recommendations concerning the care of terminally ill patients that supported selective decisions not to use special feeding mechanisms.[13] The Delaware court in the 1980 case did not require special mechanisms for feeding, in accord with the strongly held views the patient had expressed before becoming comatose.[14] In 1984 a New York court ruled that a nursing home had neither the right nor the responsibility to force nourishment on a competent 85-year-old patient, especially when the force feeding could be accomplished only through the surgical insertion of a gastric feeding tube.[15] The patient's family supported the decision.

In 1984, in the only prosecution of physicians for withholding hydration and intravenous feeding from a terminally ill patient, a California appellate court ordered the dismissal of homicide indictments against two physicians.[16] The court ruled that artificial means of feeding are treatment, not natural functions, so there is no duty to continue the treatment when it becomes ineffective. The physicians could not be criminally liable for their professional decision made in concert with the patient's family when the individual was incompetent and terminally ill, with virtually no hope of significant improvement.

Some courts may not accept withholding feeding unless it is pursuant to the wishes of the patient or other limited circumstances are present. In 1981 the highest court of New York ruled that a mother could not refuse special feeding and transfusions for her terminally ill incompetent adult son.[17] In 1985 in *In re Conroy*,[18] the New Jersey Supreme Court recognized that nutritional support through a nasogastric tube was a treatment like a respirator and that it could be discontinued in appropriate cases. The court stated that discontinuance would be appropriate pursuant to the clearly articulated wishes of an elderly nursing home patient with severe and permanent mental and physical impairments and a life expectancy of a year or less. In the absence of adequate proof of the patient's wishes, the feeding could be discontinued in cases where either (1) there was trustworthy evidence of the patient's wishes and the patient's suffering from unavoidable pain markedly outweighed any physical pleasure, emotional enjoyment, or intellectual satisfaction the patient still derived from life; or (2) there was no trustworthy evidence of the patient's wishes, the net burdens of the patient's life with treatment markedly outweighed the benefits the patient derived from life, and recurring, unavoidable, and severe pain with treatment made the administering of treatment inhumane. The emphasis that this decision places on pain can be questioned, but it is an important contribution to the legal responses to new nutritional technologies.

If the patient is not terminally ill or comatose, it is unlikely courts will order withholding feeding in an institution even at the patient's request. A California court ruled in 1983 that while a competent adult woman with cystic fibrosis could refuse feeding, she could not do so in a hospital.[19] The court refused to order the hospital not to force feed her.

Limits to the Patient's Choices

Occasionally, terminally ill patients or their families seek therapies that are outside the accepted range or seek hospitalization beyond the time necessary. These are normal responses to an extremely stressful situation. Reliance must be placed primarily on patience and tactful communications to give these patients and their families the time, information, and support to accept the limitations. Sometimes they are not able to accept the limitations, however, and other approaches become necessary.

Patients do not have a right to insist on treatment outside the accepted range of therapies. Physicians have the responsibility and authority to refuse to provide illegal and inappropriate therapies. In 1979 the Supreme Court ruled that the terminally ill have no special right to treatment that the government has declared illegal.[20] A physician who provided a legal, but inappropriate, treatment might be liable for malpractice, notwithstanding the patient's consent to such treatment. If there is a difference of opinion among reputable physicians regarding the appropriateness of legal treatment, reasonable efforts should be made to transfer the care of the patient to a physician who concurs with the patient. Sometimes, if the inappropriate treatment desired by the patient is neither illegal nor dangerous, the most prudent course may be to acquiesce, as long as the patient is willing to continue accepted therapy simultaneously.

Patients do not have a right to stay in the hospital when hospitalization is no longer required. Occasionally, terminally ill patients and their families refuse to arrange for transfers to nursing homes or other facilities when hospitalization is no longer required. They should be given a reasonable time to make appropriate arrangements. If they do not do so within a reasonable period, other remedies, including injunctions, may be sought. An injunction was sought in 1976 to transfer a teenager who had been comatose for one and one-half years from a Florida hospital bed to a nursing home, but the patient died before the final hearing.[21]

Common Law and Constitutional Right To Refuse Treatment

Competent adults have the right to refuse treatment, unless state interests outweigh that right.[22] The right to refuse is based on (a) the common law right to freedom from nonconsensual invasion of bodily integrity, reflected in the informed consent doctrine and the law of battery; (b) the constitutional right of privacy; and (c) the constitutional right to freedom of religion. The possible state interests that have been advanced include (a) preserving life; (b) protecting third parties, especially minor dependents; (c) preventing irrational self-destruction; (d) maintaining the ethical integrity of health care professionals and institutions; and (e) protecting the public health and other interests. These rights and state interests and the determination of adulthood and competence are discussed in more detail in Chapter 13. In a few situations the state's interests may outweigh the right of a competent, terminally ill adult to refuse treatment. These include cases where there is a threat to the public health or when significant harm to minor dependents can be avoided.

In some states, it is still unclear whether family disagreement can justify overriding a competent adult's directions. Numerous courts have emphasized the concurrence of the family or the absence of family in their decisions.[23] However, the few courts that have addressed actual disagreements have ruled in favor of the patient's wishes. For example, in a 1981 case, a federal court in California ordered a Veterans Administration hospital to honor a competent adult's wishes that a respirator be discontinued, despite the opposition of the patient's wife and children.[24]

A trend is also developing toward recognizing that the state's interests can seldom outweigh the seriously ill, but not terminally ill, patient's right to refuse continued treatment.[25]

The state's interest in preserving the ethical integrity of the professions should not be interpreted to permit individual professionals to impose their own standards on patients.[26]

Loss of Competence

Like virtually all adults, those who were competent when they first expressed their desire to have certain treatments withheld or withdrawn generally become incompetent before they die. The refusal of medical care must apply through the period of incompetence, or the right of these patients to make decisions regarding their own care is vitiated. Some states have attempted to address this situation through statutes that are discussed later in this chapter. In most situations, however, either there is no applicable statute or the statutory procedures have not been followed. Therefore, it is necessary to act according to the underlying common law and constitutional principles.

A distinction often is made between (1) a decision made when the person knows of the terminal condition; and (2) a decision made when the person is considering future care without reference to a known condition. The first is generally respected, while the second may be subjected to more scrutiny because less information was available at the time the decision was made. When the circumstances are substantially different from those the person anticipated in reaching the decision, there must be more latitude to act contrary to the stated wishes.

The expression of the patient's wishes does not have to be in writing. In two of the cases discussed earlier in this chapter,[27] the courts authorized carrying out the patient's orally expressed wishes. Documentary evidence of the patient's wishes should certainly be given great weight. The growing practice of preparing living wills helps to communicate those wishes clearly. Only one court has ruled that a living will is not a sufficient basis for carrying out the wishes of a terminally ill patient. The Florida Supreme Court ruled that permission of close family members or a guardian must be obtained before the wishes of an incompetent terminally ill patient may be followed.[28] When proceeding without court involvement, the situation should be considered carefully to ensure that the circumstances are not substantially different from those the patient intended to be covered. This is not a problem with most of the widely distributed versions of the living will because they generally are clearly addressed to one condition, irreversible mental incapacity, rather than to specific procedures.

When a competent patient still was able to communicate or when there is a reasonable likelihood that the patient will again be competent and able to communicate, reliance usually should not be placed on directives made before the condition was known. The patient should be given an opportunity to recover the ability to communicate and express his or her present wishes. The major exception applies to directives based on religious or other strongly held views that are intended to transcend individual conditions.

Incompetents

Some terminally ill patients who have never expressed their wishes regarding treatment become irreversibly incompetent and unable to communicate. Others have never had the opportunity to express their wishes because of youth or mental retardation. The courts that have been confronted with such cases have concluded that, since competent adults have the right to refuse treatment, there must be a means for the same right to be exercised on behalf of incompetent patients.

In the *Quinlan* decision, it was stated that all patients have a right of choice in this situation, but for the incompetent, "The only practical way to prevent destruction of the right is to permit the guardian and family of Karen to render their best judgment, subject to the qualifications hereinafter stated, as to whether she would exercise it in these circumstances."[29] The qualifications were concurrence by the attending physicians and concurrence by a hospital ethics committee or like body regarding the hopelessness of the prognosis. The court in *Saikewicz* reached the same conclusion, i.e., there is a "general right in all persons to refuse medical treatment in appropriate circumstances." The court went on to state, "The recognition of that right must extend to the case of an incompetent, as well as a competent, patient because the value of human dignity extends to both."[30]

When patients have not expressed their wishes and are unable to do so, some individual or group must be able to make decisions for them. Obviously the physician and other professionals involved in the care of the patient have an important role and are relatively easy to identify. It is sometimes more difficult to identify the proper person to represent the patient in the decision making. When there is a guardian, there is usually no problem because the guardian can make the required decisions on behalf of the patient. Occasionally, however, close family members disagree with the guardian; in such instances, guidance from a court may be needed.

When there is no guardian, it is generally accepted that the spouse or next of kin of the incompetent patient may make decisions that cannot be deferred until the patient is competent.[31] Most of the court decisions on the treatment of the terminally ill involve guardians because the appointment of a guardian is a procedural mechanism available for the courts to effectuate their judgments. However, a few courts have directly addressed whether the incompetent patient's representative must be a guardian to refuse treatment. Consistent with the general recognition of the role of the spouse or next of kin, these courts have concluded that these family members may make these decisions without being legally designated guardians.[32]

The decision-making role of the family is limited by the physician's diagnostic role and responsibility to the patient. The family can decide to withhold or withdraw treatment without court involvement only when the physician determines that the patient is terminally ill or irreversibly comatose and the physician accepts the family's treatment decision. When the physician and family concur in withholding or withdrawing treatment from an incompetent patient who is terminally ill or irreversibly comatose, the risk associated with carrying out the decision is minimal.

While it is unlikely that the courts will preclude the traditional familial decision-making role, careful analysis of specific precedents in each state is warranted to determine whether this role has been explicitly curtailed. When the hospital becomes aware of disagreement among the patient, family, and physician, the hospital administration should remember the hospital's independent duty to the patient; it should become involved to facilitate communication and to determine whether it should seek clarification from the court.

Severely Deformed or Impaired Newborns

An especially perplexing case concerns the newborn infant with severe deformities that are inconsistent with prolonged or sapient life. It has been accepted practice in many medical centers, upon the concurrence of the parents and the treatment team, to provide only ordinary care to these infants so that their suffering is not prolonged through extraordinary efforts. If the parents wish heroic measures, they are attempted. If the parents refuse treatment when the attending physician believes treatment provides a reasonable likelihood of benefit, the child neglect laws are invoked to obtain court authorization for treatment.

Health care professionals disagree as to which conditions are sufficiently severe that treatment offers no reasonable likelihood of benefit. There is general acceptance of withholding treatment when the condition is anencephaly (the absence of the higher brain) or another condition that precludes the development of sapient life or is inconsistent with prolonged life.[33] In the recent past, there was no such agreement on the surgical repair of problems associated with spina bifida. At one time, surgical treatment was frequently withheld. With improvements in treatments and outcomes, however, most physicians now believe that surgery should not be withheld except in the most severe cases. For example, a New York hospital sought and obtained a court order authorizing surgical repair of a newborn with several of the complications associated with spina bifida.[34]

Neither mental retardation, if it is at a sapient level, nor physical deformities, if they are consistent with prolonged survival, are considered to justify withholding treatment from newborns. This is illustrated by the refusal of a

Massachusetts probate court in 1978 to approve parental refusal of respiratory support and cardiac surgery, in spite of some degree of mental retardation and multiple medical problems, because the condition was not terminal and the degree of mental retardation had not been established.[35]

The Department of Health and Human Services (HHS) began in 1982 to seek to force aggressive treatment of virtually all severely deformed newborns. In May 1982 HHS sent a letter to many hospitals threatening to withhold federal funding from any hospital that permitted medically indicated treatment to be withheld from a handicapped newborn.[36] This letter was a reaction to a widely publicized case in Indiana in which an infant with Down's Syndrome (which usually results in mental retardation) was permitted to starve to death when relatively minor surgery would have permitted the newborn to live. A court order was sought to authorize the surgery, but the Indiana courts refused to intervene.[37]

In March 1983 HHS published rules (1) creating a hotline in Washington, D.C., for the reporting of suspected violations and (2) requiring notices to be posted in hospitals announcing the hotline.[38] A federal court enjoined the rules.[39] The federal intervention was criticized by the President's Commission for the Study of Ethical Problems in Medicine and Biomedical and Behavioral Research, which recommended hospital review procedures.[40] HHS published revised rules in January 1984 that continued the hotline, required notices to be posted, and recommended the creation of institutional ethics committees.[41] The revised rules were declared invalid by a federal court in 1984.[42]

In 1983 New York's highest court upheld the decision of the parents of a newborn with spina bifida and hydrocephalus to decline corrective surgery.[43] The federal government sought access to the child's medical records and the parents and hospital refused to grant access. When the government sought a court order, a federal court of appeals denied access and ruled that the federal government did not have authority under the existing handicapped rights laws to investigate this type of case.[44]

Congress then passed legislation in 1984 that required states to implement programs to address the withholding of medically indicated treatment from infants with life-threatening conditions within their child abuse prevention and treatment systems.[45] HHS promulgated implementing regulations in 1985, including recommendations for institutional infant care review committees.[46]

Even though the scope of HHS's legal authority to take action is still uncertain, the agency's efforts are another significant indication that withholding treatment is acceptable only when the deformities are inconsistent with prolonged or sapient life. It is seldom justifiable to withhold ordinary care.

These decisions will continue to be controversial, but the real exposure to potential legal sanctions is minimal if the practice is carefully limited to appropriate cases. It is important to obtain consultations regarding diagnosis, prognosis, and treatment decisions. Documenting the reasons for the decisions and the decision-making process is essential to ensure that the decision makers give principled consideration to all relevant information.

Other Minors

Minors are generally treated as incompetents for purposes of medical care decisions. When the minor is able to participate in the decision, however, the minor's wishes should be given substantial weight. This presents no difficulty when the minor and the parents or guardian agree, such as when the minor initiates the idea of withholding treatment and the parents agree. The case is more complex when there is irreconcilable disagreement. If the minor is immature, and either the minor or a parent or a guardian wants to treat, treatment should be pursued, even though court authorization is required if only the minor wants the treatment. If the minor is mature, court resolution should usually be pursued.

Role of the Courts

In most states, it is not necessary to involve courts in decisions concerning withholding or withdrawing treatment for terminally ill patients. Courts need to be involved only when there is a disagreement among those involved in the decision making. However, not all disagreements require court resolution. When a competent adult is refusing certain treatment and the physician disagrees, often the proper resolution is to transfer the care of the patient to another physician who will accept the refusal.

The Florida Supreme Court ruled in 1984 that courts do not have to be involved in these decisions in many circumstances.[47] Some of the earlier court decisions appeared to require court involvement.[48] Subsequent decisions have clarified that court involvement usually is not required.[49]

Civil Statutes and Regulations Concerning Refusal

Before the evolution of the judicial consensus regarding the rights of the terminally ill, many physicians and hospitals were reluctant to respect the wishes of terminally ill patients and their families that treatments be limited. A substantial minority of physicians still do not accept refusals of care because of either their personal ethics or their concerns regarding legal risks. To facilitate carrying out the wishes of the patient and others and to relieve the concerns of the physicians, several states have enacted laws or promulgated regulations that explicitly authorize health care personnel to honor these wishes.

Natural Death Acts

Over two-thirds of the states have enacted laws providing that a patient's wishes may be followed with some degree of immunity if the patient has executed a special directive regarding treatment of terminal illness.[50] Recognizing that, in some instances, the physician may be unwilling to follow the patient's directive, several of these laws require reasonable efforts to transfer the patient to the care of another physician who will abide by these wishes.

Other provisions of the acts vary in respect to who may sign, the content and execution of the directive, the sanctions and immunities, and the effect of the absence of a directive. Most of the natural death acts authorize only competent adults to sign directives. Thus, most of the laws do not cover a large part of the population, such as minors and incompetent adults who have not previously executed a directive.

Each of the laws specifies the precise wording of the directive or the elements that must be included. In those states that specify the wording, the patient who wants to express more detailed or different wishes must forgo the benefit of the statute and rely on common law and constitutional principles. Physicians who wish to rely on the statute should have the wording checked to determine that it satisfies the statute's requirements. Individualized documents may present problems because the intent may not be clear.

Each of the natural death acts specifies the formality with which the directive must be signed. All the acts require witnesses, and some disqualify certain people from being witnesses. Some states require that the directive be notarized. Most acts specify the means to revoke a directive. Regardless of the technicalities, it is best not to carry out a directive if there is reason to believe the patient has had a change of mind.

The effect of the directive also varies among states. In some states, the directive appears to be binding, but no sanction is specified for physicians who do not follow it. In several other states, the directive is binding, and there are sanctions for not following it if the person was diagnosed as terminally ill before the directive was signed. In most states, the directive is not binding if signed before diagnosis, so it is only to be given weight in the decisions regarding care. When the directive is binding, the physician who does not wish to follow the directive has a duty to arrange a transfer to another physician. The specified sanction for failing to arrange this transfer is medical licensing discipline for unprofessional conduct. All of the natural death acts provide some immunity for those who act or refrain from acting in accordance with a directive that complies with the act. In most states, it is questionable whether the immunity provisions offer substantially more protection than common law and constitutional principles. The primary issue in most controversies will be the diagnosis of terminal illness. Since this diagnosis is viewed as a professional responsibility for which physicians should be accountable, none of the statutes provides for any protection from liability that arises from negligent diagnosis. Of course, immunity by statute is easier to establish than immunity under common law or constitutional law principles. Thus, when practical, it is best to attempt to comply with the statutory requirements.

Most natural death acts specify that they do not affect other rights to refuse treatment. Arkansas' statute[51] could potentially be interpreted to supersede nonstatutory approaches because it is comprehensive and does not specifically preserve other approaches. With the possible exception of cases in Arkansas, it is reasonable to follow the wishes of the patient and/or family in accord with common law and constitutional principles whenever there is no valid statutory directive.

Hospices

Some terminally ill patients elect to forgo treatment for their illnesses but still require nursing care and pain medication in their homes or institutions. Special facilities, called *hospices*, are being established to provide this limited type of care along with maximal personal support to help the patient and the family cope with the dying process. Home hospice programs have been developed to provide similar support in the home. The federal government has recognized and encouraged this trend by authorizing Medicare reimbursement for hospice services. Several states regulate hospices, indicating their recognition of this practice. The Medicare reimbursement criteria and some of the state licensing regulations limit coverage to persons with a life expectancy of six months or less. This use of a six-month time limit as an administrative convenience to control expenditure of funds and utilization of facilities should not be misinterpreted as an indication that persons with longer life expectancies must accept aggressive treatment.

Civil Liability

Because of a fear of civil or criminal liability, physicians and hospitals have sometimes been reluctant to honor the wishes of terminally ill patients or their families. While liability is theoretically possible, it is not more likely that physicians and other health care providers will be held liable for withholding or withdrawing treatment than for the many other decisions and actions they must make every day.

Civil liability for withholding or withdrawing medical treatment would have to be based on negligent or deliberate failure to act in accordance with some duty to the patient. The duty to the patient is shaped by the patient's condition, and there is no duty to treat the terminally ill as if they are curable. In addition, explicit refusal by the terminally ill patient relieves the physician of further duty to provide the refused treatment. If refused treatment is given, liability for battery is possible. The same principles generally apply to refusal by the incompetent patient's representative.

There is always the possibility that a medical decision will be questioned in subsequent litigation and be found to have been negligent. The risk for decisions regarding the care of the terminally ill is no greater than that for the care of the other patients. Liability is even possible when physicians act pursuant to a court order if they are negligent in implementing the order. Limited statutory immunity has been granted in some circumstances by natural death acts, but even those provisions have broad exceptions that preserve accountability.

The best indication of the limited exposure to civil liability is the apparent absence of reported civil lawsuits brought against physicians for withholding or withdrawing medical treatment from terminally ill patients with the concurrence of the patient or the family. One of the few unreported cases arose after the physician and the patient's husband decided to discontinue the patient's dialysis at a Minnesota hospital.[52] Six months after the wife's death, the husband died. Three years later, the patient's children sued the physician for her death, but a jury found in favor of the physician.

Liability exposure is likely in cases of misdiagnosis of terminal illness or unjustifiable failure to obtain the concurrence of the patient or the family, but no reported liability cases address those issues. Exposure to civil liability is probably greater from refusing to honor the wishes of the patient and the family. Several suits have been brought against providers who continued treatment for a prolonged period after refusal.

For example, in Ohio the husband of a terminally ill woman requested that she be taken off a respirator, but the hospital refused to permit the removal until a court order was obtained. After the court order was obtained,[53] the husband filed a suit against the physician and hospital claiming that her constitutional right of privacy was violated and seeking payment for his wife's pain, suffering, and medical expenses during the time the order was sought. An Ohio court refused to dismiss the suit, ruling that the providers could be sued for battery for continuing treatment for too long a period after authorization was withdrawn.[54] Another case arose in Massachusetts after the courts authorized discontinuance of dialysis for a

patient.[55] The wife of the patient sued the health care institution that had
forced the matter to be taken to court. The trial court dismissed several of
the grounds on which the suit was brought, but the jury awarded $2.5
million on the remaining grounds. After the trial court ordered a new trial, a
second jury awarded $1 million based solely on a letter, sent to a newspaper
by several institutional employees with the approval of the administration,
that opposed the court order. The letter was found to violate a statute that
prohibited certain releases of personal data. The highest court of Massachusetts reversed the award, finding that the statute did not apply to public
institutions such as the defendant in the suit.[56] These cases illustrate that
extended delay, pursuit of court orders, and vigorous advocacy of continued
treatment may increase exposure to liability.

Criminal Liability

In some decisions involving the terminally ill, the courts have discussed
the potential criminal liability for withholding or withdrawing medical treatment without proper authorization. In the *Quinlan* decision, after observing
that termination of treatment would accelerate death, the court concluded
that "there would be no criminal homicide but rather expiration from
existing natural causes." It added as a second reason, "even if it were to be
regarded as homicide, it would not be unlawful. . . . The termination of
treatment pursuant to the right of privacy is, within the limits of this case,
ipso facto lawful." It went on to discuss the constitutional dimensions:

> Furthermore, the exercise of a constitutional right such as we have
> here found is protected from criminal prosecution. [Citation omit-
> ted.] We do not question the State's undoubted power to punish the
> taking of human life, but that power does not encompass individ-
> uals terminating medical treatment pursuant to their right of pri-
> vacy. [Citation omitted.] The constitutional protection extends to
> third parties whose action is necessary to effectuate the exercise of
> that right where the individuals themselves would not be subject to
> prosecution or the third parties are charged as accessories to an act
> which could not be a crime.[57]

Thus, there is little risk of criminal liability for these actions.
The only prosecutions of physicians in the United States for the deaths of
terminally ill patients have involved alleged injections of substances to
hasten death. In all three cases that have gone to trial, the jury acquitted the
physician. The results of these cases illustrate the difficulty in obtaining
convictions when the patient is terminally ill, even in cases alleging active

euthanasia. This is one of the reasons prosecutors do not pursue cases that involve withholding or withdrawing treatment from the terminally ill. The other reason is that it would be difficult to establish a duty to provide the withheld or withdrawn treatment.

One case that did not go to trial supports this position. In 1983 two California physicians were charged with murder for terminating all life support, including intravenous feeding, of an irreversibly comatose patient upon the written request of the family. A California appellate court ordered the charges dismissed because the physicians had no legal duty to continue futile treatment and, thus, they did not unlawfully fail to fulfill a legal duty that could be the basis for a murder charge.[58]

Some investigations into the deaths of terminally ill patients have resulted in the prosecution of hospital personnel. Two nurses were accused of poisoning 11 patients at the Ann Arbor Veterans Administration Hospital by injecting a muscle relaxant into their intravenous tubes. They were convicted on several of the counts in 1977, but when the court ordered a new trial, their indictments were dismissed.[59] A Maryland nurse was accused of unilaterally disconnecting three patients' respirators and turning down the oxygen flow to a fourth. Tried for one of the disconnection cases, she surrendered her license before the trial. The jury deadlocked, and she was not convicted. All charges were then dropped.[60] These cases demonstrate the importance of proper documentation of the circumstances under which medical treatment may be withheld or withdrawn so that authorized actions can be distinguished from unauthorized actions. Nurses and other hospital personnel should seek and hospitals should require appropriate documentation of decisions by the physician and patient or family before withholding or withdrawing medical treatment to assure appropriate care and to avoid the risk of investigation or prosecution in the absence of documented medical authorization of the actions. As mentioned in the section on DNR orders, hospitals have been investigated for permitting actions to be taken without appropriate written orders.[61]

Suggested Dimensions of Hospital Protocols

Hospitals, with the assistance of their medical staffs, should develop guidelines for managing the difficult situations associated with the dying process. Guidelines are not required by law, but they can help to avoid controversies that can add to the strain on patients, families, and staff in the already stressful situation of terminal illness. The guidelines should preserve flexibility within the outer limits of propriety because the situations surrounding terminal illness are as individualistic as the full lives that preceded the illness.

The core of the guidelines should be reaffirmation that decisions are to be made by the physician and the patient. If the patient is unable to participate or desires family involvement, the patient's family should be consulted. The nature of the patient and family involvement should be discussed in the guidelines, along with the alternatives available when they are unable to be involved.

The use of consultants in difficult cases should be encouraged and facilitated because consultation provides some protection for both the physician and the hospital if questions concerning the diagnosis are later raised. Consultation can be facilitated by a committee with members who may be consulted individually or collectively. Some persons have advocated that a committee be given an approval role because they do not trust decisions made by physicians, patients, and families. Other persons have opposed mandatory committee decision making because it interferes with the physician-patient relationship and is difficult to enforce, potentially increasing risk of liability in situations in which the committee is not involved. A few states require committee involvement in some decisions regarding the terminally ill. Based on local circumstances, a hospital could reasonably conclude that it should require confirmation by a committee. Even if confirmation is not required, prudent physicians seek the support of a committee or other consultants voluntarily because "concurrence of qualified consultants may be highly persuasive on issues of good faith and good medical practice."[62]

Proper documentation should be required. The minimum documentation should be an order or note in the medical record specifying the treatment to be withheld or withdrawn and an indication of the concurrence of the patient and/or family (or the reasons they were not involved, such as unavailability or incapacity). It is advisable to document the prognosis and any other rationale for the decision. Just as with other actions requiring written orders, emergency situations arise in which oral orders are appropriate, but they should be countersigned within a reasonable period, such as 24 hours.

The guidelines should also indicate how the medical staff should approach situations in which the patient's condition is possibly due to criminal activities. The law enforcement needs of the prosecutor and medical examiner must be accommodated.

It is advisable to have the patient and/or family sign a form stating the decision to withhold or withdraw treatment. The increasing focus of legislatures, courts, and prosecutors on these decisions and the difficulty in proving oral statements point toward more use of forms to demonstrate that actions or inactions were in accordance with the wishes of the patient and/or family.

DEFINITION OF DEATH

The question of the definition of death is distinct from the questions concerning treatment of the living. Once the patient is legally dead, there is no longer a patient. Patient care should be discontinued. The hospital becomes the custodian of a dead body with the responsibilities discussed later in this chapter.

Because of the capacity of modern technology to sustain vegetative functions of persons with irreversible cessation of brain function and the development of modern transplant surgery, irreversible cessation of brain function has been accepted as the definition of death when a patient's vital signs are being maintained artificially. The traditional definition is still applicable in all other situations.

Medical Definition of Death

For over a century, the traditional definition of death has been the cessation of respiration, heartbeat, and certain indications of central nervous system activity, e.g., response to pain and reaction of pupils to light.

Advances in technology in the 1950s and 1960s produced cardiac pumps and respirators that can maintain the first two traditional indicators of life for extended periods beyond the irreversible cessation of all detectable brain activity. Thus, medical science was forced to decide whether an individual who had irreversible cessation of brain functions was alive or dead when the first two traditional life indicators were being maintained artificially.

It was concluded that such individuals were dead and that the use of machines should be discontinued. In 1974 the House of Delegates of the American Medical Association recognized that "permanent and irreversible cessation of function of the brain constitutes one of the various criteria which can be used in the medical diagnosis of death."

The medical profession accepts that death occurs when there is irreversible cessation of all brain functions, including the brain stem. While it may be appropriate to discontinue certain treatments for patients with only brain stem functioning, it is not appropriate to declare them dead until the brain stem also irreversibly ceases to function.

There is still some debate regarding the optimal diagnostic criteria. The first widely publicized criteria were announced in 1968 by the Ad Hoc Committee of the Harvard Medical School to Examine the Definition of Brain Death. The lack of consensus at that time is reflected in the cautiously worded title of its report, *A Definition of Irreversible Coma*.[63] This title is unfortunate because it has led some to believe that the criteria can be used to assess only higher brain function, when in fact they also assess brain stem activity. Thus, despite the title, the Harvard criteria do apply to irreversible cessation of total brain function.

The report set forth the following criteria:

1. "unreceptivity and unresponsivity" to "externally applied stimuli and inner need,"
2. absence of spontaneous muscular movements or spontaneous respiration, and
3. absence of any elicitable reflexes.

A flat (isoelectric) electroencephalogram (EEG) was mentioned as having "great confirmatory value" in the diagnosis. The report also contained a warning that either hypothermia (low body temperature) or central nervous system depressants could cause the criteria to be met, so an assessment in the presence of either would not be valid. The report specified that all the criteria had to be met again at least 24 hours later.

The EEG is not a mandatory adjunct to the diagnosis, but it is helpful. Since some of the public has unfortunately identified brain death with the flat line on the EEG tracing, when appropriate EEG machines, trained operators, and trained interpreters are available in the hospital, it may be difficult to explain why they are not used (except when other technological tests of cerebral blood flow or activity are substituted). However, if all of the listed criteria are present, it is permissible to diagnose brain death without the EEG or other technological tests.

While the Harvard criteria are still widely used, various organizations have proposed modifications. In addition, the President's Commission for the Study of Ethical Problems in Medicine and Biomedical and Behavorial Research released in 1981 a set of diagnostic guidelines developed by its medical consultants.[64] Although the commission presented these solely as advisory guidelines, they can be expected to receive increasing recognition.

Some of the modifications include (1) focus on the importance of the cause of the condition, (2) changes in the length of time for the diagnosis, (3) use of other tests, and (4) other matters. The Harvard criteria focused entirely on the patient's present condition. The only reference to cause in the Harvard criteria is the statement that, if there is evidence of drug intoxication, time should be allowed for elimination of the intoxicating agent before the diagnosis is made. The commission guidelines emphasize the importance of determining cause but recognize that it is not necessary in all cases. The commission urged caution when (1) diseases or drugs that may cause total paralysis are involved; (2) metabolic abnormalities may be present; or (3) the patient is in shock.

The Harvard criteria specify that all tests must be repeated after at least 24 hours. It is now recognized that in many cases a much shorter period may be appropriate. There is growing acceptance of a 12-hour or 6-hour period in cases in which drug intoxication is not suspected. Some medical centers have eliminated the requirement of a repeat test for most cases. Some institutions use other tests to measure blood flow in the brain directly. If there is no blood flow, then the brain is dead, and no second test is required. These tests are particularly helpful to confirm the diagnosis when drug levels preclude reliance on the other tests.

The Harvard criteria do not address the age of the patient. The criteria are not as reliable in infants and young children because their recuperative potential is much greater. Great caution must be used in evaluating a child's clinical condition and in interpreting supplemental tests, including the EEG.

The Legal Definition of Death

The common law definition of death includes brain death as determined in accordance with usual medical standards. In the first years that followed the medical recognition of brain death, some lower courts had difficulty accepting brain death in suits involving organ donations for heart transplants. One California trial court refused to accept brain death as death, acquitting the person who had been charged with manslaughter in the death of the donor. Such trial court cases are now historical anomalies.

The statutory recognition of brain death not only has superseded these decisions in their jurisdictions but also has resolved the question in more than half the states. The common law definition now also includes brain death. Since 1977 the highest courts of Arizona, Colorado, Indiana, Massachusetts, Nebraska, New York, and Washington all have adopted the brain death standard.[65]

Laws that include brain death in the definition of death were passed in an effort to avoid the case-by-case approach of the common law. The early contradictory trial court decisions added impetus to the statutory trend. Many of these cases involved organs removed from victims of apparent homicides. Some persons accused of homicide argued that they were not responsible for the death of the victim whose organs were transplanted. To avoid this issue, many centers did not accept organ donations from victims of apparent homicide. An important factor in the passage of the statutes was that they facilitated organ donations from such victims, increasing the number of organs available to treat others and frequently helping the bereaved family to find some solace in helping others.

The details in the brain death laws vary from state to state, so familiarity with local law is necessary to assure compliance, especially with consultation and documentation requirements. Several groups have developed model legislation in an effort to secure more uniformity. In 1980 several of the major groups involved in this effort agreed on the following model: "An individual who has sustained either: (1) irreversible cessation of circulatory or respiratory functions; or (2) irreversible cessation of all functions of the entire brain, including the brain stem, is dead. A determination of death must be made in accordance with accepted medical standards."[66] Some states have enacted this model.[67]

DEAD BODIES

This section discusses the duties of hospitals and health care professionals in handling dead bodies and communicating with family and legal authorities. Autopsies and anatomical donations are discussed in the following sections.

Communications with Family

The hospital in which a patient dies has a duty to inform an appropriate member of the family of the death. This is not only ethically necessary but legally necessary to permit appropriate arrangements to be made for disposition of the body. Information regarding deaths should be confirmed before being communicated. Erroneous notification of death will be upsetting to the family and may cause them to make expenditures for funeral arrangements, possibly resulting in a lawsuit. The hospital could be liable for the emotional harm and expenses. However, mistaken notification will not result in liability when an error in identity is due to a good faith reliance on identification by the police at the scene of an accident.[68] Failure to make reasonable efforts to notify the appropriate member of the family within a reasonable time can also result in liability.

The method by which the family is informed also is important. In 1977 a New Jersey court ruled that a hospital could be sued for the method in which a mother had been informed of the death of her baby.[69] While still in the hospital where the birth occurred, the mother had been telephoned by a person from the hospital to which her baby had been transferred for specialized care. The caller, who was otherwise unidentified, told her the baby was dead, and the mother became hysterical. In addition to the potential liability issues, this case illustrates the humanitarian reasons for thoughtful communications with the family. If it can be avoided, family should not be informed of unexpected deaths by telephone unless someone is with them to provide support. Obviously, when death is anticipated, there may be less need for immediate support.

Medical Examiner's Cases

All states have laws providing for legal investigation of certain suspicious deaths by a legal officer, such as a medical examiner or coroner. Most of the laws require a report to the medical examiner by the physician in attendance at a death known or suspected to be of the type requiring investigation. One typical example is the Iowa requirement that physicians report any "death which affects the public interest," which is defined to include

a. Violent death, including homicidal, suicidal, or accidental death.
b. Death caused by thermal, chemical, electrical, or radiation injury.
c. Death caused by criminal abortion including self-induced, or by sexual abuse.
d. Death related to disease thought to be virulent or contagious which may constitute a public hazard.
e. Death that has occurred unexpectedly or from an unexplained cause.
f. Death of a person confined in a prison, jail, or correctional institution.
g. Death of a person if a physician was not in attendance within 36 hours preceding death, excluding prediagnosed terminal or bedfast cases, for which the time period is extended to 20 days.
h. Death of a person if the body is not claimed by a relative or friend.
i. Death of a person if the identity of the deceased is unknown.
j. Death of a child under the age of two years if death results from an unknown cause or if the circumstances surrounding the death indicate that sudden infant syndrome may be the cause of death.[70]

Each state's list is somewhat different, so it is important for hospital personnel to be familiar with their state's list and with the local medical examiner's practices concerning the cases expected to be reported. It is a crime in many states not to make the required report to the official or officials specified in the statute.

Physicians who are not sure whether to report should make a report. The medical examiner can decide whether further investigation is warranted. When it is clearly not a medical examiner's case, however, a report is inappropriate. When it is determined that the death is a medical examiner's case, all health care providers have a duty to cooperate with the investigation. The first requirement is not to move the body without the permission of the medical examiner, except as authorized by law. Some states authorize moving bodies, if necessary, to preserve the body from loss or destruction, to permit travel on highways or other public transportation, or to prevent immediate danger to the life, safety, or health of others. Not all states have the same exceptions, so health care providers must become familiar with the laws of their own states.

Release of the Body

Upon the death of a patient, the hospital becomes the temporary custodian of the body. The hospital is responsible for releasing the body in the proper condition to the proper recipient in accordance with state law. Thus, hospital staff should be familiar with state law applying to handling and releasing bodies.

In general, the proper recipient of the body has a right to its prompt release in the condition at death, unless the deceased has directed otherwise or the body is being retained or examined in accordance with law. Thus, the major issues are (1) the scope of the deceased's authority; (2) the authority of others to act in the absence of binding directions by the decedent; (3) the timing of the release of the body; and (4) the condition of the body when it is released.

Deceased's Authority

Some state statutes give individuals broad authority to direct the disposition of their remains.[71] All states have now enacted a version of the Uniform Anatomical Gift Act,[72] so individuals can donate their bodies or certain organs for various purposes. When the situation is not covered by statute and the person entitled to dispose of the body is not willing to carry out the decedent's wishes, the common law determines whether the individual's wishes can be enforced. Most courts have recognized a right to direct disposition of the body by will,[73] but they have recognized many exceptions. While courts have taken other documents or statements into account, they have been more likely to defer to such directions when they are in a will or a document authorized by statute. The one direction that the common law generally enforces is an autopsy authorization.

Authority of Others to Control Disposition

In the absence of binding directions by the deceased, the surviving spouse is recognized as the person who controls the disposition of the remains. However, in some states, if the surviving spouse has abandoned and is living apart from the deceased, the right is waived. If there is no surviving spouse or if the surviving spouse fails to act or waives the right, then control passes to the next of kin. Unless statute or common law precedent in the jurisdiction establishes a different order of kinship, the priority is generally recognized to be adult child, parent, and adult sibling. If the person with the highest priority either fails to act or waives the right, the next priority level becomes the highest priority level and has control.

Timing of Release of the Body

The person who is entitled to control of the body for disposition is entitled to have it released promptly, i.e., as soon as the person can show entitlement to the body and has satisfied any legal requirements, including permits. The hospital can retain the body long enough to transport it from the place of death to the usual place for releasing bodies and long enough to confirm that the person claiming control has the highest priority of those able and willing to do so. Delay in delivery or refusal to release the body, even of a stillborn, can result in liability.

Condition of the Body

The person who is entitled to control the body is entitled to have it in the condition it was in at the time of death. The change in the condition that most frequently has led to litigation has been due to an autopsy. An autopsy that is done without proper consent or other lawful authority can result in liability for violation of the right to the body in the condition at the time of death.

Burial or Other Disposition of Remains

The ultimate disposition of the remains is seldom the direct responsibility of the hospital, either because others assume responsibility or because arrangements are made for a mortician to handle the disposition. In a few situations, some state laws permit the hospital to dispose of certain bodies directly. For example, in some states, hospitals may dispose of a stillborn when the parents elect such a disposition.

Unclaimed Dead Bodies

When there are no known relatives or friends to claim the body, the hospital must dispose of the body in accordance with applicable laws. Some states require that unclaimed bodies be buried at public expense, and a public official is assigned to make arrangements. Most states provide that such bodies may be delivered to certain types of institutions or individuals for education or scientific purposes. The hospital should notify the appropriate public official when it has an unclaimed body so that the official can make arrangements. Before notifying the public official, a reasonable attempt should be made to locate and contact relatives so that they can claim the body. Many statutes require such an inquiry; it has also been found to be common law duty.[74]

AUTOPSIES

Autopsies are the most frequent cause of litigation involving bodies and hospitals. This section describes the legal prerequisites to autopsies and the potential sources of liability involving them.

Autopsies are performed primarily to determine the cause of death. This finding can be crucial in detecting crime or ruling out transmittable diseases that may be a threat to the public health. The cause of death can affect whether death benefits are payable under insurance policies, worker's compensation laws, and other programs. Autopsies help to advance medical science by permitting the correlation of anatomical changes with other signs and symptoms of disease. They are also educational for those involved.

Community mores and religious beliefs have long dictated respectful handling of dead bodies. Societal views have now evolved to the point that a substantial portion of the population recognizes the benefit of autopsies. Out of respect to those who continue to find autopsies unacceptable, the law requires appropriate consent before an autopsy can be performed, except when an autopsy is needed to determine the cause of death for public policy purposes.

Authorization by Decedent

The laws of many states provide specific statutory procedures by which people may authorize autopsies to be performed on their bodies. In states that do not explicitly address authorization before death, the anatomical gift act can be used. The person can donate the body for the purpose of autopsy, with such conditions as are desired, by following the rules for executing an anatomical gift. Even when there clearly is valid authorization from the decedent, hospitals and physicians may find it more prudent to decline to perform an autopsy, for example, when it is contrary to the strongly held wishes of the family.

Authorization by Family or Others

When the decedent has not given legal authorization for an autopsy, authorization must be obtained from someone else. Many states have statutes that specify who may authorize an autopsy. Some states specify a priority ordering of people;[75] the available person with the highest priority may give the authorization. Other states specify that the person assuming responsibility for disposal of the body may consent to the autopsy.[76] This second type of autopsy statute does not specify a priority, so common law principles must be followed to determine the priority. In a few states autopsy authorization statutes do not establish a priority, but rather specify the priority of the duty to assume custody for disposal.[77] The duty of disposal statutes are used to determine the priority for autopsy authorization. In the absence of either an autopsy authorization or duty of disposal statute, the common law priority is followed.

The general common law rule is that the surviving spouse has the highest priority and duty to arrange for disposal and, thus, is the proper person to authorize an autopsy. If there is no surviving spouse or the spouse's right is waived, the next of kin has the responsibility and may authorize an autopsy. The most common order is child, parent, sibling, and then other next of kin. Most statutes disqualify any on the list who are not adults.

Under most statutes, the authorization of the highest priority person who can be located with reasonable efforts is sufficient, unless the objections of a person of the same or a higher priority, or of the deceased, are actually known. In these states, objections by persons of lower priority have no legal effect. A few states permit persons of lower priority to veto an authorization.[78]

Most statutes specify others who may authorize an autopsy when no spouse or next of kin is available. In most states, the final priority rests with whoever assumes responsibility for disposal of the remains. A few states permit a physician to perform an autopsy without authorization when there is neither knowledge of any objection nor anyone assuming responsibility for disposal after due inquiry.[79]

Scope of Authorization

The general rule is that whoever authorizes the autopsy may limit its scope by imposing conditions. If these conditions are not met, then the autopsy is not authorized. If the conditions are unacceptable, the physician who is to perform the autopsy may decline to do so. Examples of conditions include limits on the areas to be examined, restrictions on retention of parts of the body, and requirements that certain observers be present. Unless the authorization specifically includes permission to retain parts of the body, an autopsy authorization usually is interpreted not to permit retention. Liability may be imposed for retaining organs from authorized autopsies. However, the Iowa Supreme Court held that an authorization implied permission to retain slices of tissues in accordance with usual pathology practices, unless expressly forbidden.[80] It is prudent to include express permission for such retention in the autopsy authorization.

Form of Authorization

A few states require that an autopsy be authorized in writing. Many states include telegrams and recorded telephone permissions as acceptable forms of authorization. Common law does not require the authorization to be documented in a particular way. A written authorization or recorded telephone authorization is obviously the easiest to prove.[81]

Authorization by Medical Examiner or Other Legal Officials

In many circumstances, authorization of the deceased, a family member, or friend is not required. Determination of the cause of death is so important in some cases that statutory authority to order an autopsy has been granted to certain public officials. In addition, courts have the authority to order an autopsy.

Each state has a state or county officer, usually called a medical examiner or coroner, who is authorized to investigate certain deaths. In most states, the medical examiner has the authority to perform an autopsy when it is necessary for the investigation. In some states the power also is given to other officials, such as the industrial commissioner responsible for worker's compensation cases.

An order from a medical examiner does not ensure immunity when the order is outside the authority of the medical examiner. In many states the scope of authority is broad enough that there is little risk that the medical examiner will exceed the scope of authority, but, in other states, the scope is so narrow that the courts have imposed liability. Thus, each hospital must be familiar with the laws of its state regarding medical examiner's autopsies before permitting them to be conducted on hospital premises.

Liability for Unauthorized Autopsies

Under general principles of liability, the hospital can be liable for unauthorized autopsies by its employees and agents. Hospitals are not the insurers of the safety of dead bodies, so hospitals are not generally liable for unauthorized autopsies by persons not acting on behalf of the hospital, but they must take reasonable steps to protect the body from unauthorized autopsy.[82]

DONATION OF BODIES AND CADAVER TRANSPLANTATION

Before 1969, the uncertainty surrounding the authority of persons to make binding anatomical donations prior to death and of others to make such donations after death limited the availability of organs for transplantation. The Uniform Anatomical Gift Act was developed as a model to resolve the uncertainty.[83] It was approved by the National Conference of Commissioners on Uniform State Laws and the American Bar Association in August 1968. Laws substantially equivalent to the model were enacted in all of the states by the end of 1971. Every state now has statutory authority and procedures for anatomical gifts, so the uncertainty has been removed.

The Uniform Anatomical Gift Act specifies who may donate and who may receive anatomical gifts. It specifies the documentation required, the permitted uses of the anatomical gift, and how a gift may be revoked. It also provides some limitations on liability. Many of the states modified the Uniform Anatomical Gift Act before enactment or by subsequent amendment. For example, the age requirements for donation and the liability limitation provisions vary.

The Uniform Anatomical Gift Act has not resulted in a sufficiently high rate of donation of available organs to meet the need. Hospitals and physicians are reluctant to act without next-of-kin authorization, even when a donor card was previously signed by the decedent. Most families approached at the time of death agree to donate, but many physicians are reluctant to ask them. A few states have adopted laws requiring families to be approached unless the physician documents reasons why it would be detrimental to the family.[84]

Who May Donate?

Section 2 of the Act specifies that persons of sound mind who are 18 years of age or more may donate all or part of their bodies. Furthermore, the Act includes a priority list of who may donate a body if the deceased has not given actual notice of contrary intentions. Persons of lower priority may donate if (1) persons of higher priority are not available; and (2) persons of the same or higher priority have not given actual notice of objection. The order of priority from highest to lowest is "(1) the spouse; (2) an adult son or daughter; (3) either parent; (4) an adult brother or sister; (5) a guardian of the person of the decedent at the time of his death; (6) any other person authorized or under obligation to dispose of the body." Several states have enacted laws that differ from the model. A few states have different age requirements. Some states authorize some minors to make donations with the consent of their parents or guardians.

Conflicting Wishes

Under the Act, the authorization of the highest priority person who can be located with reasonable effort is sufficient, unless there is actual knowledge of the contrary wishes of a person of the same or a higher priority, or of the deceased. In states that have enacted the Act without modification, objections by persons of lower priority have no legal effect. However, a few states permit persons of lower priority to veto an authorization.

In 1964 the New Hampshire Supreme Court addressed a case in which the deceased donated by will her eyes to an eye bank and her body to one of two medical schools.[85] The eye donation was carried out, but the donation of the body was not. The surviving spouse and children objected, so the medical schools declined to accept the body. The court stated that the wishes of the deceased should usually be carried out. Since the medical schools had declined, however, it ruled that the surviving spouse could determine disposition.

Medical Examiner's Cases

Section 7(d) of the Act specifies that it is subject to all laws regarding autopsies. The medical examiner's responsibilities and duties are given a higher public priority than anatomical donations. In most transplant cases, it is possible to obtain the cooperation of the medical examiner in coordinating the donation with the autopsy. If the organ is in a condition appropriate for transplantation, its removal does not usually compromise the autopsy. In cases of potential criminal prosecution, it is prudent to obtain the permission of the prosecuting attorney with jurisdiction over the case, as well as the permission of the medical examiner. While the permission of the prosecuting attorney is not legally required in most jurisdictions, it avoids accusations of interference with criminal law enforcement through destruction of necessary evidence and helps to maintain the public acceptance of transplantation. Prosecuting attorneys usually grant permission when they are assured that the donation will not compromise the testimony regarding the cause of death.

In some states the medical examiner has the authority to remove some organs in the course of a legal autopsy without the consent of the next of kin. In 1984 a Michigan court found a hospital not to be liable when corneas were removed during a medical examiner's autopsy.[86] The court said that the removal was authorized by the medical examiner's power to retain body parts. A similar result was reached in a 1985 case in which a medical examiner removed corneas pursuant to a Georgia statute. The Georgia Supreme Court ruled that the legislature could authorize corneal tissue to be removed during a medical examiner's autopsy without notice to the next of kin.[87] The court noted that the next of kin's right concerning the body was a common law quasi-property right, not a constitutional right, and the legislature has the power to modify or abrogate the common law.

Limitations on Liability

Section 7(c) of the Act prohibits liability for civil damages and criminal prosecution for actions "in good faith in accord with the terms of this Act or with the anatomical gift act laws of another state or a foreign country." In 1974 the Wisconsin Supreme Court upheld the constitutionality of this section, but ruled that it did not apply to treatment of the donor prior to death.[88] In 1975 a Michigan court ruled that the section did not preclude liability for negligent failure to have a procedure to assess the potential for disease transmission from the donor.[89]

NOTES

1. In re Quinlan, 70 N.J. 10, 355 A.2d 647, 677 (1976).

2. *E.g.,* In re Spring, 380 Mass. 629, 405 N.E.2d 115, 118 (1980) [five years].

3. *E.g.,* Wanzer et al., *The Physician's Responsibility toward Hopelessly Ill Patients,* 310 NEW ENG. J. MED. 955 (1984); Grenvik et al., *Cessation of Therapy in Terminal Illness and Brain Death,* 6 CRITICAL CARE MED. 284 (1978); Critical Care Committee, *Optimal Care for Hopelessly Ill Patients,* 295 NEW ENG. J. MED. 362 (1976).

4. In re Dinnerstein, 6 Mass. App. 466, 380 N.E.2d 134 (1978).

5. *E.g.,* N.Y. TIMES, Mar. 21, 1984, at 17, col. 1 [grand jury report on unwritten orders]; Nov. 20, 1984, at 16, col. 1 [civil charges for orders by unlicensed interns].

6. Hoyt v. St. Mary's Rehab. Center, No. 774555 (Minn. Dist. Ct., Hennepin County, Feb. 13, 1981).

7. Eichner v. Dillon, 73 A.D.2d 431, 426 N.Y.S.2d 517, 527 (1980).

8. 373 Mass. 728, 370 N.E.2d 417 (1977).

9. 380 Mass. 629, 405 N.E.2d 115 (1980). For an analysis of 155 cases in which dialysis was discontinued, *see* Neu & Kjellstrand, *Stopping Long-Term Dialysis,* 314 NEW ENG. J. MED. 14 (1986).

10. 425 A.2d 156 (Del. Ch. 1980).

11. In re J.N., 406 A.2d 1275 (D.C. 1979).

12. *E.g.*, In re Conroy, 98 N.J. 321, 486 A.2d 1209, 1234-35 (1985); President's Commission for the Study of Ethical Problems in Medicine and Biomedical and Behavioral Research, DECIDING TO FOREGO LIFE SUSTAINING TREATMENT, March 1983, at 82–89.

13. Wanzer, *supra* note 3.

14. In re Severns, 425 A.2d 156 (Del. Ch. Ct. 1980).

15. Application of Plaza Health and Rehab. Center (N.Y. Sup. Ct. Onondaga County Feb. 2, 1984); N.Y. TIMES, Feb. 3, 1984, at 1, col. 3.

16. Barber v. Superior Ct., 147 Cal. App.3d 1006, 195 Cal. Rptr. 484 (1984).

17. In re Storar, 52 N.Y.2d 363, 420 N.E.2d 64 (1981).

18. In re Conroy, 98 N.J. 321, 486 A.2d 1209 (1985); *contra* Brophy v. New England Sinai Hosp., Inc., No. 85E0009-GI (Mass.Prob.Ct. Oct. 21, 1985) and Corbett v. D'Alessandro, No. 84-5627CA-JRT (Fla.Cir.Ct., Lee County Feb. 28, 1985) [withdrawal of feeding tubes not permitted. Both decisions are being appealed]; *see also* N.Y. TIMES, Nov. 14, 1985, at 21, col. 1 [first use of procedure specified in *Conroy*].

19. Bouvia v. County of Riverside, No. 159780 (Cal. Super. Ct., Riverside County Dec. 16, 1983); N.Y. TIMES, Dec. 21, 1983, at 16; MIAMI HERALD, Dec. 23, 1983, at 15A. On February 21, 1986, a court denied her request for an injunction to halt the use of a nasogastric tube for feeding; N.Y. TIMES, Feb. 2, 1986, at 6, col. 1.

20. United States v. Rutherford, 442 U.S. 544 (1979).

21. CEDAR RAPIDS (Ia.) GAZETTE, Nov. 10, 1976.

22. *E.g.*, Tune v. Walter Reed Army Medical Center, 602 F. Supp. 1452 (D. D.C. 1985) [applies in military hospitals].

23. *E.g.*, John F. Kennedy Memorial Hosp. v. Bludworth, 452 A.2d 921 (Fla. 1984).

24. Foster v. Tourtellottee, No. CV-81-5046-RMT (C.D. Cal. Nov. 18, 1981); *accord* In re Yetter, 62 D. & C. 619 (Pa. Cm. Pl. Ct., Northampton County 1973) [disagreement between patient and brother]; Lane v. Candura, 6 Mass. App. 377, 376 N.E.2d 1232 (1978) [disagreement between patient and daughter].

25. Bartling v. Superior Ct., 163 Cal.App.3d 186, 209 Cal. Rptr. 220 (1984).

26. *E.g.*, Warthen v. Toms River Comm. Memorial Hosp., 199 N.J. Super. 18, 488 A.2d 229 (N.J. Super. Ct. App. Div. 1985) [upholding termination of nurse who refused to dialyze a seriously ill patient due to moral objections].

27. In re Severns, 425 A.2d 156 (Del. Ch. Ct. 1980); In re Storar, 52 N.Y.2d 363, 420 N.E.2d 64 (1981).

28. John F. Kennedy Memorial Hosp. v. Bludworth, 452 So.2d 921 (Fla. 1984); Fla. Stat., Ch. 765 (1984), subsequently recognized living wills.

29. In re Quinlan, 355 A.2d at 664.

30. Superintendent of Belchertown v. Saikewicz, 373 Mass. 728, 370 N.E.2d 417, 427 (1977).

31. *E.g.*, Farber v. Olkon, 40 Cal.2d 503, 254 P.2d 520 (1953).

32. *E.g.*, John F. Kennedy Memorial Hosp. v. Bludworth, 452 So.2d 921 (Fla. 1984); In re Hamlin, 102 Wash.2d 810, 689 P.2d 1372 (1984).

33. *E.g.*, In re Barry, 445 So.2d 365 (Fla. Dist. Ct. App. 1984), *approved* John F. Kennedy Memorial Hosp. v. Bludworth, 452 So.2d 921 (Fla. 1984) [approval of termination of ventilatory support of infant who had only minimal brain stem function. Court review not required when diagnosis confirmed by two physicians].

34. Application of Cicero, 101 Misc.2d 699, 421 N.Y.S.2d 965 (N.Y. Sup. Ct. 1979).

35. In re McNulty, 4 Fam. L. Rptr. 2255 (Mass. Prob. Ct., Essex County Feb. 15, 1978); *see also,* Iafelice v. Luchs, 206 N.J. Super. 103, 501 A.2d 1040 (N.J. Super. Ct. L. Div. 1985) [nontreatment not permissible alternative for infant with hydrocephalus, so physician not liable on an informed consent theory for failure to disclose this alternative].

36. HASTINGS CENTER REPORT, August 1982, at 6; 34 BAYLOR L. REV. 715 (1982).

37. In re Infant Doe, No. GU 8204-00 (Ind. Cir. Ct. Monroe County Apr. 12, 1982), *writ of mandamus dismissed sub nom.* State ex rel. Infant Doe v. Baker, No. 482 S 140 (Ind. May 27, 1982). For a description of the medical status of Infant Doe, see 309 NEW ENG. J. MED. 664 (1983).

38. 48 FED. REG. 9630 (1983).

39. American Acad. of Pediatrics v. Heckler, 561 F. Supp. 395 (D. D.C. 1983).

40. President's Commission for the Study of Ethical Problems in Medicine and Biomedical and Behavioral Research, DECIDING TO FOREGO LIFE SUSTAINING TREATMENT, March 1983, at 227.

41. 49 FED. REG. 1622 (1984).

42. American Hosp. Ass'n v. Heckler, 585 F. Supp. 541 (S.D.N.Y. 1984), *aff'd,* No. 84-6211 (2nd Cir. Dec. 27, 1984), *cert. granted,* 105 S. Ct. 3475 (U.S. 1985).

43. Weber v. Stony Brook Hosp., 60 N.Y.2d 208, 469 N.Y.S.2d 63, 456 N.E.2d 1186 (1983); Parents later authorized limited surgery, N.Y. TIMES, Apr. 7, 1984, at 12.

44. United States v. University Hosp., 729 F.2d 144 (2d Cir. 1984).

45. Child Abuse Amendments of 1984, Pub. L. No. 98-457, 98 Stat. 1753.

46. 50 FED. REG. 14878 (1985).

47. John F. Kennedy Memorial Hosp. v. Bludworth, 452 So.2d 921 (Fla. 1984).

48. *E.g.,* Superintendent of Belchertown v. Saikewicz, 373 Mass. 728, 370 N.E.2d 417 (1977); Eichner v. Dillon, 73 A.D.2d 431, 426 N.Y.S.2d 517 (1980).

49. *E.g.,* In re Spring, 380 Mass. 629, 405 N.E.2d 115 (1980); In re Storar, 52 N.Y.2d 363, 420 N.E.2d 64 (1981). *See* Neu & Kjellstrand, *supra* note 9, for a discussion of cases in which treatment was discontinued without court involvement.

50. *E.g.,* Cal. Health & Safety Code §§7185–7195 (West Supp. 1985); Fla. Stat., Chap. 765 (1985); see WALL ST. J., July 2, 1985, p. 35, col. 4 [35 states and District of Columbia had laws by July 1, 1985]; *see* HOSPITAL LAW MANUAL, *Death, Dying and Dead Bodies,* for a state-by-state list of state laws.

51. Ark. Stat. Ann. §§82-3801–82-3804 (Supp. 1983).

52. Neu & Kjellstrand, *supra* note 9, at 17.

53. Leach v. Akron General Medical Center, 68 Ohio Misc. 1, 22 Ohio Op.3d 49, 426 N.E.2d 809 (Ohio C. Pl. Ct., Summit County 1980).

54. Estate of Leach v. Shapiro, 13 Ohio App.3d 393, 469 N.E.2d 1047 (1984).

55. In re Spring, 380 Mass. 629, 405 N.E.2d 115 (1980).

56. Spring v. Geriatric Auth., 394 Mass. 274, 475 N.E.2d 727 (1985).

57. In re Quinlan, 355 A.2d at 669–670.

58. Barber v. Superior Ct., 147 Cal. App.3d 1006, 195 Cal. Rptr. 484 (1984).

59. United States v. Narcisco, 446 F. Supp. 252 (E.D. Mich. 1977); Wiley, *Liability for Death: Nine Nurses' Legal Ordeals,* 11 NURSING 81, Sept. 1981, at 34.

60. Wiley, *supra* note 59, at 37; *Nurse Admits Plug-Pulling But Is Acquitted of Murder,* 20 MED. WORLD NEWS, Apr. 30, 1979, at 48. For other cases, *see* Miller, *Killings in the Hospital,* 1 TOPICS HOSP. LAW, Mar. 1976, at xxx.

61. N.Y. TIMES, Mar. 21, 1984, at 17, col. 1; Nov. 20, 1984, at 16, col. 1.

62. In re Spring, 405 N.E.2d at 122.

63. 205 J.A.M.A. 337 (1968).

64. President's Commission for the Study of Ethical Problems in Medicine and Biomedical and Behavioral Research, DEFINING DEATH, July 1981, at 159–66.

65. State v. Fierro, 124 Ariz. 182, 603 P.2d 74 (1979); Lovato v. District Ct., 601 P.2d 1072 (Colo. 1979); Swaffort v. State, 421 N.E.2d 596 (Ind. 1981); Commonwealth v. Golston, 373 Mass. 249, 366 N.E.2d 744 (1977), *cert. denied,* 434 U.S. 1039 (1978); State v. Meints, 212 Neb. 410, 322 N.W.2d 809 (1982); People v. Eulo, 63 N.Y.2d 341, 472 N.E.2d 286 (1984); In re Bowman, 94 Wash.2d 407, 617 P.2d 731 (1980); *but see* State v. Johnson, 56 Ohio St. 2d 35, 381 N.E.2d 637 (1978).

66. Horan, *Definition of Death: An Emerging Consensus,* 12 TRIAL 22, 25–26 (1980).

67. *E.g.,* Miss. Code Ann. §§41-36-1–41-36-3 (1981).

68. Hoard v. Shawnee Mission Medical Center, 233 Kan. 267, 662 P.2d 1214 (1983); *see also* Dooley v. Richland Memorial Hosp., 283 S.C. 372, 322 S.E.2d 669 (1984) [no liability for erroneous report of serious injury].

69. Muniz v. United Hosps. Medical Center Presbyterian Hosp., 153 N.J. Super. 72, 379 A.2d 57 (N.J. Super. Ct. App. Div. 1977).

70. Iowa Code Ann. §331.802 (1983).

71. *E.g.,* Cal. Health & Safety Code §7100 (West Supp. 1985).

72. 8 U.L.A. 15 (1972).

73. *E.g.,* Dumouchelle v. Duke Univ., 69 N.C. App. 471, 317 S.E.2d 100 (1984).

74. *E.g.,* Burke v. New York Univ., 196 A.D. 491, 188 N.Y.S. 123 (1921).

75. *E.g.,* Iowa Code Ann. §144.56 (1985 Supp.).

76. *E.g.,* Colo. Rev. Stat. Ann. §12-36-133 (1978 Repl.Vol.)

77. *E.g.,* Ariz. Rev. Stat. Ann. §36-831 (1975–84 Supp.)

78. *E.g.,* Minn. Stat. Ann. §145.161 (1970).

79. *E.g.,* N.Y. Public Health Law §4214 (1971 & 1984–85 Supp.).

80. Winkler v. Hawes and Ackley, 126 Iowa 474, 102 N.W. 418 (1905).

81. *E.g.,* Lashbrook v. Barnes, 437 S.W.2d 502 (Ky. 1969).

82. *E.g.,* Grawunder v. Beth Israel Hosp. Ass'n, 266 N.Y. 605, 195 N.E. 221 (1935).

83. 8 U.L.A. 15 (1972).

84. *Hospitals Blamed for Dearth of Transplant Organs,* 15 MOD. HEALTHCARE, Sept. 13, 1985, at 68.

85. Holland v. Metalious, 105 N.H. 290, 198 A.2d 654 (1964).

86. Tillman v. Detroit Receiving Hosp., 138 Mich. App. 683, 360 N.W.2d 275 (1984).

87. Georgia Lions Eye Bank, Inc. v. Lavant, 335 S.E.2d 127 (Ga. 1985).

88. Williams v. Hofmann, 66 Wis.2d 145, 223 N.W.2d 844 (1974).

89. Ravenis v. Detroit General Hosp., 63 Mich. App. 79, 234 N.W.2d 411 (1975).

Introduction to Index
of Cases

The numbers and letters after each case name tell where to find the court's decision. For example, in *Tarasoff v. Board of Regents,* 17 Cal.3d 425, 551 P.2d 334 (1976), the numbers 17 and 551 are volume numbers. They are followed by the abbreviations for the reporter systems; "Cal.3d" means the third series of the reports of the decisions of the California Supreme Court, while "P.2d" means *Pacific Reporter, Second Series.* The final numbers 425 and 334 are the page numbers in those volumes. The number in parenthesis is the date of the decision. When the abbreviation of the reporter system does not disclose the court that rendered the decision, an abbreviation of the court's name will also appear in the parenthesis. Since the "Cal.3d" tells which court rendered the decision, the name of the court does not appear in the parentheses in the example. An example where the reporter abbreviation does not disclose the name of the court is *John F. Kennedy Memorial Hosp. v. Bludworth,* 452 So.2d 921 (Fla. 1984); since the *Southern Reporter, Second series,* abbreviated "So.2d," includes cases from several states and Florida no longer has a separate reporting system for its court's decisions, it is necessary to include the abbreviation "Fla." in the parentheses to disclose that it is a decision of the Florida Supreme Court.

When there is another set of numbers and letters after the parenthesis, they refer to another court's decision concerning the same case. If the second court is a higher court, it will be preceded by letters such as *aff'd, rev'd,* or *cert. denied* which indicate the court affirmed, reversed or declined to review the lower court's decision. (See Chapter 1 for a discussion of *cert. denied.*) In some situations the order of the references is reversed, so that the higher court is listed first. In those situations the abbreviations will be *aff'ing* or *rev'ing,* indicating whether the higher court is affirming or reversing the lower court.

Index of Cases

Note: After each case name, sets of four numbers appear (for example, the first case, *Aasum v. Good Samaritan Hosp.*, is followed by "ch.7, n.13, 143, *122*") to help locate both the note where the case is referenced and the associated text. The first three numbers indicate where the case appears in the notes (in the example, chapter 7, note 13, on page 143). The last number in italics indicates the page of the text associated with the note (in the example, page *122*). When a single number appears in italics, the case is referred to on that page without a note.

H

Index

C

About the Author

Robert D. Miller, J.D., M.S.Hyg., is a graduate of Iowa State University, the Yale University Law School, and the University of Pittsburgh Health Law Training Program. After serving as the in-house legal counsel to the University of Iowa Hospitals and Clinics for eight years, he is now practicing law with the firm of Shutts & Bowen in West Palm Beach and Miami, Florida, where he assists in the representation of several hospitals, physician groups, health insurers, and other health clients.

While at the University of Iowa, he taught health care law to health administration, law, and health science students. He now teaches health administration students at the University of Miami.

Mr. Miller was a coauthor of Aspen's *Human Experimentation of the Law* (1976), author of the fourth edition of *Problems in Hospital Law* (1983), and a coauthor of Aspen's *Nursing and the Law* (1984). He is a contributor to Aspen's *Hospital Law Manual* and edits and regularly contributes to Aspen's quarterly journal, *Topics in Hospital Law*. He has frequently lectured and contributed to numerous other publications on health law topics.